NOT FOR SALE

SPECTRUM 1

• Junior Certificate English •

John Moriarty
SERIES EDITOR

MENTOR Publications
43 Furze Road,
Sandyford Industrial Estate,
Dublin 18.

Tel: 295 2112 / 3   Fax: 295 2114

All Rights Reserved

Text by Paul Gannon, Mary Hosty, John Moriarty.
Artwork by Ann O'Connell.

Edited by: John McCormack
              Annie McCarthy
              Claire Haugh
Designed by: Kathryn McKinney

© John Moriarty 1998

Printed by ColourBooks Ltd., Dublin.

ISBN: 0-947548-76-9

Contents

POETRY

Smithereens	Roger McGough	8
Snow Storm	John Clare	9
Claims	David Kitchen	11
If The Earth Should Fall Tonight	Oliver Hereford	13
The Listeners	Walter de la Mere	15
Miller's End	Charles Causley	18
Take One Home for the Kiddies	Philip Larkin	19
City Lights	Margaret Greaves	20
Blackberry-Picking	Seamus Heaney	22
Mid-Term Break		24
It Makes Me Furious!	Teresa de Jesus	26
The Hunter	Ogden Nash	27
Bodybuilders' Contest	Wislawa Szymborska	28
Poetry Workshop		29
A Recipe for Happiness	Hugh Clement	29
Orders of the Day	John Cunliffe	31
Things People Do	Kit Wright	32
Christmas Thank Yous	Mick Gowar	32
Notice	Steve Kowit	34
But You Didn't	Merrill Glass	35
A Boy Thirteen	Jeff	36
Winter Days	Gareth Owen	37
Stopping by Woods on a Snowy Evening	Robert Frost	38
Carolling Around the Estate	Wes Magee	39
Shelter	Michael Coady	40
A Crabbit Old Woman Wrote This	Anonymous	42
Old Dog	William Stafford	43
Sheepkiller	Padraig J. Daly	44
Dad	Brian McCabe	45
Mother To Son	Langston Hughes	46
Teacher	Mary E. O'Donnell	47
The Choosing	Liz Lockhead	48
Tich Miller	Wendy Cope	50
Haiku	Various	52
City Dweller	Christy Brown	54
The Great Blasket Island	Julie O'Callaghan	55
Happiness	Carl Sandburg	56

SHORT STORIES

SWALK	Sam McBratney	57
First Confession ✓	Frank O'Connor	64
Christmas Morning		71
The Secret Life of Walter Mitty ✓	James Thurber	78
Uncle Ifor's Welsh Dresser ✓	Pat Lacey	86
Letter Writing		92
The Wolves of Cernogratz	Saki	97
The Choice is Yours	Jan Mark (adapted)	102
The Giant with the Three Golden Hairs	The Brothers Grimm (adapted)	110
The Hitch-Hiker ✓	Roald Dahl	116
The Scream ✓	Elizabeth Laird	124

A Rat and Some Renovations	Bernard MacLaverty	130
The Monkey's Paw	W. W. Jacobs	133
After Twenty Years	O. Henry (adapted)	140
Short Story Workshop		145

NOVEL

Goodnight Mister Tom	Michele Magorian	155

DRAMA

Burning Everest	Adrian Flynn	175

FILM AND RADIO DRAMA

Cinema – The Early Years		228

READING & COMPOSITION

Angela's Ashes	Frank McCourt	237
Good Handwriting		242
Keeping a Diary		243
Letter to Daniel – 1	Fergal Keane	244
Elements of Grammar – Parts of Speech		247
– Nouns		247
– Pronouns		251
Letter to Daniel – 2	Fergal Keane	252
Alphabetical Order		254
Punctuation		255
Boy	Raold Dahl	258
Elements of Grammar – Adjectives		261
Personal Writing		265
Elements of Grammar – Verbs		271
– Adverbs		273
Vampires	Various	274
Capital Letters		276
A Night to Remember	Brendan Williams	279
Proverbs		280
Ghost Stories	Various	281
Elements of Grammar – Prepositions		285
– Conjunctions		286
– Interjections		286
The First Men on the Moon	Armstrong & Aldrin	287
Idioms		288
Millionaires	Unknown	290
The Apostrophe		292
Spelling Programme		294
Made In America	Unknown	296
Matt Busby: Birth of the Babes	Unknown	298
Dictionary Work		300

MEDIA STUDIES

Introduction	305
Advertising	306
Newspapers	335

Index	351
Alphabetical List of Poems and Short Stories	352

Acknowledgements

The author and publishers would like to thank the following for their kind permission to reproduce the following information:

POETRY Peters, Fraser and Dunlop for *Smithereens* by Roger McGough, The Society of Authors for *The Listeners* by Walter de la Mere, David Higham & Associates for *Miller's End* by Charles Causley, Faber & Faber for *Take One Home for the Kiddies* by Philip Larkin, *Blackberry-Picking* and *Mid-Term Break* by Seamus Heaney and *Tich Miller* by Wendy Cope, André Deutsch for *The Hunter* by Ogden Nash, Random House UK Ltd for *Stopping by Woods on a Snowy Evening* by Robert Frost.

SHORT STORIES Peters, Fraser and Dunlop for *First Confession* and *Christmas Morning* by Frank O'Connor, Blackstaff Press for *A Rat and Some Renovations* by Bernard McLaverty, The Society of Authors for *The Monkey's Paw* by W. W. Jacobs

PLAY Adrian Flynn for *Burning Everest*. Permission for performance rights to the play are not included here and interested parties should contact David Higham Associates, 5-8 Lower John Street, Golden Square, London W14 4HA.

EXTRACTS Penguin Books for two extracts from *Letter to Daniel* by Fergal Keane; HarperCollins Publishers Ltd for an extract from *Angela's Ashes* by Frank McCourt.

While considerable effort has been made to locate all of the copyright holders of the material used in this book, we have failed to contact everyone concerned. Should anyone wish to contact the publishers we will be more than happy to come to some arrangement.

Introduction

Spectrum 1 meets the requirements of the Junior Certificate English programme and is principally aimed at First Year students preparing for either the Ordinary Level or the Higher Level. With features on Reading (Non-fiction), Personal and Functional Writing, Media, Fiction, Elements of Grammar, Poetry, Drama and Film it provides a wide selection of material and offers teachers much scope in devising a variety of work to suit the needs of their particular classes. The views and advice of many experienced teachers and examiners of Junior Certificate English were taken into consideration in selecting and devising the material in this book.

Questions & Assignments

The Questions and Assignments which follow all items provide opportunities for both written and oral work. The written responses will provide students with a record of the literature they have studied and their responses to it. This in turn will clearly be a useful examination aid.

Points to Note

These follow most items and aim to highlight important features relating to style and technique. Literary terms are clearly explained in the context of the short stories, poems, plays and extracts in which they arise. A knowledge of these literary terms provides students with the technical language for discussing and writing about all forms of literature as well as a solid foundation for the new Leaving Certificate programme. An Index of key terms is also provided at the back of the book.

Answer Guidelines

The Answer Guidelines use the following formats:
- Useful words, phrases and sentence starters from which students can construct answers.
- 'Exploration'-type questions which direct students towards appropriate responses to assignments.

The purpose of the answer guidelines is not to provide pupils with an outline 'answer' but rather to 'spark off' ideas to complement those of their own. For this reason the significance of an odd word or phrase in an answer guideline may not be immediately obvious. They should be regarded as a 'fall-back' answering strategy rather than a substitute for the students' own original responses.

Word Games

The book contains a selection of word games – matching words to meanings, spell checks, cryptic puzzles, anagrams etc – which are designed to improve spelling, vocabulary, syntax and other literacy skills. These word games are intentionally demanding and some pupils may encounter difficulties. Should this occur, teachers can provide additional clues, such as the initial letters of the solutions. Answers to all word games are included in the Teacher's Handbook.

Poetry

Said the Duck to the Kangaroo,
'Good gracious! How you hop!
Over the fields and water too,
As if you never would stop!
My life is a bore in this nasty pond,
And I long to go out in the world beyond!
I wish I could hop like you!'
Said the Duck to the Kangaroo.

– from The Duck and the Kangaroo by Edward Lear

Long ago, when people could not read or write, poetry had a very important place in everyday life. It instructed people as well as entertaining them.

Poetry was used to pass on details of both great events and local happenings and to pass important information from person to person and from generation to generation. As well as recording such things as battles and heroic deeds, poetry was also used to spread information about things such as farming, navigation and medicine.

The main reason for the popularity of poetry over prose was that, with its melodic rhymes and strong rhythms, it was easy to remember. Today, however, there is no longer a need for poetry as a means of conveying information needed for everyday living. Instead, people write poetry as a way of showing their feelings about all the things that affect us in life – from the most serious to the most trivial. Poetry gives us an insight into the thoughts and feelings of others and, in doing so, often helps us to look at things in a new and different way.

Poetry is still a very powerful way of communicating. One example of this is the way advertisements use a range of poetic devices to influence people. Over the course of this section, we will learn to identify some of these devices and examine how they work in different poems. However, understanding and enjoying poetry does not depend on being able to spot poetic devices. When you read a certain poem and think to yourself 'I felt like that too about . . . ' then that poem has worked its magic on you.

Of course, some poems do not reveal their full meaning on a first reading. Like listening to a new song, a new poem may require a number of readings before it begins to 'grow' on you. Even after this, you may still not understand each line. Don't worry! The secret is to try to enjoy it and not to be put off because you're puzzled about the meaning of a few lines. As often as not, it can be the poet's fault – he or she may have been unable to find the right words to get the message across to the reader.

The following selection offers you a wide range of poetry – modern and traditional, Irish and international, straight-forward and not so easy, funny and serious. Enjoy!

Spectrum 1

THE POETRY OF ROGER McGOUGH

Roger Mc Gough was born in Liverpool in 1937. Having failed English at 'O' level, a feat he regards as an advantage, he went on to become one of Britain's most popular living poets. In 1963 he recorded one of his poems *Lily the Pink* and had a top ten hit with it. He also wrote the script for the film *Yellow Submarine* based on The Beatles' hit. Inspiration for his poetry comes from his native city.

Smithereens

I spend my days
collecting smithereens.
I find them on buses
in department stores
and on busy pavements.

At restaurant tables
I pick up the leftovers
of polite conversation.
At railway stations
the tearful debris
of parting lovers.

I pocket my eavesdroppings
and store them away.
I make things out of them
nice things, sometimes.
Sometimes odd, like this.

 — *Roger McGough*

Questions & Assignments

1 (a) What in your opinion are the *'smithereens'* to which the poet refers?
  (b) Where does he find them?
2 *'I pocket my eavesdroppings / and store them away.'* What do you understand these lines to mean?
3 What *'things'* does the poet make from his *'eavesdroppings'*?
4 What insights into the craft of poetry writing do you get from this poem?

Poetry

◤ Points to Note

All activities have their own sets of words. A mechanic understands clearly what a 'timing belt' is; a musician is familiar with the word 'octave'. These are called **technical terms**.

The study of poetry requires students to talk and write about poems and not only to read and enjoy them. Like any other activity poetry has its own set of technical terms or special words to describe its different features. Having a clear understanding of these terms will help to shape your thoughts and responses when you are asked to talk about or write about a particular poem.

In the poetry section of this book the following terms will be explained: **Onomatopoeia, Rhyme, Rhythm, Alliteration, Assonance, Repetition, Simile, Metaphor, Image, Mood, Tone and Satire.**

Snow Storm

What a night! The wind howls, hisses, and but stops
To howl more loud, while the snow volley keeps
Incessant batter at the window pane,
Making our comfort feel as sweet again;
And in the morning, when the tempest drops,
At every cottage door mountainous heaps
Of snow lie drifted, that all entrance stops
Until the beesom and the shovel gain
The path, and leave a wall on either side.

– *John Clare*

◤ Points to Note

ONOMATOPOEIA

Read *Snow Storm* again, taking special note of the following words: '*howls*', '*hisses*' and '*batter*'. All three words describe sounds, but when we say each word it actually sounds like the sound it describes. This device is called **onomatopoeia**. We could say: '*There is onomatopoeia in the first three lines in the words 'howls', 'hisses' and 'batter'*' or '*The words 'howls', 'hisses' and 'batter' are onomatopoeic.*' We could then go on to say: '*The poet uses these words to help us imagine the noises of the storm.*'

Onomatopoeia occurs frequently in poetry, helping us to 'hear' different sounds in our imagination.

Spectrum 1

RESPONSE

Often you will be asked to give a personal response to a poem. Simply stating that *'I enjoyed the poem immensely'* is not adequate; instead take the approach *'I enjoyed the poem immensely because . . .'* and then go on to give reasons for your reactions. Consider what feelings the poem stirs in you and identify the words and phrases that led to these feelings.

Questions & Assignments

1. *'What a night!'* Explain briefly what this expression means.
2. What words describe the noises made by the wind?
3. Does the snow fall silently? Explain your answer.
4. What idea does line 4 convey to you?
5. Describe, in your own words, the scene on the morning after the snow storm.
6. Did you enjoy reading this poem? Why?

Answer Guidelines

6. I enjoyed reading *Snow Storm* because the poem . . . the snow storm to life for me. I could . . . the howling wind driving the . . . against the window pane. With such . . . outside I can understand how the poet felt very . . . inside.
I also liked the morning scene; the little cottages almost . . . by snow drifts and the people . . . paths through the snow. The poet's description of this . . . reminds me of a picture on a . . .

Here are some more examples of onomatopoeic words. Fill in each of the blank spaces with a suitable word from the box.

Hissing	Patter	Sighing	Creak
Rumble	Blast	Clink	Shuffling
Beat	Ringing	Wail	Hoot
Chug	Crack	Howling	Babble
Rustling	Ticking	Buzz	Screeching

.....................of a telephone   ....of steam
.....................of a whip   ....of a stream
.....................of a train   ....of rain
.....................of an engine   ....of a drum
.....................of the wind   ....of a clock
.....................of feet   ....of the wind
.....................of a siren   ....of brakes
.....................of leaves   ....of a hinge
.....................of a coin   ....of a horn
.....................of a saw   ....of an explosion

Claims

My father had a motor car:
It was his pride and joy.
He would have taught me how to drive
If I had been a boy.

But girls grow into women
And women are to blame,
According to my father,
For each insurance claim.

We're just not built for things like cars.
Dad says we mustn't moan:
Men are built for speed and strength,
Women for the home.

My mother used to drive a bit
Until the accident:
Parking in the multi-storey,
A wing mirror got bent.

It wasn't really Mum's fault,
There simply wasn't space.
You'd think to hear my father rant
She'd damned the human race.

My mother didn't argue,
She says she saves her breath,
Dad homes in for a blazing row
Like vultures swoop on death.

'Women drivers,' said my dad
'No one need discuss:
Women should accept their lot
And meekly take the bus.'

Which makes it such a pity,
Such wretched awful luck,
That Dad has driven his new car
Half way up a truck.

Spectrum 1

What makes it worse in Dad's eyes
(And the police's book)
Is that the truck was neatly parked
And father didn't look.

His seat belt meant that he was safe,
Though the car's beyond repair;
What hurt him was the firemen laughed
As they cut him free from there.

He sometimes takes the subject up,
Explains the crash away.
My Mum and I say nothing,
Much to Dad's dismay.

But part of what Dad taught me,
I must admit, remains:
Men are built with speed and strength
But hardly any brains.

– David Kitchen

Questions & Assignments

1 Who is supposed to be speaking in this poem?
2 Why did Dad not teach his daughter to drive his car?
3 (a) Describe Dad's attitude to women and to women drivers?
  (b) What was his excuse for this attitude?
4 Describe Dad's accident. How was it different from Mum's car accident?
5 What did Dad find most painful about his accident?
6 What message or idea do you get from this poem?

Points to Note

RHYME AND RHYTHM

RHYME is the repetition of similar sounds at the end of lines and is a feature of much poetry. The lyrics of most songs have rhymes. In the poem *Claims* the first verse or stanza consists of four lines where the second line rhymes with the fourth – while the first and third lines do not rhyme. For example, in stanza one – *'joy'* rhymes with *'boy'* while *'car'* and *'drive'* do not rhyme. Check the other stanzas to see if this pattern is repeated.

The rhyming pattern or rhyming scheme of this stanza could be expressed as follows: **o, a, o, a** (o denotes a line which does not rhyme).

Read the poem aloud to 'hear' the song-like (musical) effect produced by rhymes. This repeated rhyming pattern is pleasing to the ear. It also makes the rhyming words stand out and the effect of this can sometimes be funny – note the stanza which starts with the line *'Which makes it such a pity . . .'*

RHYTHM is the word used to describe the pattern of beats or stressed syllables in a line or in a verse of poetry. As you read the poem aloud you will stress or give extra emphasis to certain words or syllables. These stresses will sound almost like drum beats and this 'pattern' of beats is called the rhythm or **metre**. Note how the rhythm pattern repeats itself in each verse, with a few slight variations. We can say that the rhythm pattern or the metre of *Claims* is **regular**. Like rhyme, rhythm also gives poems a song-like quality and is pleasing to the ear.

Rhythm can be lively or slow. A lively rhythm is often used to set a lighthearted or dramatic style, while slow rhythm can signal a more serious mood. In some poems rhythm can be used to convey the idea in the poem – by echoing the rhythm of a train, horses galloping, soldiers marching etc.

Some poets do not make use of any rhymes or rhythm to express themselves.

If The Earth Should Fall Tonight

If this little world tonight
Suddenly should fall through space
In a hissing, headlong flight,
Shrivelling from off its face,
As it falls into the sun,
In an instant every trace
Of the little crawling things –
Ants, philosophers, and lice,
Cattle, cockroaches, and kings,
Beggars, millionaires and mice,
Men and maggots all as one
As it falls into the sun . . .
Who can say but at the same
Instant from some planet far,
A child may watch us and exclaim:
See the pretty shooting star.

– *Oliver Herford*

Spectrum 1

Questions & Assignments

1 Describe the situation which the poet imagines in the first five lines of the poem.
2 What does the phrase *'little world'* suggest?
3 Why do you think the poet uses the following words:
   fall; hissing; headlong; shrivelling?
4 What are the *'little crawling things'* he refers to?
5 Make a list of all the *'little crawling things'* he mentions.
6 Why does his list include creatures ranging from the tiniest insects to the richest human beings? What point is he making about mankind? Does he use a sound device to emphasise a link between different kinds of living creatures? Explain.
7 Why does the poet repeat the phrase *'As it falls into the sun . . .'*
8 What does the poet imagine in the final four lines?
9 Explain the image of the shooting star. Trace the image through from the start of the poem to the end.

Answer Guidelines

9 In the very first line the poet compares the world to a . . . . as it falls through . . . hurtling towards . . . As it falls into the sun it . . . and in an instant all life on earth is . . . The poet says that a child from another . . . would assume that the earth was a . . . and would not be aware of all the life which exists on the planet.

RHYME　　　'Mary, Mary, quite contrary . . .'

The Listeners

"Is there anybody there?" said the Traveller,
   Knocking on the moonlit door;
And his horse in the silence champed the grasses
   Of the forest's ferny floor:
And a bird flew up out of the turret,
   Above the Traveller's head:
And he smote upon the door again a second time;
   "Is there anybody there?" he said.
But no one descended to the Traveller;
   No head from the leaf-fringed sill
Leaned over and looked into his grey eyes,
   Where he stood perplexed and still.
But only a host of phantom listeners
   That dwelt in the lone house then
Stood listening in the quiet of the moonlight
   To that voice from the world of men:
Stood thronging the faint moonbeams on the dark stair,
   That goes down to the empty hall,
Hearkening in an air stirred and shaken
   By the lonely Traveller's call.
And he felt in his heart their strangeness,
   Their stillness answering his cry,
While his horse moved, cropping the dark turf,
   'Neath the starred and leafy sky;
For he suddenly smote on the door, even
   Louder, and lifted his head: —
"Tell them I came, and no one answered,
   That I kept my word," he said.
Never the least stir made the listeners,
   Though every word he spake
Fell echoing through the shadowiness of the still house
   From the one man left awake:
Ay, they heard his foot upon the stirrup,
   And the sound of iron on stone,
And how the silence surged softly backward,
   When the plunging hoofs were gone.

– Walter de la Mare

Spectrum 1

Points to Note

ALLITERATION AND ASSONANCE

This famous and much-loved poem is based on a very brief, mysterious and dramatic incident. The sounds of the words in the poem help to create the eerie atmosphere of the poem.

ALLITERATION occurs when two or more words close together begin with the same letter or sound, e.g. – *'the forest's ferny floor'*; *'silence surged softly backward'*. The use of 'gentle' consonants such as f, l, and s convey the gentle sounds of the forest at night.

Alliteration occurs also when a particular consonant sound is repeated in the middle or at the end of two or more words. The sound of the letter 's' occurs frequently in the following phrases *'Never the least stir made the listeners, . . . through the shadowiness of the still house'*, emphasising the atmosphere of silence. This is another example of alliteration.

We often use alliteration in our everyday conversation to make a phrase stand out. Advertisers also frequently use alliteration to make a phrase or a slogan more punchy and memorable.

ASSONANCE is another device that gives language a musical quality. We can say that assonance is present in a poem when a vowel sound is repeated, but the sounds do not completely rhyme. For example, assonance is present in the lines *'But only a host of phantom listeners / That dwelt in the lone house then'* where the 'o' sound is repeated – *only, host, lone*.

Assonance and alliteration can give a poem a haunting and beautiful sound, almost like a piece of music. This 'musical effect' created by long vowel sounds often conveys a sad or gentle atmosphere . . .

Rhyme, alliteration and assonance also emphasise a connection between words.

Questions & Assignments

1. What evidence is there that the events in the poem happen at night?
2. What does the image of the bird flying up out of the turret suggest about the building?
3. Why do you think the traveller is *'perplexed and still'*?
4. Who, in your opinion, are the *'host of phantom listeners'*?
5. Who is the one man left awake?
6. What evidence is there in the final four lines to suggest that the traveller has decided to abandon his quest?
7. This poem is very rich in sound effects. Can you identify some of these and explain briefly how each of your examples contributes to the atmosphere of the poem?
8. The following are some adjectives and adverbs from the poem: *moonlit; ferny; leaf-fringed; grey; phantom; faint; empty; leafy; suddenly; softly; plunging.* (An adjective is a word that qualifies a noun, an adverb is a word that qualifies a verb.)
   In the case of each one, tell whether it is an adjective or an adverb and explain briefly

Poetry

9 What contrasts are there between the scene inside and the scene outside the house?
10 This poem captures a very brief but significant incident in the life of a man. Use your imagination to create in poetic, dramatic (play) or narrative (short story) form, another significant incident in the life of the Traveller (e.g. The day he left; when he decides to return; the story he might tell to an innkeeper shortly after leaving the empty house in the woods).
11 'The poem *The Listeners* is full of mystery and unsolved questions.' Discuss this statement with reference to the poem.
12 What in your opinion is the Traveller's connection with the listeners? Refer to the poem to support your answer.
13 Explain why the poem is called *The Listeners*.
14 Would the scene depicted in the poem work well on film?
15 Having discussed question 14, write a brief screenplay dealing with the events in the poem. (Episode 1 could show the house and its occupants in the past; Episode 2 could show the leaving; Episode 3 could show the return.)

Answer Guidelines

11 The poem leaves the reader with many . . . questions. The poem describes a brief but . . . incident of a horseman arriving at . . . at night. After knocking three times, he . . . out *"Tell them I came . . . That I kept my word"* before galloping off into the night. We are left wondering what . . . the Traveller had with the house. The phrase *'the one man left awake'* could suggest that the Traveller was . . . We don't learn why . . . , how long he . . . , why he lost . . . and why he . . . All these unanswered questions . . . mystery to the poem.

SIMILE

'. . . as small as a mouse'
'. . . as quiet as a mouse'

Spectrum 1

Miller's End

When we moved to Miller's End,
   Every afternoon at four
A thin shadow of a shade
   Quavered through the garden-door.

Dressed in black from top to toe
   And a veil about her head
To us all it seemed as though
   She came walking from the dead.

With a basket on her arm
   Through the hedge-gap she would pass,
Never a mark that we could spy
   On the flagstones or the grass.

When we told the garden-boy
   How we saw the phantom glide,
With a grin his face was bright
   As the pool he stood beside.

"That's no ghost-walk," Billy said,
   "Nor a ghost you fear to stop –
Only old Miss Wickerby
   On a short cut to the shop."

So next day we lay in wait,
   Passed a civil time of day,
Said how pleased we were she came
   Daily down our garden-way.

Suddenly her cheek it paled,
   Turned, as quick, from ice to flame.
"Tell me," said Miss Wickerby,
   "Who spoke of me, and my name?"

"Bill the garden-boy." She sighed,
   Said, "Of course, you could not know
How he drowned – that very pool –
   A frozen winter – long ago."

            – Charles Causley

Questions & Assignments

1. (a) What details of the lady's appearance led the children to believe that she was a ghost?
   (b) What else convinced the children that she was a ghost?
2. How does the poet suggest that the children had become quite friendly with Billy?
3. After talking to Billy the children speak to the woman and surprise her. Explain how.
4. Explain how she in turn surprises them.
5. Is there a suggestion in the poem that Miss Wickerby might have been a close friend of Billy? Explain.

Take One Home for the Kiddies

On shallow straw, in shadeless glass,
Huddled by empty bowls, they sleep;
No dark, no damp, no earth, no grass –
Mam, get us one of them to keep.

Living toys are something novel,
But it soon wears off somehow.
Fetch the shoe-box, fetch the shovel –
Mam, we're playing funerals now.

– *Philip Larkin*

Points to Note

REPETITION

We often find in poetry that a word or a phrase is repeated a few times. Sometimes this is done to achieve a musical effect and sometimes to emphasise a point and make it stand out. In line 3 of *Take One Home for the Kiddies* the word '*no*' is repeated four times. The purpose of this is to emphasise how deprived the little creatures in the cage were.

Questions & Assignments

1. Do you think that the title of the poem is suitable? Give a reason.
2. What animals do you think are the subject of this poem? Give reasons for your answer.
3. '*Shallow straw*', '*shadeless glass*', '*empty bowls*'. Comment on each of these images.
4. The word '*no*' is repeated in line 3. What effect does this repetition achieve?
5. As well as the poet's voice, there is another voice in this poem. Explain.
6. What message is this poem trying to get across?

Spectrum 1

City Lights

Huge round oranges of light
Ripen against the thin dark of the city sky,
Spilling their juice in warm pools
   on bare dry pavements.
Below them blink the traffic lights
   like the eyes of enormous cats
Crouching in the dark –
Crouching and breathing with the heavy purr of traffic;
And winking tail lights slide and dart
   like goldfish
In the pale streams pouring from
   shop windows.

– Margaret Greaves

Questions & Assignments

1. What are the different types of lights described in this poem?
2. To what is each type of light compared?
3. Show how the first comparison extends over the first four lines.
4. Show how the second comparison extends from line 5 to line 8.
5. Explain how the two comparisons in the last four lines are linked.
6. Does the poem have a regular rhyming pattern? Explain.

Points to Note

COMPARING THINGS – SIMILES AND METAPHORS

We often use comparisons in our everyday conversation to describe things more vividly. 'He ran like a hare'; and 'We were as warm as toast' are examples of comparisons in everyday use.

SIMILES

A **simile** is a comparison that uses the words **like**, **as**, or **than**.

We usually put little thought into the similes we use in conversation. Expressions like 'as cold as ice', 'as black as coal' and 'went out like a light' are used again and again.

One mark of a good writer is his/her ability to give the reader a clear and vivid impression of a situation. One way of doing this is to use similes that are imaginative and original.

City Lights has two similes. To what does the first simile compare the traffic lights? The second one compares . . . ? to . . . ? These are original similes and help us to picture the scene in our imagination.

Poetry

METAPHORS

Metaphors also occur a lot in our conversation. Like similes, metaphors involve comparisons. However, while a simile is a comparison which uses the words like, as or than, a metaphor is more difficult to spot.

Look at the first line of *City Lights*. If the poet had written 'street lights that looked like huge round oranges' it would have the same meaning but would be more longwinded. Instead the poet uses a metaphor. She says that the lights **are** oranges rather than saying that the lights are **like** oranges.

The poet goes on to develop the metaphor over the next two lines. Can you see how? There is a metaphor also in the final two lines. Identify it and show how the 'goldfish' simile is linked into it.

Assignment

You should be able to understand now what a metaphor is. If you are still not sure, here are a few common metaphors for you to extend into similes.

- The boy raced up the stairs.
- That singer shot to fame overnight.
- Jane had a flash of inspiration.
- Pearls of dew lay on the grass.

You will see also from the above assignment that metaphors and similes make language – both spoken and written – more colourful and descriptive by making us see things in a new way.

When you are considering a simile or metaphor in a poem look at the two parts of the comparison and ask what similarity the poet wants to bring to your notice.

METAPHOR

'A pencil of light pierced the darkness.'

Spectrum 1

THE POETRY OF SEAMUS HEANEY

Seamus Heaney was born on April 13, 1939, the eldest of nine children, to Margaret and Patrick Heaney, at the family farm, Mossbawn, about 30 miles northwest of Belfast in County Derry. He attended the local school at Anahorish until 1957, when he enrolled at Queen's University, Belfast. While at college he began to write, publishing work in the university magazines. In 1966 his first collection of poetry – *Death of a Naturalist*, from which the poem *Blackberry-Picking* is taken – was published.

In 1972 he moved his family to County Wicklow and taught for some years in Carysfort College in Dublin before becoming a full time poet.

The many literary awards he has won, the large sales of his books and the big attendances at his readings are evidence that he is undoubtedly the most popular poet writing in English today.

Heaney's work is filled with childhood memories of growing up in the countryside. Some of his most famous poems are about friends and family members who have died.

He was awarded the world's most prestigious literary award – the Nobel Prize for Literature – in 1995 'for works of lyrical beauty and ethical depth, which exalt everyday miracles and the living past'.

Blackberry-Picking

Late August, given heavy rain and sun
For a full week, the blackberries would ripen.
At first, just one, a glossy purple clot
Among others, red, green, hard as a knot.
You ate that first one and its flesh was sweet
Like thickened wine: summer's blood was in it
Leaving stains upon the tongue and lust for
Picking. Then red ones inked up and that hunger
Sent us out with milk-cans, pea-tins, jam-pots
Where briars scratched and wet grass bleached our boots.
Round hayfields, cornfields and potato-drills
We trekked and picked until the cans were full
Until the tinkling bottom had been covered
With green ones, and on top big dark blobs burned
Like a plate of eyes. Our hands were peppered
With thorn pricks, our palms sticky as Bluebeard's.
We hoarded the fresh berries in the byre.
But when the bath was filled we found a fur,
A rat-grey fungus, glutting on our cache.
The juice was stinking too. Once off the bush
The fruit fermented, the sweet flesh would turn sour.
I always felt like crying. It wasn't fair
That all the lovely canfuls smelt of rot.
Each year I hoped they'd keep, knew they would not.

— *Seamus Heaney*

Poetry

Points to Note

IMAGES

'Image' is the most frequently used term when discussing poems. Images can be single words, phrases or complete lines that appeal to one or more of our five senses.

'The weather was awful' makes a statement about the weather, but uses no image. On the other hand 'The biting wind howled furiously' also makes a statement about the weather, but uses images in such a way that when we read it we can easily imagine, from our experience of being out on very cold days, how the wind felt and how it sounded.

A poet chooses words very carefully to create an experience or sensation in our imagination. Images can be visual when a poem invites us to 'see' in our imagination; aural imagery invites us to 'hear' something in our imagination; tactile images give us a clear impression of what it is like to touch or feel something. Imagery that appeals to our sense of taste and smell occur less frequently in poetry.

Similes and metaphors are frequently used to create vivid and effective images. Can you suggest why?

Questions & Assignments

1 How does the poet introduce the subject of the poem in the first two lines?
2 Explain how the meaning of lines 3 and 4 is linked in the opening two lines
3 Explain the comparison in the phrase *'a glossy purple clot'* and say why or why not it is effective. Would you agree that the phrase is a good visual image? Explain.
4 What images in line 4 appeal to our sense of vision and our sense of touch?
5 The poem contains a number of very vivid images (word-pictures). Identify four or five which impressed you most and state why. State also to which of the senses each of the images appeals.
6 The poem contains a number of direct comparisons (similes). Identify these and explain why (or why not) you think they are effective. Can you suggest suitable alternatives?
7 Identify a number of metaphors in the poem. In the case of each, explain clearly what is being compared.
8 'This poem illustrates Seamus Heaney's memory for detail.' Discuss this statement by referring to the poem.
9 Show how the poet uses alliteration to emphasise links between certain words.
10 Show how the poet experienced two contrasting moods during the blackberry season.

[Handwritten notes:]
1. Choral Reading
2. Groups of four read
3. Write your own personal response
4. Personal memory
5. List images
6. Metaphors Similes

storylike

Spectrum 1

Mid-Term Break

I sat all morning in the college sick-bay
Counting bells knelling classes to a close.
At two o'clock our neighbours drove me home.

In the porch I met my father crying -
He had always taken funerals in his stride -
And Big Jim Evans saying it was a hard blow.

The baby cooed and laughed and rocked the pram
When I came in, and I was embarrassed
By old men standing up to shake my hand

And tell me they were "sorry for my trouble".
Whispers informed strangers I was the eldest,
Away at school, as my mother held my hand

In hers and coughed out angry tearless sighs.
At ten o'clock the ambulance arrived
With the corpse, stanched and bandaged by the nurses.

Next morning I went up into the room. Snowdrops
And candles soothed the bedside: I saw him
For the first time in six weeks. Paler now,

Wearing a poppy bruise on his left temple,
He lay in the four foot box as in his cot.
No gaudy scars, the bumper knocked him clear.

A four foot box, a foot for every year.

— *Seamus Heaney*

Questions & Assignments

1 Who is speaking in this poem? What is he telling you about?
2 At what time of year did the tragedy take place? Refer to the poem to support your answer.
3 Comment briefly on the characters of the boy's parents as they are revealed in the poem.
4 Why did the old men shake the boy's hand?
5 How did the boy respond to the tragedy?
6 What is the significance of the baby cooing and laughing in his cot?

7 Comment on the line *'Snowdrops / And candles soothed the bedside'*.
8 What does the poet suggest about his mother's feelings in the phrase *'angry tearless sighs'*?
9 What do you consider to be the most striking line in the poem? Give reasons for your answer.
10 'The poem conveys the unique sense of tragedy associated with the death of a child.' Discuss this statement with reference to the poem as a whole.
11 Consider the title *Mid-Term Break*. Might it have two meanings? Explain.
12 **Comparing Poems** *Blackberry Picking* and *Mid-Term Break*
   Discuss how these two poems 'exalt everyday miracles and the living past' (from Seamus Heaney's Nobel Prize citation.)

Answer Guidelines

6 The subject matter of *Mid-Term Break* is clearly very . . . The poet devotes most of the poem to describing the . . . of the tragedy on the dead child's family and neighbours. However the . . . the baby cooing and laughing to . . . how even in the midst of tragedy, life goes on. The . . . of the baby also signifies hope for the future and the continuity of . . . It . . . that in the midst of death we are in . . . The image is also . . . because it contrasts sharply with all the other images in the poem.

10 Identify a number of details from the poem that together build up a picture which enables you to 'see' or 'experience' in your imagination what the poet experienced. The first one might be – *The image of the poet, as a teenager, sitting 'in the college sick bay' . . . means that he was probably called out of class and told the news of his brother's death.*
(Note how the exact words "sorry for my trouble" are marked off by quotation marks.)

• Now say something about the detail — what does it convey about the subject matter of the poem? *This conveys the sudden and unexpected nature of such tragedies. A knock on a classroom door brings news that will make that day live forever in the poet's memory.*

• Go on now to select two or three more details and show how they focus on different aspects of the tragedy. *The image of the poet's father crying . . .*

• Finish off by referring to the question. If possible, use words or phrases from the question to construct your concluding sentence. *All these images convey, in a very powerful manner, how the death of the poet's brother affected his family.*

Spectrum 1

It Makes Me Furious!

When I come upon a child
sad, dirty, skinny
it makes me furious!

When I see food
tossed into the garbage
and a poor man poking around in case
it isn't rotten yet
it makes me furious!

When a toothless woman
hunched and old tells me
she's 26
it makes me furious!

When a little old man sleeps
by his final corner
it makes me furious!

When the poor wait
for the rich man to finish his business
to ask him
for last week's salary
it makes me furious!

– Teresa de Jesus

Points to Note
MOOD AND TONE

People's moods vary. We can feel happy, sad, angry, lighthearted or a range of other emotions. Our friends can detect the kind of mood we are in from the things we say and the tone of voice in which we speak. Poems can also convey a particular tone or mood, which reflects the writer's attitude towards the subject of the poem.

Imagine the poet reciting *It Makes Me Furious!* We can imagine her speaking in an angry tone as she describes . . . ? Therefore we can say that the tone of the poem is one of anger.

Poems can have more than one mood. When discussing the mood of a poem watch out for changes of mood.

Poetry

Questions & Assignments

1. List all the things which make the poet furious.
2. Why do you think the poet chooses the following words:
   skinny; tossed; poking; furious; hunched?
3. Why does seeing the man poking in the garbage make her furious?
4. Why is the poet furious about the woman in stanza three?
5. Explain the reason for the poet's anger in the final stanza.
6. How does the poet portray the poor in the poem? How does she portray the rich?
7. Why do you think the poet repeats the title of the poem at the end of each stanza?
8. What do you learn about the poet from reading her poem?
9. Are there aspects of modern life which you consider to be unjust or unfair? Make a list of them and say why you think they are unjust.
10. What is the poet's tone of voice? Where do you think it is most strongly expressed?

The Hunter

The hunter crouches in his blind
'Neath camouflage of every kind,
And conjures up a quacking noise
To lend allure to his decoys.
This grown-up man, with pluck and luck,
Is hoping to outwit a duck.

— *Ogden Nash*

Points to Note

SATIRE

This poem is a satire. That means the poet is making fun of his subject, in this case a duck hunter. By ridiculing the hunter, the poet wants to show us that he does not like what the hunter does.

Questions & Assignments

1. Describe in your own words what the hunter does.
2. What is the hunter hoping to achieve?
3. What do the following words suggest about the hunter?
   crouches; camouflage of every kind; allure?
4. Why does the poet draw our attention to the fact that the hunter is a grown man?
5. Explain the phrase *'with pluck and luck'*.

6 The word *'pluck'* means courage. Do you think the poet really regards the hunter as brave or courageous? Explain your answer.
7 Does the hunter seem foolish to you? Explain why.

Bodybuilders' Contest

From scalp to sole, all muscles in slow motion.
The ocean of his torso drips with lotion.
The king of all is he who preens and wrestles
with sinews twisted into monstrous pretzels*.

Onstage, he grapples with a grizzly bear
the deadlier for not really being there.
Three unseen panthers are in turn laid low,
each with one smoothly choreographed blow.

He grunts while showing poses and paces.
His back alone has twenty different faces.
The mammoth fist he raises as he wins
is tribute to the force of vitamins.

– Wislawa Szymborska

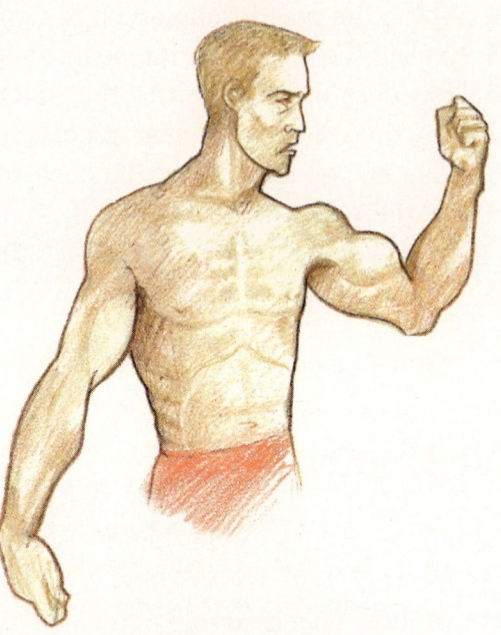

*pretzels – *large twisted biscuits in the shape of a knot*

Questions & Assignments

1 What do you think the poet means by the phrase *'From scalp to sole'*?
2 Why does the poet write the *'ocean of his torso'*? What does it suggest about the bodybuilder?
3 What does the word *'preens'* suggest about him?
4 His muscle sinews are compared to *'monstrous pretzels'*. Do you think this is a good description? Explain.
5 Read stanza two and describe in your own words what the bodybuilder does on stage. What does *'choreographed'* mean?
6 Do you think there is anything comical about his behaviour?
7 What do you understand by *'His back alone has twenty different faces'*?
8 Is *'mammoth'* a good choice of word to describe his fist? Why?
9 According to the poem what is the reason for the bodybuilder's success?
10 What is your opinion of the bodybuilder?
11 Compose a short paragraph describing a similar occupation . . . eg. boxing, weight-lifting.

POETRY WORKSHOP

One way of developing an appreciation of poetry and the skills of the poet is to try writing some of your own. A good way to get started on poetry writing is to use other poems as models. For example, *A Recipe for Happiness*, below, by Hugh Clement will serve as a useful model for your own personal recipe for happiness.

A Recipe for Happiness

An ounce of TV
A slice of disco dancing
Mix up well
With a squeeze of summer sunbaking
Half a cup of raging on Saturday night
And a large tablespoon of tickling the dog
Add a freshly picked ticket to the Grand Final
Stir in a splash of lazing around the pool
Add the mess of records and clothes on my bedroom floor
Bake slowly with a really good late night video
Add a pinch of messing round on lazy afternoons
Sprinkle with a couple of beaut barbecues
Pour in my oldest and most favourite jeans
Serve with a real good helping of family fun.
And there you are — the recipe's done.

– Hugh Clement

The following five steps should be followed when attempting to write any poem. Use these steps now to write a poem similar to '*A Recipe for Happiness*'.

STEP 1

BRAINSTORMING Begin with a brainstorming session. For this you will need a blank page and a pen or pencil. Next let your imagination loose. List all the things which make you happy. As well as obvious things such as 'Last day of term' or 'Christmas morning', try to come up with less obvious things. Write down anything that comes into your head.

Many of the things on your list should be special to you; try to include things that may not apply to other people in the class. These can be little things, e.g. a song, a special kind of food, someone's voice, a particular sound, a certain place and time, a precious memory. Often it is these little things which will give your poem its own novel spark and will make it more memorable.

Don't worry about sentences or spellings at this stage – use single words or phrases. Fill the page.

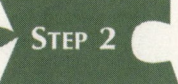

STEP 2   **SELECTING**   Next read over your list and cross out anything with which you are not entirely happy. Now take what remains on the list and decide on the order in which they will appear in the poem. There are many different ways of doing this. For example, you could start with those things that made you happy when you were very young and work your way towards the present time. You could also group all the indoor things that make you happy and then move on to the outdoor things, or you could decide to present them in random order.

STEP 3   **FIRST DRAFT**   Now make a first attempt at writing your poem. Write your effort neatly on a new page, leaving plenty of space between the lines. The purpose of this is to give you room to make changes and additions. This is called your first draft.

STEP 4   **IMPROVING YOUR FIRST DRAFT**   Here are some devices used by poets when writing poetry. You may find these useful in your efforts to prepare your final draft.

(A) CHOOSE YOUR WORDS CAREFULLY

Choose the best words – examine each word in your first draft to see if you could replace it with another word which would help the reader imagine more clearly what you are describing.

Watch out particularly for **verbs** (words that describe actions). For example the word 'strolled' is more descriptive than the word 'walked' and the phrases 'the wind whispered' or 'the wind howled' are more descriptive than the phrase 'the wind blew'. Can you replace any verbs in your draft with better ones?

Adjectives are another group of words that are useful, e.g. pale moon, golden sun, tall trees, purple heather, yellow candlelight. Adjectives tell us more about nouns. Can you add any suitable adjectives to your draft?

(B) COMPARISONS

Poets use comparisons to help us form pictures of things in our imaginations, e.g. 'the wind . . . crying like a lost child', 'as warm as toast', 'shines like a jewel', 'big as a polar bear'. Of course we also use comparisons in our everyday speech. How many times have you heard phrases such as: 'as cold as ice', 'as black as coal', 'as old as the hills'? These comparisons have become dull and stale from overuse. In your writing you should try to avoid these well-known comparisons or clichés and invent new, more exciting comparisons of your own.

(C) RHYME AND RHYTHM

Writing poems which rhyme can be difficult as it is often hard to think of a suitable word to rhyme with another. Also using a set rhythm pattern in your own poem will be quite challenging as it means getting a certain number of beats into each line. However poetry does not have to have rhymes and rhythms. When a poem has lines of varying length and no rhyming pattern it is called **free verse**. It might be a good idea to write your 'Recipe for Happiness' in free verse.

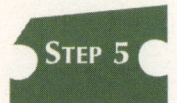 **STEP 5** **FINAL DRAFT** When you have finally made up your mind about all the changes to your first draft write the new version in very neat handwriting on a new page. This is called the final draft. You may like to draw a few suitable illustrations to 'set it off'.

Here are some extracts from a number of poems which you can use as models for some poems of your own. You should follow Steps 1-5 given above when you attempt to write any poem of your own.

1 Orders of the Day

Get up!
Get washed!
Eat your breakfast!
That's my mum,
Going on and on and on and on . . .

Sit down!
Shut up!
Get on with your work!
That's my teacher,
Going on and on and on and on . . .

Come here!
Give me that!
Go away!
That's my big sister,
Going on and on and on and on . . .

Get off!
Stop it!
Carry me!
That's my little sister,
Going on and on and on and on . . .

– *John Cunliffe*

Assignment

Think of some of the things which people always seem to be saying to you and put them in a poem. Use this poem as a model.

POETRY WORKSHOP

2 Things People Do

My brother's stripped his motorbike
Although it's bound to rain.
My sister's playing Elton John
Over and over again.

– Kit Wright

POETRY WORKSHOP

Assignment

List four more members of your family – for example Auntie Kathy, Uncle Paul, Cousin Jim, Grandad. After each name, list something they always seem to be doing. Give two lines to each person and try to follow the rhyming pattern and rhythm of the example above.

Now try similar poems featuring some people from (i) your class and (ii) your town or neighbourhood.

3 Christmas Thank Yous

Dear Auntie
Oh, what a nice jumper
I've always adored powder blue
and fancy you thinking of
orange and pink
for the stripes
how clever of you

Dear Uncle
The soap is
terrific
So
useful
and such a kind thought and
how did you guess that
I'd just used the last of
the soap that last Christmas
brought?

Dear Gran
Many thanks for the hankies

Now I really can't wait for the flu
and the daisies embroidered
in red round the 'M'
for Michael
how thoughtful of you

Dear Cousin
What socks!
and the same sort you wear
so they must be
the last word in style
and I'm certain you're right that the
luminous green
will make me stand out a mile

Dear Sister
I quite understand your concern
it's a risk sending jam in the post
But I think I've pulled out
all the bits
of glass
so it won't taste too sharp
spread on toast

Dear Grandad
Don't fret
I'm delighted
So don't think your gift will
offend
I'm not at all hurt
that you gave up this year
and just sent me
a fiver
to spend

– *Mick Gowar*

Assignment

In this poem Mick Gowar thanks some of his relations for the Christmas gifts they sent him. Read the poem and consider if he is happy with all the gifts. Would you think that his tone is a little sarcastic in places? Make up your own poem, modelled on *Christmas Thank Yous*, in which you thank some relations for the gifts they sent to you for Christmas.

Spectrum 1

Notice

This evening, the sturdy Levis
I wore every day for over a year
& which seemed to the end in perfect condition,
suddenly tore.
How or why I don't know,
but there it was – a big rip at the crotch.
A month ago my friend Nick
walked off a racquetball court,
showered,
got into his street clothes,
& halfway home collapsed & died.
Take heed you who read this
& drop to your knees now & again
like the poet Christopher Smart
& kiss the earth & be joyful
& make much of your time
& be kindly to everyone,
even to those who do not deserve it.
For although you may not believe it will happen,
you too will one day be gone.
I, whose Levis ripped at the crotch
for no reason,
assure you that such is the case.
Pass it on.

Steve Kowit

Questions & Assignments

1. What happens in the first four lines of the poem? Is the poet surprised? Why?
2. Is there any evidence that he was attached to his Levis?
3. Describe in your own words what happened to his friend Nick? Was his death unexpected? Why?
4. What is the connection between the poet's torn jeans and the death of his friend?
5. What advice does the poet give to readers? Summarise it in your own words.
6. Do you think it is good advice? Say why.
7. Why do you think the poet feels he has to pass on this advice?
8. This poem is about death. Does the poet treat the subject in a serious, doom-laden way? Explain.
9. What impression have you formed of the poet? Is he a sad person? Does he care about his friend? Is he disrespectful towards him? Does he have a good attitude to life?
10. Does the loss of his Levi jeans symbolise or stand for anything else?

But You Didn't

Remember the time you lent me your car and I dented it?
I thought you'd kill me . . .
But you didn't.

Remember the time I forgot to tell you the dance was
formal, and you came in jeans?
I thought you'd hate me . . .
But you didn't.

Remember the times I'd flirt with
other boys just to make you jealous, and
you were?
I thought you'd drop me . . .
But you didn't

There were plenty of things you did to put up with me,
to keep me happy, to love me, and there are
so many things I wanted to tell
you when you returned from
Vietnam . . .
But you didn't.

– *Merrill Glass*

Questions & Assignments

1 Why did the poet think her boyfriend would kill her in the first stanza?
2 Why did she think he would hate her in stanza two?
3 Describe the poet's behaviour in the third stanza.
4 What happens to her boyfriend in the final stanza?
5 What impression do you form of her boyfriend? . . . kind . . . tolerant . . . easy going . . . loving . . . cheerful . . .
6 What impression do you form of the poet? Do you think she loved her boyfriend?
7 From reading the poem, what sort of relationship do you think they had?
8 How would you describe the tone of the last stanza?
9 What light does this poem cast on the following issues – War . . . relationships . . . love . . . loss?

A Boy Thirteen

He had red hair,
Was thin and tall,
One could never eat as much as he,
He hiked in the sierras,
Went back-packing and even planned
a trip for the family,
Even got me to join Boy Scouts,
Always wanted me to back-pack with him,
We went to Germany,
He and I went to German schools and learned German,
Then it came time for our trip to Rome,
By train,
He and I couldn't wait to come back to
Germany and go sledding,
We passed through the Alps on the way
to Rome,
I looked up to him,
I twelve and He 'A BOY THIRTEEN',
He was five feet and nine inches tall,
I remember very well looking up and there
He was with the train window down, his head
a little way out with the wind blowing
his red hair as he watched the Alps
passing by,
He was my brother,
My only brother,
One I could play Baseball with,
Someone I could talk to.
In Germany he had bought a camera,
A single lens reflex,
He had a lot of new things going on,
Then on Feb. 6 He died.
He my only brother the one I planned to
back-pack with, the guy I wanted to sled with,
the person I looked up to, the boy that
played baseball with me, the guy with a
new camera, my brother who I could talk to, the
one who could eat as no one else, my brother that
was five feet and nine inches tall, tall and thin with
red hair 'THE BOY THAT WAS THIRTEEN'.
He died because he happened to breathe in some bacteria
that probably can only be seen under some special microscope,
I guess all I can say is I loved him and needed him and that
I don't understand.

– Jeff

In this poem Jeff writes about how he felt when his older brother, Lee, died suddenly from meningitis while they were in Rome on holidays. The boys' father recalls – 'Some days after we returned from Rome, Jeff wrote a poem. He started it one evening, worked on it steadily the next day and then took two hours to type it out on a borrowed typewriter.' The poem's strength is its honesty and simplicity, as Jeff tries to come to terms with his brother's death.

Questions & Assignments

1. What does Jeff remember about his brother's appearance?
2. Jeff recalls in some detail one special moment shared with his brother. Describe this moment in your own words.
3. What kind of activities did Jeff's brother enjoy?
4. *'He had a lot of new things going on.'* What does this line tell us about Jeff's brother?
5. Were you surprised at any point during your first reading of this poem? If so, say where you were surprised and explain why.
6. (a) What do you think of this poem? Did you find it moving, shocking or sad?
   (b) Do you think it is well written? Explain why.

Winter Days

On winter mornings in the playground
The boys stand huddled,
Their cold hands doubled
Into trouser pockets.
The air hangs frozen
About the buildings
And the cold is an ache in the blood
And a pain on the tender skin
Beneath finger nails.
The odd shouts
Sound off like struck iron
And the sun
Balances white
Above the boundary wall.
I fumble my bus ticket
Between numb fingers
Into a fag,
Take a drag
And blow white smoke
Into the December air.

– *Gareth Owen*

Questions & Assignments

1 Choose some words and phrases that best convey the coldness of the day. Explain your choices.
2 Why does the poet describe the sun as white?
3 Explain, in your own words, the final six lines of the poem?
4 Write a poem or a paragraph entitled 'Summer Days' that is set in your school playground.

Stopping by Woods on a Snowy Evening

Whose woods these are I think I know,
His house is in the village though;
He will not see me stopping here
To watch his woods fill up with snow.

My little horse must think it queer
To stop without a farmhouse near
Between the woods and frozen lake
The darkest evening of the year.

He gives his harness bells a shake
To ask if there is some mistake.
The only other sound's the sweep
Of easy wind and downy flake.

The woods are lovely, dark and deep.
But I have promises to keep,
And miles to go before I sleep,
And miles to go before I sleep.

– *Robert Frost*

Questions & Assignments

1 The poet seems relieved that the owner of the woods will not see him looking at the snow falling on the woods. Why do you think this is so?
2 How do we know that the event in the poem occurred in December? Can you give the exact date?
3 The poet stopped to gaze on a wood at the side of the road. What could he see on the other side of the road?
4 How do we know that the scene is deserted?

5 How did the horse respond when the poet decided to stop?
6 Do you think that the poet is a complete stranger or a native of the place described in the poem? Explain your answer.
7 What words suggest that the poet found the scene very peaceful and pleasant?
8 What do we learn about the poet in the final stanza?
9 Consider the final stanza. Do you think that the poet is talking about the journey and tasks that lay ahead of him on that particular evening or has it a deeper meaning? Explain.

Carolling Around the Estate

The six of us met at Alan's house
   and Jane brought a carol sheet
that she got free from the butcher's shop
   when she bought the Sunday meat.

Jeremy had a new lantern light
   made by his Uncle Ted,
and Jim had 'borrowed' his Dad's new torch
   which flashed white, green and red.

Our first call was at Stew Foster's place
   where we sang 'Three Kings' real well.
But his mother couldn't stand the row
   and she really gave us hell!

We drifted on from door to door
   singing carols by lantern light.
Jane's lips were purple with the cold;
   my fingers were turning white.

Around nine we reached the chippie shop
   where we ordered pies and peas,
and with hot grease running down our hands
   we started to defreeze.

I reached home tired out, but my mum said,
   "Your cousin Anne's been here.
She's carolling tomorrow night
   and I said you'd go, my dear."

– Wes Magee

Questions & Assignments

1. Name the carol singers. Does the poet tell us the name of every one of them? Explain.
2. What did the singers bring with them?
3. Explain the expression *'she really gave us hell'*.
4. Do you think the carol singers enjoyed the evening? Give a reason for your answer.
5. Describe the rhyming pattern of the poem.
6. Write a paragraph or a poem about your experiences of going from house to house selling raffle tickets or carol singing.

Shelter

The wind and the rain
   Are beating the windows
Lashing the tree-tops
   Beyond the dark fields

The ships and the sailors
   Are tossed on the ocean,
The fish are all hiding
   Their fins in the deep.

The small birds are clinging
   To sway of the branches,
The fox from his hunting
   Slinks back to his den

The sheep on the mountain
   Are huddled together,
The rabbits are burrowed
   Deep down in the earth.

A dog far away
   Complains in the darkness,
The brown flood is swirling
   Against the stone bridge

I hope there is no one
   Lost without shelter,
Out on the wet roads
   Or up in the hills.

I'm warm under blankets
   Safe from the weather,
Feeling my eyelids
   Surrender to sleep

The great world is turning
   Under the heavens,
This is a moment
   I wish I could keep.

– Michael Coady

Questions & Assignments

1. What words and phrases are used by the poet to capture the power of the storm?
2. The poet imagines what some creatures are doing during the storm. Explain in your own words what they are doing.
3. Say why you think the poet chose each of the following words: *slinks, huddled, complains, swirling.*
4. What are the poet's thoughts on the storm?
5. *'This is a moment / I wish I could keep'.* Why do you think the poet wants to keep that moment?

Spectrum 1

A Crabbit Old Woman Wrote This

What do you see nurses, what do you see?
Are you thinking when you are looking at me -
A crabbit old woman, not very wise,
Uncertain of habit, with far-away eyes,
Who dribbles her food and makes no reply
When you say in a loud voice – 'I do wish you'd try'.
Who seems not to notice the things that you do,
And forever is losing a stocking or shoe.
Who, unresisting or not, lets you do as you will,
With bathing and feeding, the long day to fill.
Is that what you are thinking, is that what you see?
Then open your eyes, nurse, you're not looking at me.

I'll tell you who I am as I sit here so still,
As I use at your bidding, as I eat at your will.
I'm a small child of ten with a father and mother,
Brothers and sisters, who love one another.
A young girl of sixteen with wings on her feet,
Dreaming that soon now a lover she'll meet;
A bride soon at twenty – my heart gives a leap,
Remembering the vows that I promised to keep;
At twenty-five now I have young of my own,
Who need me to build a secure, happy home;
A woman of thirty, my young now grow fast,
Bound to each other with ties that should last;
At forty, my young sons have grown and are gone.
But my man's beside me to see I don't mourn.
At fifty once more babies play round my knee,
Again we know children, my loved one and me.
Dark days are upon me, my husband is dead,
I look at the future, I shudder with dread.
For my young are all rearing young of their own,
And I think of the years and the love that I've known.
I'm an old woman now and nature is cruel –
Tis her jest to make old age look like a fool.
The body it crumbles, grace and vigour depart,
There is now a stone where I once had a heart;
But inside this old carcase a young girl still dwells,
And now and again my battered heart swells.
I remember the joys, I remember the pain,
And I'm loving and living life over again.
I think of the years all too few – gone too fast,
And accept the stark fact that nothing can last.
So open your eyes, nurses, open and see,
Not a crabbit old woman, look closer – see ME!

– *Anonymous*

A nurse in a Scottish hospital found this poem in an old lady's bedside locker after she had died.

Questions & Assignments

1. Who is speaking in this poem?
2. What does the old lady suspect the nurses think about her?
3. Give an account, in your own words, of the old lady's lifestory.
4. *'I look at the future, I shudder with dread.'* What do you understand this line to mean?
5. *'. . . and nature is cruel.'* Why do you think the old lady says this?
6. Do you think that the old lady is angry at the nurses? Give reasons for your answer.
7. What is your response to this poem? (Does it change your outlook in any way? How? Does it frighten you? Why? Will it change your view of old people? Explain.)

Old Dog

Toward the last in the morning she could not
get up, even when I rattled her pan.
I helped her into the yard, but she stumbled
and fell. I knew it was time.

The last night a mist drifted over the fields;
in the morning she would not raise her head –
the far, clear mountains we had walked
surged back to mind.

We looked a slow bargain: our days together
were the ones we already had.
I gave her something the vet had given,
and patted her still, a good last friend.

– *William Stafford*

Questions & Assignments

1. What signs are there in the first stanza that the dog is very old?
2. *'I knew it was time.'* What is meant by this line?
3. *'The last night a mist drifted over the fields.'* Why do you think the poet included this information?
4. What does the poet remember about the dog?
5. Describe the scene of the dog's final moments.
6. What were your thoughts and feelings after reading this poem?

Spectrum 1

Sheepkiller

Later that night the dog escaped
(The child could no longer bear the howling
And untied him out of pity).

Next morning he returned
And came to the kitchen door
With wool and blood on his mouth.

The uncle washed him clean;
Then, without speaking, rode with the child to the mountain
And made him face the flies and the blood.

That night the dog howled in vain;
The child fell asleep,
Listening.

– *Padraig J. Daly*

Questions & Assignments

1 How did the dog escape?
2 Why did the child pity him?
3 What happened the following morning?
4 Why do you think the uncle brought the child to the mountain?
5 Why did the dog howl in vain on the second night?
6 What is your opinion of the child? What would you have done in his situation? Explain.
7 What is your opinion of the uncle? What would you have done in his situation?
8 Was it a painful lesson for the child to learn? Can you remember ever having to learn a similarly painful lesson when you were younger? Describe the lesson in a poem or short story format.
9 Say why you think the following images are well chosen by the poet.
    'with wool and blood on his mouth'
    'the flies and the blood'.
10 How does the poet convey the viciousness of the dog's act without ever actually describing what the animal has done?
11 What light does this poem throw on the following issues – nature . . . animals . . . a tough lesson . . . childhood . . . country life?

Dad

The trouble with me is
i take everything for granted
CAMBODIA – 50,000 dead gee whizz pass the
salt.
i take wars for granted
My dad says it's all because i'm younger
than the bomb.
But the trouble with me is
i take the bomb for granted.
He says
i won't bloody well
take it for granted
when it drops on my head.

i take my head for granted.

– *Brian McCabe*

Questions & Assignments

1. Explain what you understand the poet to mean by *'take everything for granted'*.
2. What sort of things does the poet take for granted?
3. What is his reaction to the news that 50,000 people have been killed in Cambodia?
4. Why does the father think his son takes things for granted?
5. What do you understand by the following lines?
    i won't bloody well
    take it for granted
    when it drops on my head.
6. What is your opinion of the poet? What age do you think he is?
7. How would you describe the poet's attitude to life?
8. What impression do you form of his father?
9. Write a similar poem about yourself. *The trouble with me is . . . .*
10. What insights does the poem reveal about the following subjects – fathers and sons . . . war . . . being young?

Spectrum 1

Mother To Son

Well, son, I'll tell you:
Life for me ain't been no crystal stair.
It's had tacks in it,
And splinters,
And boards torn up,
And places with no carpet on the floor –
Bare.
But all the time
I'se been a-climbin' on,
And reachin' landin's ,
And turnin' corners,
And sometimes goin' in the dark
Where there ain't been no light.
So boy, don't you turn back.
Don't you set down on the steps
'Cause you finds it's kinder hard.
Don't you fall now –
For I'se still goin', honey,
I'se still climbin',
And life for me ain't been no crystal stair.

– *Langston Hughes*

Questions & Assignments

1 Who is speaking in the poem?
2 What is she telling the son about life?
3 Explain the image of the *'crystal stair'*. How is it connected to life?
4 Pick out the words in the poem which relate to the image of the stairs.
5 Do you think the woman has had an easy life? Explain.
6 What advice is she giving? Do you think it is good advice to give a young person? Why?
7 The woman says that sometimes she has gone into *'the dark / Where there ain't been no light.'* What do you think she means by that?
8 Why does she repeat the line *'life for me ain't been no crystal stair'*?
9 What is your impression of the woman?
10 What is your response to this poem?

Teacher

Summer beckons,
jostles the girls
who stare at a poem.

I'm done with them,
weary of their battle
for the warm whip of the sun,
straining to live what they read.

Blameless, of course.
Who could be still
and not anguished, giddy,

as drifts of blossom
eddy outside like pink snow?
Soon there'll be prizes, goodbyes.
I shall become again

the half-remembered voice
from a place of imprisonment,
a rudiment of chalk and red ink,

shall inhabit a cupboard
in someone's mind,
locked in the past as they ascend
inert and adult asylums.

– *Mary E. O'Donnell*

Questions & Assignments

1. Who is speaking in this poem?
2. What is the mood of the speaker? Refer to the poem to support your answer.
3. *'straining to live what they read'*. What do you understand this line to mean?
4. At what time of year is the poem set? Refer to the poem to support your answer.
5. What do you understand by the lines – *'the half-remembered voice / from a place of imprisonment'*?
6. *'locked in the past'*. To whom does this line refer? Explain.
7. Consult your dictionary for the exact meanings of *'inert'* and *'asylums'* (line 21) and then comment on the attitude of the speaker towards the girls' future lives as revealed in the final line.

Spectrum 1

The Choosing

We were first equal Mary and I
with the same coloured ribbons in mouse-coloured hair,
and with equal shyness
we curtseyed to the lady councillor
for copies of Collins' Childrens' Classics.
First equal, equally proud.

Best friends too, Mary and I
a common bond in being cleverest (equal)
in our small school's small class.
I remember
the competition for top desk
or to read aloud the lesson
at school service.
And my terrible fear
of her superiority at sums.

I remember the housing scheme
where we both stayed.
The same house, different homes,
where the choices were made.

I don't know exactly why they moved,
but anyway they went.
Something about a three-apartment
and a cheaper rent.
But from the top deck of the high school bus
I'd glimpse among the others on the corner
Mary's father, mufflered, contrasting strangely
with the elegant greyhounds by his side.
He didn't believe in high-school education,
especially for girls,
or in forking out for uniforms.

Ten years later on a Saturday –
I am coming home from the library –
sitting near me on the bus,
Mary,
with a husband who is tall,
curly haired, has eyes
for no one else but Mary.
His arms are round the full-shaped vase
that is her body.
Oh you can see where the attraction lies
in Mary's life –
not that I envy her really.

And I am coming from the library
with my arms full of books.
I think of the prizes that were ours for the taking
and wonder when the choices got made
we don't remember making.

– Liz Lochhead

Questions & Assignments

1. The first nineteen lines of this poem emphasise the similarities between the two girls. What were these similarities?
2. What caused the friendship between the two girls to fade?
3. (a) What impression do you get of Mary's father from the poem?
   (b) What lines in the poem imply that the poet's father was different?
4. (a) What kind of life does each of the girls have, ten years later?
   (b) *'not that I envy her really.'* Do you accept that the poet is being truthful here?
5. What, in your opinion, are the choices being referred to in the second last line of the poem?
6. Did you find this poem sad? Give a brief reason for your answer.

Spectrum 1

Tich Miller

Tich Miller wore glasses
with elastoplast pink frames
and had one foot three sizes larger than the other.

When they picked teams for outdoor games
She and I were always the last two
left standing by the wire-mesh fence.

We avoided one another's eyes,
Stooping, perhaps to re-tie a shoelace,
or affecting interest in the flight

of some unfortunate bird, and pretended
not to hear the urgent conference:
"Have Tubby!" "No, no, have Tich!"

Usually they chose me, the lesser dud,
and she lolloped, unselected,
to the back of the other team.

At eleven we went to different schools.
In time I learned to get my own back,
sneering at hockey players who couldn't spell.

Tich died when she was twelve.

– Wendy Cope

Questions & Assignments

1. Describe Tich Miller.
2. What do she and the poet have in common?
3. What does the poem suggest about the poet's physical appearance?
4. Describe the behaviour of Tich and the poet as they waited to be selected. How do you imagine they might have felt as they waited?
5. The poet tells us that usually she was chosen. What reason does she give for being chosen? Explain *'the lesser dud'*.
6. What happened when they were eleven?
7. What evidence is there in the poem that the writer learned to cope with her lack of skill at games?
8. What happened to Tich Miller? Is it relevant to how she was treated at school?

Poetry

9 Briefly tell the story of the poem in your own words.
10 What do you think the poet intends to convey in this poem?.

Answer Guidelines

9 The poem *Tich* . . . tells the story of two young . . . who are not very good at . . . They are always left on the sideline as both teams decide which . . . . Usually the poet is . . . and Tich Miller is left . . . We learn from the poem that Tich wore . . . and had odd . . . The poet reveals that she herself was . . . and the other children called her . . .

At the age of . . . they went to different . . . and the poet realised that although she wasn't good at . . . she could spell a lot better than some of the . . . . . . She tells us that . . . died at the age of . . . never having had a chance to overcome her physical weakness.

10 Casual cruelty of children . . . bullying at school . . . the poet's own sympathy for someone who suffered at school and never got the chance to overcome her fears as the author did . . .

Points to Note

Haiku

> A crimson berry
> Splattering softly down on
> The frost white garden.
>   – *Masoaka Shiki*

Haiku is a form of tightly structured Japanese poetry which properly has seventeen syllables arranged in three lines of five, seven and five syllables. This rule is often broken in translations of haiku into English, where stress rather than syllable counting is more important.

A haiku usually consists of two simple images or ideas which our imagination brings together. Note the contrast between the bright red berry and the white frost. The splattered berry may symbolise blood spilled, which would suggest death and the onset of winter.

Here are some more examples.

> Flashing neon light
> Blurred through a steaming window:
> A concert of colours!
>   – *J. W. Hackett*

> Alone I cling to
> The freezing mountain and see
> White cloud - below me
>   – *Ian Serraillier*

> As heavy snow falls
> He's a red-vested Batman
> On a garden fence.

> A sunny spring day,
> People are doing nothing
> In the small village.

No sky and no earth
At all. Only the snowflakes
Fall incessantly.

Through the town's centre
A little stream flows, bordered
By weeping willows.

On the temple bell
Something rests in quiet sleep.
Look, a butterfly!

Snow having melted,
The whole village is brimful
Of happy children.

The peasant hoes on.
The person who asked the way
Is now out of sight.

Questions & Assignments

1 Write a brief comment on each of the haikus on pages 52 and 53.
2 Write some haikus of your own.

Spectrum 1

City Dweller

I have never seen wild Donegal
nor the Atlantic cliffs of Kerry,
though in a haze of alcohol
I might have admired Enniskerry.

I've never dreamt beneath Ben Bulben's head,
or in a pool of poppies hid my face,
and the sweetest poems I have ever read
were down in Christchurch Place.

I've never looked down from the hills of Mourne
to the laughing sea at my feet
for the grandest of scents to my nostrils borne
came from the stalls in Moore Street.

Galway's glories rugged and raw
were in one single afternoon seen,
and the only lakes that I ever saw
were those in St. Stephen's Green.

No call of soft-vowelled curlew
came to me across evening leas,
and all the lilting strains I knew
were in The Shaky Man's on the Quays.

Yet my Liffey dreams were just as sweet
as those in a Wicklow valley,
and my heart was first forged in Merrion Street
and blinded with love in Bull Alley.

– *Christy Brown*

Questions & Assignments

1 According to the poem, has the poet travelled much outside Dublin? Explain.
2 What features of this poem amused you?
3 What point is the poet making in the second last stanza?
4 Describe the rhyming pattern of the poem.
5 What are the poet's feelings towards his native city?
6 Write about your feelings towards your native city, town or village.

The Great Blasket Island

Six men born on this island
have come back after twenty-one years.
They climb up the overgrown roads
to their family houses
and come out shaking their heads.
The roofs have fallen in
and birds have nested in the rafters.
All the whitewashed rooms
all the nagging and praying
and scolding and giggling
and crying and gossiping
are scattered in the memories of these men.
One says, 'Ten of us, blown to the winds –
some in England, some in America, some in Dublin.
Our whole way of life – extinct.'
He blinks back the tears
and looks out across the island
past the ruined houses, the cliffs
and out to the horizon.

Listen, mister, most of us cry sooner or later
over a Great Blasket Island of our own.

– *Julie O'Callaghan*

Questions & Assignments

1 Tell the story of this poem in your own words.
2 What details does the poet use to show that the island has been abandoned for some time?
3 What details show that the place was once full of life?
4 What has happened to the people who used to live on the island?
5 Explain the line: *'Our whole way of life – extinct.'*
6 Describe the reaction of the men as they return to their deserted childhood home?
7 Read the last two lines carefully. What do you think the poet means by saying that *'most of us cry sooner or later / over a Great Blasket island of our own'*?
8 Do you think this is a sad poem? Give reasons.
9 Why do you think the people had to leave their island? Why do you think they returned to visit the place?

Spectrum 1

Answer Guidelines

1 This poem tells the story of . . . who return to . . . .after . . . years. The island of their childhood is now . . . and the poet describes how the roofs have . . . and the birds have . . . The men remember all the talking, nagging and . . . that went on during their . . . Now the men feel . . . because . . . Some of them live in England, others in . . . The poem ends on a note of sadness because the poet states that we all feel sad about some lost part of our childhood.

Happiness

I asked professors who teach the meaning of life to tell me
   what is happiness.
And I went to famous executives who boss the work of
   thousands of men.
They all shook their heads and gave me a smile as though I
   was trying to fool with them.
And then one Sunday afternoon I wandered out along the
   Desplaines river
And I saw a crowd of Hungarians under the trees with their
   women and children and a keg of
   beer and an accordion.

– Carl Sandburg

Questions & Assignments

1 What question does the poet ask of professors and business executives?
2 Why do you think the poet went to professors and famous executives to find the answer?
3 What was their reaction to his question?
4 Why do you think they could not answer his question?
5 Where did the poet eventually find out what happiness was?
6 Describe in your own words, the scene which he observed.
7 Why do you think the Hungarian people were happy? What details about the scene showed they were relaxed and enjoying themselves?
8 Do you think there is a message in this poem? What is it?
9 Write a few lines giving your definition of happiness.

Short Stories

SWALK

The card he was expecting arrived a day early. Monty Quayle found it waiting for him when he got home from school on the thirteenth of February. His first impulse was to chuck it on the fire there and then and be done with it, for he had no time for this slushy, lovey-dovey St Valentine's Day nonsense; but he didn't do that. Perhaps the sheer size of the white envelope appealed to his sense of curiosity. It seemed a good deal too large for his letterbox.

'Who's your admirer, then?' his mother asked slyly as she passed through the kitchen trailing coffee fumes.

'Some twit of a girl,' he said.

'In your form?'

'How do I know?' said Monty, heading smartly for the privacy of his own room. His mother had had two questions and two answers on this subject - more than she had a right to expect.

Actually he had a pretty good idea who was torturing him in this way. In yesterday's French class Gail Summers and Anne Clarke had informed him that he would be receiving a valentine card on February the fourteenth.

'How do you know?' he'd asked in all innocence.

'A wee bird told us,' they said, adding that this card would have the French word for 'love' on it. 'L'amour,' they said, and started to laugh until Anne Clarke sounded like a camel.

In the peace and quiet of his own room Monty examined the uninvited card with as much generosity of spirit as he could muster. One of the giant red hearts on the front had a jagged split running through it, and it sickened him, that broken heart. Your heart was a thumping big muscle in the middle of your chest, it couldn't snap in two like a cheese and onion crisp and how people could ignore a simple fact like that was beyond his understanding. 'My heart longs for you,' said one of the lines inside. Hearts couldn't long for anything, they were for pumping blood and you might as well long for somebody with your left kidney. 'My brain longs for you' would be better. Not that he wanted Gail Summers' or Anne Clarke's brain to long for him either, but at least it would make sense from a biological point of view.

The whole card was a mass of scrawled verses which were so awful that he couldn't stop reading them. What could one say about:

> 'Roses are red,
> Violets are blue,
> If I had three feet,
> You'd be my third shoe'?

A long stick of French bread had been drawn in one corner with a beret on its head. It also had legs. And sunglasses. 'L'amour,' said the heart-shaped bubble escaping from the mouth of this loaf.

Those two were the guilty ones, all right.

On the reverse side of the envelope Monty noticed a word he had never seen before. It didn't even look English. SWALK. What did that mean? Was it yet more French? Monty shoved the whole lot between the pages of an atlas.

Overnight the snow came down. The cars on every road took their time that morning. Although the pavements were awash with melting slush, you could still find the makings of a snowball on the tops of walls or lying on a hedge, and Monty found himself attacked by two people as he approached the school gates. Like most of the girls he knew, those two couldn't throw a snowball to save their lives.

'You missed,' he said.

'Did you get a valentine card this morning?' shouted Anne Clarke, snorting out steam like a dragon.

'No I didn't, hard cheese.'

'Well, we know somebody who sent you one, don't we, Gail?'

'Did you send it?'

'Us?' Anne Clarke released a howl and a giggle into the morning air. 'What makes you think it was *us*?'

Monty did not understand this behaviour, so he went into school hoping that his friend Conor would be back after his dose of the flu.

During the morning he made a point of standing at the back of every line, a tactic which allowed him to go into each classroom last and so avoid Anne Clarke and Gail Summers. If he went in first, they might sit down beside him. Conor couldn't understand why he wasn't pushing and shoving for a radiator seat like everybody else.

In French he put up his hand and asked, quietly, 'Miss Peters, is SWALK a French word?'

She peered at him through the rainbow-framed glasses on the bridge of her nose. She didn't have to peer far, for Monty had been forced to take a seat at the front of the room. Under her nose, in fact.

'What?'

'SWALK, Miss, is it French?'

'Spell it.'

'S-W-A-L-K.'

Some tittering behind made him wonder whether he had asked an intelligent question.

'Are you trying to be funny, Monty Quayle?' said Miss Peters icily, then went on to describe the peculiar habits of some French verb, leaving unsolved the mystery of SWALK.

According to a powerful rumour which invaded the school at lunchtime, all the teachers were afraid of being snowed in and the place was closing early; but that didn't happen. As Conor and Monty walked home at the usual time, Conor – imitating Miss Peters – said, 'Are you trying to be funny, Monty Quayle!' Millions of his flu germs were spluttered over the slushy grey snow. 'I nearly wet myself when you asked her about SWALK.'

And Monty smiled, as if thinking up such humorous things came naturally to him.

'You didn't get a valentine card?' Conor asked shrewdly – a little dart of a question.

'You must be kidding,' said Monty. 'Me? Valentine cards?'

When he got home it was to find that a second card had been delivered to his house, by hand, without a stamp, simply pushed through his front door without so much as a by-your-leave. Monty saw no reason why that sort of thing should be legal.

'Is it from the same person?' his mother wanted to know as she hovered there.

'I don't know,' said Monty, staring at the two words written in capitals on the flap. SWALK and SWALK. Two of them. Plural swalks.

'What does SWALK actually mean?' he asked, making use of his mother.

'Sealed with a loving kiss.'

'Cut out the goo talk, Mum!'

'It does. Goo talk, indeed! S for sealed, W for with, L for loving, K for kiss. It's short for "sealed with a loving kiss".'

Hell's bells! And he'd asked Miss Peters, who now thought of him as a fool, if it was French – she'd think he was girl-mad. Sealed with a loving kiss! Oh, the shame of it, and he hated kissing; his relatives no longer tried it on because he'd put a stop to it – on TV he hated that cissy lip stuff and the horrible sucking noises made by people joined together at their mouths! The humiliation he felt was colossal – his pride all drained away.

He threw the valentine card on the fire and watched until both SWALKs were consumed by it utterly.

'Well, that's not a very nice way to go on,' his mother said. Not that he cared. She had no understanding of the situation whatsoever.

I'll send *them* a card! Monty raced upstairs. I'll send them some card, all right, and it'll be plastered with words the French never heard of. SWAFEJ, he thought. Sealed with a frog's eyeball juice. And SWAMS. Sealed with a monkey's stink. In no time at all he had over a dozen good ones - letters sealed with acid rain, elephant's wee-wee, a pelican's egg yolk, lubricating oil, mashed maggots and worse. Much worse. This line of thinking was effective in its own way, for he had calmed down quite a lot by the time he looked out of his bedroom window and saw both of them standing in the street below.

They had a spaniel-looking dog lolloping round their legs. The sight of this thing's floppy ears and its big soft belly as round as a melon inspired Monty with a cunning idea. Down the stairs he flew three at a time, calling out for Mighty Wolf to appear by his side.

Their yappy mongrel had actually been named Patch for an obvious reason, but he also answered to names like Fleabag, Lagerlout and Mighty Wolf. That dog hated every living thing that did not belong to his own family; and it hated, besides, non-living things within the family. (The hoover was its mortal enemy.) If you held up a mirror he also went berserk, which meant that Mighty Wolf was a creature who even hated himself. Monty opened the front door just enough - and let him loose. Some people were about to learn that it didn't pay to lurk.

This plan backfired horribly, as Monty had to admit when he sneaked down the path some moments later. His fool of a dog was actually showing off in front of the spaniel with a display of athletic twirls and frisky jumps. In between the twirls and jumps there occurred some rubbing of noses. SWALK, thought Monty – bitterly – again. It was as if the creature knew it was St Valentine's Day.

'Your dog likes Sheila,' said Anne Clark.

'He's just friendly,' lied Monty, scooping up the animal into his arms. This was to stop the disgusting smelling of behinds that was now going on.

'Did you get a valentine card?'

'Yes I did.' He was flustered, and could not duck the question.

'We know who sent it even though there's no name on it, don't we, Gail?'

Gail Summers blushed until her cheeks glowed; and then the beast within the cradle of Monty's arms began to whine with desire. A stump of a tail flicked backwards and forwards in front of his face like a windscreen wiper.

'It wants its tea,' Monty explained, retreating smartly up the path and into the house again, where Mighty Wolf got told in no uncertain terms what a big soft wet pudding he had degenerated into.

About the same time on the following day there came a knock at the front door which Monty, to his regret, left for his mother to answer.

She returned saying, 'It's young Gail

Summers. She wants to know: is your dog coming out? And you needn't look at me like that – go and speak to her.'

There she stood on his step, with spaniel, wearing a woollen hat and a scarf that seemed to go round her neck at least three times. Not much of her face could be seen, actually.

'Is Patch coming out?' she asked.

Patch, he thought. And how did she get to know Fleabag's real name? No doubt enquiries had been made.

'He's got a thorn in his foot.'

'Is it sore?'

'We had to bathe it.'

'Did you use hot water?'

'And disinfectant,' Monty assured her, while holding on to the door in case Mighty Wolf put in an appearance.

'Well, bye-bye, then,' said Gail, with a twist at Sheila spaniel's lead, 'I'll see you in school tomorrow.'

'Goodbye,' said Monty, as if he was leaving that night for Australia.

This business about the valentine cards forced him to take a look at himself in the long mirror that evening, and to ask: what could there be about that person on the other side of the looking glass to drive someone to send him a card that was sealed, not once, but twice, with a loving kiss? Surely such magnetism in a human being would be recognisable? All the same, he couldn't find it. After viewing himself from many angles he remained none the wiser.

Going to school next day he noticed Gail Summers on the road ahead of him. Now it was certainly a treacherous morning for walking, and ridges of frozen slush glittered in the early sunlight; but he knew fine rightly that she was not walking slowly because of the ice. The idea was that he should catch up with her, which he did.

'Daddy had to break the ice on our pond this morning,' she said.

'Goldfish?' he said.

'No. It's for wildlife. Goldfish eat tadpoles. One slurp and they're gone.'

'My girlfriend has goldfish,' Monty suddenly blurted out. 'They're big ones as long as your foot, I'd say.'

'Who is she?'

The sheer cheek of this question – the colossal amount of nosiness involved in it – allowed Monty to glare at her angrily.

'It's none of your business who she is.'

'You haven't got one, that's why.'

'That's where you're wrong.'

'Well, who is she, then?'

She didn't believe him! In spite of the fact that he'd even described his girlfriend's goldfish, his word on this important subject was not good enough for her!

'She's Glenda Finch, if you must know.'

Glenda was a rough sort, the sort who pulled hair and who wouldn't take kindly to someone who tried to steal her boyfriend. On the spur of the moment she was a very good choice, Monty was thinking. As he parted company with Gail Summers he felt that he had solved his problem, for anybody with any sense would now find another person to pursue.

At breaktime Conor told him that Glenda Finch was looking for him.

'What for?'

'Dunno,' said Conor. 'Something to do with rumours and goldfish. She says you're saying things about her and she's going to squash you like a grub. You know what she's like.'

Oh God. Only too well, he knew what Glenda was like. No matter which point of the compass she approached from you heard her coming, and you heard her go. She went through life making mountains out of molehills and molehills out of mountains.

Rather like a mole himself, Monty went underground for the rest of the morning. Great care had to be taken while crossing the playground, and he longed for a periscope to enable him to see round corners and down corridors. Often he reflected on the treachery of girls like Gail Summers, who could send you a letter sealed with a loving kiss on a Tuesday and then land you right in it the day after.

At lunchtime Glenda Finch trapped him in the crowded room where people went to eat their sandwiches. There was, in fact, an open window to hand, but only a genuine coward could have done a bunk like that.

'You're saying things about me, Monty Quayle! You said I'm your *girlfriend*!'

The whole situation – he saw as one detached – was just completely crazy. And the craziest thing of all was that, yes, somehow he *had* said that. My girlfriend is Glenda Finch, he'd said. And why? He must have been temporarily insane. Glenda could never be anyone's girlfriend, for crying out loud, it would be too dangerous.

'And you said I sent you a valentine card! You'd better watch it, Quayle. I wouldn't send you a valentine card for a pension and I wouldn't be your girlfriend if you were the last person left alive after a nuclear bomb. And I haven't got *goldfish*!' she screamed, finishing on a high note. Monty wondered desperately if he could pretend that there was another Glenda Finch.

There was more. Monty fought back with such statements as 'Shut your spout, fat whale,' in order to avoid being overwhelmed completely. After the contest he felt quite tingly and invigorated – as joggers must do, he reflected.

And Gail Summers did not trouble him from that time on.

The days raced by, and the long evenings of summer came again. That was the year when the Quayle family went abroad for the first time on a camping holiday in Northern France. Part of the thinking behind the holiday was that Monty would get a chance to practise his French, but he spent the time playing with English-speaking children and got by with a few French words for sweets. While they were away Mighty Wolf attacked a moving Volkswagen in the street and banjoed his leg. The mutt recovered all right, but once arthritis set into his left hip he could hardly muster the enthusiasm to see off a stray cat.

Two more summers went by. Monty found himself looking up at the sky at night, and wondered about the distances between the stars – a thing he had never done before. It made him sense for the first time the possible insignificance of terrestrial affairs. On some occasions he experienced in the evenings what he himself described as 'the coloured peace of sunsets'; on others, he felt disturbed by vague longings which he could not name. He grew conscious of his appearance and cared especially for his hair. The thought of going thin on top like his dad scared the wits out of him.

The girl he fancied was Gail Summers. Wherever he went he carried in his mind's eye the fling of her dark hair and the swaying of her body – these were things he could not forget, and to hear her laughing in the company of other people was like hearing laughter over the wall of a scented garden from which a time warp had excluded him. In his heart – figuratively speaking, of course – he conceded that if he had three feet she'd be his third shoe: but she was now going strong with some fellow from Bell's Hill.

– *Sam McBratney*

Spectrum 1

WORD POWER

Find words in the story which have similar meanings to each of the words and phrases below. The number in brackets after each one indicates the number of letters in the answer. The words appear in the story in the same order as the meanings given below.

CLUES

1. sudden urge (7)
2. told (8)
3. getting (9)
4. uneven (6)
5. scribbled (8)
6. pushed (6)
7. came towards (10)
8. way of acting (9)
9. plan; method (6)
10. gazed (6)
11. low laughter (9)
12. unconfirmed news (6)
13. embarrassment; shame (11)
14. working well (9)
15. gave an idea (8)
16. playful (6)
17. momentarily confused (9)
18. very dangerous (11)
19. shone brightly (9)
20. spoke on impulse (7)
21. very big (8)
22. help (6)
23. traitor-like behaviour (9)
24. refreshed; energetic (11)
25. keen interest (10)
26. unimportance (14)
27. earthly (11)
28. perfumed (7)
29. kept out (7)
30. admitted; gave in (8)

Questions & Assignments

1. How does the author attempt to capture our interest in the opening paragraph of the story?
   Does he succeed in sustaining this interest throughout the story? Explain.
2. What are Monty's feelings about the hearts on the valentine cards? Do you agree with him on these? Give a reason for your answer.
3. Would you agree that there is a good deal of humour in this story? Explain
4. Why was Monty ashamed when he found out what the letters SWALK mean?
5. Comment on the characters of Gail Summers, Anne Clarke and Glenda Finch. Do you regard them as realistic creations? Give reasons for your answer.
6. Describe the relationship between Monty and his mother, i.e. discuss how he treats her and how she treats him.
7. What is your attitude towards Monty's behaviour during the events around Valentine's Day? How has he changed two years later?
8. Do you think that the story provides important insights on the problems of growing up? Support your answer by referring to the story.
9. What features of the author's descriptive powers impressed you?

SWALK

Answer Guidelines

3 Authors generally use three methods to create humour in a . . .
  (i) **Language:** descriptions and phrases that are funny. Consider the types of comparisons (similes) the author uses . . . The initials Monty would like to put on envelopes . . . the description of the dog . . . the description of Glenda Finch . . .
  (ii) **Characters:** people that do and say funny things. In most cases the funny characters take themselves very seriously. Very often characters that would be very disagreeable to live with in real life are the source of much humour in stories. Comment on one or two characters in the story.
  (iii) **Situations:** when characters end up in situations that make them look silly. The situations are usually caused by mix-ups and misunderstandings and are generally of the character's own making. How he learns what the letters SWALK mean . . . the behaviour of the dog . . . the lie he tells Gail . . . the behaviour of Glenda Finch . . . Monty's feelings about Gail two years later . . .

Personal Writing

1 Write a description of your own dog (real or imaginary). Try to use some of the techniques used in the story.
2 'Valentine's Day is an opportunity for greeting card manufacturers, flower shops, restaurants and other businesses to make lots of money by playing on people's feelings. It should be abolished!' Write a essay explaining your views on this statement.

POETRY WORKSHOP

Compose some original verses for Valentine's Day cards.

'Roses are Red.

Violets are Blue.

. . .'

First Confession

All the trouble began when my grandfather died and my grandmother – my father's mother – came to live with us. Relations in the one house are a strain at the best of times, but to make matters worse, my grandmother was a real old countrywoman and quite unsuited to the life in town. She had a fat, wrinkled old face, and to Mother's great indignation, went round the house in bare feet – the boots had her crippled, she said. For dinner she had a jug of porter and a pot of potatoes on the table and ate them slowly, with great relish, using her fingers by way of a fork.

Now, girls are supposed to be fastidious, but I was the one who suffered most from this. Nora, my sister, just sucked up to the old woman for the penny she got every Friday out of the old-age pension, a thing I could not do. I was too honest, that was my trouble; and when I was playing with Bill Connell, the sergeant-major's son, and saw my grandmother steering up the path with the jug of porter sticking out from beneath her shawl, I was mortified. I made excuses not to let him come into the house, because I could never be sure what she would be up to when we went in.

When Mother was at work and my grandmother made the dinner I wouldn't touch it. Nora once tried to make me, but I hid under the table from her and took the breadknife with me for protection. Nora let on to be very indignant (she wasn't, of course, but she knew Mother saw through her, so she sided with Gran) and came after me. I lashed out at her with the breadknife, and after that she left me alone. I stayed there till Mother came in from work and made my dinner, but when Father came in later, Nora said in a shocked voice: "Oh, Dadda, do you know what Jackie did at dinnertime?" Mother interfered, and for days after that he didn't speak to me and Mother barely spoke to Nora. And all because of that old woman! God knows, I was heart-scalded.

Then, to crown my misfortunes, I had to make my first confession and communion. It was an old woman called Ryan who prepared us for these. She was about the one age with Gran; she was well-to-do, lived in a big house on Montenotte, wore a black cloak and bonnet, and came every day to school at three o'clock when we should have been going home, and talked to us of hell. She may have mentioned the other place as well, but that could only have been by accident, for hell had the first place in her heart.

She lit a candle, took out a new half-crown, and offered it to the first boy who would hold one finger – only one finger – in the flame for five minutes by the school clock. Being always very ambitious I was tempted to volunteer, but I thought it might look greedy. Then she asked were we afraid of holding one finger – only one finger – in a little candle flame for five minutes and not afraid of burning all over in roasting hot furnaces for all eternity. "All eternity! Just think of that! A whole lifetime goes by and it's nothing, not even a drop in the ocean of your sufferings." The woman was really interesting about hell, but my attention was all fixed on the half-crown. At the end of the lesson she put it back in her purse. It was a great disappointment; a religious woman like that, you wouldn't think she'd bother about a thing like a half-crown.

Another day she said she knew a priest who woke one night to find a fellow he didn't recognise leaning over the end of his bed. The priest was a bit frightened – naturally enough – but he asked the fellow what he wanted, and the fellow said in a deep, husky voice that he wanted to go to confession. The priest said it was an awkward time and wouldn't it do in the morning, but the fellow said that last time he went to confession, there was one sin he kept back, being ashamed to mention it, and now it was always on his mind. Then the priest knew it was a bad case, because the fellow was after making a bad confession and committing a mortal sin. He got up to dress, and just then the cock crew in the yard outside, and – low and behold – when the priest looked round there was no sign of the fellow, only a smell of burning timber, and when the priest looked at his bed didn't he see the print of two hands burned in it? That was because the fellow had made a bad confession. This story made a shocking impression on me.

But the worst of all was when she showed us how to examine our conscience. Did we take the name of the Lord, our God, in vain? Did we honour our father and our mother? (I asked her did this include grandmothers and she said it did.) Did we love our neighbours as ourselves? Did we covet our neighbour's goods? (I thought of the way I felt about the penny that Nora got every Friday.) I decided that, between one thing and another, I must have broken the whole ten commandments, all on account of that old woman, and so far as I could see, so long as she remained in the house, I had no hope of ever doing anything else.

I was scared to death of confession. The day the whole class went, I let on to have a toothache, hoping my absence wouldn't be noticed; but at three o'clock just as I was feeling safe, along comes a chap with a message from Mrs. Ryan that I was to go to confession myself on Saturday and be at the chapel for communion with the rest. To make it worse, Mother couldn't come with me and sent Nora instead.

Now, that girl had ways of tormenting me that Mother never knew of. She held my hand as we went down the hill, smiling sadly and saying how sorry she was for me, as if she were bringing me to the hospital for an operation.

"Oh, God help us!" she moaned. "Isn't it a terrible pity you weren't a good boy? Oh, Jackie, my heart bleeds for you! How will you ever think of all your sins? Don't forget you have to tell him about the time you kicked Gran on the shin."

"Lemme go!" I said, trying to drag myself free of her. "I don't want to go to confession at all."

"But sure, you'll have to go to confession, Jackie," she replied in the same regretful tone. "Sure, if you didn't, the parish priest would be up to the house, looking for you. Tisn't, God knows, that I'm not sorry for you. Do you remember the time you tried to kill me with the breadknife under the table? And the language you used to me? I don't know what he'll do with you at all, Jackie. He might have to send you to the bishop."

I remember thinking bitterly that she didn't know the half of what I had to tell – if I told it. I knew I couldn't tell it, and understood perfectly why the fellow in Mrs. Ryan's story made a bad confession; it seemed to me a great shame that people wouldn't stop criticising him. I remember that steep hill down to the church, and the sunlit hillsides beyond the valley of the river, which

I saw in the gaps between the houses like Adam's last glimpse of Paradise.

Then, when she had manoeuvred me down the long flight of steps to the chapel yard, Nora suddenly changed her tone. She became the raging malicious devil she really was.

"There you are!" she said with a yelp of triumph, hurling me through the church door. "And I hope he'll give you the penitential psalms, you dirty little caffler."

I knew then I was lost, given up to eternal justice. The door with the coloured-glass panels swung shut behind me, the sunlight went out and gave place to deep shadow, and the wind whistled outside so that the silence within seemed to crackle like ice under my feet. Nora sat in front of me by the confession box. There were a couple of old women ahead of her, and then a miserable-looking poor devil came and wedged me in at the other side, so that I couldn't escape even if I had the courage. He joined his hands and rolled his eyes in the direction of the roof, muttering aspirations in an anguished tone, and I wondered had he a grandmother too. Only a grandmother could account for a fellow behaving in that heartbroken way, but he was better off than I, for he at least could go and confess his sins; while I would make a bad confession and then die in the night and be continually coming back and burning people's furniture.

Nora's turn came, and I heard the sound of something slamming, and then her voice as if butter wouldn't melt in her mouth, and then another slam, and out she came. God, the hypocrisy of women! Her eyes were lowered, her head was bowed, and her hands were joined very low down on her stomach, and she walked up the aisle to the side altar looking like a saint. You never saw such an exhibition of devotion; and I remembered the devilish malice with which she had tormented me all the way from our door, and wondered were all religious people like that, really. It was my turn now. With the fear of damnation in my soul I went in, and the confessional door closed of itself behind me.

It was pitch-dark and I couldn't see priest or anything else. Then I really began to be frightened. In the darkness it was a matter between God and me, and He had all the odds. He knew what my intentions were before I even started; I had no chance. All I had ever been told about confession got mixed up in my mind, and I knelt to one wall and said: "Bless me, father, for I have sinned; this is my first confession." I waited for a few minutes, but nothing happened, so I tried it on the other wall. Nothing happened there either. He had me spotted all right.

It must have been then that I noticed the shelf at about one height with my head. It was really a place for grown-up people to rest their elbows, but in my distracted state, I thought it was probably the place you were supposed to kneel. Of course, it was on the high side and not very deep, but I was always good at climbing and managed to get up all right. Staying up was the trouble. There was room only for my knees, and nothing you could get a grip on but a sort of wooden moulding a bit above it. I held on to the moulding and repeated the words a little louder, and this time something happened all right. A slide was slammed back; a little light entered the box, and a man's voice said; "Who's there?"

"'Tis me, father," I said for fear he mightn't see me and go away again. I couldn't see him at all. The place the voice came from was under the moulding and I swung myself down till I saw the astonished face of a young priest looking up at me. He had to put his head on one side to see me, and I had to put mine on one side to see him, so we were more or less talking to one another upside-down. It struck me as a queer way of hearing confessions, but I didn't feel it my place to criticise.

"Bless me, father, for I have sinned; this is

my first confession," I rattled off all in one breath, and swung myself down the least shade more to make it easier for him.

"What are you doing up there?" he shouted in an angry voice, and the strain the politeness was putting on my hold of the moulding, and the shock of being addressed in such an uncivil tone, were too much for me. I lost my grip, tumbled, and hit the door an unmerciful wallop before I found myself flat on my back in the middle of the aisle. The people who had been waiting stood up with their mouths open. The priest opened the door of the middle box and came out, pushing his biretta back from his forehead; he looked something terrible. Then Nora came scampering down the aisle.

"Oh, you dirty little caffler!" she said. "I might have known you'd do it. I might have known you'd disgrace me. I can't leave you out of my sight for one minute."

Before I could even get to my feet to defend myself she bent down and gave me a clip across the ear. This reminded me that I was so stunned I had even forgotten to cry, so that people might think I wasn't hurt at all, when in fact I was probably maimed for life. I gave a roar out of me.

"What's all this about?" the priest hissed, getting angrier than ever and pushing Nora off me. "How dare you hit the child like that, you little vixen?"

"But I can't do my penance with him, father," Nora cried, cocking an outraged eye up at him.

"Well, go and do it, or I'll give you some more to do," he said, giving me a hand up. "Was it coming to confession you were, my poor man?" he asked me.

"Twas, father," said I with a sob.

"Oh," he said respectfully, "a big hefty fellow like you must have terrible sins. Is this your first?"

"Tis, father," said I.

"Worse and worse," he said gloomily. "The crimes of a lifetime. I don't know will I get rid of you at all today. You'd better wait now till I'm finished with these old ones. You can see by the looks of them they haven't much to tell."

"I will, father," I said with something approaching joy.

The relief of it was really enormous. Nora stuck out her tongue at me from behind his back, but I couldn't even be bothered retorting. I knew from the very moment that man opened his mouth that he was intelligent above the ordinary. When I had time to think, I saw how right I was. It only stood to reason that a fellow confessing after seven years would have more to tell than people that went every week. The crimes of a lifetime, exactly as he said. It was only what he expected, and the rest was the cackle of old women and girls with their talk of hell, the bishop, and the penitential psalms. That was all they knew. I started to make my examination of conscience, and barring the one bad business of my grandmother, it didn't seem so bad.

The next time, the priest steered me into

the confession box himself and left the shutter back, the way I could see him get in and sit down at the further side of the grille from me.

"Well, now," he said, "what do they call you?"

"Jackie, father," said I.

"And what's a-trouble to you, Jackie?"

"Father," I said, feeling I might as well get it over while I had him in good humour, "I had it all arranged to kill my grandmother."

He seemed a bit shaken by that, all right, because he said nothing for quite a while.

"My goodness," he said at last, "that'd be a shocking thing to do. What put that into your head?"

"Father," I said, feeling very sorry for myself, "she's an awful woman."

"Is she?" he asked. "What way is she awful?"

"She takes porter, father," I said, knowing well from the way Mother talked of it that this was a mortal sin, and hoping it would make the priest take a more favourable view of my case.

"Oh, my!" he said, and I could see he was impressed.

"And snuff, father," said I.

"That's a bad case, sure enough, Jackie," he said.

"And she goes round in her bare feet, father," I went on in a rush of self-pity, "and she knows I don't like her, and she gives pennies to Nora and none to me, and my da sides with her and flakes me, and one night I was so heart-scalded I made up my mind I'd have to kill her."

"And what would you do with the body?" he asked with great interest.

"I was thinking I could chop that up and carry it away in a barrow I have," I said.

"Begor, Jackie," he said, "do you know you're a terrible child?"

"I know, father," I said, for I was just thinking the same thing myself. "I tried to kill Nora too with a breadknife under the table, only I missed her."

"Is that the little girl that was beating you just now?" he asked.

"'Tis, father."

"Someone will go for her with a breadknife one day, and he won't miss her," he said rather cryptically. "You must have great courage. Between ourselves, there's a lot of people I'd like to do the same to, but I'd never have the nerve. Hanging is an awful death."

"Is it, father?" I asked with the deepest interest – I was always very keen on hanging. "Did you ever see a fellow hanged?"

"Dozens of them," he said solemnly. "And they all died roaring."

"Jay!" I said.

"Oh, a horrible death!" he said with great satisfaction. "Lots of the fellows I saw, killed their grandmothers too, but they all said 'twas never worth it."

He had me there for a full ten minutes talking, and then walked out the chapel yard with me. I was genuinely sorry to part with him, because he was the most entertaining character I'd ever met in the religious line. Outside, after the shadow of the church, the sunlight was like the roaring of waves on a beach; it dazzled me; and when the frozen silence melted and I heard the screech of trams on the road, my heart soared. I knew now I wouldn't die in the night and come back, leaving marks on my mother's furniture. It would be a great worry to her, and the poor soul had enough.

Nora was sitting on the railing, waiting for me, and she put on a very sour puss when she saw the priest with me. She was mad jealous because a priest had never come out of the church with her.

"Well," she asked coldly, after he left me, "what did he give you?"

"Three Hail Marys," I said.

"Three Hail Marys," she repeated incredulously. "You mustn't have told him anything."

First Confession

"I told him everything," I said confidently.

"About Gran and all?"

"About Gran and all."

(All she wanted was to be able to go home and say I'd made a bad confession.)

"Did you tell him you went for me with the breadknife?" she asked with a frown.

"I did to be sure."

"And he only gave you three Hail Marys?"

"That's all."

She slowly got down from the railing with a baffled air. Clearly, this was beyond her. As we mounted the steps back to the main road, she looked at me suspiciously.

"What are you sucking?" she asked.

"Bullseyes."

"Was it the priest gave them to you?"

"Twas."

"Lord God," she wailed bitterly, "some people have all the luck! 'Tis no advantage to anybody trying to be good. I might just as well be a sinner like you."

— *Frank O'Connor*

WORD POWER

Find words in the story which have similar meanings to each of the words and phrases below. The number in brackets after each one indicates the number of letters in the answer. The words appear in the story in the same order as the meanings given below.

CLUES

1. not suitable (8) *unsuited*
2. creased or lined skin (8) *wrinkled*
3. over-careful or difficult to please (10) *fastidious*
4. very ashamed (9) *mortified*
5. bad luck (11) *misfortunes*
6. spoke of briefly (9) *mentioned*
7. eager to do well (9) *ambitious*
8. offer to help (9) *volunteer*
9. feeling shame (7)
10. treating cruelly (10)
11. angrily, resentfully (8)
12. finding fault with (11)
13. brief view (7)
14. distressful (9)
15. public display (10)
16. very dark (5,4)
17. surprised (10)
18. replying (9)
19. mysteriously (11)
20. bravery (7)
21. in a serious tone (8)
22. in disbelief (13)

Points to Note

First Confession is probably Frank O'Connor's best known story. The story is semi-autobiographical, i.e. some of the characters and events are from his own childhood. The grandmother in the story and the circumstances that led to her moving to the city are identical to the writer's own grandmother. The story is set in the St. Luke's area of the city where O'Connor spent part of his childhood. The church in the story is St. Patrick's with its *'long flight of steps* (from Summerhill) *to the chapel yard'*. On the other hand, Nora is a fictitious character. O'Connor was an only child, a term he chose as the title for the first volume of his unfinished autobiography, *An Only Child*. The title of the second volume of his autobiography is *My Father's Son*.

THE WORK OF FRANK O'CONNOR

Frank O'Connor (1903 -1966) is famous world-wide for his short stories. They have been translated and published in many different languages – a distinction very few authors achieve. The raw material for most of his stories was the ordinary people of his native city of Cork. O'Connor drew inspiration from their hopes and fears, their triumphs and tragedies, their decency and, more so, their follies. They were a people whom he understood and wrote about in a generous and compassionate way. Yet he succeeded in portraying them in a way that had a universal appeal, i.e. a reader from Liverpool or Munich or Moscow could enjoy the stories and identify with the characters and their situations.

Frank O'Connor was born in Cork in 1903 and his formal education ended when he left national school. He was an avid reader from childhood and, after a number of short-term jobs, he worked as a librarian in Wicklow, Dublin and Cork.

Questions & Assignments

1. Why did Jackie's grandmother come to live with his family?
2. Describe Jackie's feelings towards his grandmother.
3. Explain clearly why Jackie was punished by his father.
4. Explain how Jackie is persecuted in this story.
5. What are your views on Mrs. Ryan's methods of teaching religion?
6. Describe clearly what happened in the confession box.
7. Write an account of Nora's character.
8. Tell the story of Jackie's first confession from Nora's point of view. You could begin as follows: *'On Saturday last, mother asked me to take Jackie to make his first confession,'* or, *'I will never forget the day my brother, Jackie, made his first confession.'*
9. What aspects of the story did you find humorous? In your answer, refer to the people in the story, the situations that arose, the use of language and the style of writing.

CHRISTMAS MORNING

I never really liked my brother, Sonny. From the time he was a baby he was always the mother's pet and always chasing her to tell her what mischief I was up to. Mind you, I was usually up to something. Until I was nine or ten I was never much good at school, and I really believe it was to spite me that he was so smart at his books. He seemed to know by instinct that this was what Mother had set her heart on, and you might almost say he spelt himself into her favour.

'Mummy,' he'd say, 'will I call Larry in to t-e-a?' or: 'Mummy, the k-e-t-e-l is boiling', and of course, when he was wrong she'd correct him, and next time he'd have it right and there would be no standing him. 'Mummy, aren't I a good speller?' Cripes, we could all be good spellers if we went on like that!

Mind you, it wasn't that I was stupid. Far from it. I was restless and not able to fix my mind for long on any one thing. I'd do the lessons for the year before, or the lessons for the year after; what I couldn't stand were the lessons we were supposed to be doing at the time. In the evenings I used to go out and play with the Doherty gang. Not, again, that I was rough, but I liked the excitement and for the life of me I couldn't see what attracted Mother about education.

'Can't you do your lessons first and play after?' she'd say, getting white with indignation. 'You ought to be ashamed of yourself that your baby brother can read better than you.'

She didn't seem to understand that I wasn't, because there didn't seem to me to be anything particularly praiseworthy about reading, and it struck me as an occupation better suited to a sissy kid like Sonny.

'The dear knows what will become of you,' she'd say. 'If only you'd stick on your books you might be something good like a clerk or an engineer.'

'I'll be a clerk, Mummy,' Sonny would say smugly.

'Who wants to be an old clerk?' I'd say, just to annoy him. 'I'm going to be a soldier.'

'The dear knows, I'm afraid that's all you'll ever be fit for,' she would add with a sigh.

I couldn't help feeling at times that she wasn't all there. As if there was anything better a fellow could be!

Coming on to Christmas, with the days getting shorter and the shopping crowds bigger, I began to think of all the things I might get from Santa Claus. The Dohertys said there was no Santa Claus, only what your father and mother gave you, but the Dohertys were a rough class of children you wouldn't expect Santa to come to anyway. I was rooting round for whatever information I could pick up about him, but there didn't seem to be much. I was no hand with a pen, but if a letter would do any good I was ready to chance writing to him. I had plenty of initiative and was always writing off for free samples and prospectuses.

'Ah, I don't know will he come at all this year,' Mother said with a worried air. 'He has enough to do looking after steady boys who mind the lessons without bothering about the

71

rest.'

Well, I did my best, God knows I did! It wasn't my fault, if, four days before the holidays, Flogger Dawley gave us sums we couldn't do, and Peter Doherty and myself had to go on the lang. It wasn't for the love of it, for, take it from me, December is no month for mitching, and we spent most of our time sheltering from the rain in a store on the quays. The only mistake we made was imagining we could keep it up till the holiday without being spotted. That showed real lack of foresight.

Of course, Flogger Dawley noticed and sent home word to know what was keeping me. When I came in on the third day the mother gave me a look I'll never forget, and said: 'Your dinner is there.' She was too full to talk. When I tried to explain to her about Flogger Dawley and the sums she brushed it aside and said: 'You have no word.' I saw then it wasn't the langing she minded but the lies, though I still didn't see how you could lang without lying. She didn't speak to me for days. And even then I couldn't make out what she saw in education, or why she couldn't let me grow up naturally like anyone else.

To make things worse, it stuffed Sonny up more than ever. He had the air of one saying: 'I don't know what they'd do without me in this blooming house.' He stood at the front door, leaning against the jamb with his hands in his trouser pockets, trying to make himself look like Father, and shouted to the other kids so that he could be heard all over the road.

'Larry isn't let go out. He went on the lang with Peter Doherty and me mother isn't talking to him.'

And at night, when we were in bed, he kept it up.

'Santa Claus won't bring you anything this year, aha!'

'Of course he will,' I said.

'How do you know?'

'Why wouldn't he?'

'Because you went on the lang with Doherty. I wouldn't play with them Doherty fellows.'

'You wouldn't be left.'

'I wouldn't play with them. They've no class. They had the bobbies up to the house.'

'And how would Santa know I was on the lang with Peter Doherty?' I growled, losing patience with the little prig.

'Of course he'd know. Mummy would tell him.'

'And how could Mummy tell him and he up at the North Pole? Poor Ireland, she's rearing them yet! 'Tis easy seen you're only an old baby.'

'I'm not a baby, and I can spell better than you, and Santa won't bring you anything.'

'We'll see whether he will or not,' I said sarcastically, doing the old man on him.

But, to tell the God's truth, the old man was only bluff. You could never tell what powers these superhuman chaps would have of knowing what you were up to. And I had a bad conscience about the langing because I'd never before seen the mother like that.

That was the night I decided that the only sensible thing to do was to see Santa myself and explain to him. Being a man, he'd probably understand. In those days I was a good-looking kid and had a way with me when I liked. I had only to smile nicely at one old gent on the North Mall to get a penny from him, and I felt if only I could get Santa by himself I could do the same with him and maybe get something worthwhile from him. I wanted a model railway; I was sick of Ludo and Snakes-and-Ladders.

I started to practise lying awake, counting five hundred and then a thousand, and trying to hear first eleven, then midnight, from Shandon. I felt sure Santa would be round by midnight, seeing that he'd be coming from the north, and would have the whole of the south side to do afterwards. In some ways I was very farsighted. The only trouble was the things I was farsighted about.

Christmas Morning

I was so wrapped up in my own calculations that I had little attention to spare for Mother's difficulties. Sonny and I used to go to town with her, and while she was shopping we stood outside a toyshop in the North Main Street arguing about what we'd like for Christmas.

On Christmas Eve when Father came home from work and gave her the housekeeping money, she stood looking at it doubtfully while her face grew white.

'Well?' he snapped, getting angry. 'What's wrong with that?'

'What's wrong with that?' she muttered. 'On Christmas Eve!'

'Well,' he asked truculently, sticking his hands in his trouser pockets as though to guard what was left , 'do you think I get more because it's Christmas?'

'Lord God,' she muttered distractedly.

'And not a bit of cake in the house, nor a candle, nor anything!'

'All right,' he shouted, beginning to stamp. 'How much will the candle be?'

'Ah, for pity's sake,' she cried, 'will you give me the money and not argue like that before the children? Do you think I'll leave them with nothing on the one day of the year?'

'Bad luck to you and your children!' he snarled. 'Am I to be slaving from one year's end to another for you to be throwing it away on toys? Here,' he added, tossing two half-crowns on the table, 'that's all you're going to get, so make the most of it.'

'I suppose the publicans will get the rest,' she said bitterly.

Later she went into town, but did not bring us with her, and returned with a lot of parcels, including the Christmas candle. We waited for Father to come home to his tea, but he didn't so we had our own tea and a slice of Christmas cake each, and then Mother put Sonny on a chair with the holy-water stoup to sprinkle the candle, and when he lit it she said; 'The light of heaven to our souls.' I could see she was upset because Father wasn't in - it should be the oldest and youngest. When we hung up our stockings at bedtime he was still out.

Then began the hardest couple of hours I ever put in. I was mad with sleep but afraid of losing the model railway, so I lay for a while making up things to say to Santa when he came. They varied in tone from frivolous to grave, for some old gents like kids to be modest and well spoken, while others prefer them with spirit. When I had rehearsed them all I tried to wake Sonny to keep me company, but that kid slept like the dead.

Eleven struck from Shandon, and soon after I heard the latch, but it was only Father coming home.

'Hello, little girl,' he said, letting on to be surprised at finding Mother waiting for him, and then broke into a self-conscious giggle.

'What has you up so late?'

'Do you want your supper?' she asked shortly.

'Ah, no, no,' he replied. 'I had a bit of pig's cheek at Daneen's on my way up.' (Daneen was my uncle.) 'I'm very fond of a bit of pig's cheek . . . My goodness, is it that late?' he exclaimed, letting on to be astonished. 'If I knew that I'd have gone to the North Chapel for midnight Mass. I'd like to hear the *Adeste* again. That's a hymn I'm very fond of – a most touching hymn.' Then he began to hum it falsetto:

Adeste fideles
Solus domus dagus.

Father was very fond of Latin hymns, particularly when he had a drop in, but as he had no notion of the words he made them up as he went along, and this always drove Mother mad.

'Ah, you disgust me!' she said in a scalded voice, and closed the room door behind her. Father laughed as if he thought it a great joke; and he struck a match to light his pipe and for a while puffed at it noisily. The light under the door dimmed and went out but he continued to sing emotionally:

Dixie medearo
Tutum tonum tantum
Venite adoremus.

He had it all wrong but the effect was the same on me. To save my life I couldn't keep awake.

Coming on to dawn, I woke with the feeling that something dreadful had happened. The whole house was quiet, and the little bedroom that looked out on the foot and a half of back yard was pitch-dark. It was only when I glanced at the window that I saw how all the silver had drained out of the sky. I jumped out of bed to feel my stocking, well knowing that the worst had happened. Santa had come while I was asleep, and gone away with an entirely false impression of me, because all he had left me was some sort of book, folded up, a pen and a pencil, and a tuppenny bag of sweets. Not even Snakes-and-Ladders! For a while I was too stunned even to think. A fellow who was able to drive over rooftops and climb down chimneys without getting stuck – God, wouldn't you think he'd know better?

Then I began to wonder what that foxy boy, Sonny, had. I went to his side of the bed and felt his stocking. For all his spelling and sucking-up he hadn't done so much better, because, apart from a bag of sweets like mine, all Santa had left him was a popgun, one that fired a cork on a piece of string and which you could get in any huxter's shop for sixpence.

All the same, the fact remained that it was a gun, and a gun was better than a book any day of the week. The Dohertys had a gang, and the gang fought the Strawberry Lane kids who tried to play football on our road. That gun would be very useful to me in many ways, while it would be lost on Sonny who wouldn't be let play with the gang, even if he wanted to.

Then I got the inspiration, as it seemed to me, direct from heaven. Suppose I took the gun and gave Sonny the book! Sonny would never be any good in the gang: he was fond of spelling, and a studious child like him could learn a lot of spellings from a book like mine. As he hadn't seen Santa any more than I had, what he hadn't seen wouldn't grieve him. I was doing no harm to anyone; in fact, if Sonny only knew, I was doing him a good turn which he might have cause to thank me for later. That was one thing I was always keen on; doing good turns. Perhaps this was Santa's intention the whole time and he had merely become confused between us. It was a mistake that might happen to anyone. So I put the book, the pencil, and the pen into Sonny's stocking and the popgun into my own, and returned to bed and slept again. As I say, in those days I had plenty of initiative.

It was Sonny who woke me, shaking me to tell that Santa had come and left me a gun. I let on to be surprised and rather disappointed in the gun, and to divert his mind from it made him show me his picture book, and cracked it up to the skies.

As I knew, that kid was prepared to believe anything, and nothing would do him then but to take the presents in to show Father and Mother. This was a bad moment for me. After the way she had behaved about the langing, I distrusted Mother, though I had the consolation of believing that the only person

Christmas Morning

who could contradict me now was somewhere up by the North Pole. That gave me a certain confidence, so Sonny and I burst in with our presents, shouting:

'Look what Santa Claus brought!'

Father and Mother woke, and Mother smiled, but only for an instant. As she looked at me her face changed. I knew that look; I knew it only too well. It was the same she had worn the day I came home from langing, when she said I had no word.

'Larry,' she said in a low voice, 'where did you get that gun?'

'Santa left it in my stocking, Mummy,' I said, trying to put on an injured air, though it baffled me how she guessed that he hadn't.

'He did, honest.'

'You stole from that poor child's stocking while he was asleep,' she said, her voice quivering with indignation. 'Larry, Larry, how could you be so mean?'

'Now, now, now,' Father said deprecatingly, 'tis Christmas morning.'

'Ah,' she said with real passion, 'it's easy it comes to you. Do you think I want my son to grow up a liar and a thief?'

'Ah, what thief, woman?' he said testily. 'Have sense, can't you?'

He was as cross if you interrupted him in his benevolent moods as if they were of the other sort, and this one was probably exacerbated by a feeling of guilt for his behaviour of the night before. 'Here, Larry,' he said, reaching out for the money on the bedside table, 'here's sixpence for you and one for Sonny. Mind you don't lose it now!'

But I looked at Mother and saw what was in her eyes. I burst out crying, threw the popgun on the floor, and ran bawling out of the house before anyone on the road was about.

I understand it all, and it was almost more than I could bear; that there was no Santa Claus, as the Dohertys said, only Mother trying to scrape together a few coppers from the house-keeping; that Father was mean and common and a drunkard, and that she had been relying on me to raise her out of the misery of the life she was leading. And I knew that the look in her eyes was the fear that, like my father, I should turn out to be mean and common and a drunkard.

– *Frank O'Connor*

WORD POWER

Find words in the story which have similar meanings to each of the words and phrases below. The number in brackets after each one indicates the number of letters in the answer. The words appear in the story in the same order as the meanings given below.

CLUES

1 unable to keep still (8)
2 wild, boisterous (5)
3 feeling shame (7)
4 knowledge (11)
5 ability to see what is going to happen (9)
6 wise (8)
7 make a habit of (8)
8 aggressively (11)
9 throwing carelessly (7)
10 especially (12)
11 awful (8)
12 completely (8)
13 mixed up (8)
14 let down (12)
15 moment (7)
16 puzzled (7)
17 trembling (9)
18 disapprovingly (13)
19 kindly (10)
20 worsened (11)

Questions & Assignments

1. (a) What is it about Sonny's behaviour that annoys Larry?
   (b) Which of the two boys do you prefer? Give reasons for your answer.
2. How does Larry's mother feel about his mitching?
3. What does Larry want from Santa? How does he plan to get it?
4. How does Larry's father behave when he returns home from work on Christmas Eve?
5. Why does Larry's mother worry about him?
6. *'As I say, in those days I had plenty of initiative.'* What evidence is there in the story to show that this statement which Larry made about himself, is true?
7. *'I understand it all, and it was almost more than I could bear.'*
   (a) What did Larry understand?   (b) Why was it *'almost more than I could bear'*?
8. Would you agree that the mother in the story deserves most sympathy? Give reasons for your answer.
9. Do the events in the story mark an important milestone for Larry on the road to adulthood? Explain your answer.
10. Give a brief outline of the plot of the story.
11. (a) How, in your opinion, does Larry's attitude towards the Dohertys differ from his mother's attitude towards them?
    (b) What is your own impression of the Dohertys? Refer to the story to support your answer.

Personal Writing

Do you think that parents should lead their children to believe that there is a Santa? Give reasons for your point of view.

Points to Note

Christmas Morning is another story of childhood hopes and disappointments. While Sonny is a fictitious character, the character of the father in the story shares many traits with O'Connor's own father.

PLOT

Plot is a term used to refer to the set of events in a story and the order in which these events are presented, i.e. the 'bones' of a story. The plots of novels are usually complex, while in short stories they are generally straightforward and can be summarised in a paragraph or two. A good plot will usually have some events that are unusual, i.e. unlikely and unexpected, but nevertheless within the bounds of possibility. Plots that consist of a series of unreal events and unlikely coincidences will result in the reader quickly losing interest. Writers must also take care to arrange the stages of a plot in the order that will best hold the interest of the reader.

Christmas Morning

The plot of *Christmas Morning* could be summarised as follows:

> The story is about two brothers: Sonny, the younger and his mother's pet, and Larry who is mischievous. The family are poor as their father seems to spend a good deal of money on drink. On Christmas morning Larry wakes first and inspects the presents left by Santa. When Larry sees that he has been left a book and Sonny a gun, he switches the presents. Later when the boys wake and show their parents what Santa left for them, Larry's mother gets very angry and accuses him of stealing the gun from his brother's stocking. With a shock he realises that there is no Santa Claus and that his friends, the Dohertys, were right all along.

The Secret Life of Walter Mitty

The Secret Life of Walter Mitty is a very famous short story and has been adapted to film. In fact the phrase 'Walter Mitty' is frequently used in everyday speech to describe a particular type of person with similar traits of character to the principal character of this story.

(Note: This story has been divided into episodes. Answer the questions to Episode 1 before reading Episode II etc.)

I

"We're going through!" The Commander's voice was like thin ice breaking. He wore his full-dress uniform, with the heavily braided white cap pulled down rakishly over one cold grey eye. "We can't make it, sir. It's spoiling for a hurricane, if you ask me." "I'm not asking you, Lieutenant Berg," said the Commander. "Throw on the power lights! Rev her up to 8,500. We're going through!" The pounding of the cylinders increased: ta-pocketa-pocketa-pocketa-pocketa-pocketa. The Commander stared at the ice forming on the pilot window. He walked over and twisted a row of complicated dials. "Switch on No. 8 auxiliary!" he shouted. "Switch on No. 8 auxiliary!" repeated Lieutenant Berg. "Full strength in No. 3 turret!" shouted the Commander. "Full strength in No. 3 turret!" The crew, bending to their various tasks in the huge, hurtling eight-engined Navy hydroplane, looked at each other and grinned. "The Old Man'll get us through," they said to one another. "The Old Man ain't afraid of Hell!". . . .

"Not so fast! You're driving too fast!" said Mrs. Mitty. "What are you driving so fast for?"

"Hmm?" said Walter Mitty. He looked at his wife, in the seat beside him, with shocked astonishment. She seemed grossly unfamiliar, like a strange woman who had yelled at him in a crowd. "You were up to fifty-five," she said. "You know I don't like to go more than forty. You were up to fifty-five." Walter Mitty drove on toward Waterbury in silence, the roaring of the SN202 through the worst storm in twenty years of Navy flying fading in the remote, intimate airways of his mind. "You're tensed up again," said Mrs. Mitty. "It's one of your days. I wish you'd let Dr. Renshaw look you over."

Walter Mitty stopped the car in front of the building where his wife went to have her hair done. "Remember to get those overshoes while I'm having my hair done," she said. "I don't need overshoes," said Mitty. She put her mirror back into her bag. "We've been all through that," she said, getting out of the car. "You're not a young man any longer." He raced the engine a little. "Why don't you wear your gloves? Have you lost your gloves?" Walter Mitty reached in a pocket and brought out the gloves. He put them on, but after she had turned and gone into the building and he had driven on to a red light, he took them off again. "Pick it up, brother!" snapped a cop as the lights changed, and Mitty hastily pulled on his gloves and lurched ahead. He drove around the streets aimlessly for a time, and then he drove past the hospital on his way to the parking lot.

The Secret Life of Walter Mitty

Questions & Assignments   SECTION I

1. (i) Describe the situation outlined in the opening paragraph.
   (ii) The first paragraph is set on a plane. What do we learn about the plane? Describe the event taking place.
2. What kind of a character is the 'Commander'? What is the attitude of the crew towards him?
3. The end of the first paragraph is marked by an elipse (. . . i.e. three full stops.) This punctuation mark is sometimes used by fiction writers to indicate that a scene is fading out, similar to the film technique of fading out a scene. Pay particular attention to the use of elipses in this story. What scene 'fades out' and what scene opens in the next paragraph?
4. Explain the phrase *'the roaring of the SN202 through the worst storm in twenty years of Navy flying fading in the remote intimate airways of his mind.'*
5. What do we learn about (i) Walter and (ii) his wife in this section?
6. Why did the author use the words *'snapped'* and *'lurched'* in the final paragraph.
7. Explain briefly what happens in this section?

II

. . . "It's the millionaire banker, Wellington McMillan," said the pretty nurse. "Yes?" said Walter Mitty, removing his gloves slowly. "Who has the case?" "Dr. Renshaw and Dr. Benbow, but there are two specialists here, Dr. Remington from New York and Mr. Pritchard-Mitford from London. He flew over." A door opened down a long, cool corridor and Dr. Renshaw came out. He looked distraught and haggard. "Hello, Mitty," he said. "We're having the devil's own time with McMillan, the millionaire banker and close personal friend of Roosevelt. Obstreosis of the ductal tract. Tertiary. Wish you'd take a look at him." "Glad to," said Mitty.

In the operating room there were whispered introductions: "Dr. Remington, Dr. Mitty, Mr. Pritchard-Mitford, Dr. Mitty." "I've read your book on streptothricosis," said Pritchard-Mitford, shaking hands. "A brilliant performance, sir." "Thank you," said Walter Mitty. "Didn't know you were in the States, Mitty," grumbled Remington. "Coals to Newcastle, bringing Mitford and me up here for a tertiary." "You are very kind," said Mitty. A huge, complicated machine, connected to the operating table, with many tubes and wires, began at this moment to go pocketa-pocketa-pocketa. "The new anaesthetiser is giving way!" shouted an interne. "There is no one in the East who knows how to fix it!" "Quiet, man!" said Mitty, in a low, cool voice. He sprang to the machine, which was now going pocketa-pocketa-queep-pocketa-queep. He began fingering delicately a row of glistening dials. "Give me a fountain pen!" he snapped. Someone handed him a fountain pen. He pulled a faulty piston out of the machine and inserted the pen in its place. "That will hold for ten minutes," he said. "Get on with the operation." A nurse hurried over and whispered to Renshaw, and Mitty saw the man turn pale. "Coreopsis has set in," said Renshaw nervously. "If you would take over, Mitty?" Mitty looked at him and at the craven figure of Benbow, who drank, and at the grave, uncertain faces of the two great specialists. "If you wish," he said. They slipped a white gown on him; he adjusted a mask and drew on thin gloves; nurses handed him shining . . . .

"Back it up, Mac! Look out for that Buick!" Walter Mitty jammed on the brakes. "Wrong lane, Mac," said the parking-lot attendant, looking at Mitty closely. "Gee. Yeh," muttered Mitty. He began cautiously to back out of the lane marked "Exit Only." "Leave her sit there," said the attendant. "I'll put her away." Mitty got out of the car. "Hey, better leave the key." "Oh," said Mitty, handing the man the ignition key. The attendant vaulted into the car, backed it up with insolent skill, and put it where it belonged.

They're so damn cocky, thought Walter Mitty, walking along Main Street; they think they know everything. Once he had tried to take his chains off, outside New Milford, and he had got them wound around the axles. A man had had to come out in a wrecking car and unwind them, a young, grinning garageman. Since then Mrs. Mitty always made him drive to a garage to have the chains taken off. The next time, he thought, I'll wear my right arm in a sling; they won't grin at me then. I'll have my right arm in a sling and they'll see I couldn't possibly take the chains off myself. He kicked at the slush on the sidewalk. "Overshoes," he said to himself, and he began looking for a shoe store.

When he came out into the street again, with the overshoes in a box under his arm, Walter Mitty began to wonder what the other thing was his wife had told him to get. She had told him, twice, before they set out from their house for Waterbury. In a way he hated these weekly trips to town – he was always getting something wrong. Kleenex, he thought, Squibb's, razor blades? No. Toothpaste, toothbrush, bicarbonate, carborundum, initiative and referendum? He gave it up. But she would remember it. "Where's the what's-its-name?" she would ask. "Don't tell me you forgot the what's-its-name." A newsboy went by shouting something about the Waterbury trial . . .

Questions & Assignments SECTION II

1. Describe the setting and the situation outlined in the opening paragraph of this section.
2. (i) How do the other doctors treat Mitty? What is Mitty's attitude towards them? Why does Remington say *'Coals to Newcastle'*?
   (ii) How is Mitty contrasted with the other doctors? In your answer refer to the author's choice of words in describing actions.
3. What words are used to describe the anaesthetiser? How does Mitty solve the problem? What does this action reveal about him? Is there a similar incident in the first paragraph of the story? Explain.
4. What is (i) the parking attendant's attitude towards Walter Mitty and (ii) Mitty's attitude towards the parking attendant?
5. What do the incidents with the parking attendant and the snow chains reveal about Mitty?
6. Comment on the phrases *'insolent skill'* and *'young grinning garageman'*.
7. What do we learn about Mitty in the final paragraph of this section?

III

"Perhaps this will refresh your memory." The District Attorney suddenly thrust a heavy automatic at the quiet figure on the witness stand. "Have you ever seen this before?" Walter Mitty took the gun and examined it expertly. "This is my Webley-Vickers 50.80," he said calmly. An excited buzz ran around the courtroom. The Judge rapped for order. "You are a crack shot with any sort of firearms, I believe?" said the District Attorney, insinuatingly. "Objection!" shouted Mitty's attorney. "We have shown that the defendant could not have fired the shot. We have shown that he wore his right arm in a sling on the night of the fourteenth of July." Walter Mitty raised his hand briefly and the bickering attorneys were stilled. "With any known make of gun," he said evenly, "I could have killed Gregory Fitzhurst at three hundred feet *with my left hand*." Pandemonium broke loose in the courtroom. A woman's scream rose above the bedlam and suddenly a lovely, dark-haired girl was in Walter Mitty's arms. The District Attorney struck at her savagely. Without rising from his chair, Mitty let the man have it on the point of the chin. "You miserable cur!". . . .

"Puppy biscuit," said Walter Mitty. He stopped walking and the buildings of Waterbury rose up out of the misty courtroom and surrounded him again. A woman who was passing laughed. "He said 'Puppy Biscuit,'" she said to her companion. "That man said 'Puppy biscuit' to himself." Walter Mitty hurried on. He went into an A. & P., not the first one he came to but a smaller one farther up the street. "I want some biscuit for small, young dogs," he said to the clerk. "Any special brand, sir?" The greatest pistol shot in the world thought a moment. "It says 'Puppies Bark for It' on the box," said Walter Mitty.

His wife would be through at the hairdresser's in fifteen minutes, Mitty saw in looking at his watch, unless they had trouble drying it; sometimes they had trouble drying it. She didn't like to get to the hotel first; she would want him to be there waiting for her as usual. He found a big leather chair in the lobby, facing a window, and he put the overshoes and the puppy biscuit on the floor beside it. He picked up an old copy of *Liberty* and sank down into the chair. "Can Germany Conquer the World Through the Air?" Walter Mitty looked at the pictures of bombing planes and of ruined streets . . .

Questions & Assignments   SECTION III

1 Describe the situation in the courtroom. What features of his character emerge in the court scene? Are they similar to those of the other daydream episodes? Explain. Are some new qualities emerging? Explain.

2 *'the buildings of Waterbury rose up out of the misty courtroom.'* Explain what this means.

3 What is the significance of the action of the woman passerby on the street?

IV

"The cannonading has got the wind up in young Raleigh, sir," said the sergeant. Captain Mitty looked up at him through tousled hair. "Get him to bed," he said wearily. "With the others, I'll fly alone." "But you can't, sir," said the sergeant anxiously. "It takes two men to handle that bomber and the Archies are pounding hell out of the air. Von Richtman's circus is between here and Saulier." "Somebody's got to get that ammunition dump," said Mitty. "I'm going over. Spot of brandy?" He poured a drink for the sergeant and one for himself. War thundered and whined around the dugout and battered at the door. There was a rending of wood and splinters flew through the room. "A bit of a near thing," said Captain Mitty carelessly. "The box barrage is closing in," said the sergeant. "We only live once, Sergeant," said Mitty, with his faint, fleeting smile. "Or do we?" He poured another brandy and tossed it off. "I never see a man could hold his brandy like you, sir," said the sergeant. "Begging your pardon, sir." Captain Mitty stood up and strapped on his huge Webley-Vickers automatic. "It's forty kilometres through hell, sir," said the sergeant. Mitty finished one last brandy. "After all," he said softly, "what isn't?" The pounding of the cannon increased; there was the rat-tat-tatting of machine guns, and from somewhere came the menacing pocketa-pocketa-pocketa of the new flame-throwers. Walter Mitty walked to the door of the dugout humming 'Auprès de Ma Blonde.' He turned and waved to the sergeant. "Cheerio!" he said . . .

Something struck his shoulder. "I've been looking all over this hotel for you," said Mrs. Mitty. "Why do you have to hide in this old chair? How did you expect me to find you?" "Things close in," said Walter Mitty vaguely. "What?" Mrs. Mitty said. "Did you get the what's-its-name? The puppy biscuit? What's in that box?" "Overshoes," said Mitty. "Couldn't you have put them on in the store?" "I was thinking," said Walter Mitty. "Does it ever occur to you that I am sometimes thinking?" She looked at him. "I'm going to take your temperature when I get you home," she said.

They went out through the revolving doors that made a faintly derisive whistling sound when you pushed them. It was two blocks to the parking lot. At the drugstore on the corner she said, "Wait here for me. I forgot something. I won't be a minute." She was more than a minute. Walter Mitty lighted a cigarette. It began to rain, rain with sleet in it. He stood up against the wall of the drugstore, smoking . . . He put his shoulders back and his heels together. "To hell with the handkerchief," said Walter Mitty scornfully. He took one last drag on his cigarette and snapped it away. Then, with that faint, fleeting smile playing about his lips, he faced the firing squad; erect and motionless, proud and disdainful, Walter Mitty the Undefeated, inscrutable to the last.

– *James Thurber*

Uncle Ifor's Welsh Dresser

1.

12 The Close,
London SW.
30th January

Brewsham & Moore,
Estate Agents,
Farnfield.

Dear Sir,

Would you please send me particulars of any three bed-roomed houses for sale in the Farnfield area which are in a good state of repair, adjacent to the local primary school, near open countryside and have a good garden. Most important of all, they must have a very large kitchen.

I do hope you can help me.

Yours faithfully,
Jennifer Clarke

2.

Brewsham & Moore,
Farnfield.
3rd February

Ms J Clarke,
12 The Close,
London SW.

Dear Ms. Clarke,

Thank you for your letter. I enclose particulars of several properties, but would point out that it was impossible to comply with all your requirements. As you will see, 'Ashling', in Meadow Lane, complies with most of them; there is a primary school at the end of the lane for the children, there are open fields, at the other end of the lane, the garden is a reasonable size, although somewhat overgrown, and the kitchen, although you do not give exact specifications, is large ('Ashling' was once a farmhouse).

However, the house has been allowed to fall into a certain state of disrepair – its previous owner was an elderly lady who is now living with her daughter – although nothing, I would have thought, would be beyond the capabilities of a reasonably competent D.I.Y. enthusiast to manage alone.

If you wish to inspect the property, I will be available to show you around all week.

Yours sincerely,
David Moore

3.

12 The Close.
4th February

Dear Mr. Moore,

Thank you for your letter and enclosures.

My elderly aunt and I will arrive at Farnfield station at 10.45 this Saturday. Unless I hear that you would prefer not to have him in your car, I should like to bring Meredith, my Border Collie. He is not very big, loves trains and sulks if left at home by himself; the last time, he ate the rubber plant and was very ill. The rubber plant was not improved, either. Normally, I would have brought my own car, but it has to go in for servicing.

By the way, perhaps I should explain the reasons for my very precise requirements; the primary school is for me, as I am a teacher; the garden is for Aunt Hetty who has wanted one ever since she gave up her own to come and look after me in our flat when my parents died; the open fields are for Meredith; the kitchen is for Aunt Hetty's Welsh dresser (Uncle Ifor, who died many years ago, made it for her when they were first married and she refuses to part with it), and the good state of repair is for my fiancé Mark, who could not, I'm afraid, be described as a 'reasonably competent D.I.Y. enthusiast'. However, he is a *very* competent executive with a large oil company and is actually in the Middle East at the moment for a month. Meanwhile, I am fairly competent with a hammer and chisel, and Aunt Hetty is not above holding the nails.

I hope you will forgive these autobiographical details, but I thought it might help if you were aware of the situation. Please don't hesitate to say if you would prefer not to have Meredith. I can always leave the rubber plant with friends!

Yours sincerely,
Jennifer Clarke

4.

Brewsham & Moore.
6th February

Dear Miss Clarke,

I shall be at Farnfield station at 10.45 on Saturday, the 8th, and look forward to meeting you. Please bring Meredith – and the measurements of Aunt Hetty's Welsh dresser.

Yours sincerely,
David Moore

The Secret Life of Walter Mitty

Answer Guidelines

2 (i) *Actions:* his movements in fantasy are cool; slow; acomplished. In reality flustered and awkward. Give examples by reference to the story.

Words: in reality he is a man of few words; mild mannered; not assertive; timid; sometimes utters his thoughts aloud; In fantasy terse, confident; modest; dignified; calm; assertive. Refer to text for examples.

Attitudes of others: how do others respond to him in fantasy; in reality . . . ?

Motives/Needs: to be respected; admired; to be technically competant . . . ?

Looks/Appearance: select a few details.

Personal Writing

1 As Walter Mitty returns home, a police car speeds by with its siren blaring. Describe the daydream that follows.

2 Attempt your own 'Walter Mitty' story and set it in Ireland of the nineties. Bear in mind the following points:
- Set the action over a short period.
- Write from the omniscient point of view, i.e. you see and report the details of every fantasy.
- Base the 'fantasy' episodes on people and scenarios that are frequently in the limelight such as people from the world of sport, music, business, politics etc.
- Remember that your 'Walter Mitty' can be anybody – young, old, male, female – even yourself.

8. Observing how time and events change them for better or for worse.
9. Looking at their appearance, occupation and background.

However, both in real life and in stories, our first impressions of people can often be wrong. Generally though, we get to know people in stories much better than we do in real life because writers can tell us what characters are really thinking and feeling. Also, both in real life and in stories, people do not always mean what they say. Therefore when characters talk about themselves and others we have to think carefully about what they are saying and draw our own conclusions.

Most good authors only reveal the basic details about characters indirectly, opting instead to let the reader get to know characters through their actions and through the eyes of other characters.

Characters lack credibility if they are utterly evil or completely perfect. All solid character creations have a mixture of good points and bad points. The reader, therefore, feels that they are like real people.

Nevertheless, the characters in most stories can be broadly divided into two groups – those who win the reader's sympathy and those who arouse dislike in the reader. In each case the character has caught the reader's interest. When a character wins the reader's sympathy the reader wants that character to succeed. If the reader does not care about the characters in a story, it is unlikely that he or she will read on to find out what happened to them. When writing about characters from stories, you should remember each of the points above.

Questions & Assignments

1. The story describes an afternoon in Walter Mitty's life. Write what you imagine would be his own diary account of the day. (Limit your answer to around 150 words and refer briefly to each of the daydreams.)
2. (i) What are your impressions of Walter Mitty?
   (ii) Write a character sketch of Walter Mitty from the point of view of his wife.
3. What are your impressions of Mitty's wife?
4. What evidence is there in the story to show that it is set in America?
5. Explain briefly how the author provides links or 'bridges' to and from the real world and Mitty's fantasy world.
6. Do you consider the story to be sad or humorous? In relation to this question you should carefully consider the final daydream. Has it a deeper significance than the others?
7. Does the story offer an important comment on modern life? Explain your answer.

The Secret Life of Walter Mitty

Questions & Assignments — SECTION IV

1. Describe the setting and the situation in the opening paragraph of this section.
2. What kind of a character is 'Captain' Mitty? What is the attitude of the sergeant towards him? In what way does it contrast with his wife's attitude in the next paragraph?
3. Why does the author describe the doors as making *'a faintly derisive whistling sound'*?
4. What is happening in the final daydream?

WORD POWER

Find words in the story which have similar meanings to each of the words and phrases below. The number in brackets after each one indicates the number of letters in the answer. The words appear in the story in the same order as the meanings given below.

CLUES

1. continuous hammering (8)
2. not simple (11)
3. jobs; duties (5)
4. surprise; amazement (12)
5. extremely (7)
6. strange (10)
7. shouted (6)
8. distant; far away (6)
9. moved in a jerky manner (7)
10. without direction (9)
11. emotionally upset (10)
12. rough; worn (7)
13. joined (9)
14. glowing; glittering (10)
15. not perfect (6)
16. pathetic; contemptible (6)
17. serious (5)
18. slowly and carefully (10)
19. jumped (7)
20. cheeky; disrespectful (8)
21. smiling (8)
22. arguing (9)
23. disorder (11)
24. viciously (8)
25. threatening (8)
26. mocking (8)
27. lasting only briefly (8)
28. not moving (10)
29. feelings hidden, mysterious (11)

Points to Note

BRINGING CHARACTERS TO LIFE

Characters is the term used to refer to people in a story or play. Getting to know characters in stories is like getting to know people in real life. When we come across somebody for the first time in life – or in a story – we begin forming a judgement of them by:

1. Listening to what they say about themselves.
2. Listening to what others say about them.
3. Observing their actions and behaviour.
4. Noticing their attitudes and opinions on different matters.
5. Learning of their goals, needs and ambitions.
6. Observing how they treat others in the story.
7. Noting how they react in a crisis or deal with a difficult decision.

Uncle Ifor's Welsh Dresser

5.
12 The Close.
10th February

Dear David,

Thank you for being so kind to us on Saturday. I had no idea that estate agents could be so helpful. I must apologise again about the hole Meredith made in your car seat. I think he was over-excited after the journey. You *must* let me pay for it.

Both Aunt Hetty and I loved Ashling. And I am sure Mark would, too. If only the kitchen was two inches longer! However, Aunt Hetty still seems to think we can get her dresser in and suggests that she re-takes the measurements and we try again this Saturday. Perhaps I could collect the key from the office this time, to save you the bother? I shall have my car back tomorrow.

Yours sincerely,
Jenny.

6.
Lyndhurst,
The Rise, Farnfield.
10th February

Dear Jenny,

I feel I must write and set your mind at rest about the slight tear Meredith made in my car seat cover. It's nothing that a patch won't take care of!

I'm so glad you like Ashling. As I explained, the old lady to whom it belongs is my grandmother; she is in no hurry to sell as long as it goes to someone who'll love it as much as she does.

I can quite understand why your Aunt Hetty wants to keep your uncle's Welsh dresser. Clearly, it was a labour of love. If only he had made it two inches shorter! However, I don't think the problem is insurmountable. My grandmother tells me that the inside kitchen wall was put up about twenty years ago in order to make the breakfast room, and could easily be removed without harming the original structure. Perhaps you and Aunt Hetty would like to come down again and see what I mean. What about this Saturday?

*Yours sincerely,
David.*

7.
12 The Close.
16th February

Dear David,

Thank you for yesterday. Meredith and I both adored our walk. I think early spring is always the best time for woods, don't you? Mind you, in a few months' time I shall be saying the same thing about the summer! I do hope I shall be able to see the daffodils that you say grow down by the stream. Oh, why didn't Uncle Ifor make Aunt Hetty a nice little coffee table or a set of dining-room chairs!

However, even though we've now found out that it's too high as well as too long, Aunt Hetty is still hopeful! She wants to come down yet again to see if we can take the floor tiles up or cut a hole in the ceiling! Could you bear it? I must say, she and your grandmother seemed to have got on very well. Now she knows there are gentians in the rockery, she's more determined than ever to live at Ashling.

Meredith sends his love and says he's not really afraid of rabbits. But being a town dog, he'd just never seen one before!

Yours,
Jenny

P.S. Mark will be home in a fortnight. Perhaps he will have a bright idea about the dresser.

8.
Lyndhurst,
Farnfield.
16th February

Dear Jenny,

That was a splendid walk we had yesterday! I haven't been in Bramble Woods for years – not since Gran used to get us to go blackberrying for her. I'm sorry Meredith was frightened by that rather ferocious rabbit.

It's a shame about Uncle Ifor's dresser. I suppose we couldn't saw a bit off the bottom? Ask Aunt Hetty what she thinks and then come down and we'll measure once more.

If you could manage Saturday again, there's an old James Stewart film on at the local cinema club. I remember you saying how much you liked him. Mum says she and Gran would love to look after Aunt Hetty and Meredith.

*Yours,
David*

9.
                Lyndhurst,
                Farnfield.
                23rd February

Dear Jenny,
I hope you enjoyed the film. Too bad Aunt Hetty forgot to bring the new measurements. What about next Saturday? I promise I won't try to kiss you again. I don't know what came over me. At least, that's not strictly true - you looked so pretty in that fluffy thing you were wearing, I just didn't think twice. I certainly forgot you were an engaged woman. Please forgive me! I'll make sure it doesn't happen again.

Yours,
David

10.
                12 The Close,
                London SW.
                27th February

Brewsham & Moore,
Estate Agents,
Farnfield.

Dear Mr. Moore,
  I am writing to make an appointment for my fiancé Mark Johnson to view Ashling, Meadow Lane. I trust that 10.30 a.m. next Wednesday would be convenient? If I do not hear to the contrary, I will arrange for him to meet you at the house.

Yours sincerely,
Jennifer Clarke

11.
                12 The Close,
                London SW.
                6th March

Brewsham & Moore.

Dear Sir,

<u>Ashling, Meadow Lane, Farnfield</u>

  Please note that I am no longer interested in the purchase of this property.

Yours faithfully,
J. Clarke

12.
                12 The Close.
                6th March

David,
  I am sending this to your home address because there are one or two things I must say that would not be suitable for your secretary to read. To begin with, there was absolutely no need for you to point out to Mark all the things that needed doing at Ashling - and then try to sell him a newer house. You'd never even mentioned to me that the roof leaked!
  And there was no necessity for you to be so pessimistic about Uncle Ifor's dresser! I'm sure we could have found a way, somehow. Not that we'll have the chance now, as Mark and I are no longer speaking to each other, and our engagement is off. As I couldn't possibly manage the mortgage repayments on my own, the purchase of Ashling is off, too. Aunt Hetty has taken to her room and refuses to talk about it.
  I never thought you could be so underhand and deceitful. I can only imagine that your feelings clouded your professional judgement.

Jenny

P.S. There is no point in coming to see us. Anyway, I won't be here – I am going to stay with friends in Norfolk.

13.
                Lyndhurst.
                8th March

Dear Jenny,
I hope that Aunt Hetty will send this letter on to you.
I was very sorry indeed that you felt you must break off negotiations for Ashling. And I can assure you that I had nothing at all to do with Mark's reaction. I didn't even go with him to view it, but sent our junior partner Stephen Watson, instead.
I must admit that my feelings for you over the last few weeks have grown far beyond the limits of a business relationship, but your happiness will always come first. Under the circumstances, I quite understand why you do not wish to continue with the purchase of Ashling, but I hope very much that we will not lose touch.

David

14.   Norfolk.
                                        13th March

Dear David,

   Aunt Hetty sent on your letter. I'm sorry I'd got it all wrong. It never occurred to me that someone else would show Mark around Ashling and he wouldn't know you from Adam.

   I'm still very mixed up about everything. Aunt Hetty says it's bound to take time. Thank you for everything.

Jenny

15.   *Lyndhurst.*
                                   8th September

Dear Jenny,
   I thought you might like to know that Ashling has now been sold, but that the new owner has had it converted into two separate flats, one of which is available for rent. Would you and Aunt Hetty be interested? I'm sure Meredith would! Please come and see for yourselves. How about Saturday?

Yours,
David

P.S. You missed the daffodils but the blackberries are early this year in Bramble Woods.

16.   12 The Close.
                                   14th September

Darling David,

   It was wonderful to see you again. And the blackberries are out of this world. As you say, the ground floor would be best for Aunt Hetty.

   You didn't have to be so devious! I would have come to see it, even if I had known you would be our landlord! See you next Saturday. Come for the day, if possible, and I'll book a
theatre.

Love,
Jenny

P.S. Strange – but Aunt Hetty hasn't even mentioned the dresser!

17.   *Lyndhurst.*
                                 19th September

Dearest Jenny,
   I think you know how happy I am that you and Aunt Hetty will be coming to live at Ashling. See you on Saturday.

All my love,
David

P.S. I didn't dare mention the dresser – d'you think Aunt Hetty has forgotten about it?

18.   *Lyndhurst.*
                                 22nd September

My dear Aunt Hetty,
   Jenny has passed on your congratulations on our engagement. Thank you! You know how pleased I am that you will be occupying the groundfloor flat while Jenny and I have the top.

   It is most kind to want to give us Uncle Ifor's dresser for a wedding present but I really don't think we would get it up that narrow staircase.

Your affectionate
nephew-to-be,
David

19.   12 The Close.
                                 24th September

Dear David,

   No one has ever given my Ifor credit for being the excellent craftsman that he was!

   The whole thing will take apart and bits can be left out or added, to make it narrower, shorter, taller, without altering its basic design.

   I never told either you or Jenny this because it made a good excuse for continuing to visit Ashling while you got to know each other better (I never did think Mark a suitable match for her). Certainly, there would be no problem in getting it up your stairs! However, it has served its purpose and I've decided to spare you. Much better if you and Jenny buy the furniture you really want.

   So I shall have it downstairs in my kitchen, and send you a cheque instead.

Your devious but loving,
Aunt Hetty

– Pat Lacey

Spectrum 1

WORD POWER

Find words in the story which have similar meanings to each of the words and phrases below. The number in brackets after each one indicates the number of letters in the answer. The words appear in the story in the same order as the meanings given below.

CLUES

1. details; information (11)
2. close by (8)
3. meet with; satisfy (6)
4. average (10)
5. covered in weeds (9)
6. precise (5)
7. measurements (14)
8. last; one before (8)
9. old (person) (7)
10. capable; efficient (9)
11. a person with a particular interest (10)
12. check out; look over (7)
13. rather (6)
14. displays a bad mood (5)
15. routine repair work (9)
16. needs (12)
17. a piece of furniture for holding delph (7)
18. partner engaged to be married (6)
19. express regret (9)
20. unable to be solved (14)
21. damaging (7)
22. first; at the beginning (8)
23. keen (10)
24. enjoyable; excellent (8)
25. very fierce (9)
26. an arrangement to meet (11)
27. suitable (10)
28. buying (8)
29. remarked (9)
30. looking on the gloomy side (11)
31. dishonest (9)
32. business discussions aimed at reaching an agreement (12)
33. changed (a building) (9)
34. a person who rents a flat or house (8)
35. cunning (7)

Questions & Assignments

1. What do you learn about Jennifer Clarke from her first letter?
2. Explain the phrase *'it was impossible to comply with all your requirements'*.
3. Outline briefly the good and bad points about the house 'Ashling', as outlined in the second letter.
4. What does Jennifer reveal about herself, her fiancé and her aunt in the third letter?
5. Basing your answer on the second, fourth and fifth letters only, what do the letters reveal about the character of David Clarke?
6. Describe briefly what happened during the visit on the 8th of February.
7. What indication in the letters of the 10th of February suggests that Jennifer Clarke and David Moore are becoming friendly?
8. What happens when they meet again on the 15th of February?
9. At this stage in the story what are your expectations? What do you hope will happen? What is likely to cause a problem?
10. Write a letter you imagine that Jenny writes to her fiancé after her trip to Farnfield on the 15th of February.

Uncle Ifor's Welsh Dresser

11 Describe the tone of David's letter of the 23rd of February and and the tone of Jennifer's letters of the 27th February and 6th of March. In each case show how the use of particular words and phrases helps to establish the tone.

12 At what stage in the developing friendship between David and Jenny do complications set in? Explain how.

13 Write the dialogue that you imagine takes place between Stephen Watson and Mark when he comes to view the house.

14 (a) What phrase does David use in his letter of the 8th March which suggests that he is in love with Jenny?

   (b) How does Jennifer react to to his letter?

15 Explain briefly how things finally work out for David and Jenny and comment on Aunt Hetty's role in the affair.

LETTER WRITING

FORMAL AND INFORMAL LETTERS

In general, informal letters are those which you would write to people with whom you are on first name terms, while formal letters are those which you would write to people with whom you are only distantly acquainted or not at all.

Informal letters are friendly, chatty letters which you would write to friends and relatives. Occasionally, though, you might have to write an informal letter in less than friendly terms.

Formal letters include those you might send to organisations or businesses seeking information, making complaints or suggestions, and applying for work.

LAYOUT OF LETTERS

Informal

Formal

A The **address** from where you are writing. Addresses can either be written with a vertical or with a sloped margin.

e.g. 13 Oakfield Rd.,　　27 Greendale Ave.,
　　　Perrystown,　　　　Coolara,
　　　Dublin 12.　　　　　Co. Kildare.

Each word in an address begins with a capital letter. Any shortened words are followed by a full stop. Each line of the address ends with a comma except for the final line, when a full stop is used.

B The **date** on which the letter is being written.

  e.g. 15/3/19_ _ or 3 June 19_ _

C The **name** of the person (if known), their **title**, e.g. Manager, Secretary etc, and the **address** of the organisation to whom you are writing. **(This applies to formal letters only and should not be included in informal letters.)**

D The **greeting**. In informal letters you can be quite casual, e.g. *Dear Anne, Hi Anne* or simply *Anne* are all acceptable. However, in a formal letter never use the first name of the person to whom you are writing, even if you know it. You will generally use one of the following:

Dear Mr. Murphy, Dear Mrs. Murphy, Dear Miss Murphy, Dear Ms. Murphy.

If you are writing to a large organisation and you do not know the name of the person who will deal with your letter, then you begin with *Dear Sir/Madam*.

E The **body** of the letter. Unless your letter is very short you should divide it into paragraphs. Each paragraph could deal with a different point.

F The **complimentary close** and **signature**. Again formal and informal letters differ here.

 e.g. **Informal**
  Best wishes/Lots of love/
  See you soon/Regards
  are just some of the many
  phrases that can be used here.

 Formal

If you used Dear Sir/Madam **or** in your greeting:	If you used an actual name, e.g. Mr. Brown, in your greeting:
Yours faithfully,	*Yours sincerely,*
Peter Murphy	*Mary Ashley*

(Note: If your signature cannot be read easily, write your name in block capitals underneath it).

LETTER WRITING

Assignment

In the case of each of the following assignments you must firstly decide if they are formal or informal letters and then use the correct layout for each one.

In each case when you have completed the letter draw a rectangle in your copy to represent an envelope and in it write the name and address as you would on a real envelope. Where names and addresses are not given make them up.

LETTER WRITING

SAMPLE ENVELOPE

Ms. Angela Davis
13 Gardener's Hill,
Cork

Now it's your turn . . .

1. Your godmother Angela Davis, who lives in 13 Gardener's Hill, Cork, sent you twenty pounds for your birthday. Write and thank her. Tell her how you spent your birthday and what you intend to do with her present.

2. Write to the manager of a local bank or building society seeking support for a sponsored cycle in aid of Gorta Famine Relief. You do not know the manager's name.

3. Your brother is in college in Dublin. He is a bit lonely. Write a letter to him telling him the latest family news and try to cheer him up. He lives in Flat 4, 34 Upper Rathmines Road, Dublin 6.

4. Write to the controller of television programmes in RTE explaining why you think that The Late Late Show should be broadcast on Monday evenings instead of in its usual slot.

5. Write to the presenter of a local radio show you enjoy. You may have a few suggestions to improve it.

6. Mrs Donavan, a neighbour of yours, is spending a few weeks with her daughter Emma who lives at 34 Willow Park, Jordan Hill, Oxford OX2 8EJ in England. Write to her with the news that you accidentally broke the roof of her greenhouse.

7 You are secretary of your local youth club. Write to the secretary of your local G.A.A. club asking for the use of their pitch for your club's annual sports day.

8 Your uncle, Tom Browne, who lives at 3 Avondale Drive, Clifden, County Galway, invites you to go on a camping holiday with his wife and children to France. Their children are aged five and seven and you have always found them difficult to get along with. Write to your uncle declining the invitation.

9 You are on holiday with your cousin in a different part of the country. Write home, telling your parents the good points and the bad points about the holiday, as well as some reminders about those things which you asked them to look after while you are away.

10 You had arranged to meet your cousin Andrew O'Neill, who lives in 3 Curragh Close, Newbridge, County Kildare, in Planet Hollywood in Dublin on Saturday last.
(i) You didn't turn up. Write and explain why.
or
(ii) He didn't turn up and has not contacted you. Write to him on the matter.

11 Novelists, poets and dramatists like to receive letters from children who enjoy their work. Write to a writer whose work you enjoyed, telling her or him why you enjoyed it. You may also wish to find out something about the author. (You can address the letter to the publisher, e.g. Tom Elliot, c/o Apple Publishers, 34 Grafton Street, Dublin 2. (c/o – this stands for 'care of' . . .)

12 A sign at the entrance to your local park reads 'No ballgames, no picnics, no bikes, no radios, all dogs on leads'. You do not agree with some – or all – of these rules. Write a letter to the Parks' Superintendant of your local county council or corporation. State the reason why you are complaining (you may have a dog, or like mountainbiking, or play football etc). Try to make a sensible suggestion for solving the problem.

LETTER WRITING

Sample Letters

Letter Writing

10 Beech Park
Lucan
Co. Dublin
13 - 5 - 19 _ _

Dear Aunt Mary,
    Thank you for a wonderful birthday present. When I opened the wrapping paper and saw the Sony Walkman inside I gave a cry of joy.
    It's a beautiful gift. Not only does it have a cassette player but it also has a radio. My friend Anne has a walkman but it doesn't have a radio. When she saw what you sent me she said that I was very lucky. She wishes that her walkman sounded as good as mine.
    You promised me something special for my fourteenth birthday and you certainly kept your promise. Again, many thanks for your very generous gift. I am looking forward to meeting you soon and thanking you in person.

Your loving niece
Joan

---

38 Castle Terrace,
Callan,
Co. Kilkenny.
24 - 9 - 19 _ _

Dear Margaret,
    I have just heard your sad news.
    I know that, at times such as this, even the words of a friend cannot make your grief any easier. I still had to write to tell you how deeply I feel for you and how much you are in my thoughts at this moment.
    Your father was always a kind and friendly man. I will always remember how he made me welcome whenever I visited you.
    There is no need to reply to this letter but if you feel like some company don't hesitate to call me.

Yours sincerely,
Jane

---

18 Oak Park,
Castleconnell,
Limerick.
11 - 6 - 19 _ _

The Manager,
Raleigh Cycles,
Station Rd.,
Limerick.

Dear Sir,
    I am writing to you to ask you to sponsor me in a 10k race. The race is being held to raise funds for Concern. As you probably know Concern is an organisation which helps famine victims in Africa.
    I look forward to hearing from you on this matter.

Yours faithfully,
Tony Smith.

The Wolves of Cernogratz

"Are there any old legends attached to the castle?" asked Conrad of his sister. Conrad was a prosperous Hamburg merchant, but he was the one poetically-dispositioned member of an eminently practical family.

The Baroness Gruebel shrugged her plump shoulders.

"There are always legends hanging about these old places. They are not difficult to invent and they cost nothing. In this case there is a story that when any one dies in the castle all the dogs in the village and the wild beasts in the forest howl the night long. It would not be pleasant to listen to, would it?"

"It would be weird and romantic," said the Hamburg merchant.

"Anyhow, it isn't true," said the Baroness complacently; "since we bought the place we have had proof that nothing of the sort happens. When the old mother-in-law died last springtime we all listened, but there was no howling. It is just a story that lends dignity to the place without costing anything."

"The story is not as you have told it," said Amalie, the grey old governess. Everyone turned and looked at her in astonishment. She was wont to sit silent and prim and faded in her place at table, never speaking unless some one spoke to her, and there were few who troubled themselves to make conversation with her. Today, a sudden volubility had descended on her; she continued to talk, rapidly and nervously, looking straight in front of her and seeming to address no one in particular.

"It is not when *any one* dies in the castle that the howling is heard. It was when one of the Cernogratz family died here that the wolves came from far and near and howled at the edge of the forest just before the death hour. There were only a few couple of wolves that had their lairs in this part of the forest, but at such a time, the keepers say, there would be scores of them, gliding about in the shadows and howling in chorus, and the dogs of the castle and the village and all the farms round would bay and howl in fear and anger at the wolf chorus, and as the soul of the dying one left its body a tree would crash down in the park. That is what happened when a Cernogratz died in his family castle.

But for a stranger dying here, of course no wolf would howl and no tree would fall. Oh, no."

There was a note of defiance, almost of contempt, in her voice as she said the last words. The well-fed, much-too-well dressed Baroness stared angrily at the dowdy old woman who had come forth from her usual and seemly position of effacement to speak so disrespectfully.

"You seem to know quite a lot about the von Cernogratz legends, Fräulein Schmidt," she said sharply; "I did not know that family histories were among the subjects you are supposed to be proficient in."

The answer to her taunt was even more unexpected and astonishing than the conversational outbreak which had provoked it.

"I am a von Cernogratz myself," said the old woman, "that is why I know the family history."

"You a von Cernogratz? You!" came in an incredulous chorus.

"When we became very poor," she explained, "and I had to go out and give teaching lessons, I took another name; I thought it would be more in keeping. But my grandfather spent much of his time as a boy in this castle, and my father used to tell me many stories about it, and, of course, I knew all the family legends and stories. When one has nothing left to one but memories, one guards and dusts them with especial care. I little thought when I took service with you that I should one day come with you to the old home of my family. I could wish it had been anywhere else."

There was a silence when she finished speaking, and then the Baroness turned the conversation to a less embarrassing topic than family histories. But afterwards, when the old governess had slipped away quietly to her duties, there arose a clamour of derision and disbelief.

"It was impertinence," snapped out the Baron, his protruding eyes taking on a scandalised expression; "fancy the woman talking like that at our table. She almost told us we were nobodies, and I don't believe a word of it. She is just Schmidt and nothing more. She has been talking to some of the peasants about the old Cernogratz family, and raked up their history and their stories."

"She wants to make herself out of some consequence," said the Baroness; "she knows she will soon be past work and she wants to appeal to our sympathies. Her grandfather, indeed!"

The Baroness had the usual number of grandfathers, but she never, never boasted about them.

"I dare say her grandfather was a pantry boy or something of the sort in the castle," sniggered the Baron; "that part of the story may be true."

The merchant from Hamburg said nothing; he had seen tears in the old woman's eyes when she spoke of guarding her memories — or, being of an imaginative disposition, he thought he had.

"I shall give her notice to go as soon as the New Year festivities are over," said the Baroness; "till then I shall be too busy to manage without her."

But she had to manage without her all the same, for in the cold biting weather after Christmas, the old governess fell ill and kept to her room.

"It is most provoking," said the Baroness, as her guests sat round the fire on one of the last evenings of the dying year; "all the time that she has been with us I cannot remember that she was ever seriously ill, too ill to go about and do her work, I mean. And now, when I have the house full, and she could be useful in so many ways, she goes and breaks down. One is sorry for her, of course, she looks so withered and shrunken, but it is intensely annoying all the same."

"Most annoying," agreed the banker's wife, sympathetically; "it is the intense cold, I expect, it breaks the old people up. It has been unusually cold this year."

"The frost is the sharpest that has been known in December for many years," said the Baron.

"And, of course, she is quite old," said the Baroness; "I wish I had given her notice some weeks ago, then she would have left before this happened to her. Why, Wappi, what is the matter with you?"

The small, woolly lapdog had leapt suddenly down from its cushion and crept shivering under the sofa. At the same moment an outburst of angry barking came from the dogs in the castle-yard, and other dogs could be heard yapping and barking in the distance.

"What is disturbing the animals?" asked the Baron.

And then the humans, listening intently, heard the sound that had roused the dogs to their demonstrations of fear and rage; heard a long-drawn whining howl, rising and falling, seeming at one moment leagues away, at others sweeping across the snow until it appeared to come from the foot of the castle walls; All the starved, cold misery of a frozen world, all the relentless hunger-fury of the wild, blended with other forlorn and haunting melodies to which one could give no name, seemed concentrated in that wailing cry.

"Wolves!" cried the Baron.

Their music broke forth in one raging burst, seeming to come from everywhere.

"Hundreds of wolves," said the Hamburg merchant, who was a man of strong imagination.

Moved by some impulse which she could not have explained, the Baroness left her guests and made her way to the narrow cheerless room where the old governess lay watching the hours of the dying year slip by. In spite of the biting cold of the winter night, the window stood open. With a scandalised exclamation on her lips, the Baroness rushed forward to close it.

"Leave it open," said the old woman in a voice that for all its weakness carried an air of command such as the Baroness had never heard before from her lips.

"But you will die of cold!" she expostulated.

"I am dying in any case," said the voice, "and I want to hear their music. They have come from far and wide to sing the death-music of my family. It is beautiful that they have come; I am the last von Cernogratz that will die in our old castle, and they have come to sing to me. Hark, how loud they are calling!"

The cry of the wolves rose on the still winter air and floated round the castle walls in long-drawn piercing wails; the old woman lay back on her couch with a look of long-delayed happiness on her face.

"Go away," she said to the Baroness; "I am not lonely any more. I am one of a great old

Spectrum 1

family...."

"I think she is dying," said the Baroness when she had rejoined her guests; "I suppose we must send for a doctor. And that terrible howling! Not for much money would I have such death-music."

"That music is not to be bought for any amount of money," said Conrad.

"Hark! What is that other sound?" asked the Baron, as a noise of splitting and crashing was heard.

It was a tree falling in the park.

There was a moment of constrained silence, and then the banker's wife spoke.

"It is the intense cold that is splitting the trees. It is also the cold that brought the wolves out in such numbers. It is many years since we have had such a cold winter."

The Baroness eagerly agreed that the cold was responsible for these things. It was the cold of the open window, too, which caused the heart failure that made the doctor's ministrations unnecessary for the old Fräulein. But the notice in the newspapers looked very well –

"On December 29th, at Schloss Cernogratz, Amalie von Cernogratz, for many years the valued friend of Baron and Baroness Gruebel."

– Saki

WORD POWER

Find words in the story which have similar meanings to each of the words and phrases below. The number in brackets after each one indicates the number of letters in the answer. The words appear in the story in the same order as the meanings given below.

CLUES

1. rich, wealthy (10)
2. businessman (8)
3. particularly; notably (9)
4. in a self-satisfied manner (12)
5. sense of worth; respect (7)
6. amazement (12)
7. stiffly formal; distant (4)
8. lacking smartness, shabbily dressed (5)
9. state of not being noticed (10)
10. expert (10)
11. insulting or provoking jibe (5)
12. unbelieving (11)
13. mockery (8)
14. insolence (12)
15. bulging; sticking out (10)
16. importance (11)
17. laughed slyly and mockingly (9)
18. celebrations (11)
19. stirred up; awoken (6)
20. measures of distance (7)
21. sad; pitiful (7)
22. protested; remonstrated (12)
23. embarrassed (11)

The Wolves of Cernogratz

Questions & Assignments

1. Outline (a) the differences in Baroness Gruebel's and Amalie's version of the legend and (b) the differences in their attitudes towards the legend.
2. Comment briefly on the phrase *'The well-fed, much-too-well dressed Baroness.'*
3. What characteristics of the Baron and Baroness are revealed in the story? Refer to the story to support your points.
4. When the old governess had finished speaking *'the Baroness turned the conversation to a less embarrassing topic than family histories . . .'* Can you suggest why the author used the adjective *'embarrassing'* here.
5. Outline your impression of when and where the story is set.
6. Identify one feature of the writer's style that you found interesting in his description of the howls of the wolves.
7. (a) How did the Baroness respond when the wolves were heard?
   (b) Did some wolves actually arrive outside the castle? Refer to the story to support your answer.
8. The old governess ordered the Baroness to leave the window open in *'a voice that for all its weakness carried an air of command such as the Baroness had never heard before from her lips'*. What, in your opinion, is the significance of this phrase?
9. *"That music is not to be bought for any amount of money."* Explain the irony in Conrad's words.
10. Did the banker's wife understand the significance of the tree falling? Explain your answer.
11. From what viewpoint is the story told?
12. Why does the writer say that the notice in the newspapers *'looked very well'*?

✏️ Functional Writing LETTER WRITING

Write a letter that you imagine the Baroness would have written to her sister outlining the events of the evening.

The Choice is Yours

(Note: This story has been divided into 4 episodes. Answer the questions to Episode I before your read Episode II etc.)

I

The Music Room was on one side of the school yard and the Changing Room faced it on the other. They were linked by a corridor that made up the third side, and the fourth was the view across the playing-fields. In the Music Room Miss Helen Francis sat at the piano, head bent over the keyboard as her fingers ran from note to note. At the top of the Changing Room steps Miss Marion Taylor stood with one hand on the doorknob and a whistle dangling on a string from the other; quivering with eagerness to be out on the field and inhaling fresh air. They could see each other. Brenda, standing in the doorway of the Music Room, could see them both.

"Well, come in, child," said Miss Francis. "Don't *dawdle*. If you must *dawdle*, don't do it in the doorway. Other people are trying to come in."

Brenda moved to one side to make way for the other people, members of the choir who would normally have shoved her out of the way and pushed past. Here they queued in patient silence. Miss Helen Francis favoured the noiseless approach. Across the school yard the Under-Thirteen Hockey team jostled noisily, and Miss Marion Taylor failed to intervene. Miss Francis observed all this with disapproval and looked away again.

"Brenda dear, are you coming in, going out, or putting down roots?"

The rest of the choir was by now seated. They all sat up straight, as trained by Miss Francis, and looked curiously at Brenda who should have been seated too, among the first sopranos. Her empty chair was in the front row, with the music stacked on it, all ready. Miss Francis cocked her head to one side like a budgie that sees some birdseed in the offing.

"Have you a message for us, dear? From above?" She meant the headmistress, but by her tone it could have been God and His angels.

"No, Miss Francis."

Miss Francis sighed a sigh that turned a page on the music stand.

"Two minutes, Brenda. We'll wait," she said venomously, and set the metronome ticking on the piano so that they might all count the two minutes, second by second.

Miss Taylor still stood upon the steps of the Changing Room. While they were all counting, they could turn round and watch Brenda tell Miss Taylor that she was not allowed to attend hockey practice.

Tock.

Tock.

Tock.

Brenda closed the door on the ticking and began to run. She would have to run to be there and back in two minutes, and running in the corridors was forbidden.

"Practice begins at twelve fifty," said Miss Taylor as Brenda came towards her. "I

102

The Choice is Yours

suppose you were thinking of joining us?"

Brenda began to cringe all over again.

"Please, Miss Taylor, Miss Francis says I can't come."

Questions & Assignments   Section I

1. What details in the first paragraph of the story tell us that (a) Miss Francis was the music teacher and (b) Miss Taylor was the P.E. teacher?
2. The third paragraph tells how the characters of the two teachers differ in one respect. Briefly explain how they differ. Refer to the third paragraph to support your answer.
3. At the end of this episode how does the author succeed in tempting the reader to continue reading the story?

II

"Does she? And what's it got to do with Miss Francis? Are you in detention?"

"No, Miss Taylor. I'm in choir."

"You may only be the goalkeeper, Brenda, but we still expect you to turn out for practices. You'll have to explain to Miss Francis that she must manage without you for once. I don't imagine that the choir will collapse if you're missing."

"No, Miss Taylor."

"Go on, then. At the double. We'll wait."

Brenda ran down the steps, aware of the Music Room windows but not looking at them, and back into the corridor. Halfway along it she was halted by a shout from behind.

"*What* do you think you're doing?"

Brenda turned and saw the Head Girl, Gill Rogers, who was also the school hockey captain and had the sense not to try and sing as well.

"Running, Gill. Sorry, Gill."

"Running's forbidden. You know that. Go back and walk."

"Miss Taylor told me to run."

"It's no good trying to blame Miss Taylor; I'm sure she didn't tell you to run."

"She said at the double," said Brenda.

"That's not the same thing at all. Go back and *walk*."

Brenda went back and walked.

"Two minutes and fifteen seconds," said Miss Francis, reaching for the metronome, when Brenda finally got back to the Music Room. "Sit down quickly, Brenda. Now then – I said sit down, Brenda."

"Please, Miss Francis –"

A look of dire agony appeared on Miss Francis's face – it could have been wind so soon after her lunch – and she held the metronome in a strangler's grip.

"I think you've delayed us long enough, Brenda."

"Miss Taylor said couldn't you please excuse me from choir just this once as it's such an important match," said Brenda, improvising rapidly, since Miss Taylor had said nothing of the sort. Miss Francis raised a claw.

"I believe I made myself perfectly clear the first time. Now, sit down, please."

"But they're all waiting for me."

"So are we, Brenda. I must remind you that it is not common practice in this school to postpone activities for the sake of Second Year girls. What position do you occupy on the team? First bat?" Miss Francis knew quite well that there are no bats required in a hockey game, but her ignorance suggested that she was above such things.

"Goalkeeper, Miss Francis."

"Goalkeeper? From the fuss certain

103

Spectrum 1

persons are making, I imagined that you must be at least a fast bowler. Is there no one else in the lower school to rival your undoubted excellence at keeping goal?"

"I *did* get chosen for the team, Miss Francis."

"Clearly you have no equal, Brenda. That being the case, you hardly need to practise, do you?"

"Miss Taylor thinks I do," said Brenda.

"Well, I'm afraid I don't. I would never, for one moment, keep you from a match, my dear, but practice on a *Thursday* is an entirely different matter. Sit down."

Brenda, panicking, pointed to the window. "But she won't start without me."

"Neither will I. You may return very quickly and tell Miss Taylor so. At once."

Brenda set off along the corridor, expecting to hear the first notes of '*An die Musik*' break out behind her. There was only silence. They were still waiting.

"Now run and get changed," said Miss Taylor, swinging her whistle, as Brenda came up the steps again. "We've waited long enough for you, my girl."

"Miss Francis says I can't come," Brenda said, baldly.

"Does she, now?"

"I've got to go back." A scarcely suppressed jeer rose from the rest of the team, assembled in the Changing Room.

"Brenda, this is the Under-Thirteen Eleven, not the Under-Thirteen Ten. There must be at least sixty of you in that choir. Are you really telling me that your absence will be noticed?"

"Miss Francis'll notice it," said Brenda.

"Then she'll just have to notice it," said Miss Taylor under her breath, but loudly enough for Brenda to hear "Go and tell Miss Francis that I insist you attend this practice."

"Couldn't you give me a note, please?" said Brenda. Miss Taylor could be as insulting as she pleased in a note, thought Brenda . . . .

"A note?" Brenda might have suggested a dozen red roses thrown in with it. "I don't see any reason to send a note. Simply tell Miss Francis that on this occasion she must let you go."

Brenda knew that it was impossible to tell Miss Francis that she must do anything, and Miss Taylor knew it too. Brenda put in a final plea for mercy.

"Couldn't you tell her?"

"We've already wasted ten minutes, Brenda, while you make up your mind."

"You needn't wait –"

"When I field a team, I field a team, not ten-elevenths of a team." She turned and addressed the said team. "It seems we'll have to stay here a little longer," her eyes strayed to the Music Room windows, "while Brenda arrives at the momentous decision."

Questions & Assignments   SECTION II

1 "*On the double*" means: (a) to run (b) to return (c) to hurry (d) to walk slowly?
2 Why do you think the author said that Gill Rogers '*had the sense not to try and sing as well*'?
3 What was Miss Francis' attitude to sport? Refer to the story to support your answer.
4 (i) '*Goalkeeper? From the fuss certain persons are making . . .*' Who are the '*certain persons*' that Miss Francis refers to here?
   (ii) Why did she not mention them by name?
5 (i) Explain clearly why Brenda asked Miss Taylor for a note.
   (ii) Why do you think Miss Taylor refused to give Brenda a note?
6 What problem faces Brenda at this point in the story?

III

Brenda turned and went down the steps again.

"Hurry UP, girl."

Miss Taylor's huge voice echoed dreadfully round the confining walls. She should have been in the choir herself, singing bass. Brenda began to run, and like a cuckoo from a clock, Gill Rogers sprang out of the cloakroom as she cantered past.

"Is that you again?"

Brenda side-stepped briskly and fled towards the Music Room, where she was met by the same ominous silence that had seen her off. The choir, cowed and bowed, crouched over the open music sheets and before them, wearing for some reason her *indomitable* expression, sat Miss Francis, tense as an overwound clockwork mouse and ready for action.

"At last. Really, Brenda, the suspense may prove too much for me. I thought you were never coming back." She lifted her hands and brought them down sharply on the keys. The choir jerked to attention. An over-eager soprano chimed in and then subsided as Miss Francis raised her hands again and looked round. Brenda was still standing in the doorway.

"Please sit down, Brenda."

Brenda clung to the door-post and looked hopelessly at Miss Francis. She would have gone down on her knees if there had been the slightest chance that Miss Francis would be moved.

"Well?"

"Please, Miss Francis, Miss Taylor says I *must* go to the practice." She wished that she were at home where, should rage break out on this scale, someone would have thrown something. If only Miss Francis would throw something; the metronome, perhaps, through the window.

Tock . . . . tock . . . . tock . . . . CRASH! Tinkle tinkle.

But Miss Francis was a lady. With restraint she closed the lid of the piano.

"It seems," she said, in a bitter little voice, "that we are to have no music today. A hockey game is to take precedence over a choir practice."

"It's *not* a game," said Brenda. "It's a practice, for a match. Just this once . . . . ?" she said, and was disgusted to find a tear boiling up under her eyelid. "Please, Miss Francis."

"No, Brenda. I do not know why we are enduring this ridiculous debate but I thought I had made myself quite clear the first time you asked. You will not miss a scheduled choir practice for an unscheduled hockey practice. Did you not explain to Miss Taylor?"

"Yes I did!" Brenda cried. "And she said you wouldn't miss me."

Miss Francis turned all reasonable. "Miss you? But my dear child, of course we wouldn't miss you. No one would miss you. You are not altogether indispensable, are you?"

"No, Miss Francis."

"It's a matter of principle. I would not dream of taking a girl from a hockey team, or a netball team or even, heaven preserve us, from a hopscotch team, and by the same token I will not allow other members of staff to disrupt my choir practices. Is that clear?"

"Yes, Miss Francis."

"Go and tell Miss Taylor. I'm sure she'll see my point."

"Yes, Miss Francis." Brenda turned to leave, praying that the practice would at last begin without her, but the lid of the piano remained shut.

This time the Head Girl was waiting for her and had her head round the cloakroom door before Brenda was fairly on her way down the corridor.

"Why didn't you come back when I called you, just now?"

Brenda leaned against the wall and let the tear escape followed by two or three others.

"Are you crying because you've broken

rules," Gill demanded, "or because you got caught? I'll see you outside the Sixth-Form Room at four o'clock."

"It's not my fault."

"Of course it's your fault. No one forced you to run."

"They're making me," said Brenda, pointing two-handed in either direction, towards the Music Room and the Changing Room.

"I daresay you asked for it," said Gill. "Four o'clock, please," and she went back into the Senior cloakroom in the hope of catching someone smoking or breaking another rule.

Questions & Assignments — SECTION III

1 Explain why Gill Rogers is compared to a cuckoo in a clock.
2 The author uses a comparison (simile) to describe Miss Taylor. Identify this comparison and give your views on it.
3 In your opinion which of the teachers should have given in? Refer to the story to support your answer.
4 (i) Miss Francis says *"I will not allow other members of staff to disrupt my choir practices."* Was she bluffing? Explain.
   (ii) *"Go and tell Miss Taylor. I'm sure she'll see my point,"* said Miss Francis. Do you think Miss Francis really believed this? Explain why.
5 Describe the powers that the Head Girl has.
6 Do you think the Head Girl treats Brenda fairly? Give a reason for your answer.

IV

This last injustice gave Brenda a jolt that she might otherwise have missed, and the tears of self-pity turned hot with anger. She trudged along to the Changing Room.

"You don't exactly hurry yourself, do you?" said Miss Taylor. "Well?"

"Miss Francis says I can't come to hockey, Miss Taylor."

Miss Taylor looked round at the restless members of the Under-Thirteen eleven and knew that for the good of the game it was time to make a stand.

"Very well, Brenda, I must leave it to you to make up your mind. Either you turn out now for the practice or you forfeit your place in the team. Which is it to be?"

Brenda looked at Miss Taylor, at the Music Room windows, and back to Miss Taylor.

"If I leave now, can I join again later?"

"Good Lord. Is there no end to this girl's cheek? Certainly not. This is your last chance, Brenda."

It would have to be the choir. She could not bear to hear the singing and never again be part of it, Thursday after Monday, term after term. If you missed a choir practice without permission, you were ejected from the choir. There was no appeal. There would be no permission.

"I'll leave the team, Miss Taylor."

She saw at once that Miss Taylor had not been expecting this. Her healthy face turned an alarming colour, like a ripe tomato.

"Then, there's nothing more to say, is there? This will go on your report, you understand. I cannot be bothered with people who don't take things seriously."

She turned her back on Brenda and blew the whistle at last, releasing the pent-up team from the Changing Room. They were followed, Brenda noticed, by Pat Stevens, the reserve, who had prudently put on the shin-pads in advance.

Brenda returned to the Music Room. The lid of the piano was still down and Miss Francis's brittle elbow pinned it.

"The prodigal returns," she announced to the choir as Brenda entered, having seen her approach down the corridor. "It is now one fifteen. May we begin dear?"

"Yes, Miss Francis."

"You finally persuaded Miss Taylor to see reason?"

"I told her what you said."

"And?"

"She said I could choose between missing the choir practice and leaving the team."

Miss Francis wore a look of triumph on her face.

"I see you chose wisely, Brenda."

"Miss Francis?"

"By coming back to the choir."

"No, Miss Francis . . . ." Brenda began to move towards the door, not trusting herself to come any closer to the piano. "I'm going to miss choir practice. I came back to tell you."

"Then you will leave the choir, Brenda. I hope you understand that."

"Yes, Miss Francis."

She stepped out of the room for the last time and closed the door. After a long while she heard the first notes of the piano, and the choir finally began to sing. Above the muted voices a whistle shrilled, out on the playing-field. Brenda went and sat in the Junior cloakroom, which was forbidden in lunch hour, and cried. There was no rule against that.

– *Jan Mark* *(Adapted)*

Questions & Assignments   SECTION IV

1 (i) What choice does Miss Taylor force Brenda to make?
  (ii) What does Brenda choose to do?
2 Why does the author compare the colour of Miss Taylor's face to a *'ripe tomato'*?
3 Explain why Miss Francis' face wore *'a look of triumph'*.
4 Give your views on the behaviour of both teachers in the story.
5 (i) What were your feelings towards Brenda?
  (ii) What would you have done if you found yourself in a situation similar to Brenda's?
6 Did you find this story sad or funny – or both? Give reasons for your answer.
7 Would a Head Girl or a Head Boy with similar powers to the one in the story, be a good idea in your school? Explain why or why not.

Spectrum 1

WORD POWER

Find words in the story which have similar meanings to each of the words and phrases below. The number in brackets after each one indicates the number of letters in the answer. The words appear in the story in the same order as the meanings given below.

CLUES

I

1. hanging loosely (8) *dangling*
2. trembling; shaking (9) *quivering*
3. breathing in (8) *inhaling*
4. step in (to control a disorder or a fight) (9) *intervene*
5. watched; noticed (8) *observed*
6. drew a long deep breath to indicate weariness (6) *sighed*
7. very spitefully (10) *venomously*
8. permitted (7) *allowed*
9. shrink back in fear (6) *cringe*

II

10. fall apart (8)
11. stopped (6)
12. instrument that keeps a regular beat (9)
13. making up something on the spur of the moment (11)
14. put off until later (8)
15. lack of knowledge (9)
16. kept back (10)

17. urgent request (4)
18. of great importance (9)

III

19. galloped slowly (8)
20. very quickly (7)
21. suggesting future trouble (7)
22. subdued (5)
23. unyielding (11)
24. tension; excitement (8)
25. fell away (8)
26. self-control (9)
27. putting up with (8)
28. planned for a certain time (9)
29. unable to be done without (13)

IV

30. walked wearily (7)
31. give up (7)
32. put out (7)
33. wisely (9)
34. easily broken (7)
35. hushed (5)

✎ *Functional Writing* LETTER WRITING

Write a letter from Brenda's parents to the principal about the incident.

✎ *Dialogue Writing*

Write in dialogue form the interview with Brenda's father and the two teachers about the incident. Suggestion – make her father a very forceful character, who uses much sarcasm.

✎ *Personal Writing* ASSIGNMENTS

1. Following the remark "*And?*" from Miss Francis in the final section of the story compose a different ending. Perhaps Brenda could bring a different message from the one that she was instructed to bring?
2. Write about a difficult choice that you had to make.
3. Describe the importance of music or sport in your life.

4 Write about some of the various games, activities and 'crazes' that you enjoyed over the course of your childhood – street games, hopscotch, conkers, marbles . . . or any others that you remember enjoying.

Answer Guidelines

You may find the following openings helpful when attempting Personal Writing assignments 2 and 3.

2 'Gary,' said Peter to me as we cycled towards the school, 'the sun is shining, the sky is blue. Isn't it a beautiful day?'
'True,' I replied. I wasn't sure what Peter was getting at.
'It's much too nice a day to spend at science, maths and geography.'
'I agree – but we have no choice,' I said. I knew then what was coming next.
'Of course we have a choice. We can choose to go to school or we can choose not to. It's as simple as that,' he said.
It wasn't as simple as that for me. If I got one more complaint . . .

3
- Around the time I made my confirmation, marbles were 'in'. I loved marbles. They were a slow relaxing game, perfect for sunny days. For twenty pence you could buy . . . .
- All last summer, hopscotch was the rage with the girls on our street. All you needed to play was a stick of chalk to mark out the squares and an old shoe-polish tin. Each player had to . . . The winner was the girl who . . . .

The Giant with the Three Golden Hairs

Once upon a time there was a poor woman whose son was born with a mole on his cheek, and so it was foretold of him that in his fourteenth year he should marry the King's daughter. As it happened the King soon after came into the village, quite unknown to any one, and when he asked the people what news there was, they answered, "A few days since a child with a mole on his cheek was born, which is a sure sign that he will be very lucky; and, indeed, it has been foretold of him that in his fourteenth year he will marry the King's daughter."

The King had a wicked heart, and was disturbed by this prophecy, so he went to the parents, and said to them in a most friendly manner, "Give me up your child and I will care for him." At first they refused, but the stranger begged for the child with much gold, and so at last they consented and gave him the child, thinking, "It is a luck-child, and, therefore, everything must go on well with it."

The King laid the child in a box and rode away till he came to a deep water, into which he threw the box, saying to himself, "This fellow now has no chance of marrying my daughter."

The box, however, did not sink, but floated along like a boat, and not one drop of water penetrated it. It floated at last down to a mill two miles from the King's palace, and in the mill-dam it stuck fast. The miller's boy, who was fortunately standing there, observed it, and drew it ashore with a hook, expecting to find a great treasure. When, however, he opened the box, he saw a beautiful child alive and merry. He took it to the people at the mill, who, having no children, adopted it for

The Giant with the Three Golden Hairs

their own saying, "God has sent him to us." They took good care of the child, and he grew up a steady, good lad.

It happened one day that the King went into the mill for shelter during a thunderstorm, and asked the people whether the boy was their child. "No," they answered; "he is a foundling, who, fourteen years ago, floated into our dam in a box, which the miller's boy drew out of the water." The King observed at once, that it was no other than the luck-child whom he had thrown into the water, and so said to them, "Good people, could not the youth carry a letter to my wife the Queen? If so I will give him two pieces of gold for a reward."

"As my lord the King commands," they replied, and ordered the youth get ready.

Then the King wrote a letter to the Queen, in which he said, "So soon as this boy arrives with this letter, let him be killed and buried, and let all be done before I return."

The youth set out on his journey with the letter, but he lost himself, and at evening came into a great forest. In the gloom he saw a little light, and going up to it he found a cottage, into which he went, and saw an old woman sitting by the fire. As soon as she saw the lad she was terrified, and exclaimed, "Why do you come here; and what would you do?"

"I am come from the mill," he answered, "and am going to my lady the Queen to carry a letter; but because I have lost my way in this forest, I wish to pass the night here."

"Poor boy!" said the woman, "you have come to a den of robbers, who, when they return, will murder you."

"Let who will come," he replied, "I am not afraid: I am so weary that I can go no further;" and, stretching himself upon a bench, he went to sleep. Presently the robbers returned, and asked in a rage what strange lad was lying there. "Ah," said the old woman, "it is an innocent youth, who has lost himself in the forest, and whom I have taken in out of compassion. He carries with him a letter to the Queen."

The robbers seized the letter and read it, and understood that as soon as the youth arrived he was to be put to death. Then the robbers also took compassion on him, and the captain tore up the letter and wrote another, in which he declared that the youth upon his arrival was to be married to the Princess. They let him sleep quietly on his bench till the morning, and as soon as he awoke they gave him the letter and showed him the right road.

When the Queen received the letter she did as it commanded, and ordered a splendid marriage feast to be prepared, and the Princess was given in marriage to the luck-child, who, since he was both young and handsome, pleased her well, and they were all very happy. Some little time afterwards the King returned to his palace and found the prophecy fulfilled, and his daughter married to the luck-child. "How did this happen?" he asked. "In my letter I gave quite another command."

Then the Queen handed him the letter, that he might read for himself what it stated. The King saw at once that it had been forged by another person, and he asked the youth what he had done with the original letter that had been entrusted to him. "I know nothing about it," he replied; "it must have been changed in the forest where I passed the night."

Full of rage the King answered, "Thou shalt not escape so easily; he who would marry my daughter must fetch for me three golden hairs from the head of the Giant: bring these to me and then you can stay on here as my son-in-law."

The King hoped by this means to get rid of him, but he answered, "The three Golden hairs I will fetch, for I fear not the Giant," and so he took leave and began his wanderings.

The road led him by a large town, where the watchman met him at the gate asked him what trade he had and what he knew. "I know everything," replied the youth.

"Then you can do us a kindness," said the watchman, "if you tell us the reason why the fountain in our market-place, out of which wine used to flow, now, all at once, does not even give water."

"That you shall know," was the answer; "but you must wait till I return."

Then he went on further and came to a rather large city, where the watchman asked him, as before, what trade he had, and what he knew. "I know everything," he replied.

"Then you can do us a kindness, if you tell us the reason why a tree growing in our town, which used to bear golden apples, does not now even have any leaves."

"That you shall know," replied the youth, "if you wait till I return," and so saying he went on further till he came to a great lake, over which it was necessary that he should pass. The ferryman asked him what trade he had, and what he knew. "I know everything," he replied.

"Then," said the ferryman, "you can do me a kindness, if you tell me why, for ever and ever, I am obliged to row backwards and forwards, and am never to be released." "You shall learn the reason why," replied the youth; "but wait till I return."

As soon as he got over the water he found the entrance into the Giant's kingdom. It was black and gloomy, and the Giant was not at home; but his old grandmother was sitting there in an immense armchair. "What do you want?" said she, looking at him fixedly. "I want three Golden hairs from the head of the Giant who lives in these regions," replied the youth, or "else I cannot obtain my bride."
"That is a bold request," said the woman; "for if he comes home and finds you here it will be a bad thing for you; but still you can remain, and I will see if I can help you."

The old woman, who had magic powers, then changed him into an ant, and told him to creep within the fold of her gown, where he would be quite safe.

"Yes," he said, "that is all very well; but there are three things I am desirous of knowing: – why a fountain, which used to spout wine, is now dry, and does not even give water – why a tree, which used to bear golden apples, does not now have leaves – and why a ferryman is always rowing backwards and forwards and never gets released."

"Those are difficult questions," replied the old woman; "but do you keep quiet, and pay attention to what the Giant says when I pluck each of the three golden hairs."

As soon as evening came the Giant returned, and scarcely had he entered, when he remarked that the air was not quite pure. "I smell! I smell the flesh of man!" he exclaimed; "all is not right." Then he peeped into every corner and looked about, but could find nothing. Presently his old grandmother began to scold, screaming, "There now, just as I have dusted and put everything in order, you are pulling them all about again! Sit down and eat your supper."

When he had finished he felt tired, and the old woman took his head in her lap, and said she would comb his hair a bit. Presently he yawned, then winked, and at last snored. Then she plucked out a golden hair and laid it down beside her.

"Bah!" cried the Giant, "what are you doing?"

"I have had a bad dream," answered the old woman, "and so I plucked one of your hairs."

"What did you dream, then?" asked he.

"I dreamt that a market-fountain, which used to spout wine, is dried up, and does not even give water: what is the matter with it, pray?"

"Why, if you must know," answered he, "there sits a toad under a stone in the spring, which, if any one kills, the wine will gush out as before."

Then the old woman went on combing till he went to sleep again, and snored so that the windows shook. Presently she pulled out a second hair.

"Confound it! what are you doing?" exclaimed the Giant in a passion.

"Don't be angry," said she; "I did it in a dream."

"What did you dream about this time?" he asked.

"I dreamt that in a certain royal city there grew a fruit-tree, which formerly bore golden apples, but now has not a leaf upon it: what is the cause of it?"

"Why," replied the Giant, "at the root of the tree a mouse is gnawing. But if they kill it golden apples will grow again; if not, the mouse will gnaw till the tree dies altogether. However, let me go to sleep in peace now; for if you disturb me again you will catch a box on the ears."

Nevertheless the old woman, when she had rocked him again to sleep, plucked out a third golden hair. Up jumped the Giant in a fury and would have ill-treated her, but she pacified him and said, "Who can help bad dreams?"

"What did you dream this time?" he asked, still curious to know.

"I dreamt of a ferryman, who is forever compelled to row backwards and forwards, and will never be released. What is the reason?"

"Oh, you simpleton!" answered the Giant. "When someone comes who wants to cross over, the ferryman must give the oar into his hand; then will the other person be obliged to go to and fro, and the ferryman will be free."

Now, since the old woman had plucked the three golden hairs, and had received answers to the three questions, she let the Giant lie in peace, and he slept on till daybreak.

As soon as he went out in the morning the old woman took the ant out of the fold of her gown, and restored him again to his human form.

"There you have the three golden hairs from the Giant's head, and what he replied to the three questions you have just heard."

"Yes, I have heard, and will well remember," said the luck-child; and, thanking the old woman for her assistance in his trouble, he left those regions, well pleased that he had been so lucky in everything. When he came to the ferryman he had to give him the promised answer. But he said, "First row me over, and then I will tell you how you may be freed;" and as soon as they reached the opposite side he gave him the advice, "When another comes this way, and wants to pass over, give him the oar in his hand."

Then he went on to the first city, where stood the barren tree, and where the watchman waited for the answer. So he said to him, "Kill the mouse which gnaws at the root of the tree, and then it will again bear golden apples." The watchman thanked him, and gave him for a reward two asses laden with gold, which followed him. Next he came to the other city, where the dry fountain was, and he told the watchman as the Giant had said, – "Under a stone in the spring there sits a toad, which you must uncover and kill, and then wine will flow again as before."

The watchman thanked him, and gave to him, as the other had done, two asses laden with gold.

Now the lucky youth soon reached home, and his dear bride was very glad when she saw him return, and heard how capitally everything had gone with him. He brought the King what he had desired – the three golden hairs from the head of the Giant – and when his Majesty saw the four asses laden with gold he was quite pleased, and said, "Now the conditions are fulfilled, and you may have my daughter: but tell me, dear son-in-law, from whence comes all this gold? This is, indeed, bountiful treasure."

"I was ferried over a river," he replied, "and there I picked it up, for it lies upon the shore like sand."

"Can I not fetch some as well?" asked the King, feeling quite covetous.

"As much as you like; there is a ferryman who will row you across and then you can fill your sacks on the other side."

The covetous King set out in great haste upon his journey, and as soon as he came to the river beckoned to the ferryman to take him over. The man came and asked him to step into his boat, and as soon as they reached the opposite shore, the ferryman asked the King to hold the oars for a moment while he tied up the boat. The King took the oar into his hand and the ferryman sprang on shore, a free man at last.

So the King was obliged to take his place, and there he is obliged to row to and fro forever for his sins.

And there he still rows, for no-one has yet come to take the oar from him.

– *The Brothers Grimm*
(adapted)

GRIMMS' FAIRY TALES

In Germany, at the beginning of the nineteenth century, two brothers, Jacob and Wilhelm Grimm, set about collecting folk tales. They travelled the countryside, persuading the people to tell them old stories which they then wrote down. In those days there was, of course, no radio or television. Even books were not very plentiful and, in any case, few people could read well. During the long winter nights people sat around the fireside and told stories, stories which had been handed down from generation to generation. The result of the brothers' efforts was the world-famous book – *Grimms' Fairy Tales*.

Many of the stories in the collection, such as *Cinderella, Hansel and Gretel, Sleeping Beauty, Snow White* and *Little Red Riding Hood*, have delighted children all over the world. Some of the stories are dark and frightening however and not suitable for young children.

Many of the stories feature witches, giants, goblins, sacks of gold, kings, palaces, brave handsome princes, as well as poor tailors and woodcutters whose sons often end up marrying beautiful princesses!

During their work the Grimm brothers discovered many different versions of the same stories. For example, there were over three hundred different versions of *Cinderella* in Germany alone. Of course many of the tales collected by the brothers were common to other countries, spread by sailors and travellers. Quite a number of the tales were probably inspired by living conditions of the time. For example *Little Red Riding Hood* was probably first told when wolves roamed freely throughout Europe, threatening the lives of ordinary people.

The Giant with the Three Golden Hairs is one of Grimms' lesser-known fairy tales.

The Giant with the Three Golden Hairs

Questions & Assignments

1. What details in the title and first paragraph suggest that the story to follow is a 'fairy story'?
2. Why did the King want to adopt the child?
3. Explain why the King's first attempt at killing the child failed.
4. Describe the second meeting between the King and the boy. Explain how the boy managed to escape death a second time.
5. Outline the King's next plan to get rid of the boy, who was now his son-in-law.
6. The boy met three people on his journey to the Giant's kingdom. Who were these people and what did they each want to know?
7. Describe briefly how the boy managed to get the Giant's hairs.
8. Imagine that the boy kept a diary of his return journey. Make up a number of entries that you think he might have written into that diary.
9. Explain clearly how the boy tricked the King.
10. Suggest a number of ways in which this story is like the stories of some modern science-fiction films such as *Batman*, *Superman* or *Star-Trek*.
11. List a number of events in the story which could not happen in the real world.
12. Imagine that you are a judge in a short story competition. Mark the story out of ten and explain briefly why you marked it as you did.

Personal Writing FAIRY STORIES

Make up a short 'fairy story' suitable for a young child.

THE HITCH-HIKER

I had a new car. It was an exciting toy, a big BMW 3.3 Li, which means 3.3 litre, long wheelbase, fuel injection. It had a top speed of 129mph and terrific acceleration. The body was pale blue. The seats inside were darker blue and they were made of leather, genuine soft leather of the finest quality. The windows were electrically operated and so was the sun-roof. The radio aerial popped up when I switched on the radio, and disappeared when I switched it off. The powerful engine growled and grunted impatiently at slow speeds, but at sixty miles an hour the growling stopped and the motor began to purr with pleasure.

I was driving up to London by myself. It was a lovely June day. They were haymaking in the fields and there were buttercups along both sides of the road. I was whispering along at seventy miles an hour, leaning back comfortably in my seat, with no more than a couple of fingers resting lightly on the wheel to keep her steady. Ahead of me I saw a man thumbing a lift. I touched the footbrake and brought the car to a stop beside him. I always stopped for hitch-hikers. I knew just how it used to feel to be standing on the side of a country road watching the cars go by. I hated drivers for pretending they didn't see me, especially the ones in big cars with three empty seats. The large expensive cars seldom stopped. It was always the smaller ones that offered you a lift, or the old rusty ones, or the ones that were already crammed full of children and the driver would say, 'I think we can squeeze in one more.'

The hitch-hiker poked his head through the open window and said, 'Going to London, guv'nor?'

'Yes,' I said. 'Jump in.'

He got in and I drove on.

He was a small ratty-faced man with grey teeth. His eyes were dark and quick and clever, like a rat's eyes, and his ears were slightly pointed at the top. He had a cloth cap on his head and he was wearing a greyish-coloured jacket with enormous pockets. The grey jacket, together with the quick eyes and the pointed ears, made him look more than anything like some sort of huge human rat.

'What part of London are you headed for?' I asked him.

'I'm goin' right through London and out the other side,' he said. 'I'm goin' to Epsom, for the races. It's Derby Day today.'

'So it is,' I said. 'I wish I were going with you. I love betting on horses.'

'I never bet on horses,' he said. 'I don't even watch 'em run. That's a stupid silly business.'

'Then why do you go?' I asked.

He didn't seem to like that question. His little ratty face went absolutely blank and he sat there staring straight ahead at the road, saying nothing.

'I expect you help to work the betting machines or something like that,' I said.

'That's even sillier,' he answered. 'There's no fun working them lousy machines and selling tickets to mugs. Any fool could do that.'

There was a long silence. I decided not to question him any more. I remembered how irritated I used to get in my hitch-hiking days when drivers kept asking me questions. Where are you going? Why are you going there? What's your job? Are you married? Do you have a girl-friend? What's her name? How old are you? And so on and so forth. I used to hate it.

'I'm sorry,' I said. 'It's none of my business what you do. The trouble is, I'm a writer, and most writers are terrible nosey parkers.'

'You write books?' he asked.

'Yes.'

'Writin' books is okay,' he said. 'It's what I call a skilled trade. I'm in a skilled trade too. The folks I despise is them that spend all their lives doin' crummy old routine jobs with no skill in 'em at all. You see what I mean?'

'Yes.'

'The secret of life,' he said, 'is to become very very good at somethin' that's very very 'ard to do.'

'Like you,' I said.

'Exactly. You and me both.'

'What makes you think that I'm any good at my job?' I asked. 'There's an awful lot of bad writers around.'

'You wouldn't be drivin' about in a car like this if you weren't no good at it,' he answered. 'It must've cost a tidy packet, this little job.'

'It wasn't cheap.'

'What can she do flat out?' he asked.

'One hundred and twenty-nine miles an hour,' I told him.

'I'll bet she won't do it.'

'I'll bet she will.'

'All car makers is liars,' he said. 'You can buy any car you like and it'll never do what the makers say it will in the ads.'

'This one will.'

'Open 'er up then and prove it,' he said. 'Go on, guv'nor, open 'er right up and let's see what she'll do.'

There is a roundabout at Chalfont St Peter and immediately beyond it there's a long straight section of dual carriageway. We came out of the roundabout on to the carriageway and I pressed my foot down on the accelerator. The big car leaped forward as though she'd been stung. In ten seconds or so, we were doing ninety.

'Lovely!' he cried. 'Beautiful! Keep goin'!'

I had the accelerator jammed right down against the floor and I held it there.

'One hundred!' he shouted . . . 'A hundred and five! . . . A hundred and ten! . . . A hundred and fifteen! Go on! Don't slack off!'

I was in the outside lane and we flashed past several cars as though they were standing still – a green Mini, a big cream-coloured Citroën, a white Land-Rover, a huge truck with a container on the back, an orange-coloured Volkswagen Minibus . . .

'A hundred and twenty!' my passenger shouted, jumping up and down. 'Go on! Go on! Get 'er up to one-two-nine!'

At that moment, I heard the scream of a police siren. It was so loud it seemed to be right inside the car, and then a policeman on a motorcycle loomed up alongside us on the inside lane and went past us and raised a hand for us to stop.

'Oh, my sainted aunt!' I said. 'That's torn it!'

The policeman must have been doing about a hundred and thirty when he passed us, and he took plenty of time slowing down. Finally, he pulled into the side of the road and I pulled in behind him. 'I didn't know police motorcycles could go as fast as that,' I said rather lamely.

'That one can,' my passenger said. 'It's the same make as yours. It's a BMW R90S. Fastest bike on the road. That's what they're usin' nowadays.'

The policeman got off his motor-cycle and leaned the machine sideways on to its prop stand. Then he took off his gloves and placed them carefully on the seat. He was in no hurry now. He had us where he wanted us and he knew it.

'This is real trouble,' I said. 'I don't like it one bit.'

'Don't talk to 'im any more than is necessary, you understand,' my companion said. 'Just sit tight and keep mum.'

Like an executioner approaching his victim, the policeman came strolling slowly towards us. He was a big meaty man with a belly, and his blue breeches were skintight around his enormous thighs. His goggles were pulled up on to the helmet, showing a smouldering red face with wide cheeks.

We sat there like guilty schoolboys, waiting for him to arrive.

'Watch out for this man,' my passenger whispered. ''Ee looks mean as the devil.'

The policeman came round to my open window and placed one meaty hand on the sill. 'What's the hurry?' he said.

'No hurry, officer,' I answered.

'Perhaps there's a woman in the back having a baby and you're rushing her to hospital? Is that it?'

'No, officer.'

'Or perhaps your house is on fire and you're dashing home to rescue the family from upstairs?' His voice was dangerously soft and mocking.

'My house isn't on fire, officer.'

'In that case,' he said, 'you've got yourself into a nasty mess, haven't you? Do you know what the speed limit is in this country?'

'Seventy,' I said.

'And do you mind telling me exactly what speed you were doing just now?'

I shrugged and didn't say anything.

When he spoke next, he raised his voice so loud that I jumped. *'One hundred and twenty miles per hour!'* he barked. 'That's *fifty* miles an hour over the limit!'

He turned his head and spat out a big gob of spit. It landed on the wing of my car and started sliding down over my beautiful blue paint. Then he turned back again and stared hard at my passenger. 'And who are you?' he asked sharply.

'He's a hitch-hiker,' I said. 'I'm giving him a lift.'

'I didn't ask you,' he said. 'I asked him.'

''Ave I done somethin' wrong?' my passenger asked. His voice was as soft and oily as haircream.

'That's more than likely,' the policeman answered.

'Anyway, you're a witness. I'll deal with you in a minute. Driving-licence,' he snapped, holding out his hand.

I gave him my driving-licence.

He unbuttoned the left-hand breast-pocket of his tunic and brought out the dreaded books of tickets. Carefully, he copied the name and address from my licence. Then he gave it back to me. He strolled round to the front of the car and read the number from the number-plate and wrote that down as well. He filled in the date, the time and the details of my offence. Then he tore out the top copy of the ticket. But before handing it to me, he checked that all the information had come through clearly on his own carbon copy. Finally, he replaced the book in his tunic pocket and fastened the button.

'Now you,' he said to my passenger, and he walked around to the other side of the car. From the other breast-pocket he produced a small black notebook. 'Name?' he snapped.

'Michael Fish,' my passenger said.

'Address?'

'Fourteen, Windsor Lane, Luton.'

'Show me something to prove this is your real name and address,' the policeman said.

My passenger fished in his pockets and came out with a driving-licence of his own. The policeman checked the name and address and handed it back to him. 'What's your job?' he asked sharply.

'I'm an 'od carrier.'

'A *what*?'

'An 'od carrier.'

'Spell it.'

'H-O-D C-A-. . .'

'That'll do. And what's a hod carrier, may I ask?'

'An 'od carrier, officer, is a person 'oo carries the cement up the ladder to the bricklayer. And the 'od is what 'ee carries it in. It's got a long 'andle, and on the top you've got two bits of wood set at an angle. . .'

'All right, all right. Who's your employer?'

'Don't 'ave one. I'm unemployed.'

The policeman wrote all this down in the black note-book. Then he returned the book to its pocket and did up the button.

'When I get back to the station I'm going to do a little checking up on you,' he said to my passenger.

'Me? What've I done wrong?' the rat-faced man asked.

'I don't like your face, that's all,' the policeman said. 'And we just might have a picture of it somewhere in our files.' He strolled round the car and returned to my window.

'I suppose you know you're in serious trouble,' he said to me.

'Yes, officer.'

'You won't be driving this fancy car of yours again for a very long time, not after we've finished with you. You won't be driving any car again come to that for several years. And a good thing, too. I hope they lock you up for a spell into the bargain.'

'You mean prison?' I asked, alarmed.

'Absolutely,' he said, smacking his lips. 'In the clink. Behind the bars. Along with all the other criminals who break the law. And a hefty fine into the bargain. Nobody will be more pleased about that than me. I'll see you in court, both of you. You'll be getting a summons to appear.'

He turned away and walked over to his motor-cycle. He flipped the prop stand back into position with his foot and swung his leg over the saddle. Then he kicked the starter and roared off up the road out of sight.

'Phew!' I gasped. 'That's done it.'

'We was caught,' my passenger said. 'We was caught good and proper.'

'I was caught, you mean.'

'That's right,' he said. 'What you goin' to do now, guv'nor?'

'I'm going straight up to London to talk to my solicitor,' I said. I started the car and drove on.

'You mustn't believe what 'ee said to you about goin' to prison,' my passenger said. 'They don't put anybody in the clink just for speedin'.'

'Are you sure of that?'

'I'm positive,' he answered. 'They can take your licence away and they can give you a whoppin' big fine, but that'll be the end of it.'

I felt tremendously relieved.

'By the way,' I said, 'why did you lie to him?'

'Who, me?' he said. 'What makes you think I lied?'

'You told him you were an unemployed hod carrier. But you told me you were in a highly skilled trade.'

'So I am,' he said. 'But it don't pay to tell everythin' to a copper.'

'So what *do* you do?' I asked him.

'Ah,' he said slyly. 'That'd be tellin', wouldn't it?'

'Is it something you're ashamed of?'

'Ashamed?' he cried. 'Me, ashamed of my job? I'm about as proud of it as anybody could be in the entire world!'

'Then why won't you tell me?'

'You writers really is nosey parkers, aren't

you?' he said. 'And you ain't goin' to be 'appy, I don't think, until you've found out exactly what the answer is?'

'I don't really care one way or the other,' I told him, lying.

He gave me a crafty little ratty look out of the sides of his eyes. 'I think you do care,' he said. 'I can see it on your face that you think I'm in some kind of a very peculiar trade and you're just achin' to know what it is.'

I didn't like the way he read my thoughts. I kept quiet and stared at the road ahead.

'You'd be right, too,' he went on. 'I *am* in a very peculiar trade. I'm in the queerest peculiar trade of 'em all.'

I waited for him to go on.

'That's why I 'as to be extra careful 'oo I'm talkin' to, you see. 'Ow am I to know, for instance, you're not another copper in plain clothes?'

'Do I look like a copper?'

'No,' he said. 'You don't. And you ain't. Any fool could tell that.'

He took from his pocket a tin of tobacco and a packet of cigarette papers and started to roll a cigarette. I was watching him out of the corner of one eye, and the speed with which he performed this rather difficult operation was incredible. The cigarette was rolled and ready in about five seconds. He ran his tongue along the edge of the paper, stuck it down and popped the cigarette between his lips. Then, as if from nowhere, a lighter appeared in his hand. The lighter flamed. The cigarette was lit. The lighter disappeared. It was altogether a remarkable performance.

'I've never seen anyone roll a cigarette as fast as that,' I said.

'Ah,' he said, taking a deep suck of smoke. 'So you noticed.'

'Of course I noticed. It was quite fantastic.'

He sat back and smiled. It pleased him very much that I had noticed how quickly he could roll a cigarette. 'You want to know what makes me able to do it?' he asked.

'Go on then.'

'It's because I've got fantastic fingers. These fingers of mine,' he said, holding up both hands high in front of him, 'are quicker and cleverer than the fingers of the best piano player in the world!'

'Are you a piano player?'

'Don't be daft,' he said. 'Do I look like a piano player?'

I glanced at his fingers. They were so beautifully shaped, so slim and long and elegant, they didn't seem to belong to the rest of him at all. They looked more like the fingers of a brain surgeon or a watchmaker.

'My job,' he went on, 'is a hundred times more difficult than playin' the piano. Any twerp can learn to do that. There's titchy little kids learnin' to play the piano in almost any 'ouse you go into these days. That's right, ain't it?'

'More or less,' I said.

'Of course it's right. But there's not one person in ten million can learn to do what I do. Not one in ten million! 'Ow about that?'

'Amazing,' I said.

'You're darn right it's amazin',' he said.

'I think I know what you do,' I said. 'You do conjuring tricks. You're a conjurer.'

'Me?' he snorted. 'A conjurer? Can you picture me goin' round crummy kids' parties makin' rabbits come out of top 'ats?'

'Then you're a card player. You get people into card games and deal yourself marvellous hands.'

'Me! A rotten card-sharper!' he cried. 'That's a miserable racket if ever there was one.'

'All right. I give up.'

I was taking the car along slowly now, at no more than forty miles an hour, to make quite sure I wasn't stopped again. We had come on to the main London-Oxford road and were running down the hill towards Denham.

Suddenly my passenger was holding up a black leather belt in his hand. 'Ever seen this before?' he asked. The belt had a brass buckle of unusual design.

'Hey!' I said. 'That's mine, isn't it? It is mine! Where did you get it?'

He grinned and waved the belt gently from side to side. 'Where d'you think I got it?' he said. 'Off the top of your trousers, of course.'

I reached down and felt for my belt. It was gone.

'You mean you took it off me while we've been driving along?' I asked, flabbergasted.

He nodded, watching me all the time with those little black ratty eyes.

'That's impossible,' I said. 'You'd have had to undo the buckle and slide the whole thing out through the loops all the way round. I'd have seen you doing it. And even if I hadn't seen you, I'd have felt it.'

'Ah, but you didn't, did you?' he said, triumphant. He dropped the belt on his lap, and now all at once there was a brown shoelace dangling from his finger. 'And what about this, then?' he exclaimed, waving the shoelace.

'What about it?' I said.

'Anyone around 'ere missin' a shoelace?' he asked, grinning.

I glanced down at my shoes. The lace of one of them was missing. 'Good grief!' I said. 'How did you do that? I never saw you bending down.'

'You never saw nothin',' he said proudly. 'You never even saw me move an inch. And you know why?'

'Yes,' I said. 'Because you've got fantastic fingers.'

'Exactly right!' he cried. 'You catch on pretty quick, don't you?' He sat back and sucked away at his home-made cigarette, blowing the smoke out in a thin stream against the windshield. He knew he had impressed me greatly with those two tricks, and this made him very happy. 'I don't want to be late,' he said. 'What time is it?'

'There's a clock in front of you,' I told him.

'I don't trust car clocks,' he said. 'What does your watch say?'

I hitched up my sleeve to look at the watch on my wrist. It wasn't there. I looked at the man. He looked back at me, grinning.

'You've taken that, too,' I said.

He held out his hand and there was my watch lying in his palm. 'Nice bit of stuff, this,' he said. 'Superior quality. Eighteen-carat gold. Easy to flog, too. It's never any trouble gettin' rid of quality goods.'

'I'd like it back, if you don't mind,' I said rather huffily.

He placed the watch carefully on the leather tray in front of him. 'I wouldn't nick anythin' from you, guv'nor,' he said. 'You're my pal. You're giving me a lift.'

'I'm glad to hear it,' I said.

'All I'm doin' is answerin' your questions,' he went on. 'You asked me what I did for a livin' and I'm showin' you.'

'What else have you got of mine?'

He smiled again, and now he started to take from the pocket of his jacket one thing after another that belonged to me – my driving-licence, a key-ring with four keys on it, some pound notes, a few coins, a letter from my publishers, my diary, a stubby old pencil, a cigarette-lighter, and last of all, a beautiful old sapphire ring with pearls around it belonging to my wife. I was taking the ring up to the jeweller in London because one of the pearls was missing.

'Now *there's* another lovely piece of goods,' he said, turning the ring over in his fingers. 'That's eighteenth century, if I'm not mistaken, from the reign of King George the Third.'

'You're right,' I said, impressed. 'You're absolutely right.'

He put the ring on the leather tray with the other items.

'So you're a pickpocket,' I said.

'I don't like that word,' he answered. 'It's a coarse and vulgar word. Pickpockets is coarse and vulgar people who only do easy little amateur jobs. They lift money from blind old ladies.'

'What do you call yourself, then?'

'Me? I'm a fingersmith. I'm a professional fingersmith.' He spoke the words solemnly and proudly, as though he were telling me he was the President of the Royal College of Surgeons or the Archbishop of Canterbury.

'I've never heard that word before,' I said. 'Did you invent it?'

'Of course I didn't invent it,' he replied. 'It's the name given to them who's risen to the very top of the profession. You've 'eard of a goldsmith and a silversmith, for instance. They're experts with gold and silver. I'm an expert with my fingers, so I'm a fingersmith.'

'It must be an interesting job.'

'It's a marvellous job,' he answered. 'It's lovely.'

'And that's why you go to the races?'

'Race meetings is easy meat,' he said. 'You just stand around after the race, watchin' for the lucky ones to queue up and draw their money. And when you see someone collectin' a big bundle of notes, you simply follows after 'im and 'elps yourself. But don't get me wrong guv'nor. I never takes nothin' from a loser. Nor from poor people either. I only go after them as can afford it, the winners and the rich.'

'That's very thoughtful of you,' I said. 'How often do you get caught?'

'Caught?' he cried, disgusted. '*Me* get caught! It's only pickpockets get caught. Fingersmiths never. Listen, I could take the false teeth out of your mouth if I wanted to and you wouldn't even catch me!'

'I don't have false teeth,' I said.

'I know you don't,' he answered. 'Otherwise I'd 'ave 'ad 'em out long ago!'

I believed him. Those long slim fingers of his seemed able to do anything.

We drove on for a while without talking.

'That policeman's going to check up on you pretty thoroughly,' I said. 'Doesn't that worry you a bit?'

'Nobody's checkin' up on me,' he said.

'Of course they are. He's got your name and address written down most carefully in his black book.'

The man gave me another of his sly, ratty little smiles. 'Ah,' he said. 'So 'ee 'as. But I'll bet 'ee ain't got it all written down in 'is memory as well. I've never known a copper yet with a decent memory. Some of 'em can't even remember their own names.'

'What's memory got to do with it?' I asked. 'It's written down in his book, isn't it?'

'Yes, guv'nor, it is. But the trouble is, 'ee's lost the book. 'Ee's lost both books, the one with my name in it and the one with yours.'

In the long delicate fingers of his right hand, the man was holding up in triumph the two books he had taken from the policeman's pockets. 'Easiest job I ever done,' he announced proudly.

I nearly swerved the car into a milk-truck, I was so excited.

'That copper's got nothin' on either of us now,' he said.

'You're a genius!' I cried.

''Ee's got no names, no addresses, no car number, no nothin',' he said.

'You're brilliant!'

'I think you'd better pull in off this main road as soon as possible,' he said. 'Then we'd better build a little bonfire and burn these books.'

'You're a fantastic fellow,' I exclaimed.

'Thank you guv'nor,' he said. 'It's always nice to be appreciated.'

– *Roald Dahl*

Points to Note

SETTING

Setting is the term used to refer to the place and time that the events in a story occur. When discussing the setting of a story you approach it at two levels. Firstly, there is the broad general setting – we could say *The Hitch-Hiker* is set in Britain in modern times.

Secondly, there is the more specific setting – we could say the action in the story takes place over the course of a summer's afternoon in a fast car on a motorway to London.

Setting is an essential element in all stories. As a starting point, the reader needs to have a clear impression of the time and place of the events of a story to fully understanding the significance of characters' actions.

An author will use descriptive passages to establish a setting and capture the atmosphere of the time and place in which the action takes place.

In a novel an author has space to create a detailed setting or a variety of settings. Short stories, however, usually unfold against the backdrop of a single setting. The short story writer will aim to sketch only the important details of the setting, leaving it to the imagination of the reader to fill in other details.

Most writers prefer to base the settings of their stories in a world familiar to them – their own neighbourhood, town, school etc. Only very experienced authors are successful at creating a setting of which they have not had first hand experience. This is usually achieved, as in the case of good historical novels, by a good deal of careful research.

Questions & Assignments

1. What luxury features could be found in the narrator's car?
2. Why did the author use the phrase *'whispering along at seventy miles an hour'*?
3. Why did the narrator always stop for hitch-hikers?
4. In what ways did the hitch-hiker remind the narrator of a rat?
5. What puzzled you about the hitch-hiker as you read the story for the first time?
6. What was the hitch-hiker's view on betting on horses?
7. What made the hitch-hiker decide that the narrator was a successful writer?
8. *'The big car leaped forward as though she'd been stung.'* What point is being made in this sentence?
9. Would you agree that the policeman spoke sarcastically to the narrator? Explain.
10. What details are given about the policeman which are likely to make the readers dislike him?
11. Describe clearly what the policeman did with his book of tickets.
12. The hitch-hiker claimed that he was a hod-carrier. Did you believe him? Explain why.
13. (a) Why did the author describe the way in which the hitch-hiker rolled and lit his cigarette as a *'remarkable performance'*?
    (b) Did you suspect anything when you read this description for the first time? Explain.
14. At what point in the story do we learn exactly how the hitch-hiker made his living?
15. Describe how you felt about the way the story ended.
16. Imagine that you are a judge in a short story competition. Mark the story out of ten and explain briefly why you marked it as you did.

THE SCREAM

The playground at the end of the park is the usual sort of thing. A couple of swings, a slide, a ramp for roller skating, and an old climbing-frame with metal bars and tubes, quite good, actually, if you're young enough for it.

I hadn't been down there for ages, and it was only by chance that I went past it that day. I was on the way back from my friend's house, and I'd decided to do a detour round by the High Street and take a look at the new video releases.

It was a dull, cold day, and no one much was around. The playground was empty except for a bunch of kids, standing in a group in the far corner, away from the swings and slides, almost out of sight behind a tree.

I nearly walked right past them. It wasn't what they were saying that stopped me in my tracks. It was the way they sounded. Their voices were tense with excitement. Filled with violence.

Four boys, about nine or ten years old, were standing round a little kid, smaller than most of them, taunting him and jeering at him.

'Little scruff, aren't you, Paul?'

'Yeah, didn't you know, his mum gets all his clothes at the Oxfam shop.'

'No, she doesn't. She gets the stuff Oxfam won't take.'

The kid called Paul didn't look like much. His face was grey and strained. His eyes were darting about, looking for a way out of the tight ring that swayed round him. He must have thought a gap was opening up, because he made a jump towards it, but too slowly and hesitantly, as if he knew they'd stop him.

They did. One of them lunged forward and caught hold of his collar, pulling it away from the kid's scrawny little neck with one finger and thumb, and pretending to inspect it.

'Wah, look at this. Disgusting! He stinks! His mum never does any washing!'

'Nah, didn't you know, his mum likes him dirty. She's dirty herself. She washes his head down the toilet.'

'You ever been to his house?'

'Who, me? Course not. Might catch something.'

'They got things crawling out of their fridge.'

'They got green stuff growing on their walls.'

The kid's face was puckering up.

Don't cry! I thought. Whatever you do, don't cry! Laugh. Say something cool. Walk away.

But he didn't. I never had.

'Get off me!' he wailed. 'It's not true! My house is much cleaner than yours. My clothes all come from Marks and Spencers. Look at the label if you don't believe me!' He was choking on his tears.

They moved in closer.

'Marks and Spencers! Yeah, sure.'

'It's true! Get off me! Leave me *alone*!'

They were pretending to stand loose and casual, but they were really as taut as guitar strings. They'd smelled blood.

124

'Leave you alone? We haven't touched you!'

'You starting something?'

'You want a fight, or what?'

None of them had seen me. I stood there helplessly, willing my thoughts across the tarmac, trying to get them into the kid's terrified brain.

Don't look so scared! I was silently shouting at him. Put your hands in your pockets. Shrug your shoulders. Smile. For heaven's sake, *smile*!

One of them flicked at the kid's shoulder as if he was brushing something off it, but the flick was as hard as a punch. The kid staggered backwards, and trod on the foot of a tall boy in a green jacket, who had been closing in behind him. The tall boy began to hop about, faking agony, clutching at his foot.

'He stamped on my foot! Go on, Des, get him!'

My own heart was pounding now. My hands were clammy. I knew what was going to happen next.

I could go over and stop them, I told myself. They're only small. I could take them on easily. They had the smell of violence on them. I knew it. I feared and hated it. I didn't want to walk on, but my feet carried me away of their own accord.

The kid must have made some kind of desperate move, trying to pull away, or push through the circle or something, because I heard one of them shout, 'That's *it*, he pushed me! I'll *do* you for that!' and the others cheered him on.

'Yeah, go on, Des. Kill him!'

'Kick his head in!'

I was shaking.

He's got to learn, I remember thinking to myself. He's got to stand on his own two feet. But I knew the real reason that stopped me going in. I was scared of being marked out by them, scared of their dads and their big brothers, scared of them.

I tried not to hear the scuffling, scrabbling sound of their feet on the concrete, but I couldn't help hearing the kid scream. It wasn't the kind of scream that kids do deliberately, to attract attention and get an adult to rush on to the scene. It was a scream of pure loneliness and terror. It was the scream I'd felt time and again, deep inside, the kind of scream that only dares to come out when all hope has gone.

I was already round the corner by the time I heard it, out on the main road. I stood still for a moment, not knowing what to do, feeling miserable, rotten and guilty.

The pavement was crowded. Women pushed past me, bumping their shopping bags into me.

People were picking over the racks outside the shoe shop, and gawping through the windows of the TV shop at twenty identical football games.

It's too late, anyway, I told myself. They'll have finished with him by now.

A bus pulled up at the stop just beside me. I don't know why I glanced along the upstairs windows. Habit, I suppose. I always used to have to check out the number 93 before I dared get on, in case Steve was on it. And it just so happened that he was. I stood, rooted to the pavement, and watched him.

When I was seeing him every day, before he was expelled from school, he'd always had at least one hanger-on with him, some little crawler who'd do whatever Steve said, and laugh whenever Steve tried to be funny, but he was on his own for once.

Perhaps I'd grown, or perhaps I'd always thought he was bigger than he really was. Anyway, he looked smaller now. He didn't see me at once. He was sitting hunched up, his face white and pinched.

I'd never noticed before that he was really quite thin. His shoulders were narrow and his arms looked puny. I flexed mine. I'd been working out a lot recently, and swimming twice a week. I felt good and strong.

Then he turned his head and looked right

down at me. For a split second he actually looked pleased, as if he'd been lonely or something and was quite glad to see a face he knew. He almost smiled. At least, I think he did. I'd never seen him smile before, so I wasn't sure what it would look like.

He snapped out of it almost at once. He lunged his bullet head towards the window, baring his teeth and staring hard at me through narrowed eyes, his fingers jabbing the air obscenely. He looked like one of those vicious dogs that bark hysterically and strain to get at you when you walk past the place they think they're guarding.

Before, whenever I'd seen Steve, I'd pretended not to notice him. I'd always crossed the road, or turned to look in at a shop window, avoiding him as much as possible, getting out of his way as fast as I could. But quite suddenly, for the first time in my life, I wasn't afraid of him any more.

You're pathetic, I thought. Stupid. Alone. Out of the action. Out of my nightmares. No more screams for me.

I waved at him. His daft face dropped, and he gaped at me. Then, before he had time to get hold of himself, I turned round and began to dart back, down the side street, away from the main road, towards the playground.

I was strong. I was ready.

It seemed as if I'd been gone for hours, but actually it can't have been more than a minute or two.

They'd got the kid down on the ground, and he was feebly lashing out at them with his feet. He had his arms over his head and was trying to protect himself from the stabbing kicks of the smallest boy, whose body was so taut with anger I could almost feel it crackle, like electricity, from the other side of the playground.

'Beat him up, Des!' the other boys were shouting.

'Kick him hard!'

It was Des I would have to deal with.

They didn't hear me coming. I sprinted across the playground, grabbed Des by one shoulder and spun him round.

'Stop that. Stop it, you little . . .'

The other boys, concentrating on the kid on the ground, looked up, startled. One of them had been spitting on Paul's head. He wiped a slick of spittle off his chin. They began to back away, trying to resume their usual casual, swaggering posture. I only saw them out of the corner of my eye. I was watching Des.

He was sizing me up, turning an insolent shoulder towards me, balling his fists.

'Get off! Leave me alone! What's it got to do with you?'

The others saw him squaring up to me, took courage and came in nearer again. If Des went for me, they all would. If Des backed off, they'd all be too scared to touch me. It was only mental force that would drive them off, not violence. They wanted violence. They were good at it.

I looked Des up and down, pretending to recognise him.

'I know you. You beat up small kids all the time.'

He moved back a step.

'Nah. You don't know me. Never seen me.'

'Paul pushed him,' said one of the others.

'He stamped on my foot,' said the boy in the green jacket. 'Asking for it.'

'Oh yeah?' I looked down at Paul. He wasn't even trying to get up off the ground. He'd covered his head with his jacket and his whole body was shaking with sobs. A cut on his hand was bleeding. 'Him? Asking for it? All of you against him?'

Two of them dropped their eyes and started kicking the toes of their trainers into the tarmac.

'Four against one? Think you're hard?'

'What's it to you? Who are you, anyway? What have I done?'

A whining note had crept into Des's voice. I didn't relax, but I felt more confident.

'I've been watching you,' I said, and I

found myself using Steve's old trick, staring close down into Des's eyes, moving my head gradually closer to his and forcing him to step back.

'My brother's going to get you,' he said, trying to bring the snarl back into his voice. 'He'll knife you.'

'Nobody's going to knife me.' I found to my surprise that I was enjoying myself. I bent down, pulled the jacket off Paul's head and dragged him to his feet. 'You're going to leave this kid alone, see? I'm going to make sure of that. You're going to be watched. You beat up anyone else and you'll be in trouble. Real trouble. Not just from me. You haven't seen my mates when they get angry. It's not a very nice thing to see.'

They were moving away step by step, cursing and threatening, their voices getting bolder and louder as the distance between us grew.

'I know you, Des,' I called after them. 'I know all of you. I've had a good look at you. Me and my friends'll be watching you.'

They didn't like that. They didn't like hearing me say Des's name. They speeded up. I heard their swearing get fainter as they went round the corner, and fade altogether into the roar of traffic on the High Street.

I turned back to Paul. He'd stopped crying. He was rubbing at his smeary nose with his sleeve.

'They done you before?'

He shook his head, not wanting to speak to me. I remembered exactly how he was feeling.

Humiliation. Hatred. Shame.

'They're nothing,' I said, trying to make him look up. 'They're pathetic. You're worth more than they are. You mustn't show them you're scared.'

'Leave me alone.' He was threatening to cry again. 'You don't know what it's like. You don't understand.'

I went over to one of the swings and sat down on it, letting it move me gently backwards and forwards.

'I do, as a matter of fact. It used to happen to me. Even in this playground once. A boy called Steve. Not any more, though. Never again.'

The clouds were beginning to lift. A group of mums and toddlers were coming into the playground. Paul turned away to hide his red eyes. The mums looked disapprovingly at me.

'It gets better,' I said, pushing the swing higher. 'Much better. You see through them in the end, see how stupid they are. You'll find that out one day. Anyway, they've done you over now, and they won't do it again. They'll leave you alone. If they don't they'll have me to . . .'

'Oi! Get down off that swing!'

I looked round. I'd been talking to myself. Paul had gone, and in his place was the park-keeper, red-faced. I braked with my feet.

'Can't you read? No kids over fourteen allowed in this playground.'

'Where? I didn't see a notice.'

'Over there! By the gate!'

He was used to dealing with thugs like Steve and Des. He was working himself up, expecting trouble. I'd had enough for one day. I wasn't about to take him on.

I jumped off the swing and put my hands up.

'OK, OK!' I said. 'Don't shoot! I surrender!'

I walked past him, smiling at the row of frowning mums.

'And don't let me catch you in here again,' he shouted after me.

I went out of the playground and the gate swung shut behind me with a satisfying click. I felt extremely happy.

'Don't worry,' I said. 'I won't come back. Ever.'

– Elizabeth Laird

Spectrum 1

WORD POWER

Find words in the story which have similar meanings to each of the words and phrases below. The number in brackets after each one indicates the number of letters in the answer. The words appear in the story in the same order as the meanings given below.

CLUES

1. longer route (6)
2. moved forward suddenly (6)
3. thin; skinny (7)
4. wrinkling (9)
5. cried; moaned (6)
6. stretched tightly (4)
7. walked unsteadily (9)
8. pretending (6)
9. holding tightly (9)
10. beating loudly (8)
11. reckless; despairing (9)
12. on purpose (12)
13. similar in every way (9)
14. a person who stays near another to gain some advantage (6-2)
15. looking cold, pale and thin (7)
16. small and weak (4)
17. poking; stabbing (7)
18. disgustingly (9)
19. spiteful; fierce (7)
20. useless; inadequate (8)
21. silly (4)
22. weakly (6)
23. ran at top speed (8)
24. surprised, alarmed (8)
25. position; pose (7)
26. rude; insulting (8)
27. very young children (8)
28. give in (9)

Questions & Assignments

1. What four details does the author give to help the readers visualise the playground?
2. What conclusions would you draw about the narrator from the second paragraph?
3. What two verbs does the author use to describe the way the victim was being addressed by the bullies? How do they differ in meaning from each other?
4. How does the author convey the terror felt by the victim?
5. *'They were pretending to stand loose and casual but they were really as taut as guitar strings. They'd smelt blood.'* State in your own words the idea that the author is attempting to communicate here.
6. What difficult decision is the narrator faced with in this story? How does the author convey that this was a particularly difficult decision?
7. Eventually he comes to a decision, only to reverse it a short time later. Explain clearly how he comes to the original decision and why he reverses it?
8. At what stage in the story do we get the first clue that the narrator was also a victim of bullying?
9. What characteristics of Steve emerge from the story?
10. *'It was Des I would have to deal with.'* Explain why the narrator came to this conclusion.
11. As he confronts Des the narrator confesses that he was enjoying himself. Suggest why this was so.

12 *'Humiliation. Hatred. Shame.'* Why do you think that the narrator chooses these words to describe how the victim felt after the gang had gone. In your answer refer to each word.
13 What feelings do you think that Des and his friends experienced as they left the scene?
14 There are a number of references to the weather in the story. Suggest how these references reflect the theme in some way.
15 Do you think that this story provides a good insight into how bullies operate? Give reasons for your answer by referring to the story as a whole.

A Rat and Some Renovations

Almost everyone in Ireland must have experienced American visitors or, as we called them, 'The Yanks'. Just before we were visited for the first time, my mother decided to have the working kitchen modernised. We lived in a terrace of dilapidated Victorian houses whose front gardens measured two feet by the breadth of the house. The scullery, separated from the kitchen by a wall, was the same size as the garden, and just as arable. When we pulled out the vegetable cupboard we found three or four potatoes which had fallen down behind and taken root. Ma said, 'God, if the Yanks had seen that.'

She engaged the workmen early so the job would be finished and the newness worn off by the time the Yanks arrived. She said she wouldn't like them to think that she got it done up just for them.

The first day the workmen arrived they demolished the wall, ripped up the floor and left the cold water tap hanging four feet above a bucket. We didn't see them again for three weeks. Grandma kept trying to make excuses for them, saying that it was very strenuous work. My mother however managed to get them back and they worked for three days, erecting a sink unit and leaving a hole for the outlet pipe. It must have been through this hole that the rat got in.

The first signs were discovered by Ma in the drawer of the new unit. She called me and said, 'What's those?' I looked and saw six hard brown ovals trundling about the drawer.

'Rat droppings,' I said. Ma backed disbelievingly away, her hands over her mouth, repeating, 'It's mouse, it's mouse, it must be mouse.'

The man from next door, a Mr Frank Twoomey, who had lived most of his life in the country, was called – he said from the size of them, it could well be a horse. At this my mother took her nightdress and toothbrush and moved in with an aunt across the street, leaving the brother and myself with the problem. Armed with a hatchet and shovel we banged and rattled the cupboards, then when we felt sure it was gone we blocked the hole with hardboard and sent word to Ma to return, that all was well.

It was after two days safety that she discovered the small brown bombs again. I met her with her nightdress under her arm, in the path. She just said, 'I found more,' and headed for her sister's.

That evening it was Grandma's suggestion that we should borrow the Grimleys' cat. The brother was sent and had to pull it from beneath the side-board because it was very shy of strangers. He carried it across the road and the rat-killer was so terrified of the traffic

A Rat and Some Renovations

and Peter squeezing it that it peed all down his front. By this time Ma's curiosity had got the better of her and she ventured from her sister's to stand pale and nervous in our path. The brother set the cat down and turned to look for a cloth to wipe himself. The cat shot past him down the hall, past Ma who screamed, 'Jesus, the rat', and leapt into the hedge. The cat ran until a bus stopped it with a thud. The Grimleys haven't spoken to us since.

Ma had begun to despair. 'What age do rats live to?' she asked. 'And what'll we do if it's still here when the Yanks come?' Peter said that they loved pigs in the kitchen.

The next day we bought stuff, pungent like phosphorus and spread it on cubes of bread. The idea of this stuff was to roast the rat inside when he ate it so that he would drink himself to death.

'Just like Uncle Matt,' said Peter. He tactlessly read out the instructions to Grandma who then came out in sympathy with the rat. Ma thought it may have gone outside, so to make sure, we littered the yard with pieces of bread as well. In case it didn't work Ma decided to do a novena of masses so she got up the next morning and on the driveway to the chapel which runs along the back of our house she noticed six birds with their feet in the air, stone dead.

Later that day the rat was found in the same condition on the kitchen floor. It was quickly buried in the dust-bin using the shovel as a hearse. The next day the workmen came, finished the job, and the Yanks arrived just as the paint was drying.

They looked strangely out of place with their brown, leathery faces, rimless glasses and hat brims flamboyantly large, as we met them at the boat . . . Too summery by half, against the dripping eaves of the sheds at the dock-yard. At home by a roaring fire on a July day, after having laughed a little at the quaintness of the taxi, they exchanged greetings, talked about family likenesses, jobs, and then dried up. For the next half hour the conversation had to be manufactured, except for a comparison of education systems which was confusing and therefore lasted longer. Then everything stopped.

The brother said, 'I wouldn't call this an embarrassing silence.'

They all laughed, nervously dispelling the silence but not the embarrassment.

Ma tried to cover up. 'Would yous like another cup of cawfee?' Already she had begun to pick up the accent. They agreed and the oldish one with the blue hair followed her out to the kitchen.

'Gee, isn't this modern,' she said.

Ma, untacking her hand from the paint on the drawer, said, 'Yeah, we done it up last year.'

– Bernard MacLaverty

WORD POWER

Find words in the story which have similar meanings to each of the words and phrases below. The number in brackets after each one indicates the number of letters in the answer. The words appear in the story in the same order as the meanings given below.

CLUES

1 shabby; in bad repair (11)
2 tiring and difficult (9)
3 putting together, building up (8)
4 found (10)
5 rolling (9)
6 an idea put forward (10)
7 timid in the presence of others (3)
8 very frightened (9)
9 went with caution (8)
10 strong-smelling (7)
11 very noticeably; colourfully (12)
12 chat; talk (12)
13 getting rid of (10)
14 way of talking (6)

Spectrum 1

Points to Note

A person who writes a story is called an **author**. An author can make up a story entirely from his or her imagination or can base a story on things which actually happened without having to stick to the facts.

The author of the story you have just read, *A Rat and Some Renovations*, is Bernard MacLaverty. However the events in the story may or may not have happened to him when he was a boy. He may have used his imagination to make up the whole story or it may have happened to his family. It is also possible that something similar might have happened to somebody he knew, and he then invented a few more details to make it more enjoyable.

The author chose to let a character – the son of the household – tell the story. This character is called the **narrator**. The author could have chosen the mother to tell the story instead. If he had done so we would probably have a slightly different version of the story.

Questions & Assignments

1. Why did the narrator's mother decide to have the kitchen renovated?
2. What is your opinion of:
   (i) the workmen
   (ii) Frank Twoomey?
3. Describe the episode with the cat.
4. What signs were there that the rat poison worked?
5. (i) Describe the 'Yanks" visit in your own words.
   (ii) Do you think it was worth doing up the kitchen for the 'Yanks'? Give reasons for your answer.
6. Give your impression of the character of:
   (i) the narrator
   (ii) his mother.
7. What parts of the story did you find particularly funny?
8. Write about an event which caused panic in your home.
9. Imagine that you are a judge in a short story competition. Mark the story out of ten and explain briefly why you marked it as you did.

THE MONKEY'S PAW

Without, the night was cold and wet, but in the small parlour of Lakesman Villa the blinds were drawn and the fire burned brightly. Father and son were at chess, watched by the white-haired old lady knitting placidly by the fire.

"Listen to the wind," said Mr. White, who, having seen a fatal mistake after it was too late, wanted to distract his son and prevent him from seeing it.

"I'm listening," said the latter, grimly surveying the board as he stretched out his hand. "Check."

"I should hardly think that he'd come tonight," said his father, with his hands poised over the board.

"Mate," replied the son.

"That's the worst of living so far out," bawled Mr. White, with sudden and unlooked-for violence; "of all the beastly, slushy, out-of-the-way places to live in, this is the worst. Pathway's a bog, and the road's a torrent. I don't know what people are thinking about. I suppose because only two houses on the road are left, they think it doesn't matter."

"Never mind, dear," said his wife soothingly; "perhaps you'll win the next one."

Mr. White looked up sharply, just in time to intercept a knowing glance between mother and son. The words died away on his lips, and he hid a guilty grin in his thin grey beard.

"There he is," said Herbert White, as the gate banged loudly and heavy footsteps came towards the door.

The old man rose with hospitable haste, opened the door and welcomed the new arrival, a tall burly man with beady eyes and a ruddy face.

"Sergeant-Major Morris," he said, introducing him.

The sergeant-major shook hands, and, taking the proffered seat by the fire, watched contentedly while his host got out whiskey and tumblers and stood a small copper kettle on the fire.

At the third glass his eyes got brighter, and he began to talk, the little family circle regarding with eager interest this visitor from distant parts, as he squared his broad shoulders in the chair and spoke of strange scenes and dangerous deeds, of wars and plagues and strange peoples.

"Twenty-one years of it," said Mr. White, nodding at his wife and son. "When he went away he was a slip of a youth in the warehouse. Now look at him."

"He don't look to have taken much harm," said Mrs. White politely.

"I'd like to go to India myself," said the old man, "just to look round a bit, you know."

"Better where you are," said the sergeant-major, shaking his head. He put down the empty glass and, sighing softly, shook it again.

"I should like to see those old temples and fakirs and jugglers," said the old man. "What was that you started telling me the other day about a monkey's paw or something, Morris?"

"Nothing," said the soldier hastily. "Leastways, nothing worth hearing."

"Monkey's paw?" said Mrs. White curiously.

"Well, it's just a bit of what you might call magic, perhaps," said the sergeant-major offhandedly.

His three listeners leaned forward eagerly. The visitor absentmindedly put his empty glass to his lips and then set it down again. His host filled it for him.

"To look at," said the sergeant-major, fumbling in his pocket, "it's just an ordinary little paw, dried to a mummy."

He took something out of his pocket and proffered it. Mrs. White drew back with a grimace, but her son, taking it, examined it curiously.

"And what is there special about it?" inquired Mr. White, as he took it from his son and, having examined it, placed it upon the table.

"It had a spell put on it by an old fakir," said the sergeant-major, "a very holy man. He wanted to show that fate ruled people's lives, and that those who interfered with it did so to their sorrow. He put a spell on it so that three separate men could each have three wishes from it."

His manner was so impressive that his hearers were conscious that their light laughter jarred somewhat.

"Well, why don't you have three, sir?" said Herbert White cleverly.

The old soldier looked at him for a few moments before he spoke. "I have," he said quietly, and his blotchy face whitened.

"And did you really have the three wishes granted?" asked Mrs. White.

"I did," said the sergeant-major, and his glass tapped against his strong teeth.

"And has anybody else wished?" inquired the old lady.

"The first man had his three wishes, yes," was the reply. "I don't know what the first two were, but the third was for death. That's how I got the paw.

His tones were so grave that a hush fell upon the group.

"If you've had your three wishes, it's no good to you now, then, Morris," said the old man at last. "What do you keep it for?"

The soldier shook his head. "Fancy, I suppose," he said slowly. "I did have some idea of selling it, but I don't think I will. It has caused enough mischief already. Besides, people won't buy. They think it's a fairy tale, some of them, and those who do think anything of it want to try it first and pay me afterward."

"If you could have another three wishes," said the old man, eyeing him keenly, "would you have them?"

Morris took the paw, and dangling it between his front finger and thumb, suddenly threw it upon the fire. White, with a slight cry, stooped down and snatched it off.

"Better let it burn," said the soldier solemnly.

"If you don't want it, Morris," said the old man, "give it to me."

"I won't," said his friend doggedly. "I threw it on the fire. If you keep it, don't blame me for what happens. Pitch it on the fire again, like a sensible man."

The other shook his head and examined his new possession closely. "How do you do it?" he inquired.

"Hold it up in your right hand and wish aloud," said the sergeant-major, "but I warn you of the consequences."

"Sounds like the Arabian Nights," said Mrs. White, as she rose and began to set the supper. "Don't you think you might wish for four pairs of hands for me?"

Her husband drew the talisman from his pocket and then all three burst into laughter as the sergeant-major, with a look of alarm on his face, caught him by the arm.

"If you must wish," he said gruffly, "wish for something sensible."

Mr. White dropped it back into his pocket, and placing chairs, motioned his friend to the table. In the business of supper the talisman was partly forgotten, and afterward the three sat listening in an enthralled fashion to a second instalment of the soldier's adventures in India.

"If the tale about the monkey's paw is not

more truthful than those he has been telling us," said Herbert, as the door closed behind their guest, just in time for him to catch the last train, "we shan't make much out of it."

"Did you give him anything for it, Father?" inquired Mrs. White, regarding her husband closely.

"A trifle," said he, colouring slightly. "He didn't want it, but I made him take it. And he pressed me again to throw it away."

"Likely," said Herbert, with pretended horror. "Why, we're going to be rich, and famous, and happy."

Mr. White took the paw from his pocket and eyed it dubiously. "I don't know what to wish for, and that's a fact," he said slowly. "It seems to me I've got all I want."

"If you only cleared the house, you'd be quite happy, wouldn't you?" said Herbert, with his hand on his shoulder. "Well, wish for two hundred pounds, then, that'll just do it."

His father, smiling shamefacedly at his own credulity, held up the talisman, as his son, with a solemn face somewhat marred by a wink at his mother, sat down at the piano and struck a few impressive chords.

"I wish for two hundred pounds," said the old man distinctly.

A fine crash from the piano greeted the words, interrupted by a shuddering cry from the old man. His wife and son ran toward him.

"It moved," he cried, with a glance of disgust at the object as it lay on the floor. "As I wished it twisted in my hands like a snake."

"Well, I don't see the money," said his son, as he picked it up and placed it on the table, "and I bet I never shall."

"It must have been your fancy, Father," said his wife, regarding him anxiously.

He shook his head. "Never mind though, there's no harm done, but it gave me a shock all the same."

They sat down by the fire again while the two men finished their pipes. Outside, the wind was higher than ever, and the old man started nervously at the sound of a door banging upstairs. A silence unusual and depressing settled upon all three, which lasted until the old couple rose to retire for the night.

"I expect you'll find the cash tied up in a big bag in the middle of your bed," said Herbert, as he bade them good night, "and something horrible squatting up on the top of the wardrobe watching you as you pocket your ill-gotten gains."

In the brightness of the wintry sun next morning as it streamed over the breakfast table, Herbert laughed at his fears. There was an air of wholesomeness about the room which it had lacked on the previous night, and the dirty, shrivelled little paw was pitched on the sideboard with a carelessness which betokened no great belief in its virtues.

"I suppose all old soldiers are the same," said Mrs. White. "The idea of our listening to such nonsense! How could wishes be granted in these days? And if they could, how could two hundred pounds hurt you, Father?"

"Might drop on his head from the sky," said the frivolous Herbert.

"Morris said the things happened so naturally," said his father, "that you might, if you so wished, attribute it to coincidence."

"Well, don't break into the money before I come back," said Herbert, as he rose from the table. "I'm afraid it'll turn you into a mean, avaricious man, and we shall have to disown you."

His mother laughed, and following him to the door, watched him down the road and returning to the breakfast table, was very happy at the expense of her husband's credulity. All of which did not prevent her from scurrying to the door at the postman's knock.

"Herbert will have some more of his funny remarks, I expect, when he comes home," she said as they sat at dinner.

"I dare say," said Mr. White, pouring himself out some beer; "but for all that, the thing moved in my hand; that I'll swear to."

"You thought it did," said the old lady soothingly.

"I say it did," replied the other. "There was no thought about it; I had just – what's the matter?"

His wife made no reply. She was watching the mysterious movements of a man outside, who, peering in an undecided fashion at the house, appeared to be trying to make up his mind to enter. In mental connection with the two hundred pounds, she noticed that the stranger was well dressed and wore a silk hat of glossy newness. Three times he paused at the gate and then walked on again. The fourth time he stood with his hand upon it, and then with sudden resolution flung it open and walked up the path. Mrs. White at the same moment placed her hands behind her and hurriedly unfastening the strings of her apron put that useful article of apparel beneath the cushion of her chair.

She brought the stranger, who seemed ill at ease, into the room. He gazed furtively at Mrs. White, and listened in a preoccupied fashion as the old lady apologised for the appearance of the room, and her husband's coat, a garment which he usually reserved for the garden. She then waited patiently for him to broach his business, but he was at first strangely silent. "I – was asked to call," he said at last, and stooped and picked a piece of cotton from his trousers. "I come from Maw and Meggins."

The old lady started. "Is anything the matter?" she asked breathlessly. "Has anything happened to Herbert? What is it? What is it?"

Her husband interposed. "There, there, Mother," he said hastily. "Sit down, and don't jump to conclusions. You've not brought bad news, I'm sure, sir," and he eyed the other wistfully.

"I'm sorry –" began the visitor.

"Is he hurt?" demanded the mother.

The visitor nodded.

"Badly hurt," he said quietly, "but he is not in any pain."

"Oh, thank God!" said the old woman clasping her hands. "Thank God for that. Thank –"

She broke off suddenly as the sinister meaning of his words dawned upon her and she saw the awful confirmation of her fears in the other's averted face. She caught her breath, and turning to her slower-witted husband, laid her trembling old hand upon his. There was a long silence.

"He was caught in the machinery," said the visitor at length, in a low voice.

"Caught in the machinery," repeated Mr. White, in a dazed fashion, "yes."

He sat staring blankly out of the window, and taking his wife's hand between his own, pressed it as he had been wont to do in their old courting days nearly forty years before.

"He was the only one left to us," he said, turning gently to the visitor. "It is hard."

The other coughed, and rising, walked slowly to the window. "The firm wished me to convey their sincere sympathy with you in your great loss," he said, without looking round. "I beg that you will understand I am only their servant and merely obeying orders."

There was no reply; the old woman's face was white, her eyes staring, and her breath inaudible; on the husband's face was a look such as his friend the sergeant might have carried into his first action.

"I was to say that Maw and Meggins disclaim all responsibility," continued the other. "They admit no liability at all, but in consideration of your son's services they wish to present you with a certain sum as compensation."

Mr. White dropped his wife's hand, and rising to his feet, gazed with a look of horror at his visitor. His dry lips shaped the words, "How much?"

"Two hundred pounds," was the answer.

Unconscious of his wife's shriek, the old man smiled faintly, put out his hands like a sightless man, and dropped, a senseless heap, to the floor.

In the huge new cemetery, some two miles distant, the old people buried their dead, and came back to a house steeped in shadow and silence. It was all over so quickly that at first they could hardly realise it and remained in a state of expectation as though of something else to happen – something else which was to lighten this load, too heavy for old hearts to bear. But the days passed, and expectation gave place to resignation – the hopeless resignation of the old, sometimes miscalled apathy. Sometimes they hardly exchanged a word, for now they had nothing to talk about, and their days were long to weariness.

It was about a week after that that the old man, waking suddenly in the night stretched out his hand and found himself alone. The room was in darkness, and the sound of subdued weeping came from the window. He raised himself in bed and listened.

"Come back," he said tenderly. "You will be cold."

"It is colder for my son," said the old woman and wept afresh.

The sound of her sobs died away on his ears. The bed was warm, and his eyes heavy with sleep. He dozed fitfully, and then slept until a sudden wild cry from his wife awoke him with a start.

"The monkey's paw!" she cried wildly. "The monkey's paw!"

He started up in alarm. "Where? Where is it? What's the matter?"

She cried and laughed together, and bending over, kissed his cheek.

"I only just thought of it," she said hysterically. "Why didn't I think of it before? Why didn't you think of it?"

"Think of what?" he questioned.

"The other two wishes," she replied rapidly. "We've only had one."

"Was not that enough?" he demanded fiercely.

"No," she cried triumphantly; "we'll have one more. Go down and get it quickly, and wish our boy alive again."

The man sat up in bed and flung the bedclothes from his quaking limbs. "Good God, you are mad!" he cried, aghast.

"Get it," she panted; "get it quickly, and wish - Oh, my boy; my boy!"

Her husband struck a match and lit the candle. "Get back to bed," he said unsteadily. "You don't know what you are saying."

"We had the first wish granted," said the old woman feverishly; "why not the second?"

"A coincidence," stammered the old man.

"Go and get it and wish," cried the old woman, and dragged him toward the door.

He went down in the darkness, and felt his way to the parlour, and then to the mantelpiece. The talisman was in its place, and a horrible fear that the unspoken wish might bring his mutilated son before him ere he could escape from the room seized upon him, and he caught his breath as he found that he had lost the direction of the door. His brow cold with sweat, he felt his way round the table, and groped along the wall until he found himself in the small passage with the unwholesome thing in his hand.

Even his wife's face seemed changed as he entered the room. It was white and expectant, and to his fears seemed to have an unnatural look upon it. He was afraid of her.

"Wish!" she cried, in a strong voice.

"It is foolish and wicked," he faltered.

"Wish!" repeated his wife.

He raised his hand, "I wish my son alive again."

The talisman fell to the floor, and he regarded it shudderingly. Then he sank trembling into a chair as the old woman, with burning eyes, walked to the window and raised the blind.

He sat until he was chilled with the cold, glancing occasionally at the figure of the old woman peering through the window. The candle end, which had burnt below the rim of the china candlestick, was throwing pulsating shadows on the ceiling and walls, until, with a flicker larger than the rest, it expired. The old man, with an unspeakable sense of relief at the failure of the talisman, crept back to his bed, and a minute or two afterward the old woman came silently and pathetically beside him.

Neither spoke, but both lay silently listening to the ticking of the clock. A stair creaked, and a squeaky mouse scurried noisily through the wall. The darkness was oppressive, and after lying for some time screwing up his courage, the husband took the box of matches and striking one went downstairs for a candle.

At the foot of the stairs the match went out, and he paused to strike another, and at the same moment a knock, so quiet and stealthy as to be scarcely audible sounded on the front door.

The matches fell from his hand. He stood motionless, his breath suspended until the knock was repeated. Then he turned and fled swiftly back to his room and closed the door behind him. A third knock sounded through the house.

"What's that?" cried the old woman, starting up.

"A rat," said the old man, in shaking tones – "a rat. It passed me on the stairs."

His wife sat up in bed listening. A loud knock resounded through the house. "It's Herbert!" she screamed. "It's Herbert!"

She ran to the door, but her husband was before her, and catching her by the arm held her tightly.

"What are you going to do?" he whispered hoarsely.

"It's my boy; it's Herbert!" she cried, struggling mechanically. "I forgot it was two miles away. What are you holding me for? Let go. I must open the door."

"For God's sake don't let it in," cried the old man, trembling.

"You're afraid of your own son," she cried, struggling. "Let me go. I'm coming, Herbert, I'm coming."

There was another knock, and another. The old woman with a sudden wrench broke free and ran from the room. Her husband followed to the landing, and called after her appealingly as she hurried downstairs. He heard the chain rattle back and the bottom bolt drawn slowly and stiffly from the socket. Then the old woman's voice, strained and panting.

"The bolt," she cried loudly. "Come down. I can't reach it."

But her husband was on his hands and knees groping wildly on the floor in search of the paw. If he could only find it before the thing outside got in. A perfect fusillade of knocks reverberated through the house, and he heard the scraping of a chair as his wife put it down in the passage against the door. He heard the creaking of the bolt as it came slowly back, and at the same moment he found the monkey's paw and frantically breathed his third and last wish.

The knocking ceased suddenly, although the echoes of it were still in the house. He heard the chair drawn back and the door opened. A cold wind rushed up the staircase, and a long, loud wail of disappointment and misery from his wife gave him courage to run to her side, and then to the gate beyond. The street lamp flickering opposite shone on a quiet and deserted road.

– *W. W. Jacobs*

morning I was off to Chicago. It seemed a more exciting town than New York, a town where a poor boy like me could make his fortune quickly. Jimmy was happy to stay in New York. It was his hometown and he never wanted to travel to get rich. Well, we agreed that night that we would meet again here in exactly twenty years. We made a solemn promise that no matter how we made out or where we lived, we would meet here."

"Interesting," remarked the policeman, "but twenty years is a long time between meetings though, it seems to me. Have you heard from your friend since that night twenty years ago?"

"For a year or two after, we wrote a few letters to each other. Then we lost track of each other. Chicago is a lively spot and I was busy trying to make it big. Didn't seem to have the time to go answering Jimmy's letters."

"You did well for yourself in Chicago then?" asked the policeman.

"You bet I did! I hope Jimmy did half as well. He was a bit of a plodder though a good fellow. Whatever he did I bet he did it well. I had to be ruthless to make my fortune. In Chicago you've got to be tough to make it."

The policeman took a step or two.

"I'll be on my way now. Hope your friend turns up. Are you going to call time on him sharp?"

"No, of course not," said the man in the doorway, "I'll give him a half an hour at least! If Jimmy is alive he'll be definitely here by then."

"Goodnight, sir," said the policeman moving on along his beat and shining his torch into doorways as he went. There was now a fine cold drizzle falling and the wind had risen. One or two people hurried by with coat collars turned high and hands in their pockets. And in the doorway, smoking his cigar and waiting, stood the man who had come a thousand miles to meet a friend of his youth. Gradually, he began to grow a little uncertain and to feel a little foolish for believing his friend would remember the meeting.

About twenty minutes he had waited when a tall man in a long overcoat with the collar turned up to his ears hurried across from the opposite side of the street. He went directly to the waiting man.

"Is that you, Bob?" he said.

"Is that you Jimmy Wells?" replied the man in the door.

The men shook hands warmly.

"It's Bob for sure!" said the newcomer. "I was wondering would you come. Well, well, well! Twenty years to the night! A long time! The old restaurant is gone. A pity! We could have had another meal here! How has the world treated you since we last met?"

"Great. I'm a rich man, richer than I ever thought I'd be. You've changed a lot Jimmy. You seem to have got taller."

"Oh, I grew a bit after I was twenty."

"Are you doing well in New York?"

"Okay. Steady job. Nothing fancy, but I get by. Come on, Bob; let's go somewhere out of this awful weather. We'll go around to a bar I know where we can see each other properly and have a good talk about the old days."

The two men started off down the misty street with Bob doing most of the talking. He talked about his success, his wealth, his power and how people looked up to him. He told the other man how he had made his fortune – gambling rackets, mostly illegal and other rackets which were certainly illegal. The other, his face sheltered in his overcoat collar listened with interest.

At the corner stood a bar, brilliant with electric lights. When they came into the glare of the lights both men turned and faced each other. The man from Chicago spoke first.

"You're not Jimmy Wells," he snapped "twenty years is a long time, but not long enough to change a man's face completely."

"Time can change some things," came the reply, "it can change a good man into a bad man. My name is Detective Breslin of the New York Police Department and I'm placing you under arrest. The Chicago police want to question you about a few little matters. Come quietly to the station or else . . ."

"Don't worry. I'll come quietly."

"Before we go here's a note I was asked to hand you. You may read it here in the light." The man from Chicago unfolded the piece of paper. His hand was steady when he began to read but it shook a little by the time he had finished. The note was rather short.

Bob – I was at the agreed place on time. When you struck the match to light your cigar I knew then that it was you the Chicago police wanted. Somehow I couldn't bring you in myself so I went around to the station and got a detective to do the job.

– Jimmy.

– O. Henry (Adapted)

Points to Note

PLOT

The plot of a story is the set of events that happen in a story. In novels, plots are often long and complicated. In short stories, plots are usually simple. However, in almost all short story plots, events take an unexpected and surprising turn at some point. This element of surprise is one reason why people enjoy reading short stories. The ending of the story *After Twenty Years* is an example of this.

POINT OF VIEW

In *After Twenty Years* the story is told from the point of view of someone who can see all the things as they happen and can see into the thoughts and minds of all the characters. For example, we learn a little of what Bob is thinking at one point in the story. When a writer is preparing to write a story he/she must make a decision about the Point of View from which he/she will tell the story.

The writer might decide to let a character from the story tell it. This is known as the **first person** point of view. For example both of Frank O'Connor's stories are told from the first person point of view. On the other hand, the writer might tell it from the point of view of an observer who sees all, who can tell us about the secret thoughts and actions of all the characters and who can be in a number of places at once. This is known as the **omniscient** point of view. We could say that *After Twenty Years* is written from the omniscient point of view.

After Twenty Years

Questions & Assignments

In the case of questions 1, 2 and 3 identify and write out the sentence in the story that supports your choice of answer.

1. The policeman walked in:
   - (a) a suspicious way
   - (b) a confident way
   - (c) a rapid way
   - (d) a lazy way.

2. The man standing in the doorway of the jewellery shop was:
   - (a) almost hidden by the thick mist
   - (b) totally hidden by his hat
   - (c) completely hidden in the doorway
   - (d) almost hidden by his coat collar.

3. The man in the doorway:
   - (a) hoped his friend would arrive
   - (b) was certain his friend would arrive
   - (c) didn't think his friend would arrive
   - (d) would recognise his friend when he arrived.

4. What details at the beginning of the story tell us that the policeman did his job well?
5. What do we learn about the policeman's youth from the story?
6. Describe briefly how his neighbourhood changed over the years.
7. "*A strange place to shelter, Sir*". Was this an unusual comment to the man in the doorway? Give a reason for your anwer.
8. What explanation did the man in the doorway offer the policeman for being there?
9. What do you think made the man in the doorway tell the policeman the full story about the agreement with his friend?
10. How did the policeman know that the jewellery shop was once a restaurant?
11. Whose fault was it that the friends lost contact with each other? Refer to the story to support your answer.
12. (i) What do you think the question "*Are you going to call time on him sharp?*" means?
    (ii) Why do you think the policeman asked this question?
13. Speaking of Jimmy Wells, the man in the doorway says "*Whatever he did, he did well*". Would you agree? Refer to the entire story to support your answer.
14. Write an imaginative account of each of the two old friends' lives over the twenty years.
15. Outline briefly the plot of the story.
16. What part or parts of the story surprised you? Give reasons.
17. Were you impressed with the policeman's action in the story? Give reasons for your answer.
18. Suggest an alternative story line from the point where the two men first meet.
19. Would the story be a difficult one to make into a film? Explain why.
20. Find words in the story that have similar meanings to the following words:
    - (a) foggy
    - (b) walked slowly
    - (c) narrow streets
    - (d) locked
    - (e) stopped
    - (f) rang
    - (g) felt
    - (h) pitiless
    - (i) tough
    - (j) great wealth
    - (k) without delay
    - (l) spoke angrily.

Spectrum 1

✎ *Personal Writing*

Retell the story *After Twenty Years* from the point of view of any one of the three characters in the story. The following openings may be useful in getting started.

1. When I reached the doorway he had already arrived. My heart sank. I was hoping that I wouldn't have to make that decision . . .
2. You won't believe how I ended up like this . . .
3. When Jimmy approached me in the squad room, he looked pale and shaken. "Pat," he said to me, "I have a big fish out there waiting to be brought in. You won't believe who it is . . .

Short Story Workshop

Before you begin writing a short story you will need to do a little planning under each of the four headings – **Setting**; **Characters**; **Constructing a Plot** and **Point of View**.

Setting

Decide where and when the events in the story take place – the setting. It's a good idea to write about places that are familiar to you. Choose the local sports ground, your classroom, school yard, local supermarket/hairdressing salon/newsagents/record shop/sports shop, main street of your town or village, Bonfire Night on the estate, a deserted beach, the graveyard, the disco – rather than the headquarters of the New York Mafia. For short stories confine the events to one or, at most, two settings. The reader needs to 'see' where the action is taking place. A descriptive paragraph with four or five carefully selected details will help the reader to imagine the entire scene.

A *The small back room was empty. No furniture. No cupboards. I bent down and looked at the floorboards. It was difficult to tell if anything could be hidden under them. And I didn't fancy looking. I didn't like rats.*

B *Rain. Rain. Rain. Was it ever going to stop? The sky was a mass of grey clouds. It was raining in a slow, lazy sort of way as if it was going to go on forever. An old lady pushed by and jabbed me in the leg with her shopping bag. People never look where they are going when it's raining.*

C *The park was a bit creepy. The rain dripped through the tall trees. Shivering, I picked my way along the path. My eyes got used to the gloom, and I began to make out the swings and the see-saw.*

D *I picked my way over the rotten floorboards and stood in the hall, or at least what was left of it, and shone the torch upwards. There were holes in the ceiling. Big beams of wood were hanging down. Most of the stairs were missing. It wouldn't be safe to try upstairs.*

Assignment — Establishing A Setting

1 Using some of the following phrases, write a short paragraph to establish the setting and atmosphere of an old graveyard.
The dreary rain cast a blanket of gloom over . . . the icy wind cut through . . . overgrown with grass and straggly weeds . . . grey slabs half hidden in the ground . . . garish plastic wreaths looking out of place . . . an old woman, her head covered and bent against the harsh weather . . . a strange silence . . . the tap-tap-tap of the rain on the headstones . . . a solitary crow cawing halfheartedly in the rain . . .

SHORT STORY WORKSHOP

CHARACTERS

It adds greatly to the readers' enjoyment to let them 'see' the characters in the story. (Three or four interesting details of a character's appearance are enough.) Long detailed descriptions of a character's appearance are not necessary. The following adjectives may be useful for this task.

Build: lanky, tall, short, stout, thin, frail, muscular, weedy, brawny.
Face: wrinkled, tanned, long, pointed, fat.
Hair: neat, curly, long, tangled, grey, brown, red, balding, bald.
Eyes clear, bright, innocent, shifty, large, small, sly, merry, twinkling, beady.
Clothes: shabby, smart, fashionable, grubby, drab, gaudy, worn, threadbare, neat.
Voice: low, gentle, friendly, soft, sharp, hoarse, deep, harsh.

A good writer will rarely tell us directly if a character is: friendly, snobbish, kind-hearted, greedy, lazy, cheerful, miserable, gloomy, honest, blunt, charming, spiteful, loyal, generous, sincere, detestable or timid . . . Instead the writer will reveal what the character is like by letting us see what the character does (actions) and hear what the character says (dialogue). Therefore a good writer can sketch an interesting character with a few well-chosen phrases, revealing the character through appearance, action and dialogue.

EXAMPLE – THE BULLY

All the boys felt uncomfortable whenever Tom Miller appeared in the playground. Once Danny Benson had even thrown up when Miller grabbed him.
'Benson,' he snarled in his quiet menacing way, 'you're a snivelling little sap.'
   Benson was trembling. He looked up into Miller's twisted sneer of a face. We could all see the knee raised to pound his hapless victim in the stomach and then Benson's mouth began to open and shut, just like a goldfish. In a moment Miller found himself covered in a sticky pungent mess. It was almost worth it to see the look of sheer horror on his face. Then he began to throttle Danny, shaking him so that his head was lolling around like a rag doll.
'I'm going to make you eat this, or worse. Just you wait, you miserable . . .'

Assignment — CREATING CHARACTERS

Try composing a similar character sketch, showing one of the following characters through action and dialogue: a biker, a football fan, a fashion model, a snob. Useful phrases for the football fan:
   A glazed, excited expression . . . fist jabbed aggressively at the air . . . anticipation, anger, hope and disappointment all flashed across his face . . . screamed abuse at the ref . . . kitted out in his club's finest designer gear . . . anxiously consulting his watch . . . chewing gum as though his life depended on it . . .

Constructing a Plot

Writers are fond of the phrase 'character is plot'. Loosely translated this means that if you create interesting characters they will make your story happen. When the plots of short stories are stripped down to their bare elements they are virtually identical, i.e. a character is faced with a problem which he or she succeeds or fails to resolve. The 'problem' is usually presented by another character. This results in conflict and confrontation. Confrontation and conflict add tension and interest to a story and are well conveyed through dialogue.

Use the plots of the stories in this book as ideas for your own plots.

Point of View

You must decide who will narrate ('tell') the story. You can opt for a character involved in the story (first person point of view) or the omniscient point of view.

When an author decides to tell a story from the point of view of a character in the story, there can only be a certain amount that we can be told – what that character experiences, sees and thinks. Everything we learn comes from the character who is narrating the story. Stories of this kind are called the first-person narrative. Most stories are written either from the omniscient point of view or else the point of view of a character in the story. Both techniques have advantages and drawbacks.

Assignment — Short Story Writing

Write a short story based on the following plan:
A character finds the courage she once had by performing a difficult or dangerous act; an act that in some way is similar to that which first resulted in the loss of courage.

Let's say the character's name is Ann and the story is written from **her** point of view.

Paragraph 1
Begin at the moment where Anne must make the choice to perform the dangerous act. What is it? Go into water . . . face a crowd . . . confront a hostile adult . . Describe her fear. . . physically . . . mentally . . . how she might appear to the others . . show her wavering about performing the task.

Paragraph 2
(Flashback) The event which caused her fear . . a friend gets into difficulties in the water . . . Anne, a champion swimmer, hesitates . . . then she goes into the water to rescue her friend . . . but the current is too strong . . . Describe the water . . . how it felt . . . what was in her mind at that moment . . . how she sees her friend being swept away.

SHORT STORY WORKSHOP

Paragraph 3
The aftermath . . . her feelings of guilt . . . the reactions of family and friends . . . her growing fear against going into water.

Paragraph 4
(*Back to the present*) . . . Joe her little brother is playing on the beach . . . describe the beach . . . the people . . . the weather . . . the water . . . everyone is preoccupied . . . nobody notices Joe toddling into the shallow waters . . . by the time someone notices he is quite far out . . . everyone is frozen in panic . . . What is Anne thinking? . . . she has failed once . . . what if she fails again? . . . everyone is waiting for her to act.

Paragraph 5
Something inside her snaps . . . she thinks of Joe . . . what sort of little boy he is . . she races towards the water . . . Joe is being swept away . . . she wades in, swimming faster than she has ever done in her life . . . she can see his little face bobbing in the water . . . then for a moment she can't see it. Finally she reaches him . . . he is submerged . . . she hauls him back to the beach and pumps the water out of his lungs . . . his eyes open and he smiles . . . their mother grabs him and hugs and scolds him.

Paragraph 6
Anne returns to the water . . . she swims out relishing the feel of the water on her skin . . . she dives . . . she floats . . . all her joy and skill as a swimmer have returned . . . she wades out smiling . . . the sun drying the cool water on her skin.

DIALOGUE

Note how conversations are set out in the short stories in this book. When a passage gives us the exact words spoken by characters in a story it is called dialogue.

Quotation marks are used to show where the words spoken by a character begin and end.

What are they called?

Wow! Look at those mountains.

I don't know. We can look at the map later.

'Wow! Look at those mountains,' said John.
'What are they called?' asked Brian.
'I don't know. We can look at the map later,' answered John.

- Note that in dialogue two types of quotation marks may be used:
  double " _____ "
  single ' _____ '

In novels and short stories you will find examples of both types. However, it is recommended that you use double quotation marks in your own writing at this stage as they will stand out more clearly. Whichever you choose remember to be consistent throughout your short story.

- Note that **question marks (?)** and **exclamation marks (!)** go inside the quotation marks.

"What time is it?" asked Anne.
'It's ten feet tall!' exclaimed Jim.

- An exclamation mark placed after a piece of dialogue shows that the words were spoken in a loud or excited manner. This could show anger, fear, surprise, joy, disappointment or a warning.

REMEMBER These are general guidelines on writing dialogue. You will find they vary a little in some books. By noting carefully how dialogue is laid out in novels and short stories you should quickly master the technique of writing dialogue.

Short Story Workshop

SHORT STORY WORKSHOP

Assignment — WRITING DIALOGUE

1 Write out the sentences below in your usual handwriting, inserting quotation-marks, capital letters and other necessary punctuation marks (full stops, question marks, apostrophes etc) in their proper places.
In all these sentences the spoken words are *at the start* of the sentence. Study the example carefully before beginning.

EXAMPLE
  i think that peter will be picked for the team said jane
ANSWER
  "I think that Peter will be picked for the team," said Jane.

(a) today is my mother's birthday she said
(b) will this rain ever stop sighed the farmer
(c) you need a proper haircut said peters mother angrily
(d) i'm telling my mammy on you wailed denis
(e) i bought this in london said keith
(f) follow me please said the nurse
(g) this is a new type of engine announced the salesman
(h) are you being looked after asked the assistant
(i) maybe mother said when i asked her if we were going to the cinema
(j) dont ever try that again snapped the teacher after he saw me melting my pen with a lighter
(k) where were you all morning enquired the manager when i arrived

Assignment

2 Again write out the sentences on page 151 in your own handwriting, inserting punctuation where necessary. In all these sentences the spoken words occur *at the end* of the sentence. Study the example carefully before beginning.

EXAMPLE
  he went up to the policeman and said i think i'm lost
ANSWER
  He went up to the policeman and said, "I think I'm lost."

(a) he looked at the boy and said you broke my window
(b) ann walked into the shop and asked how much are the brown boots in the window
(c) father often says every cloud has a silver lining
(d) she thought for a few moments and then remarked i have decided to travel after all
(e) the teacher came into the room and shouted whos responsible for this
(f) andrew replied i think you may be right
(g) i said is there a museum in this town
(h) whenever i meet the principal on the corridor she always says why are you wandering about miss collins
(i) my dad often says when i was your age things were different
(j) i asked him if he was sorry and he answered not really.

3 In these sentences the spoken words are interrupted. Study the example carefully before beginning.

> **EXAMPLE**
> we leave the school at nine sharp said the teacher those that are not here by nine will be left behind
> **ANSWER**
> "We leave the school at nine sharp," said the teacher. "Those that are not here by nine will be left behind."

(a) meet at the pitch ten minutes before the game said the captain ive a few words to say to you
(b) well andrea said the teacher i don't believe that the dog ate your maths copy
(c) put out the dog said david's mother he is not to be fed in the house
(d) if i see peter in town i'll tell him the good news said fiona if not i'll ring him tonight
(e) i am not worried about myself said the politician i am more worried about my family
(f) close the gates after you warned the farmer the cattle might wander on to the road if you don't
(g) this is my garden said the man my grandfather planted the apple trees over twenty years ago
(h) i was not asleep replied Paul the thunder has kept me awake
(i) im shocked he answered i was talking to him only yesterday is he badly injured
(j) are you angry Una asked i did not mean to hurt your feelings

Assignment — LAYING OUT DIALOGUE FOR TWO SPEAKERS

Write out each of the following passages in your own handwriting, inserting quotation-marks, capital letters and other necessary punctuation marks (full stops, question marks, apostrophes etc) in their proper places. There are two speakers in passages 1, 2 and 3.

REMEMBER

- Follow the layout of each passage by beginning a new paragraph for each speaker.
- Some paragraphs may consist entirely of dialogue and so it may not be necessary to identify the speaker after each piece of dialogue, particularly when only two people are talking.
- Quotation marks should enclose spoken words only. Read the passage carefully a number of times to work out who exactly is speaking and what words they speak before you begin writing.

PASSAGE 1

Bah cried the Giant what are you doing I have had a bad dream answered the old woman and so I plucked one of your hairs What did you dream then asked he (from *The Giant with the Three Golden Hairs*)

PASSAGE 2

A strange place to shelter Sir said the policeman could you not find somewhere more comfortable a bar or a café perhaps Im expecting a friend along replied the man in the doorway I see said the policeman The man in the doorway thought the policeman sounded suspicious I suppose you think it is a strange place and a strange time to meet a friend said the man in the doorway (from *After Twenty Years*)

PASSAGE 3

What do you think youre doing Brenda turned and saw the Head Girl Gill Rodgers who was also the school hockey captain and had the sense not to try and sing as well Running Gill Sorry Gill Runnings forbidden You know that Go back and walk Miss Taylor told me to run Its no good trying to blame Miss Taylor Im sure she didnt tell you to run She said on the double said Brenda Thats not the same thing at all Go back and walk (from *The Choice is Yours*)

USING DIALOGUE WHEN WRITING SHORT STORIES

- Only use dialogue when it is really necessary. Everybody enjoys hearing a good argument but not a conversation about the weather.
- Only write dialogue to reveal something about your character or to advance your story in some way.

Assignment — WRITING DRAMATIC DIALOGUE

Write a scene based on each of the following situations which establishes a confrontation. Use a mixture of dialogue and narrative.

1. Your friend wants you to bunk off school for the afternoon but you don't want to risk going.
2. Your big sister has decided she wants to swap bedrooms with you but you have no interest in moving.
3. A husband and wife are arguing in the car about directions.
4. You see one of your friends being bullied. You intervene only to find yourself in the middle of a major confrontation.
5. Now devise three situations of your own which lead to dramatic dialogue.

Assignment — WRITING SHORT STORIES

1. Write a fairy story suitable for reading aloud to a four-year-old. You can either make up one yourself or you can retell an old favourite such as *Jack and the Beanstalk* or *Little Red Riding Hood*.

   Writing stories for young children is not as simple as it may seem. It requires much skill and care. The story must be told in a clear and straight-forward way and the language must be easily understood by the child.

2. Write a story entitled *Tricked*. The story could be an account of a trick that was played (i) on a character (ii) by a character or (iii) one witnessed by a character.

   Here are a few ideas to get you thinking.

   - A wallet on a street . . . a bundle of five-pound notes sticking out . . . you are about to pick it up . . . afraid of being seen by some small boys nearby . . . you pass on and return after a while . . your thoughts . . . will you keep it? . . . . perhaps a reward . . . maybe no one will claim it . . you approach it and as you are about to pick it up it jumps . . .
     You might begin like this: When I spotted the wallet my heart missed a beat. It was beside a dustbin and it seemed to be bulging with fivers . . .
   - An old derelict house on a lonely road is supposed to be haunted. You and your friends pluck up courage and go in there one evening with the intention of scaring some passersby with ghostly noises . . . A twist at the end of this tale could be that somebody saw through your prank and decided to turn the tables on you and your friends.

SHORT STORY WORKSHOP

SHORT STORY WORKSHOP

3 Write a story entitled *Confrontation*.
You may wish to base your opening on one of the following ideas.
- The door burst open and in walked Mr. Nolan, the vice-principal. "Who is responsible for this?" he shouted, pointing at . . .
- It was unusual for Margaret Green to sit next to anyone except Jacinta Dunne. Now she sits with anyone except Jacinta. The reason for the split was something that happened at lunch hour yesterday.
- "David Hayes of Class Thirty is to report to my office now." My heart nearly stopped when the principal's voice came over the intercom. David Hayes – that's me! . . .
- "I'm certain you were involved. Unless you can prove otherwise I intend to tell your parents." What choice had I? I could either tell who was really involved or I could take the blame myself . . .

Use plenty of dialogue but remember! Don't keep repeating the word 'said'. Vary it by using other words such as *begged, bawled, cried, shouted, roared, whispered, muttered, explained, replied* . . . etc.

4 Write a story entitled *Lost*.

A Good Start

The opening lines of a story are very important. They should catch the reader's attention and arouse his/her curiosity. Students frequently tend to 'pad' out the opening lines of a piece of writing with information which is neither interesting nor necessary. For example the following paragraph would be dull and uninteresting:

One morning last week I got up and got dressed. After breakfast I got my school-bag ready. Just as I was about to leave for school my dad told me that Mrs. Donovan from next door was going away for a week and wanted me to mind her dog, Snowy.

Try to begin in a dramatic way that brings the reader right into the action. Aim to open with a statement or a piece of dialogue that 'grabs' the reader's interest at once. Here are two separate examples of how you could begin the same story.

EXAMPLE 1 Last night I had the most embarrassing experience of my life. I had to pass a group of my school friends. The problem was that I was not alone; I was with Snowy. Snowy is a white miniature poodle. At the time it was wearing a type of dog jacket. A bright red one to be exact.

EXAMPLE 2 "Oh! Dave, before you go," my Dad shouted. "Some good news! That fishing rod you're looking for. I've got you a nice job that will pay for it." My heart lifted.
"Mrs. Donovan, next door, has to go to London to visit her daughter and she wants you to exercise Snowy. I told her you would."
My heart sank. . . .

154

Novel

Goodnight Mister Tom
by Michelle Magorian

In 1939 a young boy called Willie Beech is evacuated to the village of Little Weirwold from the city of London because Britain is on the verge of the Second World War. Thousands of children have been sent to the country to escape the expected heavy bombing.

Willie has been neglected and abused by his mother, but with the kindness and care of old widower Tom Oakley and the neighbours in Little Weirwold, Willie flourishes both physically and emotionally.

Eventually he is forced to return to his mother in London and a living nightmare ensues for Willie, a nightmare from which only Tom can save him.

Historical Background: World War Two and Evacuation

To young people of today, the Second World War may seem like a long time ago. Yet there are still many people alive today who lived through it, in particular people like Willie, who as children were evacuated from their homes in London to the safety of the countryside.

Never before in the long history of warfare had cities to be evacuated in this way. Why did it happen in 1939? The reason was that the Second World War was the first war in which cities – and therefore civilians – were at risk from heavy aerial bombardment. By the end of the war many cities in England, Germany, Russia and Japan had been completely destroyed by bombs.

Many children in London were lucky in that they had friends or family outside of the city where they could be safe. Quite a few came to stay with relatives in Ireland. However for a large number of children such as Willie Beech and Zach, a new-found friend, there was no other option but to be sent to stay with people they didn't know. These children were known as **evacuees**.

Themes and Issues in the Novel

A good novel tells a good story. A really good novel tells a good story and gives us something to think about as well. In *Goodnight Mister Tom* the author tells a good story and also deals with several interesting and important issues and themes. These include:
- **Friendship** – Willie and Zach, Willie and George, Carrie.
- **The healing power of love** – Mister Tom and Willie.
- **The vulnerability of children** – Willie and his mother, Willie in hospital.
- **The contrasting effects of cruelty and kindness on children** – Mrs Beech v Mister Tom.
- **Happy and unhappy childhood** – Willie and his friends, Willie in Little Weirworld and Salmouth v Willie in London.
- **Toughness and bullying in contrast to moral and physical strength** – Mrs Beech and the nurses in hospital v Mister Tom and his neighbours.
- **Coming to terms with loss** – Mister Tom, Willie, Geoffrey.
  Watch out for these issues as the story progresses.

Developing Characters

The main characters (**protagonists**) in a novel develop as the story progresses. That is partly what makes them interesting to the reader. People who remain the same throughout a story lose our interest after a while. In *Goodnight Mister Tom* watch how the characters of Tom and Willie change and develop as the story progresses.

Setting

The setting of a novel is very important because it gives the story added interest and it sometimes causes the characters to act in a certain way. *Goodnight Mister Tom* is set in England during the early stages of the Second World War. We learn about the war and how it affected the lives of ordinary people. We also see people doing certain things because of the war. For instance everybody has to build an Anderson air raid shelter in their back gardens as protection against bombs.

In her description of Little Weirwold, the writer gives us a vivid picture of everyday English village life during the war. The chapters set in London are equally vivid, recalling the squalor of slum life and the chaos and horror which the Blitz rained down on the capital city and its inhabitants.

Goodnight Mister Tom – A Modern Fairy Tale

There are four essential ingredients in traditional fairy tales:
(a) The good people suffer at the hands of the wicked
(b) The good people overcome the wicked and find untold riches
(c) The wicked people are punished
(d) The good people live happily ever after.

When you have read the story ask yourself if *Goodnight Mister Tom* is a modern fairy tale. If not are there elements of a fairy tale in it? If so what are they?

Goodnight Mister Tom – Novel

Central Characters

There are many other characters in this book and each of them has some small role in Willie's life. However, it is not necessary to know them all. The important ones are Willie Beech (aged 9), Tom Oakley (aged 60+), Mrs. Beech (Willie's mother) and Zach (another evacuee who soon befriends Willie).

Points to Note — POINT OF VIEW

Goodnight Mister Tom is told from the author's point of view. It is as though she is looking down at the events of the story and describing to us the important parts of what happens. This is called the **omniscient** or all knowing point of view. In this way she can show us what all the main characters think and do. If the story was told from a single point of view, e.g. Tom's, we would only get to see what Willie does when he is with Tom and we would never get any insight into Willie's mind. This would clearly set limits on the telling of the story.

When you next read a story or watch a film, try to figure out from what point of view the story is being told, for example *Bank Robbery*: the robber – the cop – the bank clerk – the innocent bystander – or all of these.

Questions & Assignments — CHAPTER ONE MEETING

1. (i) Why is Willie brought to stay in Tom's house?
   (ii) What does Tom notice about Willie's leg?
   (iii) Who does Willie meet when he goes for a walk in the graveyard?
2. (i) What are your first impressions of Tom? (surly – cantankerous – blunt – impatient – rude – perceptive – tactful – strong . . . ?) Give reasons to support your answer.

(ii) What are your first impressions of Willie? (thin – sickly – nervous – polite – sad – vulnerable . . . ?)

3 What evidence is there in this chapter that Tom is kind? (clothes peg – tea – says nothing about the bruises – caring to the dog)

4 What are your first impressions of Tom's house? (simple – warm – cosy – pipe – books)

5 What background information are we given about Willie? (mother – church – lodgers – London . . .)

6 What background information are we given about Tom? (loner – reader – lost his wife and child . . .)

7 Though we do not meet Willie's mother until much later in the novel, the author conveys a very strong impression of what she is like. What have we learnt about her? (cruel – abusive – overly strict – hypocritical – takes advantage of his vulnerability . .)

8 Imagine that you are either Willie or Tom. What would you be thinking during your first meeting?

9 Rewrite the scene in Chapter One where Tom and Willie meet for the first time, first from Tom's point of view and then from Willie's viewpoint (about ten lines will do).

10 Imagine that Willie began keeping a diary when he arrived at Mister Tom's. As you read the book, write the entries that you imagine Willie would make in his diary. As a general guideline, each entry should be approximately 150 words in length and should cover the significant events of a single chapter.

Questions & Assignments — CHAPTER TWO LITTLE WEIRWOLD

1 What does Tom ask Mrs Fletcher to do? Why?
2 Willie sees new sights in Chapter 2. What are they?
3 Why does Tom go to see Ivor?
4 What does Willie's paper bag contain?
5 Why is Tom angry when he reads Mrs Beech's letter?
6 How do you know that Willie is not used to sleeping in a bed?

GENERAL QUESTIONS ON CHAPTERS ONE AND TWO

1 From reading the first two chapters, what are your impressions of Little Weirwold? (Friendly – peaceful – simple – homely . . .? Support your points with evidence.)

2 What evidence can you find in Chapter 2 to show that Willie has been neglected and badly treated?

3 Read Mrs Beech's letter again. Can you read between the lines and tell what it reveals about her?

4 Have the characters of Tom and Willie developed in Chapter 2. Show how.

5 Does the author succeed in making us like Tom, despite the fact that he is cranky and rude at first? Explain.

6 What is Willie's opinion of himself? What is Tom's opinion of him?

Goodnight Mister Tom – Novel

Questions & Assignments — CHAPTER THREE SATURDAY MORNING

1. Why does Willie keep apologising at the start of Chapter 3?
2. What is Willie referring to when he talks about the *'marks of his sins'*?
3. Describe the boy that Willie sees at the post office. What impression do you form of him?
4. In what way does Willie find the village very different from London? Does it seem like a pleasant place? Why?
5. What evidence is there in the story so far that Tom is not all that highly regarded by his neighbours?
6. Has Willie developed or made any progress by the end of this chapter? Explain.
7. Has the author succeeded in arousing your interest in the story at this stage? Explain.

Answer Guidelines

7. Consider the following points in your answer:
   Would this story be more or less interesting if: (i) Willie was a well cared for and happy nine-year-old; (ii) Tom was an ordinary contented middle-aged man with a family of his own? Explain. Part of the reason the story is interesting is that both characters appear to have very little in common and both are thrown together in unusual circumstances beyond their control. Each of them is a fish out of water. This creates an interesting dramatic situation. We want to know how they sort it out.

Questions & Assignments — CHAPTER FOUR EQUIPPED

1. Why does Willie not want to look in the toy shop?
2. Why does Tom's heart sink when Willie wants to look at the art shop?
3. Make a list of all the places that Tom visits in the town.
4. Which book does Miss Thorne pick for Willie?
5. What evidence is there in this chapter of preparations for war?
6. *"Poor boy, away from his loving home and now dumped with an irritable old man."* What is your opinion of Miss Thorne's statement.

Questions & Assignments — CHAPTER FIVE 'CHAMBERLAIN ANNOUNCES'

1. Willie is surprised by several things in church. What are they?
2. What two events in this chapter emphasise the outbreak of war?
3. Why does Willie want to keep his jumper on while building the shelter?
4. What do we learn about Willie's life with his mother in this chapter?

Spectrum 1

Questions & Assignments — CHAPTER SIX ZACH

This chapter introduces a new and important character.
1. What do we learn about Zach?
2. What does Zach say that causes Willie to drop the clod of earth?
3. How do we know that Willie has never had a bath before?
4. What are your first impressions of Zach? Compare him with Willie.
5. Different characters use different types of language. Comment on the language used by Willie and Zach and suggest what it reveals about them.

Points to Note

CONFLICT

There are three basic types of conflict: conflict between characters, conflict within a character's own mind (**internal conflict**) and conflict between a character and his environment. In most novels we come across all three.

Conflict between characters adds to the interest of a story. If everybody in a story agreed all the time and everybody was perfectly happy with themselves, it would be a dull story.

Sometimes the conflict is within the person's own mind. For instance there is an internal conflict in Willie's mind between the fear of disobeying his mother and the desire to be like his friends.

Questions & Assignments — CHAPTER SEVEN BLACKBERRIES

1. What happens to Zach when he inspects the Anderson shelter?
2. Why does George come to see Mister Tom?
3. What has Mister Tom been doing while Willie is on the picnic?
4. How does the author emphasise Willie's physical weakness in Chapter 7? How does Willie feel about his own weakness?
5. Why does Willie feel a sense of well being when he goes to bed the night after the picnic?
6. Give some examples of conflict which have occurred in the novel so far.

Questions & Assignments — CHAPTER EIGHT SCHOOL

1. Why does George think they might not have much school?
2. Whose class does Willie end up in?
3. Why do Carrie and the others come to see him later in the day?
4. What evidence is there in this chapter that Willie is making progress? Is Tom also changing for the better? How?
5. What is your opinion of Mister Ruddles? Do you think Mister Tom likes him? Explain.
6. 'With the passage of each chapter, Willie becomes more and more a part of the community.' Discuss.

Goodnight Mister Tom – Novel

Questions & Assignments — CHAPTER NINE BIRTHDAY BOY

1. What presents does Willie get for his birthday?
2. What does Willie sketch when he is in the church?
3. It is quite clear from reading the story how Tom helps Willie. Has Willie been an equally positive influence on Tom? Explain with reference to the story so far.
4. From the evidence to this point of the story, put together a profile of Mister Tom as he must have been before the arrival of Willie. (Recluse – crusty – unsociable – critical – unfriendly – unhelpful . . .)
5. Would you say there are fairy-tale elements in this chapter? Explain.
6. Imagine what Willie's birthday might be like if he was in London with his mother.

Points to Note

HOPES AND FEARS

As we become involved with the characters in a story we will hope that some things will happen to them and fear that other things might happen. Experiencing these hopes and fears is one of the pleasures of reading. A good story teller will balance our hopes and fears throughout the story.

Questions & Assignments — CHAPTER TEN THE CASE

1. Why do some of the evacuees return to London?
2. List some of the contents of Zach's suitcase.
3. Why is Mrs Little cross with Zach?
4. What evidence is there in this chapter that Tom is sensitive and tactful?
5. Since his arrival in Little Weirwold, Willie has made great progress. What are our hopes and fears for him at this point in the story?
6. 'The power of friendship is an important theme in this chapter.' Give your views on this statement, supporting the points you make by referring to the chapter.

Questions & Assignments — CHAPTER ELEVEN FRIDAY

1. What news does Zach have for the others in the group?
2. What discovery about Zach shocks Willie?
3. How does wartime effect the children of Little Weirwold?
4. Tom encourages Willie to have his friends around. Explain why this is important for both Tom and Willie.

Questions & Assignments — CHAPTER TWELVE THE SHOW MUST GO ON

1. Why does Miss Thorne have to keep recasting the play?
2. Why is Tom asked to help out with the carol service? Why does he have mixed feelings about it?
3. How does the worsening war situation affect Little Weirwold?
4. Compare Willie's acting skills with those of Zach's.

Questions & Assignments — CHAPTER THIRTEEN CAROL SINGING

1. Describe how Tom improves the performance of the choir.
2. Chapter 13 emphasises a big change in Tom's character. How?

Points to Note

FORESHADOWING

Writers often give clues or hint at what is going to happen early on in a story. This technique is called foreshadowing. For instance we know fairly early on that Mrs Beech is a cruel and violent mother. We know that when she and Willie are re-united, something unpleasant may happen.

Questions & Assignments — CHAPTER FOURTEEN NEW BEGINNINGS

1. Why is Lucy sad?
2. Why is George wearing a black armband?
3. Describe in your own words the picture which Willie draws for 'A Rainy Night'.
4. Describe Mrs Hartridge. What is Willie's opinion of her?
5. What do the others think of Carrie's ambition to go to the high school?
6. What are your hopes and fears for Willie when his mother sends for him?
7. What do you think Tom is feeling at the end of Chapter 14?
8. Are you looking forward to meeting Willie's mother?
   Yes – curious – want to see what will happen.
   No – apparently not a pleasant character – likely that she will be cruel to Willie.
9. Try to predict what will happen in the next chapter, bearing in mind what you know about Mrs Beech.

Questions & Assignments — CHAPTER FIFTEEN HOME

1. What advice does Tom give to Willie as they are parting?
2. What does Willie dream about on the train?
3. What is Mrs. Beech's first reaction when she sees her son?
4. Why does Willie's smile frighten his mother?

5 What evidence is there that the baby is neglected?
6 Compare Mrs Beech's treatment of her son with Tom's treatment of him. (Mrs Beech – critical – cruel – mistrustful – angry – bullying – selfish – hypocritical – hard. Tom – gentle – sensitive – tactful – trusting – encouraging – kind – generous – forgiving.)
7 Are there elements of a fairy tale in Chapter 15? Explain.
8 (i) Pick out some sentences from Mrs Beech's point of view.
   (ii) Pick out some sentences that reveal things from Willie's point of view.
9 Comment on the title of the chapter.

Questions & Assignments — CHAPTER SIXTEEN THE SEARCH

1 Why does Tom ask Mrs Fletcher to go to see Mrs Hartridge?
2 Why does Tom end up in an air raid shelter?
3 What is the first thing Tom and the warden notice when they break into the house?
4 Compare London with Little Weirwold. (Appearance – people – atmosphere . . .)
5 How is Mrs Beech regarded by her neighbours?

Points to Note

MORAL DILEMMA – INTERNAL CONFLICT

Mister Tom is faced with a moral dilemma. This means he has to make a very difficult moral decision. Whatever he decides may be wrong. It may be legally wrong to kidnap Willie. However, it may be morally wrong to leave him in the hospital where he will not be cared for properly. When characters in novels are faced with moral dilemmas it makes the story more interesting. We want to know what decision they will make and what will be the consequences of that decision.

Questions & Assignments — CHAPTER SEVENTEEN RESCUE

1 What reason do the nurses give for continuing to sedate Willie?
2 What is Mr Skelton's plan for Willie?
3 What has happened to Willie's baby sister?
4 The scene where Willie is discovered is very distressing. What does it emphasise? How does it arouse our sympathy for Willie?
5 What is the hospital's attitude to healing Willie? What is Tom's approach? Discuss which you think is the best approach. Give reasons for your answer.
6 What is the significance of Willie's decision regarding his name?
7 Is Mister Tom right to kidnap Willie? Discuss.

Questions & Assignments — Chapter Eighteen 'Recovery'

1. Why does Willie become upset when Zach mentions Mrs Hartridge's baby?
2. What evidence is there that the war situation is worsening?
3. This chapter shows the healing power of love and friendship. Give reasons why you do or do not agree with this view.

Points to Note

ATMOSPHERE

Atmosphere means the mood and feeling created by a piece of writing. For instance in Chapter 1 the author gives Tom's house a cosy warm atmosphere, using details such as the large range with the fire in it, the pipe, the armchair and the books. Words such as *'warm'*, *'comfortable'* and *'friendly'* add to the cosy atmosphere.

Questions & Assignments — Chapter Nineteen The Sea, The Sea,

1. How does the sea affect Willie at first?
2. In what way does Tom change his appearance in Chapter 19?
3. What do we learn about Mrs Clarence?
4. How would you describe the overall atmosphere of Chapter 19? Compare it with the atmosphere in Chapter 15. In each case select words and phrases which heighten the atmosphere.

Questions & Assignments — Chapter Twenty Spooky Cott

1. What is the strange noise the group hears from Spooky Cott?
2. What do we learn about Geoffrey Sanderton?
3. What is Willie's reaction to his mother's death?
4. Why do you think the authorities agree to let Tom adopt Willie?

Questions & Assignments — Chapter Twenty One Back At School

1. Why is Carrie very excited at the start of this chapter?
2. Why have Zach's parents remained in London?
3. Why does Zach feel that he has to return to London?
4. Why is the day following Zach's departure a special day for Willie?
5. 'Friendship is an important issue in this story.' Discuss.
   Consider some of the following points:
   Willie is bullied and has no friends in London . . .
   He is accepted and surrounded by friends in Little Weirwold . . .
   Is friendship a positive force in the story? (How – for whom?)

How does friendship help Willie? (Confidence – companionship – fun – education – learning how to mix with others – feeling accepted . . .)

Questions & Assignments — CHAPTER TWENTY TWO GRIEVING

1. What do Tom and Willie do for all the new evacuees?
2. What does Geoffrey ask Willie to paint? Why does it upset Willie?
3. When Willie finally goes to see Mrs Little, what does he ask for?
4. What part does Willie take in the play *Peter Pan*?
5. Why does Tom cry in this chapter?
6. Geoffrey tells Willie that it is *'better to accept than pretend he never existed'*. In the context of Willie's behaviour in the first half of Chapter 22, explain what Geoffrey means.
7. Describe the various stages which Willie goes through in coming to terms with the loss of someone he loves. (Despair – anger – acceptance.) Both Willie and Tom have had to come to terms with the loss of someone they love. How does each of them cope? To what extent does one help the other?

Questions & Assignments — CHAPTER TWENTY THREE POSTSCRIPT

1. Why does Carrie have to borrow Zach's old shorts?
2. Why does Willie keep books for Carrie?
3. What does Willie notice about Tom for the first time?

GENERAL QUESTIONS ON *GOODNIGHT MISTER TOM* – NOVEL

1. 'It occurred to him (Willie) that strength was quite different from toughness and that being vulnerable wasn't the same as being weak.'
   Explain clearly what is meant by this statement. How does it apply to both Willie and Tom?
2. Having reached the end of the book, read back over Chapter 1. How have Tom and Willie changed over the course of the book?

Spectrum 1

Assignment

Characters

Select at least one character from the story under each of the following headings. You may include the same character under more than one heading. In the case of each of your choices write a few sentences explaining why you made the choice.

- interesting
- amusing
- unpleasant
- cruel
- strong
- weak
- vulnerable
- tough
- old
- young
- caring
- critical

Moments

Select at least one moment from the story under each of the following headings. In each case write a few sentences explaining why you made the choice.

- exciting
- tense
- amusing
- a moment you were dreading
- a moment you were looking forward to
- a moment you weren't expecting
- sad
- lonely
- frightening
- comforting
- turning point

Feelings and Emotions

Under each of the headings below, select at least one episode from the story in which some character experiences that particular feeling or emotion. In the case of each of your choices write a few sentences explaining why you made the choice.

- Fear
- happiness
- loneliness
- sadness
- despair
- moment of insight
- confusion
- indecision
- anger
- moral dilemma
- kindness
- generosity

LIFE IN WARTIME

What have you learned about wartime life in Britain? Would you like to have lived at that time? Why? (Yes – exciting – adventurous – meeting new people. No – very dangerous – families broken up – wholesale destruction – loss of loved ones . . .)

STRUCTURE AND TIMESCALE OF *GOODNIGHT MISTER TOM* – NOVEL

Chapter Outlines

The purpose of these chapter outlines is to provide you with a convenient overview of the structure and timescale of the novel for revision purposes. In order to enjoy the novel we suggest that you <u>do</u> <u>not</u> refer to this section until you have completed a reading of the novel.

CHAPTER 1 Willie Beech, a skinny, neglected London boy is evacuated to the village house of Tom Oakley, a surly old widower in his sixties. To begin with Tom and Willie are equally suspicious of each other. Tom finds clues to Willie's harsh upbringing and despite his surliness, he finds himself helping the boy to settle in. When Tom picks up the poker Willie thinks the old man is going to hit him. He faints and Tom realises that he is frightened because he has been beaten badly at home. We realise that despite his rude exterior, Tom is a good man.

CHAPTER 2 Willie makes friends with Sammy (Tom's dog) and Tom sets about improving things for Willie. He introduces Willie to the neighbours who can already see a change in the bad-tempered old man they have been used to. Tom reads a letter from Willie's mother which reveals her heartless attitude to her son. Tom fixes a bed up for Willie in the attic room and Willie settles in for his first night in Little Weirwold.

CHAPTER 3 Tom finds more bruises on Willie's body and Willie insists on wearing his socks to keep the bruises covered. Tom discovers that the boy can't read or write and so Tom writes a card to Willie's mother to let her know that all is well. Willie is still frightened by much of what he sees around him, including the people. Tom brings him to the doctor for his bruises and then on to the post office. There Willie sees another boy who is very chatty and confident. He arouses Willie's curiosity.

Spectrum 1

CHAPTER 4 Tom brings Willie to town to buy him some clothes and equip him for his stay in Weirwold.

CHAPTER 5 Willie goes to Sunday Service with Tom and learns more about the village and its inhabitants. They all gather together in the church after the service and listen to the radio. The prime minister announces that Britain is now at war with Germany. Tom and Willie set about building an Anderson shelter with the help of the Fletcher family. Willie is delighted when he sees the boy from the post office once again.

CHAPTER 6 Willie makes friends with the boy from the post office who is called Zacharias Wrench. He too is an evacuee. Zach is very open, friendly and chatty. He helps Willie to put the finishing touches to the Anderson shelter. Meanwhile, Tom goes along to the village hall and much to the surprise of the others he volunteers for fire-watching duties. This shows that he too is changing and that having to care for the needs of Willie is making him more aware of the needs of others around him.

CHAPTER 7 William still feels bad because he is physically weak and, though he wants to run, he isn't able to run very far. Zach arrives and inspects the new shelter. Then, with George and the twins, they go blackberry picking. Gradually Willie begins to feel comfortable in the company of the other young people. When he goes to bed that night he is quite pleased with his own progress.

CHAPTER 8 Willie goes to school in Weirwold for the first time but, to his intense disappointment, he is not in the same class as his new friends since he can neither read nor write. Tom begins to teach Willie the alphabet and discovers that he is a quick learner. Some comic touches are provided by Mr Ruddles, the warden, whose job is to make sure that no light is showing through the blackouts.

CHAPTER 9 It is Willie's birthday and Tom, his new friends and many other neighbours give Willie presents. He is overwhelmed by their kindness and generosity. He goes to the churchyard to try out his new sketching equipment. Zach is full of admiration for what his friend is capable of drawing and it is clear that Willie is a gifted artist. That evening Tom arranges a party for his young evacuee and, though Willie becomes sick with the excitement of it all, he is happier than he has ever been in his life before.

CHAPTER 10 Autumn is passing and some of the evacuees return to London. Willie remains and makes good progress educationally and physically. In addition, he is now firm friends with Zach and the others. Willie enjoys the feeling of being part of a group and especially being Zach's friend. This is emphasised when Zach's case arrives from London and they all gather in Zach's room to examine its contents. They decide to form a committee and Tom agrees to let them use Willie's room for meetings.

CHAPTER 11 Mrs Fletcher notes how both Tom and Willie have changed for the better. Willie brings Zach and his other friends to his room where the strength of their friendship is further shown as they discuss the forthcoming Christmas play and carol service and their news gazette. Willie's scars have almost healed and he no longer wets the bed at night.

Chapter 12 It is now early December. Willie, much to his own and everybody else's surprise, proves to be a talented actor and lands the leading role in the Christmas play. Tom also agrees to take over the choir and play the organ for the carol service.

Chapter 13 Willie enjoys rehearsing the part of Scrooge. Together he and Tom set off to the choir practice. Though the choir begins badly, under Tom's discipline and encouragement, it makes good progress. Tom is pleased with himself that he has returned to playing the organ after so many years.

Chapter 14 Willie has made very good progress in his reading and writing and as a result he is moved into Mrs Hartridge's class along with Zach and George. At first he is nervous but he settles in well. Carrie, one of his friends applies to go to the high school. One Friday in March, Willie is very excited because he and his friends have decided to go on an adventure to Spooky Cott. At this point in the story Willie is happy, healthy, full of energy and enjoying the company of good friends. However his happiness is short-lived. When he arrives home, Tom gives him the news that his mother is ill and that she wants him back with her in London.

Chapters 15, 16 and 17 These chapters cover an important turning point in the story. Consequently the summaries of these chapters are not included. After reading the novel you may wish to write summaries of these chapters for yourself.

Chapter 18 Following his return to Tom's house, Willie is very weak and suffers some horrific nightmares. However, with Tom's care and patience, Willie gradually regains his strength. By May he is well enough to see Zach for the first time in weeks. Willie is very upset and guilty about the death of his baby sister. He is also shocked when Zach tells him how babies are formed. Trying to make sense of the baby's death, he goes to see Mrs Hartridge and her new baby. When he sees her feeding her baby and all the care a baby needs, he finally realises that he was helpless to save his little sister's life.

CHAPTER 19 In August Tom brings Willie and Zach to the seaside for a fortnight's holiday. They lodge with Mrs Clarence. The holiday strengthens the friendship between the two boys who relish the freedom and fun of being at the sea. Willie continues to progress, particularly with his drawing, and he learns to swim. When news of London being bombed reaches them, Zach becomes worried about his parents. However, he is reassured to hear that they are well. Tom and the boys return to the village, looking forward to the winter months ahead.

CHAPTER 20 Willie and Zach and their friends finally get to go to Spooky Cott. To begin with, it does sound spooky because they hear very strange noises which are explained when they meet the occupant, Geoffrey Sanderton, an artist who has lost a leg in the war. Geoffrey recognises that Willie has a special gift for painting and offers to help him out.

When Willie returns to Tom's, some visitors have arrived. They tell him that his mother is dead and that he will have to be taken into foster care. Willie refuses to go with them and it is finally agreed that Tom can legally adopt Willie as his son.

CHAPTER 21 AND 22 These chapters deal with a key episode in the story. Consequently the summaries of these chapters are not included.

CHAPTER 23 Willie and Tom are planting vegetables for the war effort when Carrie arrives to see Willie. They are both good friends and help and confide in each other. Willie is completely at ease in her company and he walks part of the way home with her. When he returns home, he hangs his cap on the peg which Tom put up for him on his very first day there, but he doesn't have to stretch to reach it any more. Willie realises that he is growing up and becoming strong. It is a moment of insight for the young evacuee, who barely a year before, had arrived on Tom's doorstep as a vulnerable little boy whose only experience of the world had been cruelty and violence and loneliness.

Drama

INTRODUCTION

The origins of drama and theatre probably go back to the dawn of history. A father and son on their return from a successful bear hunt, might act out the hunt to entertain the other members of their family. One of the hunters would play the part of the bear, wearing the bear skin to make the show more realistic.

If the actors were good, the other members of the tribe would want to see the bear hunt acted out again and again. Perhaps, as time went on, extra scenes might be put in to make it even more exciting or to make those watching it laugh. When the acting of the bear hunt became even more popular it would be performed at a particular place – probably a piece of flat ground at the foot of a hill, from where the entire tribe could see the action. Such events may have been the beginnings of theatre in primitive society.

The history of theatre and drama as we know it today began in ancient Greece. The word theatre comes from a Greek word meaning a 'seeing place'. Almost three thousand years ago plays formed part of religious services in Greece. A wooden platform was built at the bottom of a convenient hillside. The audience sat on wooden benches or stone steps built one behind the other up the hillside. The actors performed on a wooden stage on the back of which a changing room or *skene* was built. The front of the *skene* would be decorated and, thus, we get the word 'scenery' from *skene*. The plays told stories of the gods and the exploits of legendary heroes. They used primitive cranes to lower actors playing the parts of gods to the stage.

The inspiration for the Roman theatre came from Greece but the Romans introduced some new developments. They staged plays that dealt with the lives of ordinary people instead of telling stories of gods and heroes. They introduced a curtain across the front of the stage and used trap-doors and other mechanical effects. Over the period of the Roman Empire, theatre was a popular form of entertainment and the remains of Roman theatres still survive today.

The fall of the Roman Empire in the sixth century resulted in the decline of theatre in Europe. Actors and musicians were forced to take to the roads, performing plays at fairs and at other events where people gathered. Throughout the next five centuries, bands of wandering minstrels and actors travelled from town to town reciting tales of adventure and performing simple comedy sketches. By the eleventh century, minstrels and actors were being engaged by noblemen to provide entertainment at banquets.

Spectrum 1

The church, which for centuries had disapproved of wandering minstrels, gradually began to change its attitude. It saw that the ordinary people enjoyed the performances given by the wandering groups of minstrels and actors and realised that drama would be a good way of bringing the stories of the Bible and the parables to the faithful.

Priests and nuns would stage simple plays in the churches on major feast days, for example the Nativity scene at Christmas and the Sepulchre scene at Easter. These soon grew into more elaborate productions where greater numbers of actors and more space than the churches could offer were needed.

In the towns and cities of Europe, people who worked at a particular trade formed trade associations called *guilds*. The members of the various guilds now took over the task of presenting religious plays on church feast days. The plays were staged on platforms called *mansions* in the market places. Each guild chose a different story from the Bible. They were sometimes performed on wheeled stages which moved around the town, so that by waiting at one point a spectator could see the whole series, or he could follow his favourite play around the town and see it several times.

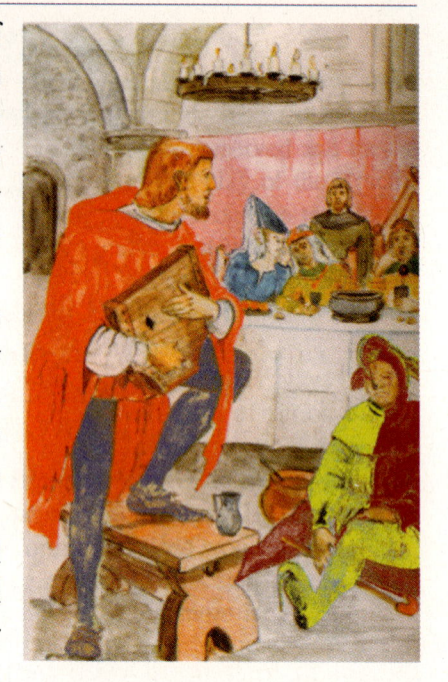

These plays were known as *Mystery* plays. There were also *Miracle* plays about the lives of the saints and *Morality* plays which showed the struggle between the forces of Good and Evil. Manuscripts of some of these plays have been preserved and they show that the plays were exciting, realistic and often humorous. The play of the Crucifixion presented at York has a scene where four Roman soldiers carry out the task of nailing Christ to the cross and then fixing the cross into the ground. Just like any soldiers who have been presented with an unpleasant task, they carry it out callously, convincingly and with black humour. Christ, in contrast, is presented with tragic dignity. In another surviving manuscript, Noah is presented as a hen-pecked husband!

The professionals also staged some of the more popular religious plays but, for the most part, they presented popular comedies and farces with a lot of action and coarse humour. In time these professionals ceased performing in the streets in favour of the courtyards of inns. Many of the old inns had an open gallery round the courtyard at first floor level where the rich people could watch the play in comfort. The common people stood in the courtyard and watched the actors perform on a raised wooden stage.

This move to the inns resulted in the richer and more educated people coming to watch the plays. In turn, this resulted in a demand for better, more intelligent plays and educated people now began to write plays. As the audience now had to pay to be admitted to the plays some actors and dramatists became comparatively rich. By the middle of the 16th century companies of actors toured from town to town performing their plays in inns and guildhalls. The guildhall in a little market town called Stratford-on-Avon in England was often the venue for companies of travelling players. It is very likely that a frequent member of the audience around the year 1580 was a teenager called William Shakespeare.

In Shakespeare's time many theatres were uncomfortable in bad weather, but by the end of the seventeenth century theatres throughout western Europe were becoming more like modern theatres. The stage was divided from the *auditorium* (the section where the audience is seated) by the *procenium* (pro-seen-ee-um) arch. A curtain hung immediately behind the procenium arch and when raised, the stage was framed in the arch like a picture and was often called a 'picture frame' stage. Scenery was more elaborate and better painted. For example, by the nineteenth century, a forest set would look like a real forest.

Drama in the eighteenth century took a new and important direction at the hands of two Irish playwrights – Richard Brinsley Sheridan and Oliver Goldsmith – who wrote some comedies, *School for Scandal* and *She Stoops to Conquer*, which are still popular today. Irish writers such as Oscar Wilde, George Bernard Shaw and Sean O'Casey continued to give English drama some of its most memorable plays in the nineteenth and twentieth centuries. Even today the works of modern Irish playwrights like Samuel Beckett (*Waiting for Godot*) and Brian Friel (*Dancing at Lughnasa*) continue to win international acclaim.

READING PLAYS

Drama is written to be performed – either on stage or on screen. When we see a play on stage or on screen the actors, their costumes, the scenery, the props and special effects all help to bring the play to life. However it is not necessary to see a production of a play to enjoy it. Reading plays can be enjoyable. Pay attention to the dialogue and stage directions and your imagination will bring the events of the play to life.

> **COSTUME** is the word used to describe the clothes a character wears. The costume of a character in a play helps the audience to understand the kind of person that the character is. The costumes play an important part in a play. They make it immediately clear who each character is – a nurse, a doctor, a policeman, a soldier, etc, all can be immediately identified by their costume. Ordinary clothes can even tell something about a character, such as whether that character is rich or poor.
>
> **SCENERY OR SET** are words that describe the painted backdrops and other objects on the stage that show the audience where the action of a play takes place. It can be elaborate and detailed or very basic.
>
> **PROPS** – short for 'properties' – is the term given to items that the actors will need to use (e.g. a telephone, a gun, a guitar etc) during a performance.
>
> **SPECIAL EFFECTS** – Many playwrights make use of lighting and sound effects. Lights can be used to mark the change from day to

Spectrum 1

> night or from night to dawn. Effects such as snow falling or lightning can also be achieved using lights. In the past, sound effects all had to be created backstage. The sound of galloping horses was created with coconut shells and thunder was created by shaking sheets of tin foil. However, since the advent of recorded sound, an endless supply of realistic sound effects is available.

LAYING OUT DRAMA

Dialogue in plays is laid out very differently from the way it is laid out in novels and stories. The main difference is that quotation marks are not used to mark off dialogue in plays. Note also how stage directions are in brackets and the names of the speakers appear on the left-hand margin.

These example will show the difference:

LAYOUT USED IN NOVELS

"What's the matter, Karen? Do you not feel well?" Miss O'Neill asked in a gentle voice.
Karen began to sob.
"I've lost my money, Miss," she replied.

LAYOUT USED IN DRAMA

Miss O'Neill: *(gently)*   What's the matter Karen? Do you not feel well?

Karen: *(sobbing)*   I've lost my money, Miss.

BURNING EVEREST

by
Adrian Flynn

Mount Everest, the highest mountain in the world, is situated along the frontier between Nepal and Tibet. For many years explorers had been trying to reach the summit. In the nineteen-twenties, world interest was aroused as several expeditions set out to conquer the mountain, among them a group led by George Leigh Mallory. Their exploits were enthusiastically followed in the pages of the daily newspapers. However, in the end, though Mallory climbed further than other previous expeditions, he never reached the summit. On his final attempt, he and his team disappeared, never to be seen again. It was not until May 1953 that the mountain was finally conquered by Edmund Hillary and Tenzing Norgay.

Since the publicity and interest which the nineteen-twenties expeditions aroused, the conquest of Everest has taken on a symbolic meaning for many people who regard it as a sign of man's struggle to match the power of nature. Many admire the bravery and perseverance of explorers who have struggled single-mindedly through great hardship and physical deprivation to achieve their aim. Their success is seen as a reminder to the world that it is possible to overcome the most challenging and difficult problems.

In the play *Burning Everest* when things are at their worst for him, Jim – the main character – daydreams about conquering Everest, like Mallory. His imaginary expedition symbolises his own struggle to overcome the difficulties in his life.

LIST OF CHARACTERS

JIM *Eanna*
TONY *Shane*
SHARON *Charmagne*
MIRANDA *Elaine*
MR WELLAND *Jeoffrey*
MRS WELLAND *Joanne*
MATT *Darren*
STUBBY *Jonathan*
MR COOPER
MR PRYME *Andrew*
MRS PRYME *Sarah*
SCHOOL HEAD *Paul*
PETER

ACT ONE

ACT ONE SCENE ONE

The stage is in darkness. There is a low wind that builds to a gale as the stage is suddenly revealed in as much white light as possible. There should be white or reflective drapes to produce a dazzling effect.
The wind abates slightly as Jim McLindon walks on. He is dressed in a faded T-shirt and torn jeans. He is aware of the wind and the cold but is more in awe of what he sees around him. He runs to the front of the stage and points behind him.

Jim Chomolungma! That's it. There, you see? Chomolungma. The highest place on earth. Never been climbed; it's never been climbed. Chomolungma . . . Oh, there is another name for it – Everest, Mount Everest, but it had a name long before the British came here. The Tibetans call it Goddess Mother of the World. Chomolungma. That's a name. That's a name for a mountain; for the mountain. She's beautiful – not 'beautiful' like a nice, sunny day in spring though. It's beauty like a drug; terrifying, taking you over, till your whole life is set on climbing her, being the first to reach the summit. You'd tear your lungs out; scramble and sweat over the frozen rock – you'd take your life in your hands and hang by a rope over a thousand feet of nothing, to stand on that peak – to be on top of the world. I should know. I've tried twice. Been beaten back by exhaustion, by the lack of air near the top. But this time I'll get there; I won't come down defeated.

For the first time Jim notices the cold and stamps to get warm.

Couldn't have had a worse day to set up base camp though; still twelve miles from the foot of the mountain. But what does the cold matter? Pitching tents, breaking open the crates and testing the oxygen equipment's going to keep us busy here. We'll soon warm up.

Jim looks for a good spot to pitch a tent. He looks out to the audience, speaking from the front of the stage.

I'm George by the way.

He calls out off stage.

Come on Irvine, come on Odell; can't you make those porters get a shift on? We don't want to lose time.

He faces the audience.

George Leigh Mallory. Perhaps you've heard of me. I've been getting mentioned too often in the papers for my liking. *The Times* kept a close eye on the '21 and '22 expeditions and they're watching this one hard as well. Everyone's convinced the 1924 expedition's the one that's finally going to crack it; get to the top. And we will. I'm going to be the first man ever to climb Everest. The first ever to climb Chomolungma – Goddess Mother of the World.

The white light fades in and out as we hear Sharon, Jim's mum from off stage.

Sharon   Jim, I can't look after you, I can't.

Jim falters at the front of the stage.

Jim   I'll climb it. I will climb it.

Sharon   I'm sorry Jim. You'll be better off without me.

There is a last blast of wind as Jim runs to the side of the stage. The drapes are flown out to reveal, on one side, the Welland's kitchen and on the other, a back gate and the back entrance of a fast food takeaway shop with a couple of dustbins outside and a neutral space downstage. Only the front of the stage is lit as Tony, Jim's social worker crosses towards Jim, who is outside a children's home.

Tony   Jim! I've been looking all over for you.

Jim   What?

Tony   Daydreaming again? Let me guess. About Everest, right?

Jim   What do you want?

Tony   You should be getting yourself ready. I'm picking you up this afternoon to take you to your new foster-parents, remember? Mr and Mrs Welland.

Jim groans.

Jim   Oh no.

Tony   They're looking forward to you coming to live with them. And you'll be seeing their daughter Miranda for the first time.

Jim   I don't want to. I want to go and live back with my mum.

Tony   Let's not go over all that again Jim. You know your mum's not able to look after you any more.

Jim   Why not? There's nothing wrong with her, is there?

Tony   Just make sure you're ready for two o'clock when I pick you up. You have got your bags packed, haven't you?

Jim   No.

Tony	Well go in and pack them.
Jim	I can't. Not now. I'm going out.
Tony	Where?
Jim	Just out.
	Jim goes off. Tony calls after him.
Tony	Make sure you're ready for two o'clock.

Questions & Assignments — ACT ONE SCENE ONE

1 What do we learn about Mt Everest in this scene?
2 What is Jim's attitude to it?
3 What impression do you form of Jim from Scene One?
4 What do we learn about George Mallory?
5 What elements of the plot are introduced in Scene One?
6 Do you think the writer's instructions for sound effects in the stage directions add to the atmosphere? What impression do you form of Jim from the way he dresses?

ACT ONE SCENE TWO

The lights come up on the Welland's kitchen and Miranda enters, carrying a shopping bag which she dumps on the table. She starts emptying the shopping onto the table, but stops when she brings out a cereal packet with a 'free gift inside' offer emblazoned over it. She reads.

Miranda 'Glow in the Dark Eyes'. Big deal. That's for kids.
She continues emptying the shopping, but is drawn back to the packet. She tries to open it discreetly and looks unsuccessfully in it for the free gift. She gets a cereal bowl and pours some out. She still can't find the gift. Inspired, she gets a large bowl from the shelves and pours out the whole packet. She picks out the 'horror eyes' and puts them on.
I'm Tharg from the planet Warg.
She bangs into the table and removes the eyes.
What a load of rubbish.
We hear Mr and Mrs Welland approaching.

Mr Welland All I'm saying is, it's going to be a bit of an upheaval.
Mrs Welland Alan, we've been through all of this.
Miranda dashes to the large bowl and tries to pour the cereal back in the box, stopping as her parents enter. They put the shopping away during the following. Mrs Welland notices the large bowl of cereal.
I didn't realise you were that hungry, Miri.
Mr Welland You're sure you're still happy about having a foster-brother, Miranda?
Miranda Yeah, I suppose.
Mr Welland You suppose? It's because you've always been going on about wanting a brother.
Miranda looks embarrassed.

Miranda	Dad.
Mr Welland	'I want a brother. Why can't I have a baby brother?'
Mrs Welland	Alan, it's a bit late to start worrying now.
Mr Welland	I'm worried. Jim McLindon's going to be a handful.
Miranda	What's wrong with him?
Mrs Welland	Nothing. Your father's just fussing as usual.
Mr Welland	He's made his mum's life hell, hasn't he?
Mrs Welland	Only since his grandmother died. She was the one who really looked after him.
Mr Welland	His last school said he was fighting all the time and when he's not fighting, he wanders round in some stupid daydream. What was it? Canoeing.
Miranda	Mountaineering.
Mrs Welland	His social worker said his great grandad had something to do with climbing Everest or something, didn't he?
	Miranda points to the shopping bag.
Miranda	I got a book out of the library on it.
Mr Welland	So we're going to have two of you nuts about it now? Great.
	He looks at the cereal.
	Miranda, what have you been doing?
Miranda	Packet was torn.
Mrs Welland	Can both of you please get out of the kitchen and let me get lunch ready? We don't want the poor lad thinking he's come into a madhouse.
Mr Welland	That's if he doesn't turn it into one.
Mrs Welland	I'm sure Jim isn't going to be that hard to handle, dear.

Questions & Assignments — ACT ONE SCENE TWO

1 What do you learn about a) Miranda; b) Mr Welland; c) Mrs Welland?
2 Explain each character's attitude to the impending arrival of Jim.

ACT ONE SCENE THREE

Lights up on the back alley. Matt, the fast food takeaway owner, is standing outside his shop holding Jim by the collar. Jim is struggling like mad.

Jim	Get off! Get off, will you!
	He tries to kick Matt.
Matt	Watch it or I'll get Samson out here. Do you remember my dog Samson?
Jim	This alley's public property.
Matt	But the back of my takeaway isn't, especially when you've been spitting on the windows.
Jim	That wasn't me.
Matt	I don't want you hanging round. That's all. All right?
	He releases Jim.

Spectrum 1

Jim I'm only waiting for my mum to come home.
He points to the back gate.
That's our house.

Matt I know where she lives and I know for a fact she doesn't want you hanging round here either. Best thing your mum ever did, getting rid of you, you little toerag.
Stubby, Jim's friend who has a prosthetic boot, comes on and watches without being noticed

Jim She didn't get rid of me. She was just a bit upset if you must know. But I'm coming back now.

Matt Dream on kid. Your mum doesn't want you; no one wants you round here.
He starts to go back into the shop.
If I can still see you out here in two minutes, I'm going to set Samson onto you. Understand?
Matt goes back into the shop. Jim lifts one of the bins and is about to tip it out when Stubby comes forward.

Stubby Jim, don't! Samson'll have your leg off.

Jim Hiya Stubbs.
He lowers the bin.
How'ya doing?

Stubby Come over here, where he can't see you . . . I hate that dog. I put superglue all over a bone for it once.

Jim Nutter.

Stubby Dog didn't get near it. Bone stuck to my hand and Mum had to take me to casualty.
Jim indicates Matt.

Jim	I'd like to put him in casualty. I told Mum not to buy takeaways off him but she's always hanging round there.
Stubby	What're you doing here anyway? I thought they'd put you in a home.
Jim	I didn't like it, so I've come back.
Stubby	Your mum taken you in again?
Jim	Not yet, but she's going to.
Stubby	She's a rotten mum to throw you out in the first place.
	Jim grabs hold of Stubby. He is furious.
Jim	Watch it!
Stubby	Give over! Get off!
Jim	I'll do you.
Stubby	All right, get off.
	Jim lets go.
Stubby	I was only saying.
Jim	Mum's all right. She was upset, that's all. 'Cos of Gran dying. And I was upset 'cos of Gran, so we didn't get on for a bit. But we'll be all right now. The minute she listens to me, we'll be all right again.
Stubby	I hope so. It was good you living here. There's no one to hang round with any more.
Jim	What about Mickey and Deano?
Stubby	Won't let me join in anything. They call me 'Spaz' and 'Plastic Man'.
	He lifts his prosthetic boot in explanation.
Jim	They never used to.
Stubby	'Cos you were here to stick up for me.
Jim	You gotta learn to stick up for yourself Stubbs.
Stubby	I know. But I wouldn't mind it if you still lived round here.
	Jim's mum comes down the alley. She pretends not to see Jim and hurries off through her back gate. Jim sees her and chases after her.
Jim	Mum! Mum! It's me. Don't shut the gate.
	He bangs hard on the gate.
Jim	Mum! I want to talk to you.
	Jim comes away from the gate and goes to the bins. He picks up two bin-lids and speaks to Stubby.
	She couldn't hear me.
	Jim takes the bin-lids to the back gate and starts banging them together.
	Mum! It's me, Jim!
Stubby	Give up, will you.
Jim	Come on, Mum!
	He bangs the lids again. Matt comes on.
Matt	You don't take telling, do you?
	He calls.
	Samson!
	There is a ferocious growl. Jim runs downstage. Matt and Stubby go off.

Spectrum 1

Points to Note

SYMPATHY TOWARDS CHARACTERS

Good dramatic characters should arouse strong feelings in us. For instance, although Jim shows a number of flaws in his character, we are still sympathetic towards him because his mother has abandoned him and he is very upset by her rejection. Matt on the other hand arouses our dislike because he is unnecessarily cruel to Jim and he is an adult who could be kinder in his treatment of the young boy.

Questions & Assignments — ACT ONE SCENE THREE

1. Why is Matt angry with Jim?
2. What impression do you form of Matt? Do you think he is a kind man? Explain.
3. Why does Jim argue with Stubby?
4. Does Jim show any likeable qualities in Scene Three?
5. How does the writer arouse our sympathy towards Jim?

ACT ONE SCENE FOUR

We hear the sound of a light wind. Jim is picked out in a white spotlight. He stops running and pants for a few moments. When he looks up, he is happy but preoccupied. He speaks from the front of the stage.

Jim It's not as easy as you think. We've hired fifty-five Tibetan porters to get our gear to the foot of Chomolungma. We've got heaps of stuff. Tents, sleeping-bags, ice-axes and these bottles of oxygen. It's not like taking a stroll up your nearest hill. Getting to the top is a regular job of work. The real journey starts from here. Camp Three. We've got three more camps to make higher up the mountain before we set out for the top. Each camp has to be properly prepared. Tents set up. Food put in place. Don't mention food. Horrible stuff. Tins of sardines. Macaroni. Pemmican. Pemmican's dried meat and fat stuck together. Horrible. But if it keeps you going, you'll eat anything. I'm not going to stop till I'm up there. On top of Chomolungma.

Questions & Assignments — ACT ONE SCENE FOUR

1. From what you have learned of Jim so far, why do you think he daydreams about climbing Mt Everest?
2. What evidence is there that he knows a great deal about climbing the world's highest mountain?

Burning Everest

ACT ONE SCENE FIVE

Tony speaks from offstage.
Tony Come on Jim.
We lose the spotlight and the wind as Tony enters with Jim's bag.
Where've you been? I've had to pack everything for you. We're due at the Wellands.
Jim looks in his bag.
Jim Where's my poster?
Tony Come on, we're running late.
Jim Where've you put it?
Tony They're expecting us at two.
Jim I'm not going without the poster.
Tony looks resigned to waiting.
Tony It's still up on the wall.
Jim goes off to collect it.
I'd been hoping you'd forget about it.

Questions & Assignments — ACT ONE SCENE FIVE

1 Jim insists on bringing a poster. From the evidence of the play so far, what do you think the poster depicts?

ACT ONE SCENE SIX

Tony follows Jim off as the lights come up on the Wellands. Mrs Welland is mixing a salad, while Miranda is engrossed in her book at the table.
Mrs Welland Is it good?
Miranda grunts.
Mrs Welland Does it mention, who is it? Mallory. The one Jim's meant to be interested in.
Miranda grunts again.
At least you'll have something to talk about.
Mr Welland enters, slightly flustered
Mr Welland They're here. Tony's parking outside.
He starts trying to tidy the table.
Mrs Welland Relax will you, Alan?
The doorbell sounds. Mr Welland goes off to answer it. Miranda hides the book. Mrs Welland crosses her fingers.
Here goes.
Jim enters, clutching a rolled-up poster. Tony and Mr Welland follow. Jim is trying to look his most yobbish and succeeds in unnerving the Wellands somewhat. He takes a disapproving look round the room. Mrs Welland goes over to him.

Spectrum 1

	Hello Jim.
	Jim ignores her. Tony looks disapproving
Tony	Jim.
	Jim responds in a lifeless way.
Jim	Hello.
	Mr Welland goes to take the poster.
Mr Welland	Shall I take that?
	Jim defends the poster.
Mrs Welland	You're just in time for lunch. You too. Tony
Jim	I don't like it here.
Tony	Give it a chance will you?
	He turns to Mrs Welland
	Thanks.
	Tony sits down. Jim follows suit as do Miranda and Mr Welland. Jim puts his poster by the table.
Mr Welland	Introduce yourself, Miranda.
Miranda	Hello Jim.
	Jim grunts something
Tony	I think this is going to take everyone a bit of time.
Mrs Welland	Of course.
	Mrs Welland puts a large bowl of food in the middle of the table.
	I bet you're starving Jim.
	Jim looks suspiciously at the bowl.
Jim	No.
Mrs Welland	Well, I hope you don't mind us eating.
	She starts serving up.
Mr Welland	It's couscous. Sort of an African meal. It's made from . . . what's it made from?
Mrs Welland	Semolina. Have you had it before, Jim?
Jim	No.
Mrs Welland	Oh.
Jim	But my hamster did.
Mrs Welland	Oh?
Jim	Then it died.
Mr Welland	We weren't sure what you'd like to eat. We're vegetarian
	Jim looks appalled
Jim	What?
Miranda	We don't eat meat.
Tony	I did tell you.
Jim	No beefburgers, no sausages, no bacon?
Mrs Welland	Of course, you'll be able to eat whatever you want.
	Jim stands up.
Jim	Beam me up, Scotty.
Tony	Jim, we've talked about this. You're not going to feel settled straightaway. It's just as strange for the Wellands, remember. You've got to get used to each other.
Jim	I don't want to get used. I don't want to be here.

Jim walks away from the table and looks out of the window.

Mr Welland We've managed to get you into Miranda's school. It's a very good one.
Jim I liked my old school.
Tony You were hardly ever there.
Jim I don't want another school.
Mrs Welland You might find you like it. Miranda does.
Miranda It's all right.
Jim Your garden's crap.
Mr Welland Nobody's perfect, Jim.

Jim turns to Tony.

Jim Can I go back to the home?
Tony You've made your mind up you're not going to like it here, haven't you?
Jim It's not me. It's this place. It's horrible.
Tony It's not your mum's home I know. But if you give it a chance, you'll start to enjoy yourself.
Jim No I won't. I won't ever enjoy it here. I hate it already.

Tony gets up and goes over to Jim.

Tony Shall we see how it goes for a week? Are you prepared to try and get along with the Wellands for a few days?
Mrs Welland We really are glad to have you here. Jim.

Jim shrugs his shoulders.

Tony It'll give you a chance to find your feet.
Jim When am I going to see Mum again?
Tony I'll try and fix something up.
Jim I want to see her. You're my social worker. You're meant to sort that out. I want to see her.
Tony I'll do what I can. She's got to want to see you as well, you know.
Jim Sort it out.

Tony moves away from Jim.

Tony I've got to make a move. That was delicious, Mrs Welland. Are you sure you'll be . . .
Mrs Welland We'll be fine.
Mr Welland We'll see you out.
Tony Give it a chance, eh Jim?

Jim ignores him. Tony, Mr and Mrs Welland go out. Jim stands looking out of the window. Miranda watches him.

Miranda There's a football team at school, if you're any good at football.
No response from Jim.
Most of the teachers are mad, but the kids are all right. They're a good laugh, some of them. What was your old school like?
Still no response.
I bet you're missing your mum. I don't blame you. I'd miss mine.
Still no response. Miranda gets up and takes the horror eyes out of a pocket.
I wish you wouldn't talk so much. You're making the eyes pop out of my head.
She puts the eyes on and walks towards Jim. She mimics him.

Spectrum 1

	I hate it already. I'm not going to like it. I'm never going to like it.
	Jim responds angrily.
Jim	Are you taking the mickey?
	Jim turns round and is taken aback by Miranda's appearance. He half laughs in spite of himself. Miranda answers defiantly.
Miranda	Yes, I am.
	She takes off the horror eyes and goes back to the table.
	What's your poster of?
	Jim goes over to it.
Jim	Leave it alone.
Miranda	All right. I only wanted to look. What is it?
Jim	Chomolungma.
Miranda	What?
	Jim unrolls it.
Jim	Mount Everest, stupid. It's really called Chomolungma.
Miranda	It'd look nice on the cupboard. There's some sticky stuff still on the back.
	She goes to put up the poster.
Jim	I'll do it.
	Jim puts the poster up.
Miranda	It's nice.
Jim	Mum bought it me.
Miranda	What's she like, your mum? I bet she's nice.
Jim	She's all right.
Miranda	Why doesn't she want you?
Jim	I dunno.
Miranda	It's not very nice of her.
	Jim is angry.
Jim	She's all right.
Miranda	She might take you back one day.
Jim	She will do. Soon as I talk to her, she'll take me back and I'll be out of this place. Away from you and your lousy parents.
Miranda	Charming.
Jim	I don't want to be here.
Miranda	How do you think I feel? I've got to put up with you here and at school.
Jim	I'm not going near you at school.
Miranda	We're in the same class.

Points to Note — ACT ONE SCENE SIX

CONFLICT

Conflict is an important element of any play. Sometimes there is conflict between characters or a character is in conflict with himself. Conflict adds tension and excitement.

Questions & Assignments

1 Describe Jim's behaviour when he first arrives in the Wellands. Do you think his behaviour is understandable?
2 Do you find any of Jim's comments in Scene Six funny? Explain.
3 Jim states that the Welland home is horrible. From the evidence so far, what is your opinion of it?
4 What do we learn about Tony the social worker?
5 How does Miranda treat Jim? Explain your answer with reference to the scene.
6 Read back over Scene Six once more. It contains a number of different points of conflict. What are they? (e.g. Jim and Miranda). Explain what is the cause of the conflict. Is the conflict resolved (ended) in this scene? If not, how do you think the conflict might be resolved later on in the play?

Act One Scene Seven

Mrs Pryme, a teacher at St Xavier's, comes on. We are in the playground of the Comprehensive. She looks at her watch and takes out a whistle, ready to blow. Before she can do so, another teacher, Mr Cooper hurries on.

Mr Cooper   Hang on, Janice. Give me a minute to get to class and get some notes up on the board.
Mrs Pryme   As well prepared as ever, Harry?
Mr Cooper   Don't you start. I've just had the Head bending my ear because I can't stay for the staff meeting this evening.
Mrs Pryme   You're not trying to wriggle out of it, are you?
Mr Cooper   I've got to get my car back from the garage and it closes at five.
Mrs Pryme   I bet Mr Bryant loved that.
Mr Cooper mimics the Head.
Mr Cooper   'You have to try and organise your life appropriately, Mr Cooper. The rest of the staff manage to organise things so they can attend staff meetings.'
Mrs Pryme   A bit of a pain?
Mr Cooper   'A bit of a pain' is putting it mildly.
Mr Bryant, the Headmaster, comes on behind Mr Cooper. Mrs Pryme tries to signal this unsuccessfully.
He's the most pompous, over-opinionated, windbag of a . . . ow!
Mrs Pryme has kicked him, as Mr Bryant draws level
Head   We're running a little late, aren't we, Mrs Pryme? I make it one minute past nine.
Mrs Pryme   I'm getting them in now.
Mrs Pryme blows the whistle as Mr Cooper slinks off.
Come on now, quickly, go straight in, straight in. Come on now.
Mrs Pryme goes off. The Head waits for a moment at the edge of the playground. Miranda hurries on at the opposite side.

Miranda	Hurry up, Jim. Hurry up!
	Jim comes on in no particular rush.
Head	You're late, Miranda.
Miranda	Yes, Sir, sorry Sir.
Head	Why's that?
Miranda	I was showing Jim the way to school.
Head	So you're Jim McLindon?
Jim	Yes.
Head	Yes, Sir.
Jim	Sir.
Head	Go in, Miranda.
	Miranda goes off
	I was just looking through the reports on you from your last school, Jim. They don't make very impressive reading, do they?
Jim	Don't they, Sir?
Head	No, they don't. Not by a long chalk. You have a reputation for being a truant; or turning up late when you could be bothered to come.
Jim	That was only after my gran . . .
Head	I didn't ask you to say anything. If I want you to speak, I'll let you know. Now let's get something straight on your first day here, McLindon. This school sets itself very high standards. We're top of just about every performance table in the district and we want to keep it that way. So we expect very high standards from our pupils as well and come down hard on those who don't like to conform. Do I make myself clear?
	Jim mumbles.
Jim	Sir.
Head	Pardon?
Jim	Yes, Sir.
Head	I hope so, McLindon. For your sake. Now where are you supposed to be?
Jim	I don't know, Sir.
Head	Go through to the office.
	He indicates offstage.

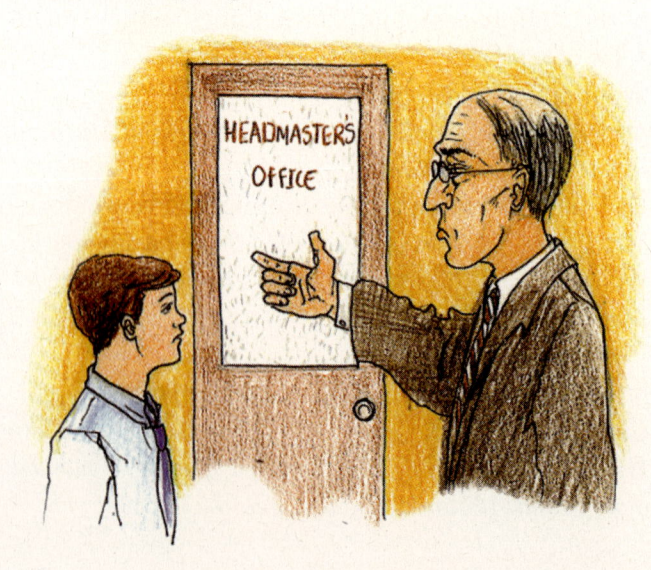

	They'll tell you. And I hope I don't have to speak to you again.
	The Head goes off. Jim is left alone onstage. The lights start to go to white and a wind begins, stopping abruptly as Miranda comes back on.
Miranda	Come on. We've got Personal Development.
Jim	What?
Miranda	Personal Development with Mrs Pryme. She kills you if you're late.
	Jim and Miranda go off as Mrs Pryme comes on followed by Peter, a pupil, carrying chairs, which he puts out. Miranda and Jim hurry on.
Mrs Pryme	Good morning, Three G . . . You must be James McLindon?
Jim	Jim.
Mrs Pryme	Jim. It's nice to have you in the class, Jim.
	Jim doesn't react. Mrs Pryme addresses the whole class.
	Now, I hope you've all had a think about your personal ambitions over the weekend, as I asked you to. Peter, what about you? Have you thought about your future?
Peter	Yes, Miss.
Mrs Pryme	What are your hopes?
Peter	Well, Miss, I intend staying on in the sixth form to take Economics, Geography and English 'A' Level. I'm going to work very hard at them, so I expect to go on to university; hopefully Oxford or Cambridge, though I mustn't be too choosy. At University, I'll study Politics, Philosophy and Economics.
Mrs Pryme	Very good.
	Peter continues hurriedly.
Peter	And while I'm there, I hope to meet a nice girl to marry, because I'm going to need a good wife who'll help me in my chosen career as a politician.
	Jim puts his fingers down his throat.
Mrs Pryme	Jim?
Jim	No, Miss.
	Peter continues as though nothing can stop him.
Peter	And I hope to become a member of the Cabinet and have a Persian cat, a Labrador and three children or some goldfish.
Mrs Pryme	That was very good, Peter. What about you, Miranda?
Miranda	I'm not sure what I want to do, Miss, but I think I want to work with children.
Mrs Pryme	Would you like to be a teacher?
Miranda	Perhaps. Or a social worker. I'd like to help children with problems no one else can help.
	Jim mimes being violently ill.
Mrs Pryme	That's a very interesting idea to have, Miranda, but it doesn't seem to meet with Jim's approval. Tell us, what are your plans for the future, Jim?
Jim	I haven't got any.
Mrs Pryme	Don't you ever think about what you're going to be in a few years' time?
Jim	A layabout.
	Peter sniggers.
Mrs Pryme	That's not much of an ambition, is it? I think that's what some people have

	told you you'll be and you've believed them. Isn't there someone in your family who does something you'd like to do? Your dad, or an uncle or someone?
Jim	I don't know who my dad was. I expect he was a layabout as well.
Peter	You don't know who your dad was!
Mrs Pryme	And there's no one you admire? No one you'd like to be like?
Jim	No.
Miranda	Miss, one of Jim's relatives climbed up Everest.
Jim	No, he didn't.
Miranda	That's what Tony said.
Jim	My great grandad was a steward on the boat that took George Mallory to India on his way to Everest, if you must know.
Mrs Pryme	Really?
Jim	Yeah. He used to serve Mallory his meals and all that.
Mrs Pryme	That's fascinating. Does anyone know who George Mallory was. Peter?
Peter	No, Miss.
Mrs Pryme	He was a very famous mountaineer. Some people say he was the first man to climb Everest, but he disappeared before he came down, so no one knows if he really got to the top or not. Are there any souvenirs in the family of all this? Any photos?
Jim	There's a couple of letters he sent my great grandma.
Peter	Liar.
Jim	Shut up!
Mrs Pryme	Peter, don't be so rude.
Peter	I bet he's just making it up to impress you, Miss.
Jim	Shut your face.
Mrs Pryme	Jim, don't take any notice. What did your great grandfather say in his letter?
Jim	Nothing much. He couldn't write very well. He just said he was sure Mallory'd make it to the top. He could stand all the cold and climbing 'cos he was hard as rock himself
Mrs Pryme	So would you like to work as a steward one day, Jim?
Jim	No. I want to climb Everest.
Peter	Miss, when I'm Prime Minister I'm going to make illegal to tell lies.
	Jim gives Peter a filthy look. The lesson bell goes. Mrs Pryme and the children go off

Questions & Assignments   ACT ONE SCENE SEVEN

1 Compare the characters of Mrs Pryme and the Head. Which character, if any, is more likeable? Why?
2 What is the Head's attitude to Jim? Do you think his treatment of the young boy is fair? Explain.
3 How do you think Jim might feel going into a new class for the first time? Write a paragraph where he outlines his thoughts and feelings.
4 What impression do you form of Peter?

ACT ONE SCENE EIGHT

Sharon McLindon's home. Her hairdressing equipment is out, ready to be packed into carrying cases. Sharon enters, followed by Tony. Sharon carries on preparing to go out.

Tony   Thanks for agreeing to see me, Mrs McLindon.
Sharon   It's all right.
Tony   I can see you're busy.
Sharon   I'm giving an old lady a rinse and perm in fifteen minutes.
Tony   If you'd rather I came back another time . .
Sharon   You've got something to say, haven't you? So say it.
Tony   Jim's keen to see you, Mrs McLindon.
Sharon just carries on.
He really does want to see you.
Sharon   I'd love to see him, but it's too early, isn't it? He hasn't had time to settle in with the . . . who did you say they were?
Tony   The Wellands.
Sharon   He's got to get used to them. If he saw me now, he'd think there was a chance of coming back.
Tony   I think it's important you stay in touch with him.
Sharon stops packing.
Sharon   I know it's important! Don't talk to me like I'm thick or something . . .
Tony   I'm sorry if . . .
Sharon   Jim's my son. I know. My responsibility. But I had him too young. I was sixteen. What sort of life do you think I've had since then? Have you thought about that?
Tony   No one's trying to accuse you of anything, Mrs McLindon.
Sharon   Well it feels like you are. But you're not going to make me feel guilty. Because I don't. I'm doing the right thing. I'm making a life for myself at last.
Tony   Perhaps you could phone him. He'd appreciate a phone call.
Sharon   It'd upset him.
Tony   I don't think so . . .
Sharon   Then it'd upset me. I've had to cope with my mother dying. It's not easy setting up this business and there's . . . other things in my life.
Tony   I know. I understand . . . All the same, how would it be if I picked you up on Saturday morning? Took you round to the Wellands for an hour, just to talk?
Sharon   You don't give up, do you?
Tony   Will you at least think about it? For Jim's sake?
Sharon   I've got to go out.
Tony   I'll give you a ring later in the week.

Spectrum 1

Questions & Assignments — ACT ONE SCENE EIGHT

1 What do we learn about Sharon? What is her attitude to her son?
2 What reasons does she give for not wanting to see her son?
3 Do you think Tony is more sympathetic towards Sharon or towards Jim? Explain.

ACT ONE SCENE NINE

Lights up on Mr Cooper who is dressed in an outrageous shellsuit and carrying a cassette recorder, which he switches on. He starts performing some eurythmics to new age music. He looks ridiculous.
Peter, one of the pupils, dressed expensively, comes on and joins in enthusiastically. Miranda, also well presented, comes on and is about to join in, when Jim enters. He is dressed in a heavy metal T-shirt and cut-off jeans. He looks in amazement.

Jim Bloody'ell.
He goes up to Miranda.
What's all this?
Miranda Eurythmics. Movement to music.
Jim Dancing like the fairies, more like.
Mr Cooper No talking. Come round here and join in.
Mr Cooper looks at Jim's clothes distastefully. He switches off the music and tugs at the T-shirt.
What do you call this, James?
Jim We call it a T-shirt on my planet, Sir.
Mr Cooper Don't try and be insolent . . . Well, boys and girls, it seems we've had a trendsetter join the school. All these years I've asked pupils to turn up in clean smart sports clothes, it seems I've been mistaken. You should've been coming in dirty old jeans with the legs cut off.
Peter sniggers dutifully.
Jim No one said anything at my last school.
Mr Cooper No, I don't imagine they did. But you're at St Xavier's now and we do things differently here. I'm sure your mother would be horrified to know that you were the scruffiest boy in the class, wouldn't she?
Miranda Sir . . .
Mr Cooper Be quiet, Miranda. I take it your mother does take an interest in the way you look, doesn't she, Jim? I'm sure she cares about you.
Jim kicks the cassette recorder over and runs off.
Come back here. Come back at once, McLindon!
Miranda That's not fair, Sir. Jim's staying with us at the moment and my mum couldn't buy him anything till she knew his size.
Mr Cooper Were you asked to speak, Miranda Welland?
Miranda No, Sir.
Mr Cooper Then don't. I'll let the Head know about Master McLindon's behaviour later. In the meantime, let's all relax and flow in harmony to the music.

Questions & Assignments   ACT ONE SCENE NINE

1 Read the stage instructions at the beginning of Scene Nine. Do you think they might be amusing to watch on stage? Explain.
2 Describe Mr Cooper's treatment of his new pupil.
3 From the evidence of the play so far, does Jim make life unnecessarily difficult for himself? Explain. (Insulting remarks, sarcastic comments, lack of interest in others . . .) Do we sympathise with his behaviour? Explain.

ACT ONE SCENE TEN

Lights come up on the Welland's kitchen.
Mr Welland is working on some papers at the table. Mrs Welland comes in with a large sports shop carrier bag.

Mrs Welland	Darling, what do you think of these?
	She takes a selection of sports clothes out of the bag.
Mr Welland	Very nice.
Mrs Welland	I hope Jim likes them. And I've bought a mountain of beefburgers
Mr Welland	Anything to cheer him up. He had a face like a dead dolphin going off to school this morning.
Mrs Welland	Poor lad.
Mr Welland	Miserable little so and so.
	Mrs Welland looks disapproving
Mrs Welland	Alan.
Mr Welland	He could make some effort, couldn't he?
	Miranda enters with school bag.
Mrs Welland	Miri, look at these. They're for Jim.
	She holds up the sports clothes.
Miranda	Not bad. It's a pity he didn't have them today. Mr Cooper really showed him up for not having the right stuff and then the Head gave him a telling off after school.

Mrs Welland	That's not fair.
Miranda	The Head's never fair.
Mr Welland	Where's Jim now?
Miranda	He went straight upstairs. He's in a bit of a mood. It was a real telling off.
	Mrs Welland goes to the door.
Mrs Welland	Jim, can you come down a moment?
	She comes back into the kitchen and picks up the sports clothes.
	He'll look as smart as Linford Christie.
Miranda	Linford Lunchbox.
Mr Welland	Miri.
	Jim comes in.
Mrs Welland	Look at these, love. What do you think?
	Jim shrugs.
Mr Welland	These cost a bit, you know.
Mrs Welland	I'm sorry you didn't have them for today. Miranda said you got into a bit of bother about it.
Jim	Nothing I couldn't handle.
Mr Welland	I hope you didn't use that tone with the Headmaster.
Mrs Welland	Do you want to go and try them on?
Jim	Not especially.
Mrs Welland	I'll need to get them changed if they don't fit. It'd only take you a minute.
Jim	I don't want to.
Mr Welland	Jim, do as you're told!
	With a great sigh, Jim takes the clothes and goes upstairs.
Mrs Welland	There was no need to lose your temper with him.
Mr Welland	He seems to think everyone exists to run after him. Did I tell you his social worker was on the phone earlier?
Mrs Welland	No.
Mr Welland	He's finally persuaded Jim's mum to come round and see him.
Mrs Welland	That's good.
Miranda	I wonder what she's like.
Mr Welland	We'll find out on Saturday. It's probably best if I take you ice-skating then to give them a bit of privacy.
Miranda	Oh! I wanted to see what she looks like.
	Mrs Welland speaks to Miranda.
Mrs Welland	Jim's all right, isn't he?
Miranda	He's OK.
Mr Welland	As long as you don't start picking up his bad habits.
Miranda	What would you be like, Dad, if you were in a strange house and at a strange school?
Mrs Welland	Exactly. He's just frightened.
Mr Welland	I hope so. Because I'm beginning to wonder if it was such a good idea having him come here after all.
Mrs Welland	It'll just take time.
	Jim comes in with the clothes in the bag.
Mrs Welland	Well?

Jim	They didn't fit.
Mrs Welland	Never mind. We can get them changed.
Jim	So I tried to make them fit. With the scissors.
	He takes the clothes out. He's deliberately shredded them and they hang in tatters.
Mr Welland	How dare you!
Mrs Welland	Alan . . .
Miranda	What did you do that for?
Mr Welland	Have you any idea how much they cost?
Mrs Welland	Alan!
	She speaks deliberately.
	We can always buy you some more clothes, Jim.
Jim	Then you're going to need to buy a lot. I'm good with scissors.

Questions & Assignments — ACT ONE SCENE TEN

1 What evidence is there in Scene Ten that Mrs Welland is doing her best for her new foster son?
2 Are you surprised by Jim's reaction to her kindness? Why do you think he reacts in such a hurtful way? Who do you sympathise with most – Mrs Welland or Jim? Explain.
3 Where does Mr Welland plan to take his daughter on Saturday?
4 How do Mr and Mrs Welland's attitudes to Jim differ?

ACT ONE SCENE ELEVEN

Tony and Sharon enter. They're on the street outside the Wellands'. Sharon is admiring the outside of the house.

Sharon	It's beautiful.
Tony	Quite nice.
Sharon	No, it's beautiful. It's a really beautiful house.
Tony	We ought to go in. We're rather late as it is.
Sharon	He's never lived anywhere like this. Look, I shouldn't 've come. I'll only show him up.
Tony	No, you won't, Mrs McLindon. He'll be really pleased to see you.
Sharon	I shouldn't've listened to you.
Tony	He's expecting you now. Let's go in.
Sharon	I want you there all the time. Don't leave me alone with him.

Questions & Assignments — ACT ONE SCENE ELEVEN

1 What, in your opinion, is the purpose of this scene?
2 What is Sharon's attitude to the Welland's home?

Act One Scene Twelve

Lights up on the Wellands' kitchen. Jim's brushing his hair. He's very nervous. The doorbell goes. Jim puts the brush away. He tries to find a position to stay in. Mrs Welland comes into the room.

Mrs Welland Visitors.
She shows Sharon and Tony in, then withdraws.
Jim You're late.
Tony Unavoidable.
There is a slight pause.
Sharon Hello, Jim.
Jim moves towards his mum. She ignores this and sits down at the table. Tony finds a corner.
How've you been?
Jim All right.
Sharon What's your new school like?
Jim All right, I suppose.
Sharon looks round the kitchen.
Sharon Nice here.
Jim It's OK.
Sharon It's more than OK. It's nice. Real nice.
Jim Mum.
Sharon You'll love it here, I bet.
Jim Mum.
Sharon It's much better than my tatty old dump, isn't it?
Jim Can I come home?
Sharon sighs.
Sharon No, Jim.
Jim Go on, Mum. I'll be good.
Sharon No.
Jim Why not?
Sharon We'd drive each other mad.
Jim We wouldn't.
Sharon You drove me mad after Gran died. I couldn't handle it.
Jim It'd be different.
Sharon speaks to Tony.
Sharon He was fighting; shoplifting, everything.
Jim I was upset.
Sharon You think I wasn't?
Jim You're my mum. I want to live with you.
Sharon speaks to Tony again.
Sharon I thought he understood he can't come back.
Tony That's not what this morning's about, Jim.
Jim speaks to Sharon.
Jim I hate it here.
Sharon Can't you find him anywhere else?

Jim	I'd hate it anywhere. I want to go home.
Tony	Your mother feels she wouldn't be able to look after you properly, Jim.
Jim	I'd look after myself.
Sharon	I'm working all hours now. The hairdressing's really taken off.
	Jim speaks to Tony.
Jim	You tell her. Mums are meant to look after their children, aren't they? That's what mums are for.
	Sharon gets up. We hear a door open offstage. She speaks to Tony.
Sharon	Why don't you get in touch with his father, if you can find him? He hasn't done anything for Jim in twelve years.
	Miranda comes bursting into the kitchen carrying a pair of iceskates.

Miranda	Whoo! I'm starving!
	We hear Mrs Welland speak from offstage.
Mrs Welland	Miri!
	Miranda sees what's happening.
Miranda	Soz. Don't mind me.
	Sharon gets ready to leave.
Jim	Don't go yet, Mum.
	Sharon speaks to Tony.
Sharon	I knew it'd be a waste of time coming round.
	She fishes in her purse and takes out a tenner.
	Look, Jim, this is for you. Buy yourself something nice.
Jim	I want to go home, Mum. I want to go home.
	Sharon stands uncertainly for a moment, then shakes her head.
Sharon	I'm sorry . . . I'm sorry.
	She puts the money on the table and hurries out, brushing past Miranda.
Jim	Mum!
	Jim stands in shock. Tony moves towards him.
Tony	Jim, I know you must feel awful.
Jim	Shut up! This is all your lousy fault!
	He dashes off

Questions & Assignments — ACT ONE SCENE TWELVE

1. Why do you think Jim is nervous at the beginning of the scene?
2. Why is there conflict in the scene between Jim and Sharon?
3. What reasons does Sharon give for not wanting to have her son at home? Are her reasons convincing? Explain.
4. Do you sympathise with Jim at the end of the scene? Give reasons.

Act One Scene Thirteen

The Himalayan winds start gusting very strongly as the neutral area is bathed in white light. Jim comes into the light and addresses the audience from the front of the stage.

Jim I never expected it to be easy. Climbing any mountain's hard, but this one, Chomolungma, is the hardest thing in the world. So I'm caught in a little tent at twenty-six thousand feet; the wind's trying to blow me clean off the mountain and the snow is gusting over in sheets. So what? I have to sit tight for another day, that's all.
He tugs at his collar and continues.
It's getting hard to breathe . . . The oxygen's thin here and it's going to get worse. When the blizzard ends and I start out again, every step's going to be a nightmare – the mountain's treacherous. You see what looks like a nice easy route and set off, crunching across the snow like a Boxing Day Walk. But there's ice under the snow and you can slip. An avalanche'll start and you're swept away, hundreds of feet in a matter of seconds. Between here and the top, death is sitting and watching – deciding whether to let me pass by, or catch hold of me for daring the impossible. To climb Chomolungma, you have to risk everything. Everything.
The wind gusts. Then we lose the white light as Jim goes off

Questions & Assignments   Act One Scene Thirteen

1 From your reading of the play so far, do you think Jim's imaginary attempt to get to the top of Everest might be related to other events in his life? Explain.
2 Would you say he has a good imagination? Give reasons.

Act One Scene Fourteen

The lights come up on the dustbins and the alley. Stubby is playing with a basketball and gives the following commentary.

Stubby And it's Jordan again. It's like the ball's tied to his hand. He's dribbling round everyone and that's with his eyes closed . . . But surely even Jordan can't score from here.
Stubby lifts a bin-lid and slam-dunks the ball in. He celebrates.
That's an incredible fifty points to Michael Jordan and they've only been playing for five minutes.
Jim comes on as Stubby takes the ball out of the bin.

Jim Stubbs!
Stubby passes the ball to Jim. They interchange a couple of passes, then Jim throws the ball close to the Takeaway window and Stubby has to make a desperate save.

Stubby	Careful!
Jim	Do him good to have his window out.
	Stubby, very deliberately, sits down with the ball. Jim comes and sits next to him.
Stubby	What're you doing here?
Jim	Nothing.
Stubby	Come to see your mum?
Jim	Seen her.
Stubby	She taking you back?
	Jim shrugs.
	I bet she'll be round here soon. She's always hanging round there these days.
	He indicates the Takeway.
Jim	I just wanted to get out. They drive me mad where I am.
Stubby	My mum's doing my head in an' all. 'Get your room tidied up. It looks like the Corporation Tip.'
Jim	They make me sick. I ripped up all these clothes they bought me and they didn't even get mad.
Stubby	What you do that for?
Jim	And there's a girl. Miranda. She's horrible.
Stubby	Yeah. Girls usually are.
Jim	It's really boring there.
Stubby	It's really boring here.
Jim	Well, let's do something.
Stubby	What?
Jim	I dunno.
Stubby	You're the one with ideas.
	Jim thinks for a moment, then grabs the basketball. He holds it up like a globe and points.
Jim	There.
Stubby	What?
Jim	Tibet. The Himalayas.

Stubby	You what?
Jim	We're going to the Himalayas to climb Mount Everest
Stubby	I promised me mam I'd be back for tea.
Jim	It's a game, you daft chissick. We could do it in the Quarry. I'll be George Mallory and you can be his best mate, Sandy Irvine.
Stubby	OK.
Jim	They both disappeared on the mountain.
Stubby	I don't want to disappear. We've got a 'Star Trek' video for tonight.
Jim	All right. You can be Odell. He got back off the mountain . . . We can pretend that big, sticky-out bit of rock is Everest . . . I've never seen anyone climb out on that. We can be the first.
Stubby	What about my leg?
Jim	What about it? If you could get up there, all the other kids'd have to shut up calling you 'Plastic Man'.
Stubby	All right, let's go.
	Miranda enters.
Miranda	Where're you off to?
Jim	What you doing here?
Miranda	I'm just here.
Jim	Well go away again.
Stubby	Who is she?
Miranda	Where're you going?
Jim	Somewhere that doesn't concern little girls.
Miranda	Oh, I am sorry. I didn't recognise you, Mr Schwarzenegger.
Stubby	Come on.
	Jim wants to make a point in front of Miranda. He speaks to Stubby.
Jim	Yeah. As soon as I've scored one past you. In there.
	Jim points to the bin. He starts showing off with the basketball, then tries dribbling round Stubby. They have a tussle which leads to Stubby crashing into the bins. Matt comes out, enraged.
Matt	What the bloody hell are you playing at?
Jim	It was an accident.

Matt	You're not wanted round here. Now clear off and take your little spastic friend with you.
	Jim is furious.
Jim	Don't call him that!
Matt	Well he is, isn't he?
Jim	Don't ever call him that.
Stubby	Let's get off.
Matt	Now move it.
Jim	I'll get you for that. For calling him that.
Matt	Oh yeah?
	He calls.
	Samson, Samson!
	A rottweiler growls offstage. Stubby grabs Jim's arm and pulls him offstage. Matt looks at Miranda.
	You don't want to hang round with him. He belongs in here . . .
	He indicates the bin.
	With the rest of the rubbish.
	Miranda goes off in the direction Jim and Stubby took. Matt goes off.

Questions & Assignments — ACT ONE SCENE FOURTEEN

1. What is Stubby doing at the start of the scene?
2. What does Jim suggest they should do to pass the time? Is Stubby enthusiastic about the plan? Why?
3. How does Jim convince Stubby to take part in the game?
4. Why does Jim threaten to get Matt?

ACT ONE SCENE FIFTEEN

The Quarry – a large structure with different levels is brought on. There are odd bits of junk by the foot of it – part of a bicycle, some tin cans, a length of rope. Jim enters, followed by Stubby.

Jim	Base camp.
Stubby	What?
Jim	We'll stop here for a bit.
Stubby	Oh good. I'm knackered.
	Stubby sinks down on the ground by the rubbish and looks through it rather absently.
Jim	We can't stop too long. The weather conditions'll be against an attempt on the summit.
Stubby	You what?
Jim	It's going to pee down in a minute. We'll have to set up some camps on the mountain. We can't get to the top all in one go. We've got to put up tents and lay in supplies part way up.

Stubby	We haven't got any tents.
Jim	Use your imagination. This is Mount Everest – a huge ferocious mountain.
Stubby	It's Bailey's Quarry, where everyone dumps everyone else's bike.
	Stubby picks up the rope and twirls it round his head.
	Yee-ha!
Jim	Stubbs! You're a genius.
Stubby	No, I'm a Capricorn. My birthday's January the eighth.
	Jim grabs the rope. Miranda enters unnoticed.
Jim	This'll be perfect. Come on.
Stubby	I'll carry on playing when I've had a rest. I'm starving. You got anything to eat?
Jim	No.
	Miranda holds out some bars of chocolate.
Miranda	Have one of these.
	Stubby takes a piece.
Stubby	Ta.
	Miranda offers one to Jim.
Miranda	Want one? You can pretend it's pemmican.
Jim	What're you doing here?
Miranda	Thought I'd take a walk.
Jim	You been following us?
	Miranda offers the chocolate to Jim again.
Miranda	Do you want one or not?
	Jim takes it.
Jim	What do you mean, I can pretend it's pemmican?
Stubby	Don't introduce me, or owt polite like that.
Miranda	I'm Miranda Welland.
Stubby	I'm Terry Redshaw. Everyone calls me Stubby.
	He speaks to Jim.
	She's not horrible.
Miranda	What?
Stubby	Not that Jim said you were.
Jim	How do you know about pemmican?
Miranda	You're climbing Everest, aren't you? That's one of the things they ate.
Jim	Yeah, but how do you know?
Miranda	I read about it in a book. About George Mallory.
Jim	You've read about him?
Miranda	Yeah.
Jim	He was brilliant. Did you know that my great grandad . . .
Miranda	Was on the boat that took Mallory to India? Yeah, I think you've told everyone in town that.
Jim	I never met anyone who's read about Mallory before.
Stubby	So they all ate chocolate and called it pemmican. Why?
Miranda	Pemmican's dried meat and fat.
Jim	It lasts for ever. That's why they take it on expeditions.
Stubby	It's very nice. Have you got any more of them pemmican bars?

Jim	Come on! If we don't hurry, a blizzard'll set in.
Stubby	Wish I'd put me vest on.
Miranda	Can I join in?
Jim	There weren't any girls on the Everest expedition.
Miranda	There weren't any thirteen-year-old boys either.
Stubby	He's Mallory, I'm Odell. Who are you going to be?
Miranda	I'll be Sandy Irvine. I'll be in charge of the oxygen masks.
Stubby	You know you have to mysteriously disappear if you're Irvine.
Jim	I wish she would.
Stubby	Let's get cracking then. Who's going up first?
Jim	Odell's got to be first. He takes supplies to the last camp before the summit so Irvine and Mallory don't have to carry so much.
Stubby	Cheers.
Jim	You wanted to be Odell. You can make a camp there.
	Jim points up to a ledge on the quarry.
Stubby	What supplies am I going to take up?
	Miranda holds out the last chocolate bar.
Miranda	I've got this.
Jim	Right, that'll do. And no eating it on the way up.
	Miranda takes off her cardigan.
Miranda	And we can use my cardigan for a flag.
	Jim goes to the foot of the quarry, carrying the rope.

Jim	Get a move on.
Stubby	Listen to him.
	Jim climbs to the first level, followed by Stubby then Miranda.
Jim	Careful, the ice is treacherous.
	Stubby looks down. He is suffering from vertigo already.
Stubby	I shouldn't be up here. I get dizzy standing on a brick.
Jim	Right. We're roping up.
	He puts the rope round his waist, ties it on, feeds it out and then starts to tie it round Stubby.

Stubby	Yow! You're tickling.
Jim	Now, I want you to go up and make Camp Six.
Stubby	Do I have to?
Jim	We'll pass the flag up to you.
Miranda	Stubby shouldn't go first.
Jim	Why not?
Miranda	Because of his . . .

Miranda trails off as she becomes aware of Stubby waiting for her answer.

Jim	Go on, Odell. I'll give you a leg up. You've a couple of decent handholds there.
Stubby	Right, Mallory.

Stubby makes his ascent to the next level. For someone without a disabled foot it wouldn't be that difficult, but it is a major challenge to Stubby. He's extremely nervous and falters once or twice. The others encourage him – 'Go on, Odell', 'Keep going, Stubby', etc. Finally Stubby makes it and is able to sit and get his breath back. Miranda and Jim cheer.

Miranda	Well done!
Stubby	It was a piece of cake actually.
Jim	Now make the camp. Here!

He takes Miranda's cardigan and throws it up to Stubby.

Put the chocolate under a rock.

Stubby	Do I have to?
Miranda	We can share it later.

Reluctantly Stubby stashes the chocolate.

Jim	Now hold onto the rope, Odell. I'm coming up.
Stubby	Hang on, it's tea-time. Me mam'll hammer me if I'm late.
Jim	You can't just come down Everest for your tea.
Stubby	I'll have to. It's me favourite. Steaklet and chips. Give us a help down.

Stubby climbs down to the first level

Miranda	We'd better get home as well, Jim. We'll come back another day.
Jim	All right.

He calls out.

I'll be back, Chomolungma. Back to Base camp.

They climb down to the foot of the quarry.

Stubby	That was good. I enjoyed it.
Jim	We'll get right to the top next time.
Stubby	Yeah . . . Mam'll be doing her nut. I'll see you, Jim. See you, Miranda.

Stubby hurries off. Miranda and Jim start walking, as we lose the quarry.

Miranda	I thought that would kill him, climbing up there.
Jim	Stubby?
Miranda	Yeah.
Jim	I was a bit afraid for him myself.
Miranda	Then why did you make him do it?
Jim	Dunno . . . Everyone knocks him because of his leg. It's not right. He can do all sorts when he wants to
Miranda	He did all right in the quarry . . . He's left my cardigan up there!
Jim	Do you want to go back?

Miranda	It's only an old one. Mum'll never notice.
Jim	I bet he didn't leave the chocolate.
Miranda	Why do people make fun of each other?
Jim	Don't ask me.
Miranda	Everyone does it though. Like Mr Cooper showing you up because of your shorts. It's not your fault your mum didn't look after you properly.
Jim	Shut up!
Miranda	I didn't mean it nastily. I just mean people pick on things you can't do anything about.
Jim	No one makes fun of you.
Miranda	You told Stubby I was horrible.
Jim	Well, yeah . . .
Miranda	Didn't you?
Jim	I wasn't making fun. I didn't mean it. No one makes fun of you.
Miranda	They would if they knew.
Jim	What?

Miranda stops walking. Jim stops too.

Miranda	If I tell you something, you won't ever tell anyone else?
Jim	What?
Miranda	You've got to promise.
Jim	All right. Promise.
Miranda	Sometimes my dad gets ill.
Jim	So does everyone.
Miranda	No. Ill up here.

She touches her head.

Jim	What, mad?
Miranda	No. Just, sort of depressed. He won't come out of his room. Mum brings him up all of his meals. She tells me he's working, like I don't know there's something wrong.
Jim	How often does it happen?
Miranda	He can go ages without it happening. Then something stupid'll set him off; he'll get upset over nothing and disappear into his room for a week.
Jim	Must be creepy for you.
Miranda	You won't ever tell anyone, will you?
Jim	No.
Miranda	Promise?
Jim	Promise.

They start walking again.

Miranda	If you ever let on at school, they'd make life hell for me.

The bins and alley are lit.

Jim	Don't worry. I keep my promises. Always.
Miranda	We'd better hurry up.
Jim	You go on home.
Miranda	What?
Jim	I'll be back soon.
Miranda	What're you going to do?
Jim	Nothing.
Miranda	Jim?

Jim	I've got to see someone, that's all. I'll be back soon. Go on.
Miranda	All right . . . We'll go up that mountain another day, yeah?
Jim	Yeah.

Reluctantly Miranda goes off. Jim goes to the alley and picks up one of the bins.

Spastic, is he? You should've seen him halfway up that quarry. You wouldn't've had the guts. I'll show you spastic.

Jim throws the bin through the Takeaway window, setting off an alarm. Jim turns and walks slowly downstage, as the lights turn to white and the alarm crossfades with the Himalayan wind. Over, we hear the following voices, repeating and overlapping.

Matt	Your mum doesn't want you. No one wants you round here.
Sharon	I thought he understood he wouldn't be coming back.
Mr Cooper	I take it your mother does care about you, doesn't she?
Sharon	Sorry. . . I'm sorry.

Jim draws into himself, becoming as small as possible as the winds gust furiously.

[End of Act One]

Questions & Assignments — ACT ONE SCENE FIFTEEN

1 Read the stage directions at the start of the scene. Suggest some more details which might make the scene more realistic.
2 What is Stubby's attitude to Miranda?
3 From the evidence of the play so far, would you say that Miranda is a strong character? Does she have a sense of humour? Is she easily put off?
4 Although the three young people are only climbing a high rock in a quarry, what details does Jim mention to suggest they are climbing Everest?
5 Why does Miranda think Stubby shouldn't go first? Why do you think Jim disagrees with her?
6 What does Miranda reveal to Jim? Why do you think she reveals her secret?
7 Read back over the scene. How has the relationship between the two changed?
8 What does Jim do at the end of Scene Fifteen? Do you think he has thought out the possible consequences? Explain.
9 What is the effect of hearing the voices speaking over the sound of the wind? What do the voices suggest about Jim's state of mind?

GENERAL QUESTIONS ON *BURNING EVEREST* – ACT ONE

1 Write character sketches of each of the following:
   Jim; Miranda; Sharon; Tony; Mr Welland; Mrs Welland; Matt.
2 'Most of the adults whom Jim encounters make no attempt to understand or help him.' Discuss this statement with reference to Act One.
3 'Jim's escape into a fantasy world is a way of helping him cope with the real world.' Discuss.
4 'Jim makes no attempt to adapt himself to his difficult circumstances.' Discuss.
5 'Although he is capable of actions which are mean and hurtful, we remain sympathetic to Jim throughout Act One.' Discuss.

ACT TWO

ACT TWO SCENE ONE

The stage is in darkness with a high, gusting wind for some moments. A spotlight comes up on the poster of Everest. The wind fades as the lights come up on the Wellands' kitchen.

Jim is sitting on a chair downstage of the table. He is facing the audience and away from Mr and Mrs Welland, who are standing. Tony is seated at the table. Miranda is sitting cross-legged in a corner of the room, cleaning her ice-skating boots.

Jim is in disgrace. There is a long silence.

Mrs Welland	That's the first time, the first time ever . . .
Mr Welland	All the neighbours were at the window, couldn't see enough of it.
Mrs Welland	A police car outside this house!
Mr Welland	Do you know how lucky you are, Jim? . . . I said, do you know how lucky you are?

No response from Jim.

Tony	Jim.

Jim shifts in his chair, half-looks back over his shoulder, then stares expressionlessly again.

Mrs Welland	Smashing a window! What got into you?
Mr Welland	If he'd brought charges against you, you'd have a criminal record now.
Mrs Welland	I suppose you haven't thought of the money we've got to find to pay for the damage?
Tony	I think you owe Mr and Mrs Welland an apology, Jim, don't you?
Jim	I didn't ask them to have me.
Tony	That's not the point
Mr Welland	You're not making things any easier you know.
Miranda	It's not all his fault. That man called Jim's friend a spastic.
Mrs Welland	We're not saying the owner's not at fault.
Mr Welland	You don't try and sort things out that way. Do you think smashing his window's going to make him any better towards handicapped people?
Jim	Stubby's not handicapped!
Mr Welland	We're not talking about Stubby.
Jim	Then don't call him handicapped.

Tony addresses the Wellands.

Tony	Can I have a word with Jim in private?
Mrs Welland	Of course.

The Wellands go off Tony goes over to Jim.

Tony	How're you feeling?
Jim	OK?
Tony	Really?
Jim	I'm OK.
Tony	You know, if your mum hadn't been able to talk the Takeaway owner out

	of prosecuting you, you'd be in big trouble.
Jim	So what?
Tony	It's lucky she gets on so well with him.
Jim	I wouldn't mind if the police had taken me away. I wouldn't mind if I had been put in prison. Couldn't be worse than this.
Tony	You don't know what you're talking about, Jim. The Wellands care about you, you know that?
Jim	No one asked them to.
Tony	But they do. All of them. And if you gave yourself a chance, if you stopped trying to fight the whole world, you might actually start to enjoy life a bit . . . Your mum's not going to take you back again, Jim. It's not going to happen. You've got to get on with the rest of your life.
Jim	I'm not bothered about my mum.
Tony	In her own way, she does still love you.
Jim	Oh yeah?
Tony	Yes . . . so why don't you give her a son that's worth loving? One who's not in trouble at school all the time. One who doesn't have the police chasing after him. You never know; if she hears you're a pretty smart lad, she might just understand what she's missing after all.
	Jim looks at him for the first time.
	Give it a try, eh? One time, just give it a try.
	Tony puts his hand on Jim's shoulder then goes off. After a moment, Miranda comes in with her school bag, which she dumps on the table. She takes a couple of books out and starts to work. Jim goes over to the table and looks at what she's doing. Miranda looks annoyed.
Miranda	What do you want?
Jim	Is that homework? Have we got some?
Miranda	Homework?
Jim	Yeah.
Miranda	I didn't think you bothered.
Jim	Yeah, well . . . I thought I might have a go. What is it?
	Miranda is furious.
Miranda	Jim, can you just leave me alone! I've had enough of you for one day. Mum and Dad are arguing with each other again and it's all your fault.
Jim	I'm sorry, I'm sorry.
Miranda	The next thing, Dad'll get in one of his moods and do you know what happens next?
Jim	I didn't want to upset anyone.
Miranda	This house'll become hell. He'll lock himself away. He doesn't get dressed; he just sits in his dressing-gown for days. It's horrible.
Jim	I guess so.
	Miranda is close to tears.
Miranda	Last time it happened, I went in. Mum told me not to, but I did. He was sat on the bed. He'd got some scissors in his hand and he was holding a fish or something he'd cut out of paper. All over the bed was little fish.
Jim	I didn't mean to wind everyone up.

Burning Everest

Miranda	Well you have.
Jim	I know what it's like.
Miranda	No, you don't.
Jim	I do. My mum's really weird sometimes. Like she isn't my real mum at all. She won't talk to me. She doesn't want to know me.
Miranda	That's your problem, isn't it?
Jim	Yeah, I suppose it is. Look, what is this homework?
	Miranda blows her nose.
Miranda	Maths.
Jim	I'll have a go at that.
	He sits down next to her.
Miranda	Do you have to do it here?
Jim	I'll be as quiet as a mouse.
	Miranda carries on with her work.
	You got a bit of paper?
	Miranda looks annoyed
	Eek, eek.
	Despite herself, Miranda laughs.

Questions & Assignments — ACT TWO SCENE ONE

1. Read the writer's directions at the beginning of the scene. What does the position of the characters and the long silence tell you about their feelings and the atmosphere in the room?
2. What arguments does Tony use to persuade Jim to improve his behaviour and attitude? Do you think Tony is talking sense? Explain.
3. What evidence is there to show that Jim is trying to be better?
4. What do we learn about Mr Welland? Why is Miranda close to tears?

ACT TWO SCENE TWO

The staffroom of St Xavier's. Mrs Pryme and Mr Cooper are sitting down. Mrs Pryme takes a set of exercise books out of her bag and starts to mark them methodically.

Mr Cooper gets out a pile of exercise books, spills them on the floor and groans. He picks one up, opens it and tries to read it. He turns it upside down, then sideways, but still can't read it. He marks it.

Mr Cooper	D - . . .
	He picks up a handful of books and starts marking them very rapidly.
	Simms, C+ . . . Bashley, B . . . Whitfield, A+ . . . Walgrave, E please see me.
Mrs Pryme	Harry?
Mr Cooper	Yes, Janice?

Spectrum 1

Mrs Pryme	Are you marking those without reading them first?
Mr Cooper	I've had this lot for two years. I know what marks they get.
Mrs Pryme	Don't you think that's a bit . . .
Mr Cooper	Don't worry. They don't take the slightest notice of what I write anyway.
	The Head comes in. Mr Cooper hurriedly tidies up his spilt books.
Head	Both of you teaching this afternoon?
	Mrs Pryme and Mr Cooper reply hurriedly.
Mrs Pryme and Mr Cooper	Yes.
Head	Pity. I'm rather busy and I'm supposed to be taking 3G for history. I'd let them get on with some silent reading of their own, but that awful Jim McLindon's in the class.
Mrs Pryme	Actually, Jim's work for me is improving.
	The Head ignores her.
Head	It was a mistake letting him join the school in the first place. What on earth do you do with a boy like that?
Mr Cooper	Boil him in oil and serve him with chips.
Head	What? That's not such a bad idea.
Mrs Pryme	I think he is trying to make an effort, Mr Bryant.
Head	A leopard can't change his spots, Janice.
	The bell goes.
	Oh well, I'll just have to try and hammer some facts into that thick head of his.

Questions & Assignments — ACT TWO SCENE TWO

1 Do you think Mrs Pryme and Mr Cooper differ in their approach to their students? Explain.
2 Briefly explain how the three teachers have differing attitudes to Jim.

ACT TWO SCENE THREE

	A classroom. Jim, Miranda and Peter come on with their books and bags.
Head	Good afternoon, 3G.
All	Good afternoon, Headmaster.
Head	Your homework was to write about achievement in the twentieth century. I'll collect your work now.
	Peter and Miranda hand in their homework. Jim is getting his exercise book out of his bag.
Head	There's no use expecting homework from you, is there, McLindon?
Jim	I've done it, Sir.
Head	What's your excuse this time?

Jim	I've done it.
Head	You realise you'll have to complete the homework in detention anyway?
Jim	It's here, Sir.
Head	What?
Jim	I spent three hours doing it last night.

The Head looks very suspicious.

Head	Show me.

Jim opens his exercise book.

Head	Copied out of a library book, I'll bet.
Jim	I did it myself.
Head	Then read some of it out. I can always tell when a pupil's copied something.
Jim	Do I have to?
Head	I wouldn't've asked you if you didn't. Stand up to read.

Reluctantly, Jim gets up.

Jim	It's about George Leigh Mallory, the mountaineer.
Head	Get on with it, McLindon. I'm sure we're all waiting for the words of wisdom to pour forth from your lips.

Peter sniggers sycophantically. Jim reads.

Jim	George Leigh Mallory is remembered as one of the greatest explorers which ever came from the British Isles . . .
Head	'Whoever', McLindon, not 'Which ever'.

Jim continues reading.

Jim	Above all else, he is remembered for his courageous attempt to be the first man to climb Mount Everest. When asked why he wanted to do it, he simply said, 'Because it's there.' This sets an example to all of us not to be afraid of trying to do things what seem impossible . . .
Peter	Like writing good English.

The Head reproves Peter.

Head	Peter.

Jim continues to read.

Jim	Whether he ever reached the top of the mountain, we'll never know. He was last seen eight hundred feet from the summit, climbing strongly with his companion, Sandy Irvine. Then cloud came down and they were hidden from view. They were never seen again and their bodies were never found.

The Head interrupts.

Head	It's certainly too badly written to have been copied. Give it here.

Jim hands in his book. The Head glances through it. Miranda whispers across to Jim.

Miranda	It was good, Jim.

Jim whispers back, indicating the Head.

Jim	I hate him.

Miranda whispers.

Miranda	Never mind. Think about later. Mum and Dad are taking us ice-skating for a treat.

Jim forgets to whisper and bursts out.

Jim   Ice-skating? Bloody hell!
Head   McLindon!

Questions & Assignments   ACT TWO SCENE THREE

1 Why is the headmaster suspicious of Jim's work?
2 What is the head's attitude to Jim's work? Is he being fair?
3 'This sets an example to all of us not to be afraid of trying to do things what seem impossible.' What do you understand by this statement? How does it relate to Jim's own life?

ACT TWO SCENE FOUR

We hear a loud burst of ice-arena music. The lights come up upon Mr and Mrs Welland, wearing skates and carrying spare pairs for Jim and Miranda.
While the children are putting their skates on, Mr and Mrs Welland start a Torvill and Dean style routine. The effect should be exaggerated and funny. Miranda gets her skates on quickly and joins in. She is a skilled skater. Jim has much more trouble. He gets up and falls straight down.

Jim   Help!

Mr and Mrs Welland pick him up and start taking him round the rink. They reduce their support for him and he starts to skate alone.
Slow at first, he quickly gets the hang of it and is putting in twirls and jumps. The others stop to watch. He finishes with a great leap and twirl. As he lands, the others applaud.

Am I good or what?

Jim slips over. The music stops and the lights fade to blackout.

Questions & Assignments   ACT TWO SCENE FOUR

1 How do the Wellands treat Jim in the ice skating rink?

Act Two Scene Five

The lights up on the alley and the bins. Stubby is bouncing a basketball from hand to hand. After a moment, Jim comes on, holding a letter.

Jim Hiya, Stubbs.
Stubby ignores him and carries on bouncing the ball.
What's the matter? Not talking?
Stubby It's not me not talking, is it?
Jim What's that supposed to mean?
Stubby Nothing.
Jim Look, I've been busy. I've had things to do.
Stubby We was meant to be going back to the quarry, remember?
Jim I haven't had time.
Stubby I told everyone I was going to climb it.
Jim We will.
Stubby Now Deano keeps getting on at me. 'Climbed Everest yet, Plastic Man?'
Jim We will do. Promise.
Stubby Today?
Jim Not today.
Stubby, disappointed, goes back to bouncing the ball
I've got something to do today. I need your help.
Stubby What?
Jim holds out a letter.
Jim I want you to give this to my mum.
Stubby What is it?
Jim Nothing. Just a letter. I saw her down the shops. She'll be back soon.
Stubby Give it her yourself.
Jim I don't want to. She doesn't take things right from me. Go on.
Stubby When're we going back to the quarry?
Jim This Saturday, honest.
Stubby All right.
He takes the letter.
Jim Look, here she is. Give it to her.
Jim dives out of sight as Sharon enters and goes to her back gate.
Stubby Mrs McLindon, Mrs McLindon!
Sharon What is it?
Stubby holds out the letter.
Stubby It's for you.
Sharon Who from?
Stubby Dunno. Someone just asked me to give it to you.
Sharon takes the letter and exits through the back gate. Stubby waits a minute, then signals Jim to come out.
Jim Did she take it?
Stubby nods.
Did she read it?
Stubby shrugs.

The lights go down on Jim and Stubby, who freeze, as Sharon is lit. She takes off her coat and starts to open her hairdressing carry-case. She decides she will read the letter. She takes it from her coat and starts to read

Sharon   Dear Mum,
This is just to say that I miss seeing you and think about you everyday.
Jim's voice is heard continuing.

Jim   I can understand about you not wanting to see me. I know I've been very bad and a lot of trouble. I'm sorry about smashing that window. I've tried being better since then. My teachers say I'm not as bad as I was.
I do love you, Mum. Please stay friends with me.
Please still be my mum.
Love, Jim.
Sharon looks for a moment out of an imaginary window, down towards Jim. The lights come down on her and up on Jim and Stubby.

Jim   Think she'll take any notice?
Stubby   Search me.
Jim   I want her to.
Stubby   You can't tell. Not with mums. They're not like ordinary people.
Sharon comes on quickly, then pulls herself up.
Jim   Mum?
Sharon takes a step towards him.
Mum?
Sharon holds out her arms. Jim runs into them and she hugs him. Matt comes out of the Takeaway with a bin bag.
Matt   What's going off here then?
Sharon releases Jim.
I thought we had an agreement, Sharon.
Sharon   We do.
Matt   Then what you hugging him for? I let him off smashing my window – you don't see him again.
Sharon   I know, Matt.
Matt   An agreement's an agreement.
Sharon   He just came round.
Matt   I told you: I don't want lumbering with someone else's kid when we get married.
Jim is horrified
Jim   Mum?
Sharon   I was going to tell you.
Jim   You're marrying him?
Matt   That's right. Next month, all right? And you aren't part of the picture, so get that straight in your head for starters.
Sharon   Jim, it's the best thing for all of us. You'd feel out of place, especially when Matt and me start a family of our own. The Wellands'll bring you up better than I ever could. They've got all those books and paintings. I was going to tell you. It's for the best.
Sharon moves to put her arm round Jim again. He backs away. Stubby goes up to him.

Stubby Come on, let's go to my place.
Jim Get off! Get off all of you!
Jim runs off. Stubby looks at Sharon and Matt.

Questions & Assignments — ACT TWO SCENE FIVE

1 Read Jim's letter to his mother. What does it show about his character?
2 Briefly explain what Jim discovers in this scene.
3 Comment on Sharon's behaviour. Do you sympathise with her?
4 Comment on Matt's attitude to Jim. What is your opinion of Matt?
5 What do you imagine Jim's feelings are at the end of the scene?

ACT TWO SCENE SIX

A fierce wind starts and the lights are brilliant white. Jim enters in the thick of the storm.

Jim I was so close. So close to the top of Chomolungma. Goddess Mother of the World. Eight hundred feet. Four hours walking. I could see the peak up above me. Every step I took, crunching into the treacherous snow, I imagined myself there – on top of the world. It had been a hard slog, the last few days, but early on June the eighth, I set out from Camp Six full of hope and determination. All the sweat, the pain was going to be worth it. The air was pitifully thin. It burned my lungs but I didn't mind. My legs and arms ached with exhaustion but it didn't matter any more. Everything I wanted in life was going to be mine. I could see it. I could see it. And then the cloud came in. The blizzard started with blinding fine snow that cut into my eyes and mouth. I couldn't see anything any more. I was lost. Chomolungma wanted to destroy me.

Questions & Assignments — ACT TWO SCENE SIX

1 Read Jim's imaginary description of his attempt to climb Everest. Explain how each stage relates to some recent event in his life.
2 How would you describe his mood here? Angry, sad, bitter, disappointed, disillusioned? Give reasons.

ACT TWO SCENE SEVEN

The school bell rings in the school playground.
Jim sits down slowly on the ground. Miranda crosses behind him.

Miranda Come on, Jim, we'll be late for Maths.
No response from Jim.
Maths!
She goes off. Jim stays sitting.
The Head comes on.

Head McLindon! What are you doing there?
Still no response from Jim.
McLindon!
No response.
Get up!
Jim gets up slowly.
Where are you meant to be now?

Jim I don't know.

Head Sir.
Jim responds lifelessly.

Jim Sir.

Head What on earth do you think you're playing at, hanging round here when you should be in class? Well? . . . I asked you a question, boy.

Jim I don't know . . . Sir.

Head Don't get clever with me, young man, or I'll get clever with you and, believe me, you'll come off the worse. Are you ill or something?

Jim No.

Head But you don't know which class you're supposed to be in?

Jim No.

Head Sir! I've had just about as much of your bad manners as I'm going to take, McLindon. I didn't think much of you when you came here and I've seen nothing since to make me change my mind. Mrs Pryme sticks up for you; she seems to think she's seen a change in you, but I'm afraid Mrs Pryme is rather too good-hearted. I'm different; I'm an old hand, McLindon, and I've seen it all before. You're no good, right the way through. You're no good at school and you're no good at home.

Jim Sod off!

Head What did you say?

Jim You heard me.

Head	How dare you! How dare you address a teacher like that. I've a good mind to . . .
Jim	Oh sod off!
	Jim runs off. The Head looks after Jim, absolutely astonished. No one has ever spoken to him like that before.

Questions & Assignments   ACT TWO SCENE SEVEN

1 Why do you think Jim tells the head to *'sod off'*?
2 Comment on the head's treatment of his student.

ACT TWO SCENE EIGHT

Lights up on the Wellands' kitchen. Mr Welland is on the phone. Mrs Welland is listening in.

Mr Welland	Yes . . . yes . . . Like I say, he's not at home at the moment, but the minute Jim comes in, I'll have a very serious talk with him. Yes, we'll come up and discuss his future at St Xavier's. Sorry about the trouble, Mr Bryant.
	He puts the phone down.
	I'll throttle Jim; I will, I'll throttle him.
Mrs Welland	Alan, calm down. We don't want it triggering you off.
	Mr and Mrs Welland exchange glances.
Mrs Welland	He'll expel Jim, of course.
Mrs Welland	Do you think so?
	The front door opens offstage.
	That'll be the kids.
Mr Welland	Right. I'm going to sort that little tyke out once and for all.
Mrs Welland	I'll deal with it, Alan. You just keep quiet.
Mr Welland	If you don't sort it, I will.
	Miranda comes in. She is trying extra hard to be cheerful.
Miranda	Hiya.

Mrs Welland	Hello, love.
Mr Welland	Where's Jim?
Miranda	I think he's gone up to his room. What's for tea, Mum? Anything nice?
Mr Welland	What happened at school today?
Miranda	Oh nothing much. Mr Cooper fell asleep at choir practice, but there's nothing unusual about that.
Mrs Welland	What happened with Jim, love?
	Miranda responds innocently.
Miranda	Jim?
Mrs Welland	We've had the Headmaster on the phone.
Miranda	Oh, I think there was a little bit of trouble, but the Head gets on at everyone some time or other.
	Mr Welland goes to the door and calls upstairs.
Mr Welland	Jim . . . Jim!
Miranda	Dad, the Head always picks on Jim. He doesn't understand him. It's not Jim's fault.
Mr Welland	Jim get down here at once.
	Mrs Welland addresses her husband
Mrs Welland	It won't do any good to have a go at him. He's had enough of being told off for one day.
	Jim enters and stands in the doorway.
Mr Welland	Come and sit down, Jim.
	Miranda pleads with her father.
Miranda	Dad.
	Mrs Welland speaks to Jim.
Mrs Welland	What happened this afternoon?
Jim	Nothing.
Mr Welland	Nothing!
Mrs Welland	We've had the Headmaster on the phone for half an hour.
Mr Welland	He wants you out of St Xavier's.
Jim	Good. I don't want to stay there.
Mr Welland	Stop being so stupid.
Mrs Welland	Alan.
Mr Welland	We all understand you've been through a hard time. We all wish you and your mother got on. But it's not an excuse for you to be completely bloody-minded for the rest of your life. You've got to think of other people, not just yourself.
Jim	Why? I don't care what anyone thinks of me.
Mr Welland	That's a downright stupid attitude to take.
Jim	I might be stupid, but at least I'm not mad.
	Slight pause while everyone takes in what Jim's said
Mrs Welland	Jim.
Mr Welland	What do you mean by that?
Jim	You are, aren't you? Mad.
	Points to Miranda.
	That's what she said.

Burning Everest

Miranda	You promised you'd never . . .
Jim	You lock yourself away in your room for days with little paper fish. Say that you're working, but really you've gone mad. That's what she said.
Miranda	I didn't, Daddy, I didn't.
	She speaks to Jim.
	How could you? You promised!
Mrs Welland	I think you've said more than enough for one night, don't you, Jim? Go up to your room.
	Jim goes out defiantly. Miranda is mortified and close to tears.
Miranda	Daddy, I didn't say . . . I just wanted Jim to know . . . he felt so bad about his mum. I hate him! I hate him!
	Mrs Welland puts her arm round Miranda.
Mrs Welland	It's all right, Miri, it's all right.
Mr Welland	I'll get in touch with Tony first thing in the morning. That boy's not staying a moment longer.

Questions & Assignments — ACT TWO SCENE EIGHT

1 Why is Mr Welland angry at the beginning of the scene?
2 Compare Mr Welland's treatment of Jim to the head's treatment of Jim.
3 Why does Jim make the comment about Mr Welland being mad? How do you think Miranda feels at this point?
4 'Jim has behaved in a very hurtful nasty way and yet we still feel sympathy for him.' Discuss this statement.

ACT TWO SCENE NINE

Moonlight on the kitchen. Jim creeps in with a torch. He takes a quick drink of milk from a carton, pulls on a jacket, then climbs out through the window. As Jim walks downstage, we have the Everest poster lit and a central white light and wind: wilder than ever. Jim speaks from the front of the stage.

Jim A few hundred feet from the summit of Chomolungma and I'm beaten. I know I can never make it up there now. I could've turned back for Camp Six an hour or two ago and still have made it to safety before nightfall. But I didn't. I couldn't turn back. I kept slogging on through this hellish gale, knowing that I'd never get any higher. Every step I take could be my last. I can't see where I'm putting my feet. They keep slipping. I don't know what's to the side of me; most probably a drop of hundreds of feet – ice and rock below waiting to smash my body to pulp. Night must come and with it, a cold that'll stop my heart beating and freeze my blood to ice. I know this and still I climb on. Because there's nothing for me down there. My whole life was a dream – the dream of climbing Chomolungma. It drove me on – made me wake up, day after day, excited to be living, preparing to make my dream come real . . . And now it's over. I can't breathe. My lungs are exhausted. There's no strength in my legs to lift my feet. The others, Odell, Somervell, none of them can help me now. They'll never know what happened. They'll say it was an accident. Bad luck. I slipped and fell to my death. They don't know what I feel inside now. My life is over before my body's died. None of them understands what the mountain means to me. It's everything.

    Already it's getting dark. Colder. A cold I can feel inside each bone. I'm turning to ice. My breath is freezing on my lips. All there is left is black, winter night. And for me to walk into it.

A great howl of wind. The quarry appears and Jim walks to the foot of it. We hear Stubby shouting over from offstage.

Stubby   Jim! Jim! . . . Jim! . . . Jim!
Stubby runs on. The light and wind become normal
I knew you'd be here. I knew it . . . Boy, are you in trouble. There's police out looking for you everywhere. The Wellands phoned them as soon as they found you were missing. Two of them came to our house. Huge great copper one of them. Mum nearly choked on her cornflakes.

Jim   You didn't tell them about here?

Stubby   Course not. Said I didn't see you much these days anyway. And I made sure they didn't follow me here. I doubled back down our alley in case they were following. What're you going to do?

Jim   Nothing. Go away, Stubbs.

Stubby   It's all right. I don't mind getting into trouble with you. They're bound to find us and then you're for it.

Jim   No one knows about this place except you and Miranda. She won't tell them. She wants rid of me, same as the rest of them.

Stubby   You're dead brave, running away. I want to an' all.
Jim starts climbing the quarry face. Stubby moves towards the foot of the quarry.
I won't tell anyone. I'll bring some food after school. We've got some tins of Spaghetti Hoops. We'll have to eat them cold . . . Jim?
Jim keeps on climbing. Stubby starts up the quarry face.
Jim!
Jim keeps climbing and turns around.

Jim   Go away!

Stubby   I'll run away with you. It'll be great. I'm sick of it round here. Everyone making fun.

Jim   Go home, Stubbs.

Stubby   Two's better than one. They'll never find us.

Jim   I don't want anyone else with me.

Stubby   I'll be whosit . . . Odell . . . I'll make all the camps, lay in the supplies.

Jim   That was just a game, stupid.

Stubby   Well, games are better than real life then. We'll be a team. We'll climb Everest.

Jim   I don't want you with me.

Stubby   Go on.

Jim	No.
Stubby	Let me stay.
Jim	No.
Stubby	You can't stop me coming up if I want to.
Jim	Go home!
Stubby	Why won't you let me?
Jim	Because you're useless.
Stubby	I won't go away.

Jim's voice turns nasty.

Jim	Stubby, I don't want a plastic man with me.

Stubby is shattered He looks disbelievingly up at Jim.

Stubby	Jim?
Jim	Go on. Clear off, Plastic Man.

Slowly Stubby moves away. He takes a last look at Jim, who turns away. Stubby goes off. Jim climbs on and picks up the cardigan left by Miranda. He thinks about throwing it down, then throws it over his shoulder and climbs on a little way to a new ledge.

Questions & Assignments — ACT TWO SCENE NINE

1. What event in Mallory's life is Jim imagining himself into? How does it relate to his own life?
2. Are you concerned for Jim's future in this scene? Explain why.
3. In his speech Jim says 'none of them understands'. Do you agree with this statement? Explain.
4. Describe Jim's treatment of Stubby.

ACT TWO SCENE TEN

The Wellands' kitchen. Mr Welland is on the phone. Tony, Miranda and Mrs Welland are listening

Mr Welland	No one's got any idea. Have you asked the other pupils in his class? Yes, of course. Well, if you hear anything. Thanks. Bye.

He puts the phone down.

Mrs Welland	Nothing?
Mr Welland	The damned Headmaster's delighted Jim's missing if you ask me.
Miranda	That's typical of Mr Bryant.
Tony	Jim didn't say anything last night? Didn't give any idea of where he'd go to?
Mrs Welland	Tony, if he had, we'd've told you.
Tony	You should've got in touch with me if you thought there were problems.
Mr Welland	We were managing very well, thank you.
Tony	You can't've managed that well, if Jim's done a runner. You've landed me right in it. I had to fight to get permission for him to be fostered.

Mrs Welland	Is that all you can think about? The poor boy might be in danger.
Mr Welland	Miranda, get off to school.
Miranda	Do I have to?
Mr Welland	Yes. You'll just be in the way here.
Tony	There's bound to be an enquiry.

Miranda speaks reluctantly.

Miranda	Dad.
Mrs Welland	Where can he be? You tried his mother?

Tony snaps back.

Tony	Of course I did.
Mrs Welland	I'm only asking.
Tony	Sorry. The police have looked everywhere. Miranda, do you know anywhere Jim liked going? Anywhere he might try and hide out?

There is a slight pause before Miranda answers.

Miranda	No.
Mr Welland	Then where the hell is he? People don't just disappear, do they?

Questions & Assignments — ACT TWO SCENE TEN

1 Why in your opinion does Miranda not reveal Jim's hideout?
2 Describe Mr Welland's behaviour.

ACT TWO SCENE ELEVEN

The quarry. Jim is at the highest point. There is a brilliant white light, but no wind. Jim addresses the audience.

Jim This'll be the last place. On top of the world.

Jim waves Miranda's cardigan slowly, like a flag. He wraps it over his shoulders.

I'll just wait. Wait for it all to finish. I'll sleep or something and it'll all stop. It's so cold. I can't feel anything. I can't feel pain anymore. Nothing. I'm frozen; as hard and cold as ice. Nothing matters. No one matters anymore. There's only me and a mountain that doesn't even know I'm here. Chomolungma.

He steps towards the edge and looks out into space. He is contemplating jumping. Miranda enters, but doesn't see him. She calls out.

Miranda Jim! . . . Jim!

No response from Jim. Miranda keeps looking, then sees him.

Jim! It's me.

No response.

Mallory! Mallory, can you hear me?

Jim looks vacantly towards her, but doesn't speak.

Mallory, I've come with the rescue party. When you disappeared, we all came looking for you. You're safe. Step back from the edge.

Burning Everest

Jim	Leave me alone.
Miranda	Come down. We'll go back together. It'll be all right.
Jim	Please leave me alone.
	Miranda starts climbing the foot of the quarry. She pauses to find a safe foothold
Miranda	I can get so far, but you'll have to meet me halfway.
Jim	Don't come up here. It's not safe.
	Miranda climbs to the camp Stubby made.
	It's not safe.
Miranda	You got up.
Jim	Stay there.
	Miranda, short of breath, sits down in the camp. She picks up the chocolate Stubby stashed
Miranda	Look, I've found the pemmican we left. We can share it when I get to the top.
Jim	You shouldn't be here.
Miranda	You can't climb mountains on your own.
Jim	I don't want you here.
Miranda	I know. I came because I wanted to.
Jim	Don't pretend you want to help me, because you don't. I gave away your secret. You hate me, don't you?
Miranda	Do you want me to?
Jim	Yes.
Miranda	You want everyone to hate you, don't you? Mum, Dad, all the teachers at school. Me.
Jim	Yes.
Miranda	That's why I won't.
	She stands up again.
Jim	Don't come up here.

Miranda	Did Mallory die on Everest?
Jim	Yeah, course he did.
Miranda	What killed him?
Jim	He was caught in a blizzard, most probably. Froze to death.
Miranda	He needn't have. He could've turned back.
Jim	No, he couldn't! He had to keep going. He had to try and climb Everest.
Miranda	But he must've known near the top he couldn't make it.
Jim	He couldn't come down. It was the only mountain in the world for him.
Miranda	Then it was the wrong mountain.

She starts to climb higher.

Jim	You'll fall if you try and come up here. The rock's crumbly.
Miranda	Which way should I go?
Jim	Back down.
Miranda	I'm coming up one way or another.

She starts to move again.

Jim	To your left. There's a handhold there.

Miranda moves to the narrow ledge and looks down.

Miranda	Oooh . . . I don't like heights.
Jim	Don't look down. You'll get giddy.

Miranda looks nervous about falling.

Miranda	You know what I always wanted, Jim? I always wanted a brother. To do things like this with.
Jim	You're crazy.
Miranda	I love Mum and Dad, but sometimes it's so lonely at home. 'Cos I'm a girl, they don't let me do anything exciting. They think girls break easily or something.
Jim	Watch your feet!
Miranda	Mum and Dad said they'd tried, but they couldn't. It's funny; I don't like boys much, but it had to be a brother. I always wanted a brother who'd call me 'sis'. Isn't that stupid? 'Sis'? That's why I didn't mind you coming. Didn't know what we were letting ourselves in for.

She starts moving again.

Jim	Don't try coming across!
Miranda	I'm halfway there.
Jim	It's too dangerous.
Miranda	It's as dangerous to go back.

She takes another step. Part of the quarry gives way and she slips. She clutches at a tenuous handhold and dangles. It's clear she can't hold on for long.

Help! Help me!

Jim moves towards her.

Jim	Hang on.
Miranda	I can't.
Jim	Hang on!
Miranda	I'm slipping.

Jim inches towards her.

Jim	Give me your hand.

Miranda I can't.
Jim Come on.
Miranda I can't let go.
Jim inches closer, holding out his hand
Jim Come on. You're all right.
Miranda holds out her hand As Jim takes hold of it, more of the rockface gives way. Jim manages to hold on and she scrambles back up. They find safe footholds and take a couple of moments to calm down. They look at each other.
Jim You dropped the chocolate then?
Miranda nods. Slight pause.
Miranda I'd've been dead if you hadn't grabbed me.
Jim You shouldn't've come up.
Miranda Thanks very much.
Jim No, but . . . well . . . thanks. We can climb up onto the top. I'll take you home.
Miranda is extremely frightened
Miranda I'm not moving another step.
Jim It's only a bit further and it's not too slippy.
Miranda I'm not moving!
Jim I'll go up on the top. Go for help.
Miranda grabs his arm.
Miranda You're not going anywhere.
Jim It won't take long.
Miranda You are not leaving me here alone. All right?
Jim All right . . . So what are we going to do?
Miranda I don't know.
Jim Better not try tap dancing, eh?
Miranda Jim, I'm scared.
Jim Me too, sis.
They hold hands for comfort. They start to cry for help.

Questions & Assignments — Act Two Scene Eleven

1 Describe briefly in your own words how Miranda saves Jim.
2 What does the scene reveal about her character?
3 What do you understand by her comment '. . . *it was the wrong mountain.*'?
4 How would you describe the atmosphere as Miranda struggles to save Jim?
5 Would this be an exciting scene to stage or film? Explain.
6 If you were filming the scene, describe what shots and camera angles you might use. Would sound effects be effective? Could you cut away to another scene to heighten suspense?

Act Two Scene Twelve

The Wellands' kitchen.

Mr Welland Thank God for you, Stubby. Telling the police where Jim was hiding.
Stubby He'll kill me.
Tony I don't think so.
Mr Welland From the look on his face when they finally brought him and Miri back up, I think he might actually have learned something today.
Stubby It must've been dead good fun getting winched up.
Tony They were scared out of their wits, Stubby.
Stubby What'll happen to Jim?
Mr Welland Nothing much. I think he's had enough of a scare to keep him out of mischief for a while.
Tony We'll make arrangements for him to go back to the children's home first thing tomorrow.
Mr Welland Don't you dare. After all the trouble Miri went to finding him, I think he's with us for good.

Miranda comes on, wiping her hair with a towel.

Miranda Stubby, you're a hero!
Stubby Am I?
Miranda Absolutely.
Stubby Jim didn't mind me going to the coppers?
Miranda He thinks you're brilliant.

Mrs Welland comes on with Jim, who is looking the smartest we've ever seen him. He's carrying the poster of Everest.

Mrs Welland You're staying for supper, aren't you, Stubby?

Stubby looks worried about Jim's reaction.

Stubby I don't know.
Jim You've got to. It's chocolate mousse.
Stubby Oh, right.
Mrs Welland Sit down everybody, then I can serve up.
Jim Yeah, in a minute. I gotta do something first.

Jim walks into the neutral space, which is now the back garden.

Mr Welland Miri, keep an eye on him.

Miranda goes to look. Jim is unrolling the poster and putting a vertical crease in it to keep it open. Miranda indicates to the others to come out and join them. Jim looks back over his shoulder at them.

Jim What it is . . . is . . . I want to say . . . because I was rotten to Stubby. I said things . . . And to you, Mr Welland. I'm sorry what I said.
Mr Welland I didn't hear him say anything, did you, Stubby?
Stubby No.
Jim Yeah but . . . Like I've been and the way you've been.
Miranda Jim, do shut up so we can get on with our dinner.
Jim All right, Sis. Wrong mountain, that's all.

He sets fire to the poster. As it burns, the lights fade.

The End

Questions & Assignments — ACT TWO SCENE TWELVE

1. Describe Mr Welland's feelings at the start of the scene.
2. What suggestion does Tony make? Why does Mr Welland reject it? Does it show a significant change in his attitude?
3. Comment on Jim's behaviour in the Welland house. Does it show a significant change in his attitude to them?
4. What does Jim do at the end of the play? Do you think his action has any symbolic meaning?

GENERAL QUESTIONS ON *BURNING EVEREST*

1. Comment on the ending of the play. Is it a happy-ever-after ending? Is it a realistic ending? Consider alternative endings.
2. Now that you have read the play from beginning to end, write character sketches of each of the following:
   Jim; Miranda; Sharon; Matt; Stubby; Mr Welland; Mrs Welland.
3. Does the play deal with real life issues? (Isolation, family problems, fear of rejection, the meaning of love, forgiveness, acceptance of things which cannot be changed, friendship.)
4. 'Jim's greatest struggle is not trying to be reunited with his mother. It is in learning to accept the inevitable and in making the most of his new friends and circumstances.' Discuss.
5. 'For Jim the adult world is a harsh, unfriendly place.' Discuss.
6. 'None of the characters in *Burning Everest* is totally good or completely bad. Each of them is complex enough to hold our interest to the end.' Discuss.
7. A good play hinges on interesting characters involved in events which create drama and suspense. Do you think *Burning Everest* is a good play?

Film and Radio Drama

Cinema – The Early Years

In 1903 an event took place in America which, in time, would draw people away in huge numbers from live theatre. The first film drama was screened.

It was an eight-minute silent film entitled *The Great Train Robbery* which was enthusiastically received by the public. Other 'movies' soon followed.

By 1912 subtitles were shown on the screen to lead the audience through the story and to show a few important pieces of dialogue. In each cinema a pianist played throughout the performance, matching the mood of the music to the mood of the film.

Another milestone in the development of cinema drama came in 1915 with a three-hour film *The Birth of a Nation*, a story about the American Civil War. This was a very successful film and it held audiences of the time spellbound. One of the reasons for its success was the imaginative camera techniques used in filming. These included dramatic close-ups and impressive long shots which gave the historical setting and the drama of the war a new level of realism.

Cinemas had begun to open all over America and Europe. Dublin's first cinema was called *Cinematograph Volta*. It was situated in Mary Street and was managed for a time by James Joyce.

As well as showing complete feature films, the fledgling cinemas showed serials to maintain audiences from week to week. These serials were divided into twenty minute episodes and a new episode was shown each week. Each episode would end with the hero or heroine facing a dangerous predicament. The serials were called 'cliff hangers' because they would sometimes end with a character actually hanging from a cliff. The audience had to wait until the following week to see what happened. Many of the techniques used in today's television serials can be traced back to these early serials of the silent screen.

In the early years of the 1920's cinema had become a big business. Most films were produced by a small number of big companies. Among these were Warner Brothers, Universal Studios, Paramount and United Artists. By 1920 all these companies had based themselves in Hollywood in California.

From the beginning of cinema, the public were particularly interested in the leading actors and actresses. These became known as *movie stars*. The success of a film depended largely on who was *starring* in it. The first crop of Hollywood stars included such names as Charlie Chaplin, Buster Keaton, Gloria Swanson, Rudolph Valentino, Mary Pickford and Douglas Fairbanks. Hollywood soon acquired the reputation for glamour and overnight fame that has made it a famous name throughout the world.

Radio Drama

By 1925 cinema was threatened by a new rival – radio. There was a big decline in cinema audiences as people turned to the new medium for entertainment. As well as broadcasting music, radio also broadcast drama. On a radio play scenery could not, of course, be shown. Instead it had to be suggested through the dialogue of the play and through sound effects. Radio plays could not have a lot of characters as this would confuse the audience. Actors were chosen on the basis of their vocal talents rather than on their appearance. However, radio drama could easily be set anywhere and at any time without having to go to the trouble of creating a series of expensive and elaborate sets. A few simple sound effects, good dialogue and a small number of characters, each with a distinctive accent, were sufficient to capture the interest of the audience and help them to create scenery in their imaginations. Today radio drama is still alive and well and operating on these simple principles.

Modern Cinema

The advent of radio did not pose a threat to the cinema for long. The reason for this was the discovery of a method of adding sound to films. In 1927, *The Jazz Singer*, a film starring Al Jolson, was released. It contained three songs and a couple of lines of spoken dialogue but the public flocked to see it, fascinated by the picture that talked. The *'talking film'*, or *talkies*, marked the birth of modern cinema. Studios and cinemas had to quickly adapt to these new technical changes. There were other problems in producing pictures with dialogue; actors with good speaking voices as well as good appearances had to be recruited and playwrights were needed to write 'screen plays'. These dramatists were no longer confined to the limitations of a stage in a theatre. They could now write dialogue or scripts to be spoken by actors on the roof of a moving train or on horseback in the middle of a prairie. As well as writing the lines to be spoken, the script writer would also indicate how each scene would be filmed. For example, an expression of surprise or contempt on a character's face could be an important element in the plot of a film. This would require a close-up shot of the actor's face.

A long-shot is used to show, for example, an entire street scene while a medium shot is used to show a few characters together. All the techniques of film drama that were developed in the past are now also used in television drama.

Serials

TV serials are viewed by larger audiences than any other type of TV drama. The story in TV serials runs from episode to episode.

Spectrum 1

Questions & Assignments

1. Name your favourite TV serial. Write a brief description of all the main characters and describe the setting.
2. TV serials always have a number of loosely linked plots developing at the same time. Describe briefly each of the plots which are presently being developed in your favourite serial. In the case of any one, suggest the direction you think it is most likely to take.
3. What serials are on television at present? Which ones would you regard as being (a) true to life (b) far-fetched? Give reasons for your answers in each case.
4. Certain TV serials have occasionally been accused of highlighting values and attitudes which are at odds with those of the Irish people. Are such accusations justified? Refer to a number of serials that are being broadcast currently. In approaching this you should consider the attitudes of (a) the 'good' characters to issues such as success, wealth, responsibilities, duties, their families, alcohol, etc. and (b) the 'bad' characters to similar issues. Review also the manner in which members of each group attain their aims.

CRIME DRAMA

Another very popular type of television programme is the crime/detective series. In each episode, the setting and principal characters are the same and a complete story is told.

Questions & Assignments

1. Name your favourite series and describe briefly the main character and setting.
2. Watch an episode and outline the main points of the plot.
3. Are the plots of most crime/detective series broadly similar? Explain your answer.
4. What are the qualities that (a) the heroes and (b) the villains display in the majority of crime/detective series? Refer to the characters from a number of these series when answering this question.

SITUATION COMEDY

The most popular form of comedy drama on television is the situation comedy – or sit-com. Generally, the plot of each episode is self-contained; the principal characters and setting don't vary.

Plots are usually based on a group of people, such as a family, of which one or more get involved in some kind of a peculiar situation. Much of the humour arises from the events and circumstances that led the characters into the situation and their efforts to get out of it. Much of the dialogue can be funny too, with devices such as heavy sarcasm, ambiguity and dramatic irony.

FAWLTY TOWERS

by
John Cleese/Connie Booth

INTRODUCTION

Here are three short extracts from one of the most popular television comedy series ever – *Fawlty Towers*. The series is unusual in that it was written by the actors John Cleese and Connie Booth, who both play leading roles in the series.

Note how the stage directions, the characters' names and the dialogue are laid out in the following extracts. All twelve episodes of *Fawlty Towers* are available on video.

EXTRACT 1

Basil changes his attitude towards a guest...
(**Basil** *hurries bad-temperedly into the lobby.* **Melbury** *is standing there.*)

Basil	Yes, yes, well, yes?
Melbury	... Er, well, I was wondering if you could offer me accommodation for a few nights?
Basil	*(very cross)* Well, have you booked?
Melbury	... I'm sorry?
Basil	Have you booked, have you booked?
Melbury	No.
Basil	*(to himself)* Oh dear!
Melbury	Why, are you full?
Basil	Oh, we're not full ... we're not <u>full</u> ... of course we're not <u>full</u>!!
Melbury	I'd like, er ...

231

Spectrum 1

Basil	One moment, one moment, please . . . yes?
Melbury	A single room with a . . .
Basil	Your **name**, please, could I have your name?
Melbury	Melbury.
	The phone rings; Basil picks it up.
Basil	*(to **Melbury**)* One second please. *(to phone)* Hello? . . . Ah, yes, Mr O'Reilly, well it's perfectly simple. When I asked you to build me a wall I was rather hoping that instead of just dumping the bricks in a pile you might have found time to cement them together . . . you know, one on top of another, in the traditional fashion. *(to **Melbury**, testily)* Could you fill it in, please? *(to phone)* Oh, splendid! Ah, yes, but when, Mr O'Reilly? *(to **Melbury**, who is having difficulty with the register)* there – there!! *(to phone)* Yes, but <u>when</u>? Yes, yes . . . ah! . . . the flu! *(to **Melbury**)* <u>Both</u> names, please. *(to phone)* Yes, I should have guessed, Mr O'Reilly, that and the potato famine I suppose . . .
Melbury	I beg your pardon?
Basil	Would you put both your names, please? . . . *(to phone)* Well, will you give me a date?
Melbury	Er . . . I only use one.
Basil	*(with a withering look)* You don't have a first name?
Melbury	No, I am <u>Lord</u> Melbury, so I simply sign myself 'Melbury'.
	There is a long, long pause.
Basil	*(to phone)* Go away. *(puts phone down)* . . . I'm so sorry to have kept you waiting, your lordship . . . I do apologise, please forgive me. Now, was there something, is there something, anything, I can do for you? Anything at all?
Melbury	Well, I have filled this in . . .
Basil	Oh, please don't bother with that. *(he takes the form and throws it away)* Now, a special room? . . . a single? A double? A suite? . . . Well, we don't have any suites, but we do have some beautiful doubles with a view . . .
Melbury	No, no, just a single.
Basil	Just a single! Absolutely! How very <u>wise</u> if I may say so, your honour.
Melbury	With a bath.
Basil	Naturally, naturally! *Naturellement!* *(he roars with laughter)*
Melbury	I shall be staying for one or two nights . . .
Basil	Oh please! Please! . . . Manuel!! *(he bangs the bell; nothing happens)* . . . Well, it's . . . it's rather grey today, isn't it?
Melbury	Oh, yes, it is, rather.
Basil	Of course usually down here it's quite beautiful, but today is a real old . . . er . . . rotter. *(another bang on the bell)* Manuel!!! . . . Still . . . it's good for the wheat.
Melbury	Yes, er, I suppose so.
Basil	Oh yes! I hear it's coming along wonderfully at the moment! Thank God! I love the wheat . . . there's no sight like a field of wheat waving in the . . . waving in . . . **Manuel!!!!** *(he bangs the bell as hard as he can; no result)* . . . Well, how are you? I mean, if it's not a personal question. Well, it is a

	personal . . . *(he dashes from behind the desk)* Let me get your cases for you, please allow me . . .
Melbury	. . . Oh, thank you very much, they're just outside.
Basil	Splendid. Thank you so much. I won't be one moment . . .

Questions & Assignments

1 Would you agree that this episode shows Basil Fawlty to be a very rude person? Give reasons for your answer.
2 What do we learn about O'Reilly from this extract?
3 How and why does Basil's attitude change towards Melbury?

Extract 2

The forecourt of Fawlty Towers. Basil is fiddling under the bonnet of his car, which is clearly a real mother of an old car. He makes a final adjustment and strides round to the driver's seat. He presses the starter twice, without results.

Basil	Oh come on, is it so difficult for you to start? . . . I mean it's so <u>basic</u>. If you don't go, there's very little point in having you.
	He tries again, then gives up, goes round to the front and takes a delicious-looking savoury from a small pile on the engine, – pops it in his mouth and starts fiddling again. The horn jams on; he clears it.
Basil	Now, just pull yourself together, right? Make the effort. *(he gets back in and presses the starter; it whines pitifully)* Come on . . . now look!
Manuel	*(running down the steps)* Mr Fawlty! Mr Fawlty! Telephone!!
Basil	What?
Manuel	Telephone . . . telephone. *(mimes a telephone)*
Basil	Oh . . . where's Sybil?
Manuel	. . . Qué?
Basil	Where's . . . Sy . . . bil?
Manuel	. . . Where's . . . the bill?
Basil	No! No! I own the place. I don't pay bills. Where's my <u>wife</u>?
Manuel	She not there.
Basil	She <u>is</u> there! *(Manuel looks helpless)* Oh, never mind, right, leave it to me, <u>I'll</u> do it! *(he strides towards the hotel)* <u>I'll</u> mend the car, <u>I'll</u> answer the telephone, then you can all handcuff and blindfold me and <u>I'll</u> clean the windows . . .
	He steams into the lobby. **Manuel** *gets ahead of him.*
Manuel	In here.
Basil	Yes, I know it's in here!
Manuel	*(indicating telephone)* This way, please. *(he goes into the kitchen)*

Spectrum 1

Basil	Yes, I know it's this way, I <u>own</u> the place!
	But just before he gets to the telephone, **Sybil** *appears from the office and answers it herself.*
Sybil	Hallo, Fawlty Towers . . . Oh, André, thank you for calling. Kurt's marvellous, we're absolutely delighted with him . . . really, André, he's wonderful . . .
	Basil *goes to the kitchen and leads* **Manuel** *back to the desk.*
Basil	*(pointing to* **Sybil***)* This Basil's wife. *(pointing to himself)* This . . . Basil. This . . . smack on head. *(demonstrates;* **Manuel** *slinks off)*
Sybil	Just one moment, André . . . Basil!
Basil	Yes, dear?
Sybil	Have you taken the car in yet?
Basil	Yes, I'm just dealing with it, dear.
Sybil	You're not trying to do it yourself, are you, Basil?
Basil	*(discovering a change of subject on the wall)* Have you seen this mark up here, dear?
Sybil	Did you hear what I said?
Basil	Yes I did, dear, it's a bit of a scratch . . .
Sybil	Take it into the garage, Basil.

Questions & Assignments

1 Based on this extract, briefly describe the characters of (i) Manuel and (ii) Sybil.
2 Show how Manuel's poor knowledge of English leads to some comic situations in this extract.

Extract 3

Mr. Leeman, a guest at Fawlty Towers, is not feeling well. He plans an early night and meets Basil as he makes his way upstairs to his bedroom . . .

Basil	*(appearing from the kitchen with a plate of sandwiches; to* **Leeman***)* Good night. *(***Leeman** *does not respond, moving past towards the stairs)* I said 'Good night.'
Mr Leeman	Oh, good night.
Basil	That didn't hurt, did it.
Sybil	Basil!
	Mr Leeman *disappears uncertainly as* **Basil** *crosses the lobby.*
Basil	Good manners cost nothing, dear.
Sybil	He's not feeling very well, Basil.
Basil	He only had to say 'Good night', dear. It's not the Gettysburg address.
Sybil	Basil, when you're not feeling well . . .

Basil	(*going into the bar*) Just two little words, dear, to bring a little happiness into the world.
Mr Leeman	(*coming down again*) Excuse me.
Sybil	Yes, Mr Leeman. What can I do for you?
Mr Leeman	Do you think I might have breakfast in bed in the morning.
Basil	(*coming back in*) . . . In bed?
Mr Leeman	Yes.
Sybil	Of course, Mr Leeman.
Basil	Yes, we can manage that, can't we dear?
Sybil	Yes, we can. (*to phone*) I'll call you back. (*puts the phone down*)
Basil	Is it your legs?
Mr Leeman	. . . I'm sorry?
Basil	Well, most of our guests manage to struggle down in the morning.
Sybil	A full breakfast or the continental?
Mr Leeman	Oh, er . . .
Sybil	Our chef does a very good full breakfast, eggs, bacon, sausage, tomato, fried bread . . .
Mr Leeman	The continental.
Basil	You wouldn't care for kippers?
Mr Leeman	Oh . . . fine, kippers, yes, thank you.
	***Basil** departs resignedly.*
Sybil	Toast, butter, marmalade . . .
Mr Leeman	Yes, thank you.
Sybil	Tea or coffee?
Mr Leeman	(*not feeling at all well*) Yes, er . . . tea, thank you.
Sybil	A newspaper?
Mr Leeman	Er . . . Telegraph.
Sybil	Thank you . . . Good night.
	Mr Leeman** starts to move off:* ***Sybil *goes into the office;* ***Basil*** *comes back in.*
Basil	Rosewood, mahogany, teak?
Mr Leeman	. . . I beg your pardon?
Basil	What would you like your breakfast tray made out of?
Mr Leeman	I don't really mind.
Basil	Are you sure? Fine, well you go along and have a really good night's sleep then – I'm hoping to get a couple of hours later on myself . . . (*shouting after **Mr Leeman** as he goes up the stairs*) but I'll be up in good time to serve you your breakfast in bed. (***Leeman*** *has now gone*) If you can remember to sleep with your mouth open you won't even have to wake up. I'll just drop in small pieces of lightly buttered kipper when you're breathing in the right direction, if that doesn't put you out. (*imitates **Sybil***) Basil! (*slaps his own wrist*).

Spectrum 1

Questions & Assignments

1 Imagine that Manuel discovers Mr. Leeman dead in bed on the following morning. He rushes down to break the news to Basil. Write the dialogue that you imagine would take place between Basil and Manuel.
2 Basil goes to investigate and finds that Manuel was telling the truth. Write the dialogue that you imagine would then take place between Basil and Sybil.

Reading & Composition

THE WORK OF FRANK McCOURT

At the age of 66, Frank McCourt, a retired teacher of English, published his first book, *Angela's Ashes*, an account of his childhood in Limerick in the 1930s and 1940s. The book met with instant success and won a Pulitzer Prize in 1997. As one critic wrote – 'McCourt magically retrieves love, dignity, and humour from a childhood of hunger, loss, and pain.'

In *Angela's Ashes* Frank McCourt describes, not without humour, scenes of poverty and sadness that for the vast majority of young people in today's Ireland are almost unimaginable.

McCourt was born in New York in 1930 to parents who had emigrated from Ireland a few years before. It was the time of the Great Depression when hunger and unemployment were widespread in America. He returned to Ireland with his family at the age of four and was raised in the slums of Limerick. Frank's mother, Angela, had no money to feed the children since Frank's father, Malachy, rarely worked, and when he did he drank his wages. Shortly after the outbreak of war, Malachy, like many other men from Ireland, went to England to work. He failed to send any money home, leaving his wife and children, already living in squalor, to further fend for themselves.

In this extract Frank writes about his first job, as a helper to a neighbour, Mr Hannon, a coal delivery man whose legs are 'ruined'.

(Note: The author has not used any quotation marks throughout the entire book.)

From *Angela's Ashes*

I'm dying to go around with Mr. Hannon on the great float like a real workingman. If I'm good at it they might let me stay at home from school forever but Mam says, He can do it as long as it doesn't interfere with school and he can start on a Saturday morning.

I'm a man now so I light the fire early on Saturday morning and make my own tea and fried bread. I wait next door for Mr. Hannon to come out with his bicycle and there's a lovely smell of rashers and eggs coming through the window. Mam says Mr. Hannon gets the best of food because Mrs. Hannon is as mad about him as she was the day she married him. They're like two lovers out of an American film the way they go on. Here he is pushing the bicycle and puffing away on the pipe in his mouth. He tells me climb up on the bar of his bike and off we go to my first job as a man. His head is over mine on the bike and the smell of the pipe is lovely. There's a coal smell on his clothes and that makes me sneeze.

Men are walking or cycling toward the coal yards and Rank's Flour Mills and the Limerick Steamship Company on the Dock Road. Mr. Hannon takes his pipe from his mouth and tells me this is the best morning of all, Saturday, half day. We'll start at eight and be finished by the time the Angelus rings at twelve.

First we get the horse ready, give him a bit off a rub, fill the wooden tub with oats and the bucket with water. Mr. Hannon shows me how to put on the harness and lets me back the horse into the shafts of the float. He says, Jaysus, Frankie, you have the knack of it. That makes me so happy I want to jump up and down and drive a float the rest of my life.

There are two men filling bags with coal and turf and weighing them on the great iron scale, a hundredweight in each bag. It's their job to stack the bags on the float while Mr. Hannon goes to the office for the delivery dockets. The bag men are fast and we're ready for our rounds. Mr. Hannon sits up on the left side of the float and flicks the whip to show where I'm to sit on the right side. It's hard to climb up the way the float is so high and packed with bags and I try to get up by climbing the wheel. Mr. Hannon says I should never do the likes of that again. Never put your leg or hand near a wheel when the horse is harnessed in the shafts A horse might take a notion to go for a walk for himself and there you are with the leg or the arm caught in the wheel and twisted off your body and you looking at it. He says to the horse, G'up ower that, and the horse shakes his head and rattles the harness and Mr. Hannon laughs. That fool of a horse loves to work, he says. He won't be rattling his harness in a few hours.

When the rain starts we cover ourselves with old coal bags and Mr. Hannon turns his pipe upside down in his mouth to keep the tobacco dry. He says the rain makes everything heavier but what's the use of complaining. You might as well be complaining about the sun in Africa.

We cross the Sarsfield Bridge for deliveries to the Ennis Road and the North Circular Road. Rich people, says Mr. Hannon, and very slow to put their hands in their pockets for a tip.

We have sixteen bags to deliver. Mr. Hannon says we're lucky today because some houses get more than one and he doesn't have to be climbing on and off that float destroying his legs. When we stop he gets down and I pull the bag to the edge and lay it on his shoulders. Some houses have areas outside where you pull up a trap door and tip the bag till it empties and that's easy. There are other houses with long backyards and you can see Mr. Hannon suffering with his legs when he has to carry the bags from the float to the sheds near the back doors. Ah, Jaysus, Frankie, ah, Jaysus, is the only complaint out of him and he asks me to give him a hand to climb back on the float. He says if he had a handcart he could wheel the bags from float to house and that would be a blessing but a handcart would cost two weeks' wages and who could afford that?

The bags are delivered and the float is empty, and the horse knows his workday is over. It's lovely to sit on the float looking along the length of the horse from his tail to his head rocking along the Ennis Road over the Shannon and up the Dock Road. Mr. Hannon says the man who delivered sixteen hundredweights of coal and turf deserves a pint and the boy who helped him deserves a lemonade. He tells me I should go to school and not be like him working away with the two legs rotting under him. Go to school,

Frankie, and get out of Limerick and Ireland itself. This war will be over some day and you can go to America or Australia or any big open country where you can look up and see no end to the land. The world is wide and you can have great adventures. If I didn't have these two legs I'd be over in England making a fortune in the factories like the rest of the Irishmen, like your father. No, not like your father. I hear he left you high and dry, eh? I don't know how a man in his right mind can go off and leave a wife and family to starve and shiver in a Limerick winter. School, Frankie, school. The books, the books, the books. Get out of Limerick before your legs rot and your mind collapses entirely.

The horse clops along and when we get to the coal yard we feed and water him and give him a rubdown. Mr. Hannon talks to him all the time and calls him Me oul' segosha, and the horse snuffles and pushes his nose against Mr. Hannon's chest. I'd love to bring this horse home and let him stay downstairs when we're upstairs but even if I could get him in the door my mother would yell at me that the last thing we need in this house is a horse.

. . . Mr Hannon buys me a lemonade, gives me the shilling for my morning's work and tells me I can go home now, I'm a great worker and I can help him again next week after school.

On the way home I see myself in the glass of a shop window all black from the coal, and I feel like a man, a man with a shilling in his pocket, a man who had a lemonade in a pub with two coal men and a lime man. I'm not a child anymore and I could easily leave Leamy's School forever. I could work with Mr. Hannon every day and when his legs got too bad I could take over the float and deliver coal to the rich people the rest of my life and my mother wouldn't have to be a beggar at the Redemptorist priests' house.

People on the streets and lanes give me a curious looks. Boys and girls laugh and call out, Here's the chimney sweep. How much you want for cleaning our chimney? Did you fall into a coal hole? Were you burned by the darkness?

They're ignorant. They don't know I spent the day delivering hundredweights of coal and turf. They don't know I'm a man.

. . . I can hear Mrs. Hannon through the window, Your little Frankie is a godsend to John for 'tis the climbing up and down on that float that was ruining his legs entirely.

Mam doesn't say anything and that means she feels so sorry for Mr. Hannon she'll let me help him again on his heavy delivery day, Thursday. I wash my eyes three times a day and I blink till I get a pain in my eyebrows. I blink in school when the master isn't looking and all the boys in my class are calling me Blinky and adding that to the list of names.

Blinky McCourt
beggar woman's son
scabby-eyed
blubber gob
dancing
Jap.

I don't care what they call me anymore as long as my eyes are clearing up and I have a regular job lifting hundredweights of coal on a float. I wish they could see me on Thursday after school when I'm on the float and Mr. Hannon hands me the reins so that he can smoke his pipe in comfort. Here you are, Frankie, nice and gentle for this is a good horse and he doesn't need to be pulled at.

He hands me the whip too but you never need the whip with this horse. It's all for show and I just flick it at the air like Mr. Hannon or I might knock a fly off the horse's great golden rump swinging between the shafts.

Surely the world is looking at me and admiring the way I rock with the float, the cool way I have with the reins and the whip. I wish I had a pipe like Mr. Hannon and a tweed cap. I wish I could be a real coal man with black skin like Mr. Hannon and Uncle Pa Keating so that people would say, There goes Frankie McCourt that delivers all the coal in Limerick and drinks his pint in South's pub. I'd never wash my face. I'd be black every day of the year even Christmas when you're supposed to give yourself a good wash for the coming of the Infant Jesus.

. . . I work with Mr. Hannon after school on Tuesdays and Thursdays and the half day on Saturday morning and that means three shillings for my mother though she worries all the time over my eyes. The minute I get home she washes them and makes me rest them for half an hour.

Mr. Hannon says he'll wait near Leamy's School for me on Thursdays after his deliveries on Barrington Street. Now the boys will see me. Now they'll know I'm a workingman and more than a scabby-eyed blubber gob dancing Jap. Mr. Hannon says, Up you get, and I climb up on the float like any workingman. I look at the boys gawking at me. Gawking. I tell Mr. Hannon if he wants to smoke his pipe in comfort I'll take the reins and when he hands then over I'm sure I hear the boys gasping. I tell the horse, G'up ower that, like Mr. Hannon. We trot away and I know dozens of Leamy's boys are committing the deadly sin of envy. I tell the horse again, G'up ower that, to make sure everyone heard, to make sure they know I'm driving that float and no one else, to make sure they'll never forget it was me they saw on that float with the reins and the whip. It's the best day of my life, better than my First Communion day, which Grandma ruined, better than my Confirmation day when I had the typhoid.

They don't call me names anymore. They don't laugh at my scabby eyes. They want to know how I got such a good job at eleven years of age and what I'm paid and if I'll have that job forever. They want to know if there are any other good jobs going in the coal yards and would I put in a good word for them.

Then there are big boys of thirteen who stick their faces in mine and say they should have that job because they're bigger and I'm nothing but a scrawny little runt with no shoulders. They can talk as much as they like. I have the job and Mr. Hannon tells me I'm powerful.

. . . The legs are getting so bad he has to get up an hour earlier in the morning to get the stiffness out, to put on another dressing. It's still dark one Saturday morning when Mrs. Hannon knocks at our door and asks me if I'd go to a neighbour and borrow their handcart to take on the float for Mr. Hannon will never be able to carry the bags today and maybe I'd just roll then on the handcart for him. He won't be able to carry me on his bicycle so I can meet him at the yard with the handcart.

The neighbour says, Anything for Mr. Hannon, God bless him.

I wait at the gate of the coal yard and watch him cycle toward me, slower than ever. He's so stiff he can hardly get off the bike and he says, You're a great man, Frankie. He lets me get the horse ready though I still have trouble getting on the harness. He lets me handle the float out of the yard and into the frosty streets and I wish I could drive forever and never go home. Mr. Hannon shows me how to pull the bags to the edge of the float and drop them on the ground so that I can pull them on the handcart and push them to the houses. He tells me how to lift and push the bags without straining myself and we have the sixteen bags delivered by noon.

I wish the boys at Leamy's could see me

now, the way I drive the horse and handle the bags, the way I do everything while Mr. Hannon rests his legs. I wish they could see me pushing the handcart to South's pub and having my lemonade with Mr. Hannon and Uncle Pa and me all black and Bill Galvin all white. I'd like to show the world the tips Mr. Hannon lets me keep, four shillings and the shilling he gives me for the morning's work, five shillings altogether.

Mam is sitting by the fire and when I hand her the money she looks at me, drops it in her lap and cries. I'm puzzled because money is supposed to make you happy. Look at your eyes, she says. Go to that glass and look at your eyes.

My face is black and the eyes are worse than ever. The whites and the eyelids are red, and the yellow stuff oozes to the corners and out over the lower lids. If the ooze sits a while it forms a crust that has to be picked off or washed away.

Questions & Assignments

1. (i) What are the author's feelings about starting work?
   (ii) What conditions does his mother impose before she agrees to let him work?
2. (i) State in one sentence what the second paragraph is about.
   (ii) When writers describe things they mainly appeal to the reader's sense of sight and sound. Examine the second paragraph and say what the writer wants the reader to imagine – sights . . . sounds . . . or . . . ? Explain your answer.
3. Consider the description of people on their way to work and suggest how things have changed over the years.
4. (i) Outline Mr. Hannon's duties.
   (ii) Did Mr. Hannon's employer treat him well? Give reasons.
5. (i) What advice does Mr. Hannon give the young Frank?
   (ii) In your view was it sound advice? Explain your answer.
6. How do other children treat Frank?
7. (i) How did he feel when Mr. Hannon was waiting for him outside the school?
   (ii) How did this affect the other boys?
8. Why does his mother cry when he gives her the money?
9. How does the passage convey the extent of the poverty suffered by the author?
10. What did you learn about the character of (a) Mr Hannon (b) the writer and (c) the writer's mother from your reading of the passage?
11. In his writing the author makes use of many words and phrases spoken by the people at the time. Identify a number of examples of these.

Autobiography

The reading public have always enjoyed life-stories. When a person writes about his or her own life, that work is called an **autobiography**; when a person writes about the life of another person that work is called a **biography**.

At present, biography is a very popular literary form. Many books have been published on the lives of well-known people, both living and dead. Often the writers of biographies (biographers) concentrate on uncovering unexpected – and often unpleasant – details about their subjects, in an attempt to find the 'real person' behind the public image.

PERSONAL WRITING

GOOD HANDWRITING

Write Neatly! It is always pleasing to get a postcard or a letter written in neat handwriting. It is easy to read and you get the feeling that the writer took a little extra care.

Nowadays computers and printers are widely used in both the workplace and the home. Producing a neatly printed document was never so easy.

Nevertheless neat handwriting is a very important skill. In primary school you will have been taught the basics of good handwriting. As you begin the next stage of your education you should continue to aim for a high standard of handwriting in all subjects. Good handwriting will work to your advantage in all your future examinations. Nothing is more annoying for a teacher or examiner than page after page of untidy handwriting where almost every word presents a difficulty.

The most common cause of poor handwriting is hurrying to get a passage written. When handwriting is rushed it usually results in one or more of the following:
- Individual letters badly formed;
- Letters bunched too closely together;
- Letters which are the wrong size or height in relation to other letters;
- Incorrect spacing between words;
- Words that wander above or below the line;
- Many words and letters crossed out.

> **Everyone, by taking a little care and attention, can write in a neat and readable style. The basic rule is to slow down to a pace where each word can be clearly read. Practise this and you will find that your writing speed will gradually increase without losing its quality.**

JOINED WRITING

The disadvantage of 'printing' is that you have to lift the pen off the paper after writing each letter. This is both time-consuming and tiring. Joined writing allows you to write most words without lifting the pen from the paper. Joined writing – also called **cursive** writing – simply involves joining up letters with slopes, loops and curves.

Personal Writing: Keeping a Diary

People keep diaries to help them to look back on events dating back over months or years. Many diaries, both of famous people and 'ordinary' people, have been published over the years and they provide interesting information about the day-to-day lives of their authors.

One of the earliest diarists to be published was Samuel Pepys. He kept his diary for nine years between 1660 and 1669, writing in shorthand to protect his diary from prying eyes. In 1825 a scholar at Cambridge deciphered the diary and it was published around fifty years later. He is famous for his vivid painting of historic events of the London of the day, such as the plague and the Great Fire of London.

Here are some examples of entries in diaries. The first two are fictitious and the remaining three are from the diaries of actual people.

> **Monday 1 March:** Got up. Went to school. Came home. Had fish fingers. Went to bed. Started to count up to a billion but only got up to 7,643 for the reason that my Father made me stop. He said that if he had to come up to my bedroom once more, that he would strangle me. This man is dangerous.   *(K. Waterhouse)*
>
> **Monday January 19th:** The dog is back at the vet's. It has got concrete stuck on its paws. No wonder it was making such a row on the stairs last night.
> *(Diary of Adrian Mole)*
>
> **May 23 1800:** Ironing till tea time. So heavy rain that I could not go for letters.
> *(Dorothy Wordsworth)*
>
> **March 10 1904:** Sixteen hrs march, the hottest day we have had . . . No water . . . Nearly drank from a green stinking puddle, but refrained.   *(Aubrey Herbert)*
>
> **January 6 1663:** Myself somewhat vexed at my wife's neglect in leaving of her scarf and waistcoat in the coach today that brought us from Westminster, though I confess she did give them to me to look after – yet it was her fault not to see that I did take them out of the coach.
> *(Samuel Pepys)*

✎ Personal Writing Keeping a Diary

Begin by keeping a diary for a fortnight or so. Write about the things that are important to you. Don't try to describe everything that happens. Select those of most significance to you. As your journal or diary is a personal document, you should not be afraid to experiment with a variety of forms of expression, such as poetry, dialogue, song lyrics and so on. It might provide interesting or exciting reading in a few years' time. You can write phrases rather than long sentences . . . The extracts above may give you ideas to get started.

From *Letter to Daniel – 1*
Fergal Keane

My grandfather's name was Paddy Hassett and he married my grandmother, May Sexton, in the summer of 1932. The house he built for his new bride sat in its own garden with a rockery full of flowers, several apple trees and numerous blackcurrant bushes. It was made of solid west Cork stone and, in the first year of their occupation, they planted ivy which soon spread across the walls. Every few months this had to be sheared back lest it sneak across the windows and block out the sunlight.

Like many Irish couples of the time my grandparents had a large family. There were eight children in all, of whom seven lived beyond childhood. My grandfather died when I was one year old and what I know of him has been gleaned from the stories of my family. I know that he was a quiet man who neither smoked nor drank. But he had a romantic nature and loved opera and the Irish game of hurling. More than anything he loved his children. Once a week he and my grandmother would go into town for tea and afterwards to the cinema. It was, as far as I know, the only time in the week which was not devoted to the interests and well-being of their growing brood of children.

My grandfather ran his own garage business and made a good income in the postwar years when cars began to appear for the first time on Ireland's narrow roads. He built a seaside cottage for his family near the village of Ardmore in County Waterford where he had been born, the son of a police sergeant. Every June my grandmother would load her family on to the bus and set off for the cottage where they stayed until the end of August. But it was the house at Turners Cross which remained at the centre of the family. My mother remembers it as a place crowded with children's voices and music.

Then in the early sixties my grandfather's business collapsed, a victim of recession and his own unending willingness to give credit to those who would never repay him. For a while it looked as if the bank would take the house, but then my grandfather's eldest son stepped in and took out a mortgage on the property.

My grandfather died a few months later from the effects of a stroke. I know that, close to the end, my grandmother brought me, their first grandchild, to see him in hospital and that he stroked my infant head. He wanted to speak but could not and he never left hospital. My grandmother returned alone to the house they had built on the hills above the river.

In retrospect, much of my grandmother's later life seems to have been a hard struggle for emotional survival. She had already suffered the loss of her husband and the death of a child shortly after birth. Then she lost a fourteen-year-old son, Ben, to polio. But it was the death of their third son, Michael, in a fire in New York City, which came close to destroying her faith in life. Michael had been a favourite. A talented theatre director, he had emigrated to America in the 1950s but was weeks away from returning to Ireland when a fire in his apartment claimed his life. Warm-hearted, artistic and handsome, he closely resembled my grandfather. The mention of his name would bring tears to my grandmother's eyes until the day she died.

And yet, in spite of her immense sorrow, May Hassett kept going. She still managed to smile and make us laugh. Although I suspect her own hope disappeared on the night Michael died, she communicated her love for others with such power that those around her always felt happy and wanted. I spent most of my childhood summers living with her in St Declans. My memories are of a happy place were comfort and reassurance were always at hand. Because of my father's alcoholism, my own home environment was neither happy nor secure. Taking the train to Cork and St Declans and the warm arms of my grandmother seemed to me an annual deliverance.

When my parents separated permanently in 1970, I went to live in St Declans for two years. <u>It was a traumatic time, a time of great upheaval, and I would almost certainly have become lost in bad places had the lights of my grandparents' house not beckoned</u>. I remember many things about that house: the smell of brown bread baking in the kitchen, collecting armfuls of apples in the garden for crab apple jelly, picking blackcurrants for jam, playing endless games of 'kiss or torture' with my friends' sisters, choking desperately on my first cigarette in the shed at the end of the garden while my grandmother laughed to herself in the kitchen.

On rainy afternoons my grandmother would bring down the big box of toy soldiers collected over the years by her own sons and I would lose myself in imaginary battles and conquests. Later, when I saw a girl I wanted to ask out, it was my grandmother who gave me the courage to venture forth, a teenage Romeo in brushed denim jeans, and suggest a trip to the cinema. 'The worst she can say is 'no', she told me and, as always, she was right. In fact the girl said 'Yes', and our relationship lasted, believe it or not, for eight years. When we broke up and I was plunged into extended youthful misery my grandmother was waiting in St Declans with a mug of cocoa and a sympathetic smile.

I left Cork and the world of my childhood in 1979 and began a journalistic career that would take me to places my grandparents had barely heard of. As the years went on, I saw less and less of my grandmother. Yet each time I came back to St Declans she seemed to be the strong warm person I had always known. And then, while living in Belfast, I received news that she was suffering from cancer. When I went to see her she seemed frail and suddenly old, and she told me she believed she was dying. 'I'm on the way out, Ferg,' she said and then added, 'but we all have to go some time.'

That evening I went up to St Declans and the house felt empty and strange. There were no voices now. Only her photographs on the walls, some of them fading into yellow, spoke of its crowded past. My grandmother was eventually transferred to the Royal Marsden Hospital in London where the doctors seemed more optimistic. At about the same time I was appointed BBC correspondent in South Africa, a job I had wanted from the moment I joined the Corporation. My grandmother was delighted for me and even spoke hopefully of being there to greet me at St Declans where I came home in the summer. On our way out to South Africa my wife and I stopped off in London to visit her at the Royal Marsden. There, among other old people, in a city she did not know, my grandmother seemed small and vulnerable, a little old lady for whom unseen shadows were lengthening every day. We spoke about the past and about our large group of relatives, and she told me to take care of myself and my wife, Anne. 'Mind that little girl,' she joked.

When I got up to go I noticed that my grandmother had tears in her eyes and we both knew, without saying a word, that I would never see her again. A month later she came home to die. I was given the news early one morning on a long-distance call from Ireland. I walked out into the garden and cried for a long time. And then, with the birds of the highveld singing their hearts out, I went back inside and woke my wife. We sat for hours drinking tea and remembering my grandmother, and I am happy to say that most of the memories involved laughter. After her death my uncle decided to sell St Declans and the rest of the family agreed. There seemed little point in clinging to bricks and mortar when the people we had loved, who had made the place special, had passed on.

Yet each summer when I return to Cork I cannot resist the urge to drive past St Declans. I always stop there for a few moments and lean back into warm invisible arms, imagining I can hear the sound of opera playing on the radio and children's voices rising above it, and then a woman calling them home for tea. Home as it always will be.

Questions & Assignments

1. (i) What were the attractive features of the house that the author's grandfather built?
   (ii) Why did the ivy have to be trimmed back?
2. Would you agree that both the author's grandparents come across in the extract as loving and caring people? Give reasons for your answer.
3. Explain the two underlined passages in your own words.
4. What happy memories had the author of his years in Cork?
5. Why according to the author did his grandfather's business go bankrupt?
6. (i) Had the author's grandmother a hard life? Explain your answer.
   (ii) What incident came close to destroying his grandmother's faith in life?
7. From the evidence of the passage why do you think the author had a high regard for his grandmother?
8. What do we learn about the author from the extract?
9. What parts of the passage did you find particularly moving or sad?

PARTS OF SPEECH

All activities have their own sets of words. A mechanic understands what a 'clutch' is, a printer knows what a 'folio' is and a musician appreciates the musical significance of a 'key'.

The study of English – or any language – is an activity that involves working with words. Therefore this activity has its own set of technical terms or special words to describe different kinds of words, different groupings of words and different punctuation marks.

All words belong to one of eight groups of words:

> nouns
> pronouns
> adjectives
> verbs
> adverbs
> prepositions
> conjunctions
> interjections.

These are called **parts of speech**. You cannot always tell what part of speech a word is by looking at the word on its own. For example, the word 'fly' can be a noun ('Waiter, there's a **fly** in my soup.') or a verb (Some birds **fly** to great heights). To tell what part of speech a word is, you must look at the work it does in a particular sentence.

NOUNS

The word **noun** is of Latin origin and means name. Nouns are names given to persons, places and things.

> Sentence 1:   **Peter** found **money** in the **park**.
> Sentence 2:   The **musicians** travelled to **Cork** to a **concert**.

The nouns in each of the above sentences are in bold. **Peter** and **musicians** are words that name persons; **money** and **concert** are words that name things; **park** and **Cork** are words that name places.

NOUNS – SINGULAR AND PLURAL

When we speak of one thing – The **dog** barked; The **man** arrived – we are using the **singular** form of the noun.

When we speak of more than one thing – The **dogs** barked; The **men** arrived – we are using the **plural** form of the noun.

Guidelines for forming plurals

1. The general rule is to add **s** to the singular,
   for example: house/house**s**; song/song**s**; girl/girl**s**.

2. Add **es** to the singular of words where the **s** cannot be pronounced on its own. These are usually words ending in
   - ss   class/class**es**
   - x   fox/fox**es**
   - sh   marsh/marsh**es**
   - ch   branch/branch**es**

3. If the singular ends in **y** and is preceded by a consonant, change the **y** into an **i** and add **es**,
   for example: army/arm**ies**; duty/ dut**ies**.

4. If the singular ends with **y** and is preceded by a vowel, add **s**,
   for example: boy/boy**s**; day/day**s**; key/key**s**; kidney/kidney**s**.

5. If the singular ends in **f** or **fe** change it to **ves**,
   for example: loaf/ loa**ves**; wolf/wol**ves**.
   (There are some exceptions to this rule. These include chief, fife, gulf, proof, roof, reef – where an **s** is added for the plural.)

6. If a singular ends in **o**, preceded by a consonant, add **es**,
   for example: hero/hero**es**; volcano/volcano**es**.
   (Exceptions include piano/piano**s**; solo/solo**s**; Eskimo/Eskimo**s**.)

7. In the case of compound words (a word formed from two or more words) change the **principal word** to the plural,
   for example: mother-in-law/mother**s**-in-law;
   commander-in-chief/ commander**s**-in-chief.

8. Certain words change completely in the plural, form,
   for example: man/m**en**, woman/wom**en**, foot/f**ee**t, goose/g**ee**se, tooth/ t**ee**th, mouse/m**ice**, child/child**ren**.

9. A few words such as deer, sheep and fish have the same form in both the singular and the plural.

10. A number of foreign nouns which have become part of everyday English still form their plurals according to the rules of the language from which they originated,
    for example: memorandum/memorand**a**; radius/rad**ii**;
    index/ind**ices**.
    (These are all from the Latin.)
    Other examples include:
    analysis/analy**ses**; hypothesis/hypothe**ses**; crisis/cri**ses**.

Spectrum 1

18 When they came we were delighted.
19 Farther along the path.
20 When the teacher came back, she found the class was sitting quietly.
21 Electricity can kill.
22 After reaching the top of the mountain.
23 At the foot of the hill.
24 As a result of his win.
25 Every little helps.
26 Nobody cares.

Assignment

2   All capital letters and full stops have been removed from each of the passages below. Rewrite each of the passages, putting in capital letters at the start of sentences and full stops at the end of sentences. The number of sentences in each passage is given at the end of the passage. Remember that names of people always begin with a capital letter and that the word 'I' is always a capital letter. After sentences that form questions you should insert a question mark (?) instead of a full stop.

Passage A
ben awoke to a frosty, bright christmas morning already the tiny cottage was filled with appetising smells ben fetched his bulky parcels from where he had hidden them and ran downstairs to give them to his family never had he felt so keenly the pleasure of giving
(4 sentences)

Passage B
as we were leaving the café with our hot-dogs we bumped into a kid pushing through the narrow doorway i recognised him straight away he was a punk, about seventeen years old he used to go to our school, until he'd been thrown out i had dropped my hot-dog and when i bent down to pick it up the punk slammed his boot down on my hand the hot-dog was squashed flat and ketchup oozed out between my fingers i cried out in pain
(7 sentences)

Passage C
puppets are small animal or human figures worked by a person who is called a puppet-master, or puppeteer a good puppeteer can charm an audience by making even the simplest puppet move and speak in a way that seems almost human a puppet may be only a handkerchief draped over the hand, or it may be a figure strung with wires so that it can perform many different movements there are six basic types of puppet, one of the most common is the glove puppet or hand puppet, which is worn on the hand the first finger is put into the neck, and the thumb and second finger into the arms two of the best-known puppets, punch and judy, are nearly always made as glove puppets
(7 sentences)

256

PERSONAL WRITING — PUNCTUATION

SENTENCES AND FULL STOPS

In many early manuscripts, handwritten by monks, there was no punctuation at all and this created difficulties for the reader. Punctuation was introduced to divide up unbroken sections of text into small, easily understood parts. Punctuation marks such as full stops, commas, and question marks all help to make the meaning of a piece of writing more clear. The **full stop**, used to mark the end of a sentence, is the most important punctuation mark of all.

WHAT IS A SENTENCE?

When somebody says 'The men walked down to the river' we know what is meant. However, if somebody says 'The men walked down to the river to', we would wait to hear the remainder of the statement.

✓ 'The men walked down to the river.' **is a sentence because it is complete and makes sense.**

✗ 'The men walked down to the river to' is not a complete statement and is therefore not a sentence. The statement can be completed by adding a phrase such as 'watch the boats go by'.

Assignment — RECOGNISING SENTENCES

1 There are 14 sentences in the list of 26 sentences below. Identify each sentence by its number. In the case of those that are not sentences, turn them into sentences by making suitable additions.

1. When the concert started.
2. The dog is playful and he snaps at people's legs.
3. At night the light shines through the windows.
4. If we get paid on Friday and we meet Peter.
5. Elephants live to be a good age.
6. It is shaped like a star.
7. If it had ever lived, the unicorn would have been a strange creature.
8. Pure gold is bright and shiny.
9. You will never see a live unicorn.
10. It is a mile long.
11. When they die.
12. If the rain stops.
13. The prisoners are carefully guarded.
14. Although some people are afraid of bats.
15. When the teacher returned and found the class making noise.
16. Children who fear dogs.
17. Tom is always late but.

Spectrum 1

Alphabetical Order

ABCDEFGHIJKLMNOPQRSTUVWXTZ

Lists of words are usually presented in alphabetical order. The names in a telephone directory, the words in a dictionary and the topics in an encyclopaedia are all arranged in alphabetical order. This makes it easy to find an item in a list.

Rearrange the following lists of words in alphabetical order.
1. Holland France Ireland Canada Russia Germany Austria Denmark.
2. Dog Cat Monkey Bear Giraffe Lion Tiger Elephant.
3. Cork Limerick Tipperary Antrim Donegal Sligo Mayo Galway.
4. Comerford Regan Osborne McNulty Byrne Daly Fahy Healy.

When words begin with the same letter then their second letters are used to arrange them in alphabetical order

Example 1: Box, Bet, Brown, Bag, Block
These are rearranged as follows: Bag, Bet, Block, Box, Brown.

When the first two letters of a group of words are the same, then we rearrange them in alphabetical order according to their third letter.

Example 2: Street, Stop, Stick, Stamp, Steam
These are rearranged as follows: Stamp, Steam, Stick, Stop, Street.

Assignment — Dictionary Work.

Rearrange the following lists in alphabetical order.

1.
expert	indigo	index
persuade	permit	pervade
indirect	explosion	expedition
industry	independence	indulge
parent	party	perceive
expand	expulsion	exports

2.
Romania	Jamaica	Kenmare	Kinsale	Leeds
Ireland	Spain	Dunmanway	Reading	Newcastle
Canada	Navan	Arklow	Ramsgate	Manchester
Greece	Celbridge	Youghal	Hull	Russia
Germany	Bray	Dundalk	Brighton	Columbia
Naas	Newbridge	Durham	Liverpool	Denmark
Dunsink	Carlow	Leicester	Gibraltar	Iceland
Tallow	Bolton	Bradford	Mexico	Argentina
Ardee	Windsor	Henley	France	Colchester

pressed citizens of Ulan Bator. There was a misery about the people, a doleful expression, which spoke of lives lived on the margins: a struggle to feed themselves and their families, to keep warm in freezing winters, to find jobs and get their children to school, when the money which sustained the state has drained out of the country, north across the border into Siberia.

What is saddest, is the sense of how a people's pride in themselves, in their heritage and ancestry, is being worn down in the face of economic troubles. There is a fierce sensitivity to criticism or investigation by outsiders. When we filmed groups of street children begging, we were chased by groups of angry women. 'Stop showing the world the bad side of Mongolia,' they cried.

The government is under pressure from the world's financial institutions to trim public spending, and most diplomats agree that it is doing the best it can under difficult circumstances. But with millions of roubles still owed to Russia, a vastly underdeveloped infrastructure and rising unemployment, Mongolia will find it hard to return to the days of imperial glory.

Perhaps the train conductor was right, perhaps the herdsman really did believe I was a Russian, and that kick in the leg was his only way of hitting back for all the shame and frustration of life in post-Soviet Mongolia. In the long run I suspect his wounded pride was a much more severe wound than my bruised leg.

Questions & Assignments

1 What words in the first paragraph emphasise the size and strength of the herdsman?
2 How did the guard deal with the herdsman?
3 What was the reaction of the other passengers?
4 Why had the herdsman attacked the writer?
5 Explain the phrases:
   (i) 'There is a fierce sensitivity to criticism or investigation from outsiders.'
   (ii) 'In the long run I suspect his wounded pride was a much more severe wound than my bruised leg.'

From *Letter to Daniel – 2*
Fergal Keane

**Trans-Siberian Attack
Ulan Bator, June 1995
With the collapse of Communism, Mongolia was forced to fend for itself – and found it hard to cope.**

About an hour north of Ulan Bator, the big herdsman stormed into the carriage and headed straight for where I was sitting. He wore a rough cloak fastened around the waist by a piece of rope and on his feet a pair of sturdy leather boots. I was to make the intimate acquaintance of these formidable items of footwear in just a few seconds, for as I looked away briefly, the herdsman drove his right foot, with considerable force, into my knee. In other words, he kicked me, hard.

I gasped with surprise, too taken aback and too small to mount a counter-attack. Getting into a fight with a Mongolian herdsman on the Trans-Siberian Express is not recommended, so I looked around for the train guard who had been assigned as our guide. I need not have worried. He materialized from the toilet in seconds, and, although much smaller in height and weight, launched a ferocious assault on the herdsman. He punched, kicked and swore. In a few minutes, the big man was subdued and blubbering. The train was stopped, and he was ejected into the wilderness, miles from any station or apparent human settlement.

The other passengers, mostly traders ferrying electrical goods between Moscow and Ulan Bator, took all this in their stride. In fact, most ignored the action altogether. When I inquired as to why the guard had responded in, well, what some might call an extreme fashion, he told me that this was Mongolia, and they had rough ways of dealing with trouble-makers. It seems the big herdsman thought I was a Russian, and the Russians, once the economic mainstay of Mongolia, are now despised by many, having abandoned the country that was once their effective colony, and retreated with their money and soldiers back to the motherland.

That afternoon, as the train rattled and rolled across the vast hilly terrain that stretched north in a carpet of spring green, I watched teams of horsemen, appearing out of the emptiness like ghosts, chasing in front of them the herds of horses. Some carried long poles with which they roped in the wilder of the animals and, behind them, in the wake of the horses and their fearsome-looking masters, rose trails of dust, galloped up into the air by a hundred pounding hooves. From the window, the plains of Mongolia looked forbidding, bleak, endless.

I wondered what would become of the herdsman. Was he lost now, wandering hopelessly with the night coming on, and the temperature, even in late May, sinking to freezing? I thought back to what somebody had told me in Ulan Bator before we left. I had been talking about the economic hardship which had followed the Russian withdrawal, its appalling effect on children, and the rise of social problems like alcoholism and violence. 'Yes that's true,' he said, 'but always remember, you are talking about people who once conquered China, who very nearly managed to conquer Europe. They are tough. Don't underestimate them.'

For all that, I found it hard to see the image of Genghis Khan and his Golden Horde reflected in the eyes of the hard-

Nouns

ELEMENTS OF GRAMMAR

PRONOUNS

'Pro' means 'for' in Latin. A pronoun is a word used in place of a noun, referring to a person, place or thing.

Example: Dave gave Tom a ball and **he** lost **it**.
Here the word **he** refers to **Tom** and the word **it** refers to **ball**.

I, you, he, she, it, we, they are some commonly used pronouns.

POSSESSIVE PRONOUNS

Yours, hers, its, ours, theirs are some pronouns that show possession.
(Note: Possessive pronouns do not use an apostrophe.)

✗ Incorrect – It's windscreen is broken.   ✓ This should be – **Its** windscreen is broken.
✗ Incorrect – The dog is their's.   ✓ This should be – The dog is **theirs**.

Me and *I* – Using the correct one

Example 1: The teacher told Tom and ___? to go to the office.
Is the missing word **me** or **I**? To check make two simple sentences, instead of the one above.
  Sentence 1: The teacher told Tom to go to the office.
  Sentence 2: The teacher told **me** (not **I**) to go to the office.
Answer: The teacher told Tom and **me** to go the office.

Example 2: Tom and ___? are going to the match.
  Sentence 1: Tom is going to the match.
  Sentence 2: I (not me) am going to the match.
Answer: is Tom and **I** are going to the match.

NOTE: **Me** always follows **between**. *Example:* He divided the sweets **between** Nora and **me**.

Assignment — THE CORRECT PRONOUN – I OR ME?

Choose the correct pronoun – I or me – in the following 10 sentences.
1. She knew that Peter and __I__ were in trouble.
2. There was a surprise waiting for John and __me__.
3. The prize was to be shared between Dave and __me__.
4. The principal said that Liam and __I__ were to pick up the litter.
5. The coach warned Jean and __me__ about being late.
6. Niall sent tickets for Nuala and __me__.
7. Darren and __I__ got no pocket money.
8. Between you and __me__, I think Anne will be caught.
9. Shane invited Jill and __me__ to his birthday party.
10. Tommy and __I__ are leaving soon.

251

Spectrum 1

COLLECTIVE NOUNS describe a collection or group, e.g. a **flock** of sheep; a **herd** of cattle; a **bunch** of grapes.

Assignment — COLLECTIVE NOUNS

Write out the collective noun which denotes a collection of each of the following:

- *pack* playing cards
- *crowd* spectators
- *board* directors
- *flock* birds
- islands
- *flight* steps
- pups *litter*
- wolves *pack*
- china *set*
- fish *school*
- musicians *orchestra*
- bees *swarm*

ABSTRACT NOUNS describe a **quality** (e.g. height, honesty, wisdom), a **state** (e.g. youth, pleasure, anger) or an **action** (e.g. laughter, disturbance, applause).

Assignment — ABSTRACT NOUNS

Form abstract nouns from the following words. Use your dictionary to check the spellings.

Examples

wise – wisdom   obey – obedience
angry – anger   happy – happiness
thief – theft   see – sight

quality / state / action

- think *thought*
- explode *explosion*
- deceive *deception*
- sweet *sweetness*
- wide *width*
- cold *ness*
- injure *injury*
- manage *management*
- abolish *ment*
- destroy *destruction*
- prove *proof*
- depart *departure*
- accuse *accusation*
- defy *defiance*
- translate *translation*
- applaud *applause*
- ascend *ascension*
- young *youth*
- brave *bravery*
- true *truth*
- appear *appearance*
- mock *mockery*
- pretend *pretence*
- hero *heroism*
- expel *expulsion*
- succeed *success*
- know *knowledge*
- pursue *pursuit*
- persuade *persuasion*
- admit *tance*
- conspire *conspiracy*
- grow *growth*
- approve *approval*
- advise
- behave *behaviour*
- slave *slavery*
- calculate *calculation*
- believe *belief*
- thief *theft*
- relieve *relief*
- betray *betrayal*
- reside *residence*
- complain *complaint*
- judge *judgement*
- anger *anger*
- fly *flight*
- hate ✓
- proud *pride*
- confuse *fusion*
- disturb *disturbance*
- hinder *hindrance*
- exhaust *ion*
- defend *defense*
- compensate *ion*
- occupy *occupation*
- exist *existence*
- practise ✓
- occur *ance*
- lose *loss*
- permit *permission*

250

Nouns

Assignment — THE PLURALS OF NOUNS

Write the plural form of each of the nouns in the list below. In the case of each one give the number of the rule governing it.

- 2 potato*es*
- mesh*es*
- pass*es*
- volcano*es*
- tomato*es*
- 3 kiss*es*
- 3 policy *ies*
- 5 proof*s*
- supply *ies*
- passer-by

- lunch*es*
- valley*s*
- motto*es*
- library *ies*
- injury *ies*
- jockey*s*
- loaf *ves*
- torpedo*es*
- bush*es*
- story *ies*

- fly *ies*
- factory *ies*
- trolley*s*
- mystery *ies*
- piano*s*
- buffalo*es*
- thief *ves*
- box*es*
- goose *geese*
- match*es*

- lily *ies*
- radius *i*
- crutch*es*
- hero*es*
- railway*s*
- arch*es*
- penny *ies*
- porch*es*
- calf *ves*
- roof*s*

TYPES OF NOUNS

There are four types of nouns:

> common
> proper
> collective
> abstract.

COMMON NOUNS do not refer to any one person, place or thing in particular, but are common to all things of the same kind, e.g. **boy**; **garden**; **pencil**.

PROPER NOUNS refer to one specific person, place or thing, e.g. **Peter**; **London**; **Titanic**. (In this case the word *proper* derives from the word *property*.)

Depending on how they are used, certain nouns can be either common or proper.

For example, in the sentence – Students from Killybegs National School visited the Aran Islands – the words *School* and *Islands* are **proper nouns** as they form part of the name of specific places.

However, in the sentence – Two boys from our school rowed out to one of the islands on the lake – the words *school* and *islands* are **common nouns**.

Proper nouns always begin with a capital letter. (*See* Capital Letters Rule 5 on page 276.)

Assignment — PROPER AND COMMON NOUNS

Rewrite each of the following sentences, inserting capital letters where necessary.
1. county kerry is the most scenic county in ireland.
2. trinity college in dublin is the oldest college in ireland.
3. the street where i live is the same length as grafton street in dublin.
4. the oak lodge hotel is the only hotel in the town.
5. the actor, sean connery, was offered the part of the dragon in the film *dragonheart*.
6. county cork is the largest county in ireland.
7. the connemara mountains are the nearest mountains to galway.

COMMAS

Commas have a number of uses. While full stops mark the long pauses we make in reading, commas show where the shorter pauses occur.

Example 1: Smiling happily, Mary left the room.

Example 2: John brought his coat, hat, shoes and umbrella with him.

Commas are also used to separate the items in a list of things.
   (Note that there is no comma between the final two items of a list; instead the word 'and' is used.)
   In some sentences commas can be very important to express the exact meaning. Never use a comma unless you are sure that it is necessary.

Assignment — Using Commas

Rewrite the following sentences, inserting commas where necessary.
1. Not easily frightened our dog continued to bark at the horses.
2. Although running is a good way of keeping fit one should not overdo it.
3. If I decide to go I will telephone you tomorrow.
4. Never a very reliable car the Model T was still very popular.
5. Two boys none of whom I knew arrived.
6. I decided having thought about it carefully not to travel.
7. I asked him knowing he was a local person the way to the football grounds.
8. Five passengers two of them children are still missing.
9. Tom who is five is in Peter's class.
10. Dublin a city I know well has many beautiful parks.
11. Henry Ford the famous car manufacturer had Irish ancestors.
12. In fact nobody turned up to greet us.
13. He knew that even as things were she was far happier in her new school.
14. On the other hand it may be better to travel by train.
15. Two hundred and fifty grams of mushrooms a cup of flour a knob of margarine and a stock cube are the ingredients needed to make mushroom soup.
16. Our local pet show was disappointing as only two dogs five cats three guinea-pigs and a goldfish were entered.
17. London Paris Amsterdam and Canterbury none of which I have visited all have famous buildings.
18. A group of us from my old primary school including two teachers visited a model farm in Co. Kildare which had pigs lambs goats calves and rabbits on display.
19. Tidying my room hoovering washing and drying dishes hanging out clothes on the line and ironing are just some of the jobs I hate doing.
20. Some of my favourite occupations include watching television playing with my computer walking my dog playing with my guinea pigs and chatting to my friends on the telephone.

From *Boy*
Roald Dahl

The next morning, everyone got up early and eager to continue the journey. There was another full day's travelling to be done before we reached our final destination, most of it by boat. So after a rapid breakfast, our cavalcade left the Grand Hotel in three more taxis and headed for Oslo docks. There we went on board a small coastal steamer, and Nanny was heard to say, 'I'm sure it leaks! We shall be food for the fishes before the day is out!' Then she would disappear below for the rest of the trip.

We loved this part of the journey. The splendid little vessel with its single tall funnel would move out into the calm waters of the fjord and proceed at a leisurely pace along the coast, stopping every hour or so at a small wooden jetty where a group of villagers and summer people would be waiting to welcome friends or to collect parcels and mail. Unless you have sailed down the Oslo-fjord like this yourself on a tranquil summer's day, you cannot imagine what it is like. It is impossible to describe the sensation of absolute peace and beauty that surrounds you. The boat weaves in and out between countless tiny islands, some with small brightly painted wooden houses on them, but many with not a house or a tree on the bare rocks. These granite rocks are so smooth that you can lie and sun yourself on them in your bathing-costume without putting a towel underneath. We would see long-legged girls and tall boys basking on the rocks of the islands. There are no sandy beaches on the fjord. The rocks go straight down to the water's edge and the water is immediately deep. As a result, Norwegian children all learn to swim when they are very young because if you can't swim it is difficult to find a place to bathe.

Sometimes when our little vessel slipped between two small islands, the channel was so narrow we could almost touch the rocks on either side. We would pass row-boats and canoes with flaxen-haired children in them, their skins browned by the sun, and we would wave to them and watch their tiny boats rocking violently in the swell that our larger ship left behind.

Late in the afternoon, we would come finally to the end of the journey, the island of Tjöme. This was where our mother always took us. Heaven knows how she found it, but to us it was the greatest place on earth. About two hundred yards from the jetty, along a narrow dusty road, stood a simple wooden hotel painted white. It was run by an elderly couple whose faces I still remember vividly, and every year they welcomed us like old friends. Everything about the hotel was extremely primitive, except the dining-room. The walls, the ceiling and the floor of our bedrooms were made of plain unvarnished pine planks. There was a washbasin and a jug of cold water in each of them.

Breakfast was the best meal of the day in our hotel, and it was all laid out on a huge table in the middle of the dining-room from which you helped yourself. There were maybe fifty different dishes to choose from on that table. There were large jugs of milk, which all Norwegian children drink at every meal. There were plates of cold beef, veal, ham and pork. There was cold boiled mackerel submerged in aspic. There were spiced and pickled herring fillets, sardines, smoked eels and cod's roe. There was a large bowl piled high with hot boiled eggs. There were cold omelettes with chopped ham in them, and cold chicken and hot coffee for the grown ups, and hot crisp rolls baked in the hotel kitchen, which we ate with butter and cranberry jam. There were stewed apricots and five or six different cheeses including of course the ever-present gjetost, that tall brown rather sweet Norwegian goat's cheese which you find on just about every table in the land.

After breakfast, we collected our bathing things and the whole party, all ten of us, would pile into our boat.

Everyone has some sort of a boat in Norway. Nobody sits around in front of the hotel. Nor does anyone sit on the beach because there aren't any beaches to sit on. In the early days, we had only a row-boat, but a very fine one it was. It carried all of us easily, with places for two rowers. My mother took one pair of oars and my fairly ancient half-brother took the other, and off we would go.

My mother and the half-brother (he was somewhere around eighteen then) were expert rowers. They kept in perfect time and the oars went *click-click*, *click-click* in their wooden rowlocks, and the rowers never paused once during the long forty-minute journey. The rest of us sat in the boat trailing our fingers in the clear water and looking for jellyfish. We skimmed across the sound and went whizzing through narrow channels with rocky islands on either side, heading as always for a very secret tiny patch of sand on a distant island that only we knew about. In the early days we needed a place like this where we could paddle and play about because my younger sister was only one, the next sister was three and I was four. The rocks and the deep water were no good to us.

Every day, for several summers, that tiny secret sand-patch on that tiny secret island was our regular destination. We would stay there for three or four hours, messing about in the water and in the rockpools and getting extraordinarily burnt.

In later years, when we were all a little older and could swim, the daily routine became different. By then, my mother had acquired a motor-boat, a small and not very seaworthy white wooden vessel which sat far too low in the water and was powered by an unreliable one-cylinder engine. The fairly ancient half-brother was the only one who could make the engine go at all. It was extremely difficult to start, and he always had to unscrew the sparking-plug and pour petrol into the cylinder. Then he swung a flywheel round and round, and with a bit of luck, after a lot of coughing and spluttering, the thing would finally get going.

When we first acquired the motor-boat, my youngest sister was four and I was seven, and by then all of us had learnt to swim. The exciting new boat made it possible for us to go much farther afield, and every day we would travel far out into the fjord, hunting for a different island. There were hundreds of them to choose from. Some were very small, no more than thirty yards long. Others were quite large, maybe half a mile in length. It was wonderful to have such a choice of places, and it was terrific fun to explore each island before we went swimming off the rocks. There were the wooden skeletons of shipwrecked boats on those islands, and big white bones (were they human bones?), and wild raspberries, and mussels clinging to the rocks, and some of the islands had shaggy long-haired goats on them, and even sheep.

Now and again, when we were out in the open water beyond the chain of islands, the sea became very rough, and that was when my mother enjoyed herself most. Nobody, not even the tiny children, bothered with lifebelts in those days. We would cling to the sides of our funny little white motor-boat, driving through mountainous white-capped waves and getting drenched to the skin, while my mother calmly handled the tiller. There were times, I promise you, when the waves were so high that as we slid down into a trough the whole world disappeared from sight. Then up and up the little boat would climb, standing almost vertically on its tail, until we reached the crest of the next wave, and then it was like being on top of a foaming mountain. It requires great skill to handle a small boat in seas like these. The thing can easily capsize or be swamped if the bows do not meet the great combing breakers at just the right angle. But my mother knew exactly how to do it, and we were never afraid. We loved every minute of it, all of us except for our long-suffering Nanny, who would bury her face in her hands and call loud upon the Lord to save her soul.

In the early evenings we nearly always went out fishing. We collected mussels from the rocks for bait, then we got into either the row-boat or the motor-boat and pushed off to drop anchor later in some likely spot. The water was very deep and often we had to let out two hundred feet of lime before we touched the bottom. We would sit silent and tense, waiting for a bite, and it always amazed me how even a little nibble at the end of that long line would be transmitted to one's fingers. 'A bite!' someone would shout, jerking the line. 'I've got him! It's a big one! It's a whopper!' And then came the thrill of hauling in the line hand over hand and peering over the side into the clear water to see how big the fish really was as he neared the surface. Cod, whiting, haddock and mackerel, we caught them all and bore them back triumphantly to the hotel kitchen where the cheery fat woman who did the cooking promised to get them ready for our supper.

I tell you, my friends, those were the days.

Questions & Assignments

1 What evidence is there in the second paragraph that the writer really enjoyed the journey down the Oslo-fjord?
2 Why do Norwegian children all learn to swim when they are young?
3 Describe the hotel where the writer and his family stayed.
4 Why do you think breakfast is described as the best meal of the day?
5 What did the children do when they were sitting in the rowing boat?
6 How did the daily routine change when the children grew older?
7 Mention some of the things which the children discovered on their exploration of the islands.
8 Describe the reactions of the various members of the family when the sea became rough.
9 Dahl finishes the passage by saying *'I tell you, my friends, those were the days.'* What do you understand by this statement? From your reading of the passage would you agree with him?
10 Pleasant memories from childhood are often the clearest and sharpest – even into old age. Give an account of some of your own childhood memories. In your account, say why you think the memory has stayed with you so strongly.

Adjectives

ELEMENTS OF GRAMMAR

ADJECTIVES

The word adjective derives from the Latin word for addition. An adjective is a word that tells us more about a noun or pronoun. We say that an adjective modifies (adds to the meaning of) the noun or pronoun to which it is attached.

Here are some examples of adjectives – the **broken** bottle; the **old** house; the **French** team; a **red** brick; **that** car.

Assignment — MATCHING ADJECTIVES

Each of the adjectives in the left-hand box has a synonym in the right-hand box. A synonym is a word which has the same – or almost the same – meaning as another. For example **yearly** and **annual** are synonyms.

1. In your copy, list all the words in the left-hand box in alphabetical order and leave a space after each word.
2. When you have this completed find the synonym in the right-hand box for each of the words in your list and write them in the spaces that you left. Try to complete the task without using a dictionary. Your first word will be **abrupt** and its synonym is **sudden**.

A

abrupt	grave	ample
peculiar	reluctant	brief
intoxicated	arrogant	drowsy
lofty	tranquil	stationary
gruesome	secluded	annual
amiable	industrious	courageous
mute	insane	puny
awkward	slender	invincible
prompt	energetic	rare
infuriated	invaluable	robust
prominent	jovial	cautious
avaricious	meticulous	sufficient
celebrated	motionless	wretched
courteous	abundant	indolent
eminent	sly	aggressive
accurate	melancholy	obstinate
vacant	pathetic	putrid
wealthy	perpetual	insolent
reckless	anonymous	gleaming

B

careful	busy	nameless
plentiful	angry	active
quarrelsome	mad	stubborn
sad	cheeky	greedy
friendly	polite	shining
unbeatable	cunning	rash
calm	jolly	unwilling
priceless	drunk	strong
yearly	high	lonely
haughty	still	enough
short	outstanding	empty
careful	brave	rich
sleepy	dumb	miserable
serious	odd	sudden
unending	quick	clumsy
slim	scarce	rotten
weak	famous	careful
pitiful	correct	still
horrible	lazy	plentiful

Spectrum 1

3 Each of the adjectives below are followed by a number of synonyms, but the letters have been mixed up. For example ugeh (huge) menseim (immense) and ganticig (gigantic) are all synonyms of the word 'large'. Unscramble each of the jumbled words for each adjective.

large	ugeh (huge)	menseim (immense)	ganticig (gigantic)
happy	huefcler	dencenott (contented)	htelidegd
sad	doartheewnd (downhearted)	jeteedcd (dejected)	oworfulsr
fast	seydpe	piadr	twifs (swift)
funny	cocialm	gaminus	ilusahori
new	fhesr (fresh)	naligori (original)	nelov
weak	gilfrae	faril (frail)	lictedea
dirty	fitlyh	oluf (foul)	elploutd

Forming adjectives with suffixes

4 (a) Form one adjective from each of the nouns below by adding one of the suffixes given. In some cases you will have to make some spelling changes. Use your dictionary to check your answers.
   (b) Then put each adjective into a sentence.

Suffixes

– y	– ful	– ish	– ly
– like	– less	– ent	– ic
– ous	– ed	– ible	– able

Nouns

- noise(x)
- danger(ous)
- snob(ish)
- God(ly)
- paint(ed)
- beauty(ful)
- ice
- leaf(less)
- talent(ed)
- saint(ly)
- care(ful)
- wood
- glory(ious)
- volcano
- Ireland (Irish)
- pass(ed)
- value(d)
- Spain(ish)
- doubt(ful)
- hero(ic)
- life(less)
- sunny(y)
- style(ish)
- Britain(ish)
- apology(sed)
- violence(ent)
- sense(less)
- heaven(ly)
- scenery (scenic)
- magnet(ic)
- plenty(ful)
- mud(dy)
- Australia
- fool(ish)
- drama(tic)
- cloud(en)

ADJECTIVES USED FOR COMPARISON

Adjectives can be used to compare things, e.g. the **taller** tree; the **fastest** car.
  There are three degrees of comparison.
   (i) The **positive** is the basic form of the adjective, e.g. **tall**.
   (ii) The **comparative** is used when two things are being compared, e.g. **taller**.
   (iii) The **superlative** is used when the comparison is made between three or more things, e.g. **tallest**.

PERSONAL WRITING

Have you ever chatted to your friends or family about: a time when you got into trouble; your part-time job; a person you admire; the difficulties you face in school; the school bully; how you spent the weekend; what happened on Christmas Day in your home; your favourite teacher or your favourite pop group?

Clearly your answer will be 'Yes' to one or perhaps more of these topics. You will be interested to know that all these topics were essay titles set in the Junior Certificate examination over the past few years. Students doing the exam are required to write around two pages on topics such as these – topics that come up again and again in everyday conversation. This section of the examination is called Personal Writing because – as you can see from above – all the topics relate to the kind of things that young people like you will have experienced personally.

Steps to Improve your Personal Writing

Step 1 — **Getting Ideas** Never begin an essay without first thinking about it and planning it carefully. For this you will need a blank page. Use this to jot down all the ideas you have on the topic. Try to represent each idea with a few words. Write without stopping for two or three minutes, putting down every idea that comes into your head. This is called **brainstorming**.

> *Example 1:* **The School Bully**
> swaggers; sneers; really a coward; greedy; sneaky; his/her 'gang'; picks on certain people; why?; licks up to teachers; slags; mocks; why does he/she bother?; 'ratting' on him/her a problem; my worst experience of him/her . . . etc.

> *Example 2:* **Christmas Day in My Home**
> waking up; uncle Tom singing; dog gets sick; sister's new electric guitar; presents good and not so good; no batteries; awful telly programmes; phone relatives abroad; visitors . . . etc.

Step 2 — **Planning** This stage again should only take a few minutes. Go back through all your ideas in stage one. Consider each one and cross out those that you think are are not worth following up. In the case of the remainder decide on the order in which you are going to present them.

On essays such as 'Christmas Day' or 'My Weekend' the most straightforward and effective way is to follow the natural time sequence. Don't try to cover every single moment – concentrate on the interesting episodes. If the topic does not naturally break up into blocks of time concentrate on five or six interesting aspects of the topic. When you have this stage completed the rest of the job will be easy – the essay will almost write itself!

PERSONAL WRITING

Example 1: **The School Bully**
1. Appearance/habits – build; face; clothes; sayings
2. How he/she 'licks up' to teachers (give one example or two).
3. Describe how he/she picks on other students.
4. The problem of telling . . .
5. His/her 'gang'
6. The day he/she met his/her match
7. My experience.
8. How I would solve it if I were principal . . .

Example 2: **Christmas Day in My Home**
1. Early morning – opening presents; surprises
2. Mid-morning – meeting your friends; comparing notes
3. Afternoon – phone my brother in London
4. Christmas dinner – grandad remembers
5. Evening – visitors; relations; auntie playing with computer game; party sing-song
6. My thoughts as the day draws to a close.

STEP 3

HOW NOT TO GET STUCK! When you have completed Stage 2 you will have worked out the number of paragraphs that your essay will consist of and the topic of each of these paragraphs. Now, on a new page, you simply begin writing. At this stage some students seem to seize up. 'I can't get started.' – 'I don't know what to write.' – 'I'm not able to think of a good opening sentence.' – 'I can't think of anything more to write.' – 'I'm stuck.' These are some of the more common complaints that teachers frequently hear. A useful 'trick' to get over these complaints is to imagine that you have made a 'new' friend, who is anxious to get to know you. This imaginary friend is very inquisitive. He or she is asking you about the topic of the essay. Imagine the questions that he or she would ask you. Then compose a complete answer in your head.

Each answer should be a complete sentence. 'Listen' to each sentence in your head. Make sure the words flow easily and that they get across each idea clearly. Then write the sentence down. Remember to follow your plan and to write in paragraphs. Paragraph lengths can vary from one or two sentences up to six or seven depending on the topic.

Example 1: **The School Bully**
The following questions . . .
Does he look like a bully? What does he look like – strong and tough looking? Any striking feature – shape of face, size . . . ? Does he have any noticeable habits or sayings? . . . could result in this piece of writing:

If you saw Brian Triggs you would never think that he was a bully. He is small for his age and has a pointed face, a bit like a rat's. He walks with a swagger and always has his thumbs hooked in his trouser pockets.

Example 2: **Christmas Day in My Home**
The following questions your imaginary friend might ask . . . :
Who awoke first? When did you get up? Where were your presents? How many? What was the best thing you got? What was the most unusual thing you got and what was the dullest thing you got? Did any members of your family get unusual presents? How did they react? could result in this piece of writing:
Deirdre, my little sister woke me at seven, with squeals of excitement. When I realised what day it was I hopped out of bed too. The presents, all wrapped in fancy paper, were stacked at the foot of the christmas tree.

If you are still getting 'stuck'!
- Consult your plan
- Read over the last sentence that you have written and consider the question that would follow it.
- Remember the following words that begin most questions – Who? What? When? Where? Why? How?

STEP 4 — **USING DIALOGUE** Good writing is less about 'telling' the reader and more about helping him or her 'see' and 'hear'. Readers enjoy a conversation much more when they can 'hear' it than just being told in broad terms what it was about.

One of the best ways to let a reader 'hear' a conversation is by using **dialogue**. Instead of telling the reader that somebody praised you, blamed you, advised you, threatened you or mocked you, let the reader hear the actual words that were said.
- Tell the reader how the words were spoken. Try not to depend on the verb 'said' all of the time. Think of suitable options such as: roared, whispered, hissed, snapped, smiled, snarled, bellowed etc.
- Use adverbs such as: angrily, quietly, jokingly, softly, nervously etc. This also helps the reader to 'hear' the tone of voice in which a piece of dialogue was spoken.
- Understand the rules for punctuating and laying out dialogue. These are discussed in more detail on page 149. The basic things to remember are:

PERSONAL WRITING

PERSONAL WRITING

1. Spoken words only are to be enclosed in quotation marks – '____' or "____".
2. Begin a new line for each speaker. Start each of these lines with a capital letter.
3. In a conversation between two speakers it is not always necessary to keep identifying the speakers.

The two examples below show the importance of laying out dialogue correctly. In the first example quotation marks are used incorrectly and new pieces of dialogue do not begin on new lines. The result is confusing and difficult to follow. Note how easy it is to read and understand the corrected version.

Example 1: **Incorrect Dialogue**
Over dinner my Grandad talked about his favourite subject – the Good Old Days. 'Christmas was much different when I was your age,' said Grandad. 'We know. You keep telling us,' muttered my brother. 'We had no such things as computer games in those days,' continued Grandad. 'What kind of presents did you get when you were my age, Grandad?' asked my younger sister. 'An apple and an orange if we were lucky.'

Example 2: **Correct Dialogue**
Over dinner my Grandad talked about his favourite subject – the Good Old Days.
'Christmas was much different when I was your age,' said Grandad.
'We know. You keep telling us,' muttered my brother.
'We had no such things as computer games in those days,' continued Grandad.
'What kind of presents did you get when you were my age, Grandad?' asked my younger sister.
'An apple and an orange if we were lucky.'

Finally remember to use dialogue sparingly. One or two short pieces of dialogue can add to your essay. Don't include it just for the sake of including it – and try to write dialogue that is a little dramatic. Everybody enjoys hearing a good argument but not a conversation about the weather.

STEP 5

SETTING THE SCENE The setting is where an event in a story takes place. It could be anywhere – the principal's office; a park at night; outside a take-away on a frosty night; a derelict house etc.

- Always include a sentence or two to let the reader 'see' where the action is taking place.
- Don't try to give a detailed description of a setting. Try to select one or two features that will help the reader to imagine the entire scene.

Example 1
The sky was a mass of grey clouds. It was raining in a slow, lazy sort of way as if it was going to go on for ever.

Example 2
The park was a bit creepy. The rain dripped through the tall trees. Shivering, I picked my way along the path. My eyes got used to the gloom, and I began to make out the swings and the children's slide.

STEP 6

DESCRIBING PEOPLE Again, it adds to the reader's enjoyment to let him or her 'see' the people you encounter in your essay. As in setting the scene, avoid long detailed descriptions. One or two interesting aspects of a person's appearance are sufficient. The following are some adjectives that you might find useful for this task:

Build – lanky, tall, short, stout, thin, frail, muscular, weedy, brawny.
Face – wrinkled, tanned, long, pointed, fat.
Hair – neat, curly, long, tangled, grey, brown, red, balding, bald.
Eyes – clear, bright, innocent, shifty, large, small, sly, merry, twinkling, beady.
Clothes – shabby, smart, fashionable, grubby, drab, gaudy, worn, threadbare, neat.
Voice – low, gentle, friendly, soft, sharp, hoarse, deep, harsh.
Character – friendly, snobbish, kind-hearted, greedy, lazy, cheerful, miserable, gloomy, honest, blunt, charming, spiteful, loyal, generous, sincere, detestable, timid.

Example 1
My father once told me that Doc Spencer had been looking after the people of our district for nearly forty-five years. She was a tiny woman with tiny hands and feet, and a tiny round face. Her face was as brown and wrinkled as a shrivelled apple. Nobody feared her. Many people loved her, and she was especially gentle with children.

Example 2
Lankers, our teacher, was a horrid man. He had fiery carrot-coloured hair and a little clipped carrotty moustache and a fiery temper. Carrotty-coloured hairs were also sprouting out of his nostrils and his earholes. We were all terrified of him. He sat at the top of the class making snufflung grunts like a dog sniffing at food.

PERSONAL WRITING

PERSONAL WRITING

STEP 7 — **WRITE ABOUT THE WORLD YOU KNOW** Personal Writing gives you the opportunity to write about events and people of which you have first-hand personal experience. It is a chance for you to write about places you know and things that happened to you, to your friends and family. Making up stories about people and places you saw on television or read about in novels is a difficult task and such stories rarely have a 'ring of truth' about them.

Even if you want to write a ghost story, a horror story, a science fiction story, a love story or a crime story make it happen in your own street, your own town or your own school.

STEP 8 — **BE SINCERE** One of the great pleasures of reading is learning about how other people cope with the ups and downs of everyday life. When you are writing about a personal experience don't be afraid to reveal your feelings. If something delighted you, amused you, saddened you, angered you, made you feel guilty or look silly don't be afraid to say so. It will add interest and depth to your work.

Assignment — PERSONAL WRITING

Here are some topics for essay writing.

1. Learning a new skill.
2. My views on sport.
3. A school outing.
4. School is not easy.
5. My earliest memories.
6. My pet.
7. An argument with a friend.
8. The funniest thing that ever happened in primary school
9. An adult (not a relative) whom you admire.
10. The most terrifying experience of your life.
11. Looking after a young child.
12. If you won the Lotto . . .
13. Ghosts – do they exist?
14. How you see yourself in ten years time.
15. What would you like to be good at – and why?
16. A true friend.
17. Saturdays – how I spend them.
18. Things that make me angry.
19. My friends.
20. Songs that bring back memories.
21. My unhappiest day at school.
22. My hobby.
23. A row you witnessed.
24. A sad occasion.
25. Your favourite place – and your least favourite place.
26. A time when you were treated unfairly.
27. Your town.
28. Neighbours – good and bad.

Verbs

VERBS

A word that describes an action, a state or a condition, or gives a command is known as a **verb**, for example: Peter **built** a wall; **sing** another song; Anne **arrives** home every day after work; James **studies** music.

Sometimes two words are needed to form a verb, for example: the train **has gone**; The boy **felt happy**, Sarah **looked tired**.

Every sentence must have a VERB

Assignment   VERBS

1 Pick out the verbs in each of the following passages.
   (a) It was morning. Jane and Michael climbed the hill to the castle. The old man from the cottage had already unlocked the door, so they crept down the winding stairs and peeped round at the old bed with its carved wooden post at each corner. There they saw a man asleep! He had a small, dark beard, black hair, and ragged clothes. 'A tramp!' gasped Michael, surprised.
   (b) The men gave a great pull. Slowly the wooden ship moved. It creaked and scraped, and its big square sail fluttered in the wind. With all their strength the men pulled at the ropes, dragging the ship across the strip of land, until they reached the sea on the other side. Down into the green-grey water went the ship again. Magnus laughed, for he had sailed around the island.
2 Write the verbs to match the following meanings.

1	p e _ _ _ _ _ _ _	to go on in spite of difficulties
2	f l _ _ _ _ _	to give undeserved praise
3	_ _ p _ _ _	to give somebody work
4	_ _ d _ _ _	to suffer without complaint
5	d i s _ _ _ _ _ _ _	to give out, to deliver
6	n _ _ _ _ _	to bite off little pieces
7	_ a _ _ _ _	to disappear
8	u n _ _ _ _	to expose, to make public
9	_ _ _ _ g _	to give up a position
10	_ _ j _ _ _	to disapprove or protest
11	_ _ _ _ l	a position to pray
12	_ _ v _ _ _	to use money to make more
13	h _ _ _ _ _	to crowd together
14	f _ _ _ _ _ _ _ _ _	to make easier
15	e _ _ _ _ _ _	to search, to study
16	e l _ _ _	to escape the notice of
17	_ _ i _ _ _ _	to copy
18	p _ _ _ _ _ _ _	to put off to a later time
19	_ _ _ _ _ l	to call off an event
20	_ _ _ _ _ _ s _	to knock down, to destroy

Spectrum 1

TENSES OF VERBS

The tense of a verb tells us **when** the action took place. The three most common tenses used are:

> The **past** tense (He *sang* a song)
> The **present** tense (He *sings* a song)
> The **future** tense (He *will sing* a song).

Frequently students get confused between the **past tense** of a verb and the **past participle**. A participle is, to put it simply, a word that can be used either as a verb or an adjective.

> *Example 1* **Having beaten** Kerry by a goal, the Leitrim team decided to celebrate.
> Here the words **having beaten** are used as a **verb**.
> (It would be incorrect to write 'Having **beat** Kerry . . . ')

> *Example 2* The **beaten** team were very disappointed.
> Here the word **beaten** is used as an **adjective**.
> (It would be incorrect to write 'The **beat** team . . . ')

Assignment — PAST PARTICIPLE AND PAST TENSE – AVOIDING CONFUSION

In the case of each of the verbs in the box below write out a sentence using (i) the past tense and (ii) the past participle.

Example
- steal   (i) Peter **stole** the book.   (ii) Tom found the **stolen** book.

• write	• sing	• forget	• hide	• swell
• sell	• choose	• bleed	• break	• show
• saw	• fly	• swear	• fall	• mow
• wear	• do	• grow	• speak	• eat
• rise	• draw	• throw	• give	• drink
• spring	• sow	• steal	• drive	• ring
• sink	• bite	• beat	• begin	• blow
• swim	• know	• freeze	• shake	• tear

TWO USEFUL SPELLING RULES FOR FORMING THE PAST TENSE

1 If the present tense ends in a **y** change it to an **i** before adding **ed**,
  for example: cry/cr**ied**; terrify/terrif**ied**.
2 If the present tense ends in a consonant which is immediately preceded by a single vowel double the last consonant before adding **ed**,
  for example: drip/drip**ped**; stop/stop**ped**.

ADVERBS

As its name suggests, an adverb is a word which is added to a verb to give it extra meaning. We say that an adverb *modifies* a verb, for example:
Joan walked **briskly**; John sang **tunelessly**; Peter smiled **mockingly**.

However, adverbs are also used to qualify the following parts of speech: adjectives, other adverbs and prepositions.

> *Example 1* The dog was **unusually** large. (adjective)
> *Example 2* He drove **very** slowly. (other adverb)
> *Example 3* The ball was **nearly** in the goal. (preposition)

FORMING ADVERBS

Adverbs can be formed from adjectives by adding **-ly** but spelling changes are often necessary.
- When an adjective ends in **y** change it to **i**, for example la**zy** becomes la**zily**.
- When an adjective ends in an **e** which is preceded by a double consonant the **e** is dropped, for example humbl**e** becomes humbl**y**.
- When an adjective ends in **l** the **l** is doubled, for example bruta**l** becomes bruta**lly**.

Assignment — FORMING ADVERBS

Form adverbs from each of the following adjectives.

Example: • nice   Jane spoke **nicely** about her baby brother.

- easy
- heavy
- equal
- annual
- noisy
- rare
- bitter
- patient
- angry

- responsible
- scornful
- graceful
- tidy
- honest
- new
- cautious
- frequent
- quick

- rapid
- busy
- brave
- secret
- harsh
- hungry
- gentle
- skillful
- loyal

- probable
- feeble
- immediate
- practical
- fatal
- leisure
- attentive
- noble
- sensible

- brave
- weary
- steady
- idle
- suitable
- gradual
- annual
- predictable
- pitiful

Vampires

Did you know that Dracula's creator was an Irishman? Bram Stoker (Bram is an unusual short form of Abraham) was born in Dublin and educated there. In 1866 he joined the Irish Civil Service. It must have been a rather dull life, but nevertheless he was interested enough to write some reports and books on subjects such as the work of the law courts. In 1878 he left the civil service and became Henry Irving's agent. Irving was the most outstanding figure in the London theatre in the second half of the nineteenth century. As well as acting, he also produced many plays. His favourite plays were those by Shakespeare. Henry Irving was famous for his Shakespearean roles such as Hamlet from the play of the same name, Shylock from The Merchant of Venice and Malvolio from Twelfth Night. But he also enjoyed producing and acting in melodramas. Melodramas are plays with exciting and sensational events, and which generally have a happy ending.

Perhaps that is where Bram Stoker first discovered his interest in the vampire myths. Bram Stoker's book Dracula was first published in 1897. It aroused great public interest at a time when the subject of the supernatural – ghost stories and accounts of events that cannot be explained – had come into fashion. It was an immediate success, and it was followed – and continues to be followed, thanks partly to cinema and television – by very many other stories about vampires and other supernatural creatures. Dracula was not the first story to feature vampires but it certainly is the most famous, and today the name 'Dracula' is known in nearly every part of the world.

Dracula

The Dracula story is told through the diaries of a young solicitor, Jonathan Harker, his fiancée Mina, her friend Lucy Westenra, and Dr. John Seward, the superintendent of a large lunatic asylum in Essex in England. It begins with Harker's journey from his native England to Count Dracula's eerie castle in Transylvania. He went there to help arrange the Count's purchase of Carfax, an ancient house close

Vampires

The belief in vampires is a very ancient one. In many stories, the vampire was the ghost of a dead wrongdoer. The ghost returned from the grave in the shape of a huge bat and fed on the blood of sleeping people. These people usually became vampires themselves. So long as it could get human blood in this way, the vampire would never die. But people believed in the protective power of fire, crosses and certain plants, especially garlic. They believed that the only way to kill a vampire and set its spirit free was to cut off its head and drive a sharpened stake of wood through its heart.

Transylvania

The name Transylvania comes from Latin meaning 'beyond the forests', but it is, in fact, a real place, not an imaginary one. It is located in present-day Romania, lying between western Romania and southern Hungary. It is a mountainous country, enclosed to the east and south by the Carpathian Mountains and the Transylvanian Alps, and to the west by the Bihor Mountains. Gypsies, who are among the inhabitants of the area, play a significant part in the story.

to Dr. Seward's asylum. After various horrifying experiences as a guest at Dracula's castle, Jonathan makes his way back to England. Dracula, however, manages to get there ahead of him. The rest of the book tells of the attempt to save Mina from Dracula's advances and his subsequent pursuit. The evil Count escapes back to Transylvania where, after a thrilling chase, he is beheaded and stabbed through the heart, at which point his body crumbles to dust.

Questions & Assignments

1. (i) What was Bram Stoker's first job?
   (ii) For how many years did he have this job?
2. When was *Dracula* first published?
3. Who was Henry Irving?
4. What kind of work do you think Bram Stoker had to do as Henry Irving's agent?
5. In which Shakespearean plays did Irving act? What parts did he play?
6. (i) Why was the book *Dracula* so successful?
   (ii) Name some characters from *Dracula*.
   (iii) In which countries does the action of the story take place?
7. Write down three facts about Transylvania.
8. What beliefs are associated with vampires?

Spectrum 1

PERSONAL WRITING: CAPITAL LETTERS

There are twelve basic rules for the use of capital letters. We will begin with **Rules 1 - 7**.

Capitals are used . . .

Rule 1 At the start of each sentence.
- **O**ur class won the school league.
- **I**t was late when he arrived.

Rule 2 To begin both surnames and first names.
- **M**ary, **P**aul, **J**oan, **D**aniel, **L**iam, **P**eter, **N**uala.
- **B**yrne, **D**aly, **H**anley, **M**cCarthy.

Rule 3 For initials.
- **J.D.** Smith, **T.** O'Neill.
- **RTE**, **ASTI**, **TUI**, **ESB**, **IDA**, **GAA**, **FAI**, **FIFA**.

Rule 4 For days of the week, months of the year and holidays.
- **F**riday, **S**aturday, **F**ebruary, **A**pril.
- **C**hristmas, **E**aster, **St. P**atrick's **D**ay.

Rule 5 For brand names.
- She drinks **F**anta.
- He plays a **F**ender guitar.
- They won a **S**ony cassette player and a **Y**amaha motor-cycle.

Rule 6 To begin titles that are used as part of personal names.
- **D**octor **M**cCormack
- **C**aptain **M**urphy.
- **C**ount **D**racula.
- **M**iss **D**unne.

Rule 7 To begin abbreviated (shortened) words.
- **Mr.** Murray.
- **Dr.** Brown.
- Dublin **Rd**.
- **Mrs.** Nolan.
- Botanic **A**ve.
- O'Connell **St**.

(Note that abbreviated words always end with a full stop.)

Questions & Assignments

In each of the following paragraphs all capitals and most of the punctuation have been omitted. Refer to **Rules 1–7** above to rewrite each paragraph with capital letters and punctuation correctly included. After you have rewritten each paragraph correctly, list all the words to which you gave capitals. Then write the rule number that made you decide that the word should have a capital.

Example

my neighbour, peter byrne, works for the esb sometimes he works on sundays last year he worked on easter sunday

Answer

My neighbour, Peter Byrne, works for the ESB. Sometimes he works on Sundays. Last year he worked on Easter Sunday.

Rules Used

My (Rule 1) Peter Byrne (Rule 2) ESB (Rule 3) Sometimes (Rule 1)
Sundays (Rule 4) Last (Rule 1) Easter Sunday (Rule 4)

1 liam and david like to watch utv on saturday mornings
2 on christmas day my nextdoor neighbout mr dunne phoned the esb when the power failed
3 mrs patterson sold her toyota last saturday and bought a bmw
4 the bus left patrick st and arrived at st lukes cross an hour later
5 paul sinclair claims that his uncle is the duke of sligo
6 a religion teacher in our school, fr dunne, plays the piano sometimes he brings in a casio keyboard and plays it for our class and margaret sullivan sings the headmaster, mr buckley, came in one day and sang an elvis song he was awful
7 on mayday there was a big parade in our town it was sponsored by toyota ms carbery, who teaches us maths, won first prize in the adults fancy dress competition she was dressed up as queen elizabeth the first she was interviewed by a reporter from utv and was presented with a mitsubishi camcorder her boyfriend, peter eason, went as prince charles he came second last

Capitals are used . . .

Rule 8 For the names of specific continents, countries, provinces, cities, towns, mountains, rivers, lakes, streets, parks, buildings etc.
- Europe, Ireland, France, Munster, Dublin, Cardiff, Reading, Naas, Alps, Galtees, Wicklow Mountains, Aran Islands, Liffey, River Lee, Grafton Street, Patrick Street, Phoenix Park, Hyde Park, St. Stephen's Green, Slish Woods, Greendale College, Cumberland House, Oak Drive, Willow Gardens etc.

The examples below illustrate how capital letters are used for names of specific places only.
She lives in Dublin – She lives in the city.
They travelled to Tralee – They travelled to town.
There is snow on the Galtees – There is snow on the mountains.
Our class visited the Aran Islands – The class visited islands on the lake.
I go to Glenroe Community School – I go to a community school.

Rule 9 To begin the key words in titles of books, films, plays, songs, poems, magazines, newspapers etc.
- The Day of the Jackal.
- The Phoenix.
- The Green Fields of France.
- The Irish Times.

Rule 10 To begin words in the names given to ships, aircraft, restaurants etc.
- The Titanic.
- Enterprise Express.
- The Pink Flamingo.
- The Little Chef.

Rule 11 To begin all adjectives which are formed from proper nouns.
- Irish, European, French, Edwardian, Elizabethan, Georgian.

Rule 12 To begin the first word of direct speech which is a sentence within a sentence.
- Peter suddenly remarked, 'Fishing is a lazy sport.'

Spectrum 1

Questions & Assignments — Using Capitals Correctly

In each of the following sentences all capitals have been omitted. Refer to **Rules 1-12** to rewrite each sentence with capital letters correctly included. After you have rewritten each sentence correctly, list all the words to which you gave capitals. Then write the rule number that made you decide that the word should have a capital.

1. peter donovan spent the first two weeks of june in kerry.
2. my mother has a new phillips washing machine.
3. we have a dog called blackie and she has a sore nose.
4. liam and paul went fishing for trout and salmon in the river liffey.
5. The chef turned to his assistant and said, 'too many cooks spoil the broth.'
6. the assistant replied 'many hands make light work.'
7. peter's father used to drive a ford escort, but now he has a bmw.
8. the doctor and the priest were sent for when the guards arrived at the scene of the accident.
9. when doctor o' neill arrived at st. anne's hospital, nurse nagle told him that he was to report to the children's ward.
10. findus fish fingers are advertised on television, but I have never seen an advertisement for walsh's sausages.
11. peter bought the sunday independent, the sunday mirror and the rte guide, but his brother bought irish papers only.
12. the opening of a new production of *macbeth* by w. shakespeare was attended by mr. and mrs. browne.
13. ms o'brien left cork on tuesday around ten thirty and drove to dublin airport in her toyota starlet.
14. the greek and spanish teams arrived in london airport at around midnight on saturday.
15. american wines are becoming increasingly popular in britain, although french wines are still the most popular.
16. when the jet landed, captain connolly, the pilot, relaxed and sat back in her seat.
17. the shop assistant turned to miss naughton, 'we seem to be out of daz. can I offer you any other washing powder?'
18. james enjoyed reading *black beauty* he thought it was a great book.
19. is the capital of the united states of america called new york?
20. the esb does not generate any electricity from nuclear power stations.

A Night To Remember
Brendan Williams

As bad as our storms over Christmas may have seemed, they were not the worst, by all accounts, to ever reach our shores. That honour, at least in the collective memory of folklore, goes to the storm which struck Ireland on the night of January 6th/7th, 1839. The 'Night of the Big Wind', or Oíche na Gaoithe Móire, was 159 years ago today.

From the evidence now available, we know that the *Big Wind* was caused by a very deep depression which originated over the Atlantic and passed eastwards close to the north coast of Ireland. Other explanations, however, were more popular at the time.

Some saw the violent storm as a precursor of the Day of Judgement – a sharp reminder on the part of the Almighty of the wrath of God that may await us all when the final trumpet sounds. Others formed the view that the Freemasons were behind it – that they had called the Devil out of hell and failed to get him back again. And others again blamed the fairies; their notion was that the English fairies had invaded Ireland and that our indigenous Little People had to raise a ferocious wind to blow them out again.

This last theory was at least consistent with the well-known fact that the Irish fairies have no wings and can only fly by calling up the sidhe gaoithe – the magic whirlwinds. But, whatever the reason for its coming, the damage caused to life and property by the Big Wind was exceptional by any standard.

Dublin after the storm was described as resembling a sacked city, and the splendid avenue of elms which graced the main thoroughfare of the Phoenix Park was completely levelled. Throughout the country stately demesnes were laid low, to the chagrin of the rural gentry, and indeed one of the incidental consequences of the event was the total collapse of the price of lumber, as what had previously been a valuable commodity became practically worthless overnight through oversupply.

Damage to shipping around the coast was estimated at half a million pounds, an almost unimaginable sum in those days, while on land, houses were destroyed and more than a hundred people died, either crushed by falling masonry or swept away in the floods which accompanied the raging winds.

We will never know for sure if the storm of 1839 was the worst that Ireland ever experienced. It was certainly one of the most memorable – not least because it was confined almost entirely to the hours of darkness; and, unlike most of today's big winds, it was totally unexpected.

Questions & Assignments

1. According to recorded memory, when was the worst storm ever to strike Ireland? What is the storm most commonly called?
2. What was the real cause of the storm?
3. What other reasons were put forward to explain the violence of the storm?
4. What evidence is there in the passage to show that the storm caused extreme damage?
5. In the final paragraph the writer says the storm of 1839 was Ireland's most memorable storm. What reasons does he give for making this statement?

Spectrum 1

PROVERBS

> Proverbs are sayings that contain sound advice or wise observations on life, e.g. A stitch in time save nine.

Questions & Assignments

In each of the following proverbs a word has been omitted. Find the correct word in the box to complete each proverb. When you have this completed state briefly, in your own words, what each of the proverbs mean.

Example: **7** Birds of a feather **flock** together – means – People with the same interests or attitudes enjoy each other's company.

1. Absence makes the heart grow ----------.
2. Actions speak louder than ---------.
3. As you make your bed so must you ------- on it.
4. ------------- can't be choosers.
5. A bird in the ------------ is worth two in the bush.
6. The ----------- bird catches the worm.
7. Birds of a feather --------- together.
8. Once --------- , twice shy.
9. Blood is thicker than --------.
10. You cannot get blood out of a ----------.
11. When the cat's away the mice will ----------- .
12. ------------ begins at home.
13. Don't ----------- your chickens before they are hatched.
14. Every cloud has a ------- lining.
15. Cut your ---------- according to your cloth.
16. Too many cooks --------- the broth.
17. ------- costs nothing.
18. Barking dogs seldom ----------.
19. --------- dog has his day.
20. Let sleeping dogs ----------.
21. A drowning man will clutch at any ---------.
22. Don't put all your ---------- in one basket.
23. ------------ is as good as a feast.
24. Where there's --------- there's fire.
25. A fool and his money are soon -----------.
26. A friend in -------- is a friend indeed.
27. ------------ fruit tastes sweetest.
28. God helps those who help ---------.
29. Grasp all, --------- all.
30. More ------- , less speed.

smoke
early
Every
water
Forbidden
words
lose
parted
straw
Beggars
bitten
haste
silver
coat
spoil
play
fonder
bite
lie
stone
eggs
lie
Enough
count
need
themselves
flock
Courtesy
hand
Charity

Ghost Stories

Long ago, before the advent of radio and television, storytelling was a common way of passing the long winter nights. People would gather round the fireside, swapping news and stories. Ghost stories were always popular, especially when they were set in the locality.

Stories of sightings of ghosts are very much a part of local traditions and folklore in Ireland – as in most other countries. There is hardly a parish or townland in Ireland which cannot boast of its own ghostly apparition.

There have been various traditions associated with the sightings of ghosts. The most common ones are that:

- ghosts are spirits of the dead, denied rest, until a wrong done *to* them or *by* them has been put right.
- ghosts are apparitions sent with a message or a warning to a living person.
- ghosts are evil spirits in the guise of a dead relative or friend.
- ghosts are hallucinations, the result of a guilty conscience.

Ghostly Monks at Cashel

A strange story is told about ghostly monks said to have been seen going into a churchyard near the ruins of an Old Augustinian Priory not far from Cashel, in Co. Tipperary.

Two girls from Thurles were visiting friends in Cashel. On their way home that night they drove their car through a lane alongside a field where the old Abbey ruins are located. Here they saw a little party of monks approaching, but as they had some idea that there was a religious order in the district, they thought little of it. As the monks drew nearer, however, the girls saw that they were carrying a bier (a coffin on a stand).

Since it was a funeral procession, they pulled the car on to the grass verge, switched off the engine and waited for the procession to pass. When level with the car, the whole scene disappeared.

On their return home the girls told of their weird experience, and they heard for the first time the legend of Cormac the Hunter and how his body had been borne away from that spot by monks and buried in the Priory churchyard, centuries before.

Cormac was a rich young man who lived in the district, which at that period was a desolate area. He went out hunting one day and a blizzard sprang up. He froze to death and later the monks from the nearby Augustinian Abbey, who apparently specialised in deeds of mercy, found the body and carried it back to their churchyard for burial.

Vanishing Gravediggers

They say that ghosts are rarely seen in graveyards, but that idea seems to be refuted by an alleged happening in Esker Graveyard, Lucan, Co. Dublin, early on the evening of Hallowe'en, 1930.

A little old woman, the owner of a sweet shop in the village, went to visit her husband's grave. As she walked along the path that led to the grave she heard the village church bell strike four o'clock.

The widow carried a bunch of red roses to place on the grave. As she walked along the pathway, one of the roses fell to the ground, at a spot where two young men were digging a grave. They looked up as she passed and she was struck by their good looks and the fact that they looked so much alike. She went on to her husband's grave but couldn't get rid of the feeling that they were watching her. She went about the task of tending the grave, all the while thinking about the two young gravediggers. It was very quiet in the graveyard but the setting sun helped to brighten the place. Then the caretaker's bell broke the silence, to tell visitors it was time to leave. The old woman made her way towards the cemetery gates, glancing about her to see if the two young gravediggers were still there. They were not. Then she saw the red rose she had dropped on the way in.

She stooped to pick it up, and then realised that there should have been a freshly-dug grave at the spot. But there was only a weed-covered plot over which stood a slab of stone.

On the slab was an inscription:

Sacred to the memory of the
twin Berwick brothers,
Martin and James, killed by a
falling tree outside this
cemetery during a storm on the
evening of October 31st, 1903.
R.I.P.

At the base of the slab was a photograph of the two young men she had seen an hour before, digging a grave.

POLTERGEISTS IN CORK

The son of a bank worker begins this story by recalling the first night the family spent in a rented house in Blarney Road in Cork . . .

After supper we sat by the fire, with the furniture piled up around us. The December winds moaned around the house as we finally went to bed and every few minutes window shutters clattered. Then the dogs began to howl dismally. Feeling very frightened, we children got up and scampered to our parent's room. Father was very cross but finally he decided to occupy our room and allow us to sleep with mother. 'Such utter nonsense,' he said angrily. 'The dogs are howling because they are in a strange place, and the shutters are banging because they are loose. I'll fix them first thing tomorrow.' We huddled close to our mother and dropped off to sleep about 2 a.m. when all the noises suddenly ceased.

Next morning father was up early foraging through boxes in search of tools. He came into the kitchen looking puzzled. 'That's the most extraordinary thing,' he muttered, half to himself. 'There are no shutters on the windows, and nothing that could cause that slapping sound.'

'But, mamma, we heard it,' I cried.

'Never mind,' said father thoughtfully.

'Some ordinary thing caused it. We'll fix it when we find it.'

That night about midnight, the noises began again and ended abruptly at 2 a.m. During that time dad went from room to room hearing the bang of invisible shutters but seeing everything motionless. He spent the next day moving our beds into a diningroom downstairs. There the four of us slept from that night onwards. We settled for the kitchen as living quarters, and left the remainder of the furniture piled up in the big front drawingroom.

Each night the noises were different and quite definitely increased in volume and variety as time went on. We made the big mistake of bringing the dogs into the house. They both became hysterical and frightened us far more than the noise did. One of them tried to scale the kitchen wall and foamed from the mouth when father went to hold him.

Father mentioned to his manager that there was something wrong with the house, and that night two young bank clerks came to spend a few hours with us. Mother had planned to give them supper at midnight so we would have their company during the frightening hours. When we sat to the table in the kitchen bedlam was let loose in the front room. The big window seemed to crash in and furniture clattered. The men grabbed pokers and rushed out. As they went, all the china in the pantry crashed to the floor, but nothing was broken! Father returned to the kitchen only to find he had no male company. The bank clerks had flown!

Mother called to the Donovan family to ask their help in finding another house. Mrs. Donovan and her son came rather late the following night. The moon was full, and the snow-covered garden was brighter than in daylight. They brought a friend named Fr. Tierney. We had supper in the kitchen about 10.30 p.m. and stayed at the table talking for some time after the meal ended. Our friends had not been given details of the haunting and did not know what to expect. When the racket started John Donovan jumped to his feet. 'Good heavens! What's going on here?' A piercing shriek rang out, followed by what sounded like two revolver shots.

Fr. Tierney and John Donovan stood rockstill. Mother crouched in her chair with her arms around my sister and me. Then the priest walked out and opened the front door followed by father and John. They all heard running footsteps but there was no sign of anyone. They followed the sound of the running feet around to the back door, where, except for their own footprints, the frozen snow remained unmarked. In the kitchen Mrs. Donovan leaned, faint with fear, against the table. When my father opened the back door she collapsed to the floor. He ran to her aid, while Fr. Tierney forced a few drops of brandy between her white lips.

About a week later we rented a house in Sundays Well Avenue. Fr. Tierney was a frequent visitor during our long period in the south. All that time the house on Blarney Road was left unoccupied. Many years later it was demolished and the ground used as a market garden. Fr. Tierney spoke about the occurrence in many discourses from the pulpit, and pronounced it a most extraordinary manifestation. There is no doubt the agency at work gave a special performance on the night the priest was witness.

Old people, living in the vicinity, remembered hearing about a tragedy which had taken place many years earlier when a young man shot and killed himself and his wife. Frank O'Connor's mother verified this story which she had heard from old nuns in the Good Shepherd Convent.

Questions & Assignments

1. Retell the first two ghost stories in this section from the point of view of the people who witnessed the apparitions.
2. Write an article in the form of a piece of investigative journalism on the story *Poltergeists in Cork*. Include headlines and subheadings. (If you wish, you may be unscrupulous and invent certain details and quotations.)
3. Do some research into your own local ghosts. Interview, if possible, people who claim to have sighted ghosts and write a report on your findings.
4. Write of an encounter (real or imaginary) you had with a ghost. (Use the stories in this section for inspiration and vocabulary.)

PREPOSITIONS

Prepositions are words that indicate direction, position and location Some examples are: **to**, **with**, **from**, **at**, **in**, **near**, **by**, **beside**, **above**.

> 'Never end a sentence with a preposition' is a much quoted 'rule' of grammar.

While logically there seems to be little merit to the rule, there is a substantial body of opinion against end-of-sentence prepositions. So if you want to keep the grammar purists happy, try to avoid ending sentences with prepositions.

For example, instead of writing – 'That is the car I would like to travel in.' – where the preposition **in** ends the sentence, consider – 'That is the car **in** which I would like to travel.'

On the other hand, don't let the rule make your writing clumsy or confusing; if a sentence is more graceful with a final preposition, let it stand. A sentence can become very unwieldy when it's filled with *from whom's*, and *with which's*.

Winston Churchill was once reprimanded for ending a sentence with a preposition and retorted 'This is the sort of thing up with which I will not put.'

PREPOSITIONS – SOME COMMON ERRORS

✗ Incorrect – The bus went **passed** the stop.
✓ Correct – The bus went **past** the stop
(**Past** is a preposition. **Passed** is a verb).

✗ Incorrect – He fell **in** the river from the boat.
✓ Correct – He fell from the boat **into** the river
(**Into** refers to movement from one place to another. **In** shows position.)

✗ Incorrect – That dog is different **to** ours.
✗ Incorrect – That dog is different **than** ours.
✓ Correct – That dog is different **from** ours.
(**From** always follows **different**.)

✗ Incorrect – Two teachers were there **beside** the principal.
✓ Correct – Two teachers were there **besides** the principal.
(**Besides** means **in addition to**. **Beside** refers to a position.)

AMONG
The sweets were shared **among** the class. (There are more than two people.)

BETWEEN
The sweets were shared **between** the twins. (There are only two people.)

CONJUNCTIONS

The word 'conjunction' derives from Latin and means 'something that joins'. The words **and** and **but** are the most commonly used conjunctions. Conjunctions are used to join words and sentences together.

Note: The **overuse** of conjunctions will result in very long and confusing sentences.

Here are some other words that are frequently used as conjunctions: **if, as, for, yet, that, when, since, because, while, until, though, although, whether.**

Pay particular attention to the spelling of the last five.

INTERJECTIONS

An interjection is unlike all other parts of speech because it does no work in a sentence. Here are some interjections which occur frequently in dialogue: **Gosh! Ah! Oh! Oh dear! Alas!**

However, interjections can help to give a sentence a particular mood or atmosphere.

> **Oh dear!** I've just missed my bus home.
> **Ah!** It's hot.

PREPOSITIONS

'The keys were in his pocket.'

'He put his keys into the drawer.'

The First Men on the Moon, 21 July 1969
Neil Armstrong and Edwin E. Aldrin

Apollo 11, carrying Neil Armstrong, Lieutenant-Colonel Michael Collins and Colonel Edwin Aldrin, was launched on 16 July. At 03.56 BST on 21 July Armstrong stepped off the ladder of the lunar landing vehicle, *Eagle*, on to the Moon.

Neil Armstrong: The most dramatic recollections I had were the sights themselves. Of the spectacular views we had, the most impressive to me was on the way to the Moon, when we flew through its shadow. We were still thousands of miles away, but close enough, so that the Moon almost filled our circular window. It was eclipsing the Sun, from our position, and the corona of the Sun was visible around the limb of the Moon as a gigantic lens-shaped or saucer-shaped light, stretching out to several lunar diameters. It was magnificent, but the Moon was even more so. We were in its shadow, so there was no part of it illuminated by the Sun. It was illuminated only by earthshine. It made the Moon appear blue-grey, and the entire scene looked decidedly three-dimensional.

I was really aware, visually aware, that the Moon was in fact a sphere not a disc. It seemed almost as if it were showing us its roundness, its similarity in shape to our Earth, a sort of welcome. I was sure that it would be a hospitable host. It had been awaiting its first visitors for a long time . . .

[After touchdown] The sky is black, you know. It's a very dark sky. But it still seemed more like daylight than darkness as we looked out the window. It's a peculiar thing, but the surface looked very warm and inviting. It was the sort of situation in which you felt like going out there in nothing but a swimming suit to get a little sun. From the cockpit, the surface seemed to be tan. It's hard to account for that, because later when I held this material in my hand, it wasn't tan at all. It was black, grey and so on. It's some kind of lighting effect, but out the window the surface looks much more like light desert sand than black sand . . .

Edwin E. Aldrin [on the Moon]: The blue colour of my boot has completely disappeared now into this – still don't know exactly what colour to describe this other than greyish-cocoa colour. It appears to be covering most of the lighter part of my boot . . . very fine particles . . .

[Later] The Moon was a very natural and pleasant environment in which to work. It had many of the advantages of zero gravity but it was in a sense less *lonesome* than Zero G, where you always have to pay attention to securing attachment points to give you some means of leverage. In one-sixth gravity, on the Moon, you had a distinct feeling of being *somewhere* . . . As we deployed our experiments on the surface we had to jettison things like lanyards, retaining fasteners etc, and some of these we tossed away. The objects would go away with a slow, lazy motion. If anyone tried to throw a baseball back and forth in that atmosphere he would have difficulty, at first, acclimatising himself to that slow, lazy trajectory; but I believe he could adapt to it quite readily . . .

> Odour is very subjective, but to me there was a distinct smell to the lunar material – pungent, like gunpowder or spent cap-pistol caps. We carted a fair amount of lunar dust back inside the vehicle with us, either on our suits and boots or on the conveyor system we used to get boxes and equipment back inside. We did notice the odour right away.

Questions & Assignments

1. What was the most spectacular view that Armstrong saw on the way to the moon?
2. What made the moon appear to be blue-grey in colour?
3. What did Armstrong feel like doing after touchdown?
4. What, according to Aldrin, were the attractions of working on the moon?
5. What comparison does he use to describe the smell of lunar material?
6. What words and phrases in the passage suggest that the astronauts were very excited by their experience?

PERSONAL WRITING — IDIOMS

An idiom is an expression whose meaning is not immediately clear from the actual words. If a teacher tells a parent that Johnny has been swinging the lead since September he does not mean that Johnny has been literally swinging a lump of lead for a few months! The teacher means of course that Johnny has not been studying since September.

People often use idioms in conversation and writers often use them when writing dialogue for characters. Idioms can add life and colour to a conversation or a piece of written dialogue. When used in a prose passage they give it an informal, chatty tone.

Foreigners who are learning how to speak English often have problems with idioms. Can you suggest why?

Questions & Assignments

1. Match each of the idioms in List A with the correct meaning in List B.

List A	List B
1 to paddle one's own canoe	a to behave unfairly towards some body
2 to have a bee in one's bonnet	b to do things without depending on others
3 to hit below the belt	c to be obsessed by a particular idea
4 to be a wet blanket	d to be a spoilsport
5 to have a bone to pick with someone	e to pay too much
6 to pay through the nose	f to take on a problem boldly
7 to make a clean breast of it	g to suspect something
8 to take the bull by the horns	h to have a complaint to make
9 to smell a rat	i to confess to something
10 to put the cart before the horse	j to do things in the wrong order

2 Match each of the idioms in List A with the correct meaning in List B.

List A
1. to let the cat out of the bag
2. to be under a cloud
3. to keep it dark
4. to be a dog in the manger
5. to make both ends meet
6. to have a feather in one's cap
7. to show the white feather
8. to sit on the fence
9. to play second fiddle
10. to bury the hatchet
11. to give a person the cold shoulder
12. to blow one's own trumpet

List B
a. to keep it secret
b. to reveal a secret
c. to deny something to others that is of no value to yourself
d. to be under suspicion
e. to boast
f. to show fear
g. to make friends after a quarrel
h. to refuse to take sides in an argument
i. to have achieved something worthwhile
j. to stand back while someone else leads
k. to live on what you have
l. to make somebody feel unwelcome or disliked

3 Match each of the idioms in List A with the correct meaning in List B.

List A
1. to hang one's head
2. to live from hand to mouth
3. to flog a dead horse
4. to strike while the iron is hot
5. to swing the lead
6. to turn over a new leaf
7. to be at loggerheads
8. to make a mountain out of a molehill
9. to face the music
10. to feather one's nest
11. to get into hot water
12. to throw cold water on something

List B
a. to make small problems seem like big ones
b. to spend all you have got without being able to put some by for the future
c. to look after yourself at the expense of others
d. to suggest that an idea is of no value
e. to put an effort into something which is unlikely to pay off
f. to be ashamed
g. to act while conditions are in your favour
h. to dodge work by pretending to be sick
i. to be quarrelling
j. to get into trouble
k. to face punishment or criticism with out complaint
l. to lead a better life

Millionaires

As early as the mid-1820s, Americans were talking admiringly of *millionaires*, a term borrowed from the British who had in turn taken it from the French, and by 1850 were supplementing the word with a more aggressive version of their own devising: *multimillionaires*. An American lucky enough to get in on the ground floor with an arresting invention or a timely investment might reasonably hope to become a millionaire himself. In 1840 the country had no more than twenty millionaires. By 1915 there were 40,000.

The new class of tycoons enjoyed a concentration of money and power that is almost unimaginable now. In 1891 John D. Rockefeller and Standard Oil controlled 70% of the world market for oil. J.P. Morgan's House of Morgan and its associate companies in 1912 were worth more 'than the assessed value of all the property in the 22 states and territories west of the Mississippi'. With great wealth came the luxury of eccentricity. James Hill of the Great Northern Railroad reportedly fired an employee because the man's name was Spittles. The servants at J.P. Morgan's London residence nightly prepared dinner, turned down the bed and laid out nightclothes for their master even when he was known beyond doubt to be three thousand miles away in New York. The industrialist John M. Longyear, disturbed by the opening of a railroad line past his Michigan residence, had the entire estate packed up – sixty-room house, hedges, trees, shrubs, fountains, the works – and re-erected in Brookline, Massachusetts. James Gordon Bennett, a newspaper baron, liked to announce his arrival in a restaurant by yanking the tablecloths from all the tables he passed. He would then hand the manager a wad of cash with which to compensate his victims for their lost meals and spattered attire. Though long forgotten in his native land, Bennett and his exploits – invariably involving prodigious drinking before and lavish restitution after – were once world famous, and indeed his name lives on in England in the cry 'Gordon Bennett!', usually uttered by someone who has just been drenched by a clumsy waiter or otherwise exposed to some exasperating indignity.

The indulgences of the rich become all the more insufferable when contrasted with the miserable condition of those whose labours sustained their wealth. Through the 1860s, workers in factories – or *manufactories* as they were still often called – routinely worked sixteen-hour days six days a week for less than twenty cents a day. Often they were paid in scrip, which they could spend only at the factory store. Workplaces were often ill-lit, ill-heated and filled with dangerous machinery and perilous substances. A physician in the mill town of Lawrence, Massachusetts, noted just after the turn of the century that 36% of factory workers there didn't live to see their twenty-fifth birthdays.

As America prospered, less attractive words entered the language, like *slum* (a word of uncertain origin, but probably based on a British dialectal variant of slime). Older words, too, sometimes took on new, more sinister meanings. *Tenement* originally described any tenanted dwelling. In America, where only the poor lived in shared housing, it had by the 1840s taken on the sense of a crowded, fetid building inhabited by the poor.

Out in the sunshine of prosperity, however, it was a dazzling age. A brief list of just some American inventions of the period may give an idea of the dynamism that seized the country: the passenger elevator, escalator, telephone, phonograph, air-brake, cash register, electric light, fountain-pen, linotype, box camera, pneumatic tire, adding machine, revolving door, safety pin, and typewriter. All were invented in America, mostly in the frantic last quarter of the nineteenth century, and all were designed to relieve people of some everyday inconvenience. Where other countries tied their fortunes to revolutionary industrial processes – Bessemer steel, Jacquard looms, steam presses – Americans churned out appliances that made life easier.

Questions & Assignments

1 What was the attitude of Americans to millionaires? How, according to the passage, did some people become millionaires?
2 How is the wealth of the tycoons conveyed in the first two paragraphs?
3 The writer of the passage says that their wealth made them eccentric. What does this mean? What examples of their eccentricity does he give in the passage?
4 Describe in your own words the working conditions which existed in factories as outlined in the third paragraph.
5 Explain the following statement in your own words: *'The indulgences of the rich become all the more insufferable when contrasted with the miserable condition of those whose labours sustained their wealth.'*
6 Why do you think that the writer refers to the nineteenth century as *'a dazzling age'*?

Spectrum 1

THE APOSTROPHE

The apostrophe is used to denote ownership. Remember when there is one owner keep the singular form of the noun and add **'s**.

Examples: my **brother's** keys, **Jane's** ring, the **man's** watch.

When there is more than one owner, use the plural form of the noun if it ends in **s** or **es** and simply add an apostrophe after the **s**.

Examples: the **ladies'** club, the **dogs'** kennels, the **boys'** den.

However, in a small number of cases the plural form of the noun does not end in **s** or **es**. In these cases simply add **'s**.

Examples: the **men's** club, the **women's** room, the **children's** toys.

Assignment — Using the Apostrophe to denote Possession

Change the following into the possessive form using the apostrophe.

1. the colour of the leaves
2. the dog belonging to the girls
3. the car belonging to the man
4. the shape of the leaf
5. the scent of the fox
6. the shadow of the arches
7. the mother of the children
8. the height of the window
9. the home of the hero
10. the size of the house
11. the howl of the wolf
12. the sounds of the city
13. the price of the diaries
14. the length of the stitch
15. the scent of the roses
16. the scent of the rose

The apostrophe is used also to show that one or more letters have been **omitted** from a word. In conversation people say 'It's early' instead of 'It **is** early' and 'I'd like to go' instead of 'I **would** like to go'.

Questions & Assignments — USING THE APOSTROPHE TO SHORTEN WORDS

1 Rewrite the following phrases as they would be spoken in conversation by inserting apostrophes and omitting letters where necessary.

- What is the matter?
- You are wanted in the office.
- It is not important.
- There is nobody there.
- They are late again.
- They have seen it.
- Do not attempt to run.
- They will try again.
- He cannot go.
- She would buy it.

2 Rewrite the following phrases by inserting letters in place of the apostrophes.

- That's the place.
- They've no chance.
- She's crying.
- I've lost the money.
- It's nearly midnight.
- They'd never succeed.
- We're doing our best.
- He'll return.
- Who's making that noise?
- It won't budge.
- He can't sing.
- You're never on time.

Note: Shortened word forms, using the apostrophe, should be used only when writing dialogue. For descriptive and formal writing the longer form is more appropriate.

'My hat's blue,' he said.

'The boy's thoughts are all questions.'

Spectrum 1

SPELLING PROGRAMME – (35 WEEKS)

Guidelines on Learning Spellings.
1. Look at the word carefully. Take note of parts where you might make a mistake such as 'silent' letters and double letters.
2. Say it out loud, pronouncing it accurately.
3. Spell it to yourself — preferably aloud — a few times.
4. Cover the word.
5. Write the word.
6. Check your answer carefully.

1	2	3	4	5
Absence	Accept	Accepted	Accidentally	Addresses
Achieve	Achieved	Across	Address	Advantage
Affair	Affect	Agreeable	Acquaintance	Alcohol
Almost	Already	Also	Although	Always
Amount	Anxious	Appalling	Acute	Apparent
Arctic	Argument	Associate	Athletic	Author
Awful	Awkward	Ability	Bachelor	Banister
Because	Beginning	Behaviour	Being	Believe
Bicycle	Biscuit	Bodies	Bored	Bought
Britain	Broken	Brought	Business	Ceiling

6	7	8	9	10
Category	Certain	Choice	Choose	Climbing
Character	Chimneys	College	Colour	Coming
Clothes	Comment	Committee	Corridor	Countries
Competition	Completely	Conscience	Courteous	Courtesy
Courageous	Damaged	Deceive	Decided	Decision
Definitely	Describe	Desperate	Develop	Diary
Different	Difference	Disappoint	Disastrous	Discipline
Disregard	Deteriorated	Dissatisfied	Distort	Drought
Disappeared	Discussed	Discuss	Eagerly	Eerie
Eight	Embarrass	Entered	Emigrate	Enroll

11	12	13	14	15
Equipped	Especially	Eventually	Except	Excellent
Excitement	Exaggerated	Experience	Exhausted	Existence
Extremely	February	Field	Familiar	Finally
Foreign	Forty	Friend	Fulfil	Furniture
Gaping	Genius	Glimpse	Goal	Grammar
Grieved	Gauge	Guard	Guest	Government
Handled	Harass	Height	Helpful	Heroes
Holiday	Hungry	Honourable	Hypocrisy	Humourous
Illegal	Imitate	Imagination	Interfere	Irritable
Ingenious	Immensely	Impertinent	Immediately	Incidentally

294

Spelling Programme

16
Independent
Leisure
Lose
Marriage
Manoeuvre
Occurred
Parliament
Pleasant
Received
Seize

17
Jewellery
Lightning
Losing
Medicine
Moustache
Omitted
Pastime
Professional
Recognise
Similar

18
Keenness
Likable
Loneliness
Minutes
Mischievous
Opinion
Permanent
Prejudice
Relieved
Separate

19
Knowledge
Literature
Lovable
Magnificent
Niece
Originally
Personnel
Preference
Restaurant
Severely

20
Labour
Livelihood
Lying
Museum
Necessary
Occasionally
Physical
Quiet
Rhythm
Shining

21
Sincerely
Until
Wednesday
Occasion
Paid
Practical
Privilege
Programme
Receipt
Restaurant

22
Successful
Usually
Woollen
Ordinary
Paper
Precaution
Probably
Prominent
Received
Safely

23
Surprising
Unconscious
Ninety
Occasional
Perhaps
Preferring
Procedure
Pursue
Relevant
Safety

24
Tragedy
Unnecessary
Noisy
Occurrence
Permanently
Possessive
Proceed
Queue
Recommend
Scene

25
Transferred
Valuable
Noticeable
Opportunity
Persistent
Prejudice
Procession
Quite
Rhyme
Scheming

26
Senses
Saturday
Stretched
Supplies
Travelling
Unnatural
Vicious
Worrying
Twelfth
Presence

27
Shriek
Solemn
Studying
Suspicion
Tries
Utmost
Victorian
Writing
View
Professional

28
Sizeable
Sure
Succeed
Theatre
Trolleys
Valleys
Village
Wooden
Nuisance
Quieter

29
Smiling
Something
Saturated
Tolerant
Truly
Valuable
Weather
Yacht
Operation
Responsibility

30
Soldier
Souvenir
Superstitious
Telephone
Treacherous
Vandalism
Weird
Yield
Personally
Secretary

31
Succeed
Vegetable
Beautiful
Century
Changeable
Effect
Tuesday
Irrelevant
Mantelpiece
Scarcely

32
Spiteful
Whether
Achievement
Conscious
Definite
Embarrassed
Grateful
Incidentally
Noticeable
Sentence

33
Suppose
Among
Believed
Cries
Disappointed
Exercise
Guarantee
Laid
Parallel
Plentiful

34
Technology
Appearance
Advertisement
Accommodation
Development
Expenses
Handkerchief
Loser
Planning
Benefit

35
Umbrella
Autumn
Breathe
Camouflage
Dining Room
Finished
Icy
Magazine
Really
Certainty

Made In America

In other nations, inventions emerged from laboratories. In America they came out of kitchens and tool-sheds. Everyone, it seemed, got in on the act. Even Abraham Lincoln found time to take out a patent (No. 6469: A Device for Buoying Vessels over Shoals).

Typical of the age was Charles Goodyear, the man who gave the world vulcanised rubber. Goodyear personified most of the qualities of the classic American inventor – total belief in the product, years of sacrifice, blind devotion to an idea – but with one engaging difference. He didn't have the faintest idea what he was doing. Described by one biographer as a 'gentle lunatic', Goodyear in 1834 became fascinated with rubber. It was a wonderfully promising material – pliant, waterproof, rugged and durable – but it had many intractable shortcomings. For one thing, it had a low melting-point. Boots made of rubber were fine in winter, but at the first sign of warm weather whey would gooily decompose and quickly begin to shrink.

Goodyear decided to make it his life's work to solve these problems. To say that he became obsessed only begins to hint at the degree of his commitment. Over the next nine years, he sold or pawned everything he owned, raced through his friend's and family's money, occasionally resorted to begging, and generally inflicted loving but untold hardship on his long-suffering wife and numerous children. He turned the family kitchen into a laboratory and, with only the most basic understanding of the chemistry involved, frequently filled the house with noxious gases and at least once nearly asphyxiated himself. Nothing he tried worked. To demonstrate the material's versatility, he took to wearing a suit made entirely of rubber, but this merely underlined its acute malodorousness and its owner's faltering grip on reality. Amazingly, everyone stood by him. His wife did whatever he asked of her and relatives gladly handed him their fortunes. One brother-in-law parted with $46,000 and never whimpered when all it resulted in was tubs of noisome slop. With implacable resolve Goodyear churned out one product after another – rubber mailbags, life-preservers, boots, rainwear – that proved disastrously ineffective. Even with the lavish support of friends and relatives, when his two-year-old son died, the family couldn't even afford a coffin.

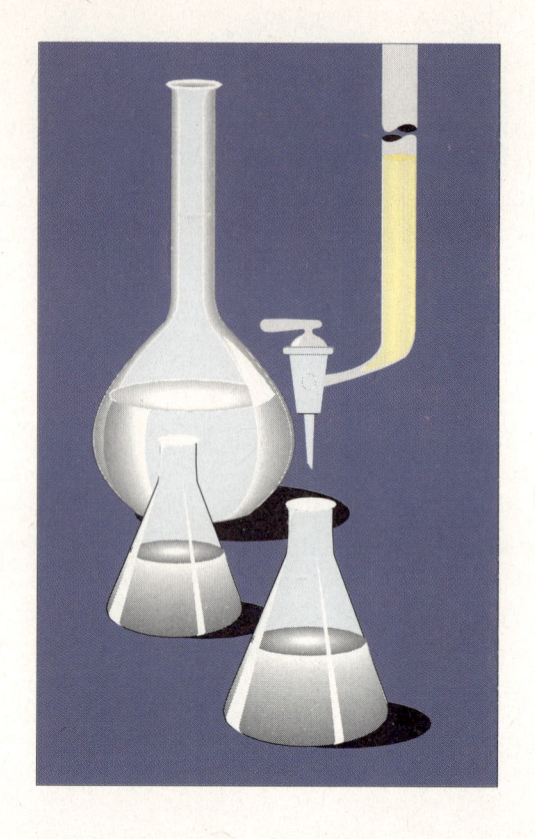

Finally in 1834, entirely by accident, he had his breakthrough. He spilled some India rubber and sulphur on the top of his stove and in so doing discovered the secret of producing a rubber that was waterproof, pliant, resistant to extremes of heat and cold, made an ideal insulator, didn't break when dropped or struck, and, above all, was practically odourless. Goodyear hastily secured a patent and formed the Naugatuck India-Rubber Company. At long last he and his family were poised for the fame and fortune that there years of sacrifice so dearly warranted.

It was not to be. Goodyear's process was so easily duplicated that other manufacturers simply stole it. Even the name by which the process became known, vulcanisation, was coined by an English pirate. Goodyear had endless problems protecting his patents. The French gave him a patent but then withdrew it on a technicality, and when he travelled to France to protest the matter, he found himself tossed yet again into a debtor's prison. He made more money from his autobiography – a book with the slightly less than compelling title Gum-Elastic – than he ever did from his invention. When he died in 1860, he left his family saddled with debts. The company that proudly bears his name, the Goodyear Tire and Rubber Company, had nothing to do with him or his descendants. It was named Goodyear by two brothers in Akron, Ohio, Frank and Charles Seiberling, who simply admired him.

Questions & Assignments

1. What did Charles Goodyear invent?
2. Explain in your own words why Goodyear was a 'classic American inventor'?
3. Why, according to the passage was he fascinated with rubber?
4. What problems did Goodyear set out to solve?
5. What evidence is there in the third paragraph that Goodyear was blindly devoted to pursuing his work?
6. What evidence is there in the passage that his family supported him?
7. How does the passage emphasise the inventor's poverty?
8. Explain in your own words how Goodyear had his big breakthrough. Why was this new discovery so important?
9. Why did Goodyear not become rich from patenting his invention?
10. How did the Goodyear tyre get its name?
11. In your view would Goodyear's life story make a good film? Give reasons for your answer by describing a number of scenes that would be dramatic, interesting or amusing.

Matt Busby: Birth of the Babes

Sir Matt Busby lent his name to the most romantic and tragic experiences of football. The 'Busby Babes' of Manchester United fired the imagination of the public as they came bounding onto the scene a few years after the Second World War. They were the creation of a remarkable manager, a man of genius and vision who was to change the face of English football.

Tragically, the Busby Babes were destroyed in the Munich air disaster of 1958 before they had reached their prime, and their manager came close to perishing with them. But he survived and Manchester United rose again from the ashes of their despair. Busby started all over again and produced more splendid teams so, as Bobby Charlton once put it, Old Trafford became a theatre of dreams.

United blazed a trail for English football in Europe. Winning the European Cup in 1968 just ten years after the tragedy at Munich was an incredible achievement and, of course, a testament to the life and work of Matthew Busby, born in 1909 in a two-roomed pitman's cottage in Orbiston, a small Lanarkshire mining village some miles from Glasgow.

The young Busby was no stranger to loss. His father and all his uncles were killed in the First World War. The result was that the remainder of the family, one by one, emigrated to America, looking for a better life than coal mining. Matt's mother was due to join her sister, and Matt himself was only waiting for a visa quota number. Then, just before he was 17, came the invitation to join Manchester City after he had played a few games for Denny Hibs, a local side.

Plans to go to the United States were scrapped, though Matt probably wished at times that he had gone, because life at Maine Road was not easy. He was homesick and he struggled to get into the first team. A switch of position to take the place of an injured player at wing half in the reserves finally launched him on a distinguished career with City and won him Scottish international honours.

He won a Cup-winners' medal in 1934 and by 1936 he was captain of City, but he decided he wanted a change and he signed for Liverpool. Like most of the Liverpool team he joined the army when the Second World War started and served in the 9th Battalion of the King's Liverpool Regiment, and eventually in the Army Physical Training Corps. After the war Liverpool wanted him back as a player and as assistant to manager George Kay. But, as Matt says: 'I got this opportunity to go as manager of Manchester United. I had a soft spot for Manchester after my City days and it attracted me.'

So began a 25-year reign in which he

produced three great teams, all different in character but reflecting his desire to create and entertain. In his time with United they won five League Championships, the FA Cup twice (from four finals), the FA Youth Cup six times, five of them on the trot as he fashioned the Busby Babes, and achieved crowning glory in 1968 with the winning of the European Cup. He was never naïve in pursuit of honours, either on the field or in the transfer jungle, but he always set responsible standards. Busby took the appalling tragedy of Munich at both personal and club level with quiet fortitude. The heady delights of football victory and the gloomy setbacks were alike treated with an admirable calm and sense of proportion.

His great gift was as a leader and manager of men. Obviously, he was a perceptive judge of players and a shrewd tactician, but he always had the additional advantage of being able to inspire. He enjoyed the respect of players, rather like the old type of headmaster. Some say Busby failed to handle George Best; but he did get nearly 500 first-team games from him – and it's quite possible that without Busby in the background Best might have burnt out in half the time he did.

Honours have been heaped upon him. He was awarded the CBE in 1958, he was given the Freedom of Manchester in 1967 and he was knighted the following year. Pope Paul conferred one of the highest civil awards in the Roman Catholic Church on him in 1972 by making him a Knight Commander of St Gregory the Great. When he retired as manager of Manchester United in 1970 he was made a director and then the club's first president. Over the years he changed little; certainly success never swayed him. As Geoffrey Green, then a distinguished reporter for *The Times*, so admiringly expressed it: 'He is a legendary eminence who has always been approachable and modest, with time to spare for everybody. It is a humility born of early struggle and given only to those who found the answer when the way ahead looked bleak and life itself seemed an insuperable mountain.

Questions & Assignments

1 Having read through the passage, why do you think the 'Busby Babes' are described as both romantic and tragic?
2 What evidence is there to suggest that Matt Busby's early life was hard?
3 What do you understand by the following: *The heady delights of football victory and the gloomy setbacks were alike treated with an admirable calm and sense of proportion*? What does it suggest about the character of Busby?
4 Why, according to the passage, was Busby a gifted manager?

Spectrum 1

Assignment — DICTIONARY WORK

Use your dictionary to find each of the following words. Each dash represents a letter.

WORD	MEANING
1 ac — —	pain
2 acet — — — — —	a gas used for cutting metals
3 ba — — — —	comes from volcanoes
4 bro — — — — —	a booklet
5 cap — — — — — —	a tiny blood vessel
6 car — — — — — — —	a lifelike picture or drawing of someone
7 de — — —	found at the mouth of a river
8 d — — — — — l	type of engine used to pull trains
9 el — — — —	a magic liquid
10 ep — — — — —	words written on a gravestone
11 f — — g	a sharp tooth
12 ga — — — — —	a large Spanish sailing ship
13 g — — — — o	a poor part of a city
14 hall — — — — — — — —	seeing something that is not there
15 hy — — — — — — — —	introduced beneath the skin
16 ic — —	image; statue
17 imp — — — — — —	cheek!
18 j — — — t	a pleasant journey
19 ju — — —	a sweet drink
20 ke — — — — — —	a dish of rice, fish and eggs
21 ke — — — — —	a small falcon
22 la — — — — —	an eel-like fish
23 li — — — —	moss-like plant
24 me — — — — — —	not very good; only ordinary
25 mo — — — —	up-to-date
26 na — — — — — —	to plot the course of a ship

300

WORD	MEANING
27 no ————————	a longing for the old days
28 ob ———————	no longer in use
29 op ————	choice
30 pa —————	to spoil someone
31 pe ————————	a useful instrument on a submarine
32 qu ————	to satisfy your thirst
33 qu ————	a sick feeling
34 rem ————————	payment for work done
35 re ————	bring back to life
36 sau ————	to walk in a relaxed way
37 sec ———————	someone employed to type letters etc
38 tu —————n	instruction
39 tra ——————	to pass over
40 unr ———	badly-behaved
41 uns ———————	generous
42 ven ——————	a long-lasting quarrel
43 v ——————	confirm
44 wh ——	sharpen
45 wr ———	seaweed
46 xy ———	plant tissue that conducts water
47 xy ————————	musical instrument
48 ye ———	long for
49 y ———	story; thread
50 z ————	striped animal
51 z —————	Polish coin

Spectrum 1

Assignment   DICTIONARY QUIZ

Use your dictionary to solve each of the following questions.

A

1. What colour is amethyst?
2. For what purpose is an anemometer used?
3. Aq —————— : a certain type of bridge. What crosses this bridge?
4. What colour is auburn hair?
5. Are you bilingual?
6. Can a beverage be eaten or drunk?
7. Is a biped a living creature or a type of machine?
8. From what word does the word budgie come?
9. Calico – a fruit?
10. Campanology – the study of camping?
11. Do carbohydrates contain oxygen?
12. Does a cedar lose its leaves in autumn?
13. What colour is cerise?
14. Cha —————— : What is unusual about this lizard?
15. Cha ————— : This person is paid to drive who?
16. Clodhopper – an insect?
17. Symbols or cymbals – Which do drummers use?
18. What two meanings has the word 'invalid'?
19. Are guinea-pigs docile animals?
20. Would you expect to find a double-bass supporting a large building or in an orchestra?

B

1. If a performer got an encore would she be pleased?
2. What type of instrument is an epigram?
3. Do fastidious people make good company?
4. Are there any fauns in Ireland?
5. Is cotton made from flax?
6. If a man's manner was described as formal would he be warm and friendly?
7. Why would a pair of galoshes be of little use on a dry day?
8. Why do we sometimes gesticulate?
9. Is gingham edible?
10. Was Gorgonzola an imaginary man-eating monster?
11. Would you find a gudgeon in the sea?
12. Is it easy to fool a gullible person?
13. Why would somebody look haggard?
14. Is the haggis a native Scottish animal?
15. Harlequin – another name for a judge?
16. Where would you expect to find a harpy?
17. What is meant by a hereditary talent?
18. Do farmers sometimes export hillocks?

19 Is a hopper a machine?
20 Why should you never cut off a hydra's head?

C

1 Ichthyology – the study of skin diseases?
2 Name a well-known fungus.
3 Why would an army officer wear insignia?
4 What makes an invertebrate different from most other creatures?
5 What is the difference between an isobar and an isotherm?
6 In what continent are ivory trees found?
7 Jasmine – a bush, a flower or a tree?
8 Is Juniper a planet?
9 Could a castle be described as a keep?
10 Why would you not go to a Kibbutz for a relaxing holiday?
11 Kittiwake or Kittihawk – a type of bird?
12 If you called somebody a knave would you be praising him?
13 Is a larch a bird?
14 Are you likely to find an orange-coloured larkspur?
15 Limo is short for what word?
16 A loganberry is like which other kind of fruit?
17 Magenta, Magnolia, Madrigal. – a tree, a colour, a ship. True or False?
18 What subjects does a reporter who covers maritime affairs write about?
19 Which falls on the earth – a meteor? a meteorite?
20 Does a millipede have a thousand legs?

D

1 Which measures time – a minute or a minuet?
2 Would a nefarious person be a good companion?
3 Where would you find an obituary?
4 Do omniverous creatures eat meat?
5 What is the difference between a panther and a puma?
6 A phial and a barrel. Are they similar?
7 What two different types of activities does the word poaching describe?
8 Troubadour – a soldier, singer, sailor?
9 Wombats are found only in Africa?
10 Which of these words describe a person who is never cheerful – sullen, doleful, disconsolate, discerning?
11 Which of these words describe a person who is rude:
civil, curt, disparaging, courteous, refined, abusive, churlish?
12 Complete each of the following words which describe a wicked person:
ras — — —, vi — — — — —, sco — — — — — — —, ro — — —
13 Which of the following words mean (i) to clean (ii) to dirty? – contaminate, purge, tarnish, defile, scour, purify, defile?

Spectrum 1

Assignment — DICTIONARY WORK – FIND THE ODD ONE OUT

Find the odd one out in each of the following

- **a** lyre, lupin, lute
- **b** organdie, osprey, otter
- **c** shrew, sleuth, skunk
- **d** toucan, terrier, teal
- **e** vole, vixen, visor
- **f** xylophone, zephyr, zither
- **g** magenta, magnolia, marigold
- **h** raffia, ragworth, refuse
- **i** sham, shamrock, shallot
- **j** moccasin, mohair, mollusc
- **k** onyx, opal, onus
- **l** parakeet, partridge, papyrus
- **m** speedwell, spatula, spruce
- **n** tulle, turbine, tunic
- **o** whippet, whelk, whey
- **p** kittiwake, kiwi, kitten
- **q** pugilist, punnet, pullet
- **r** rowan, rupee, rosemary
- **s** stockade, stile, stole
- **t** sonata, regatta, nocturne

Assignment — WORD SEARCH

List as many words as you can by simply looking at all the detail in this Circus Scene. (You should be able to find *at least* twenty words.)

To get you started: cardboard, tarpaulin, whiskers . . .

Media Studies

INTRODUCTION

The **mass media** is the term we use to describe the means through which information, ideas, entertainment or persuasion is passed on to the public. The word 'mass' means a large gathering or group of people. The word 'medium' means something through which people can communicate. We could say: Television is a popular medium with very young children. When we refer to more than one medium we say 'media' not 'mediums'. Hence the term 'mass media'. Newspapers (sometimes referred to as 'the press'), magazines, television and radio are examples of the mass media. Other media include cinemas, videos, books and outdoor posters. The Internet is a new medium that is expanding rapidly.

HOW WE DEPEND ON THE MEDIA

The mass media have five main functions:
1. To inform, e.g. news from home and abroad.
2. To educate, e.g. advice features on cookery, gardening, health, finance etc.
3. To entertain, e.g. music, drama, stories, cartoons, crosswords etc.
4. To act as a watchdog by exposing abuses of power by organisations and people in public office.
5. To provide a platform where members of the public can air their views on issues that interest them.

THE IMPORTANCE OF THE MEDIA IN OUR LIVES

The mass media are the main sources of much of our information on our world. Most of the things we 'know' about the world – a famine in an African country; a nuclear power station explodes in Russia, a rail crash in France, a football star is arrested after a fight in Milan airport – we have never witnessed at first hand but learn about through the media.

The mass media are responsible for providing people with a balanced and accurate picture of the affairs of the nation and the world. Unfortunately, they do not always meet this responsibility.

It is important to develop the habit of reading a good quality newspaper because it will help you to understand the world in which you live. On the other hand most tabloids supply their readers with a diet of scandals and sensation, giving a blurred and unreal picture of life. Success and contentment in life usually come easier to those who are well informed about the world in which they live.

Questions & Assignments

1. (a) Explain the term 'mass media'.
   (b) What section of the mass media touches your life most?
   (c) Does it affect your attitudes or views of things? Explain.
2. (a) 'Television and radio can inform and entertain the public in a way that a newspaper cannot hope to do.' Comment on this statement.
   (b) Suggest some advantages that newspapers have over television.
4. Why are the mass media important in our lives?

Advertising

Over the course of an average day in your life you will be exposed to hundreds of advertisements. It is, therefore, important to understand the methods they use to try to influence the way in which you behave. Advertisements aim to persuade people to do something; to want to own a particular car; to want to use a particular washing-up liquid; to want to go on a particular holiday; to want to support a particular charity and so on.

Advertising Agencies

Most advertisements are created by advertising agencies working for **clients**, i.e. the makers of different products that are to be advertised. Among the people who work in an advertising agency are **copywriters** who write the words (scripts, slogans and text) in advertisements; **illustrators** and **photographers** who devise and create the pictures in advertisements; **media experts** (sometimes called buyers) to advise on and purchase the best places to put the advertisement

The process of creating an advertisement begins when a client comes with a product to the agency. Following discussions and meetings during which ideas are tossed around, an **advertising campaign** is devised.

At this stage they will have agreed on the following:

1 Target Market

Advertisers aim certain products at certain groups of people. These groups of people are called target markets, i.e. groups of people who buy similar types of products. The kind of people who form the main target of the campaign will dictate the approach of the entire advertising campaign. It will influence, for example, the music used in radio and TV advertisements and the kind of headlines, illustrations and the language in print advertisements.

The target market could be farmers, teenagers, mothers of young children, or young single people in their twenties or early thirties with well paid jobs and high spending power.

2 Main Selling Point

This is what the **main selling point** – the main message – of the campaign will be. It could suggest that the product is cheaper than its competitors; that it is fashionable and trendy; that it is healthier; that it will make life easier in some way; that it will improve your appearance; that owning it will impress others and so on.

3 Facts, suggestions and opinions used to back up the main message

The copywriter now takes over. It is his or her job to get to understand the target market and how they think – their needs, fears, ambitions and hopes – and in doing so give them a good reason to want to buy the product. Members of these target groups have their own special hopes and worries. For example, mothers will want their children to be happy and healthy; older people are often anxious about a secure place to keep their savings; teenagers worry about spots and pimples. When advertisers are trying to sell to a particular target market they take the fears and needs of that market into account.

Those who make up advertisements know that people enjoy being admired by others; that people enjoy looking well; that people worry about the future and that some people like to own goods that make others jealous. We all have certain hopes and ambitions, fears and worries – and even flaws.

Advertisers know about these ambitions, hopes, worries, fears and flaws and use this knowledge to persuade us to buy certain products and services.

Lookout for new Tayto LFCs

What are *Tayto LFCs*? - They are the great new taste sensation from *Tayto* - low fat crisps! *Tayto* are confident that they have developed a low fat crisp with no taste compromise. *Tayto* in conjunction with Weightwatchers conducted research which indicated that today's health conscious consumer wanted low fat options but yet expected the same taste as their full fat counterparts.

Tayto LFCs are available in two of the most popular crisp flavours - *Cheese & Onion* and *Salt & Vinegar*, and are available in single 25g pack size and the multipack of six. There is also a healthy low fat dip recipe on the 6 pack ideal for parties and summer barbecues. Look out for a chance to sample the *LFCs* in a store near you and see for yourself that the healthy option does not mean compromising on taste.

Questions & Assignments

1. What do the letters LFCs stand for?
2. What is meant by *'no taste compromise'*?
3. Why were LFC's produced?
4. How do Tayto intend to promote their new product.
5. At what kind of people is this product aimed?

Win a Super Vintage deluxe VW Beetle with LYNX and the LYNX effect

Lynx, the biggest selling male deodourant bodyspray in Ireland, is offering its customers the chance to win a fabulous lime green, chrome finished, vintage *Volkswagon Beetle* plus hundreds of runners up prizes of fashionable club clothing this summer.

Customers can enter the competition by filling out the form attached to special *Lynx* products which will be on shelf from 11th August for 4 weeks. The competition ends on 31st October. First prize will be awarded to the correctly completed entry with the best tie-break slogan, which will be judged on originality.

Questions & Assignments

1 What do we learn about Lynx from this advertisement?
2 What method is being used to tempt people to buy the product?

Spectrum 1

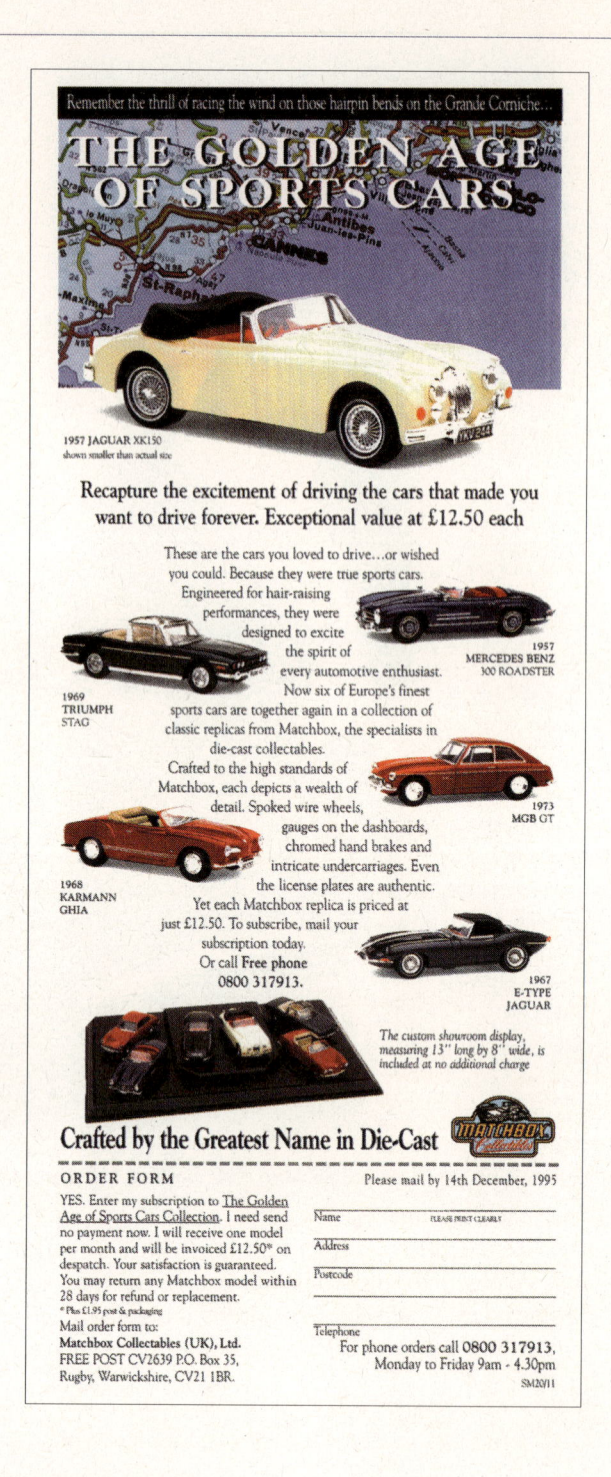

Questions & Assignments

1 Is this advertisement aimed at children? Give a reason for your answer.
2 Do you find any aspects of this advertisement misleading? Give reasons for your answer.
3 Do the terms of the advertisement enable people to buy a single car?
4 How much money would you have to spend to buy all six cars?
5 What words and phrases are used to make the products seem attractive?
6 Explain clearly how you can order the products.

Questions & Assignments

1. What is the main message about Jersey in this advertisement?
2. Do you think that the illustration in the advertisement underlines the message? Explain.

Spectrum 1

> "You want to
> make sure
> you're eating well
> in this weather"

> "Mum –
> it's ninety degrees
> outside!"

See how they're getting on in Australia.

Give them a call now.

call and see

TELECOM EIREANN

Questions & Assignments

1. What product or service is being advertised here?
2. At what group of people is it aimed?
3. Is the picture effective in getting the message across? Explain.
4. Comment on the text in the brown panels.

Advertising

DO AS THE ROMANS DO.

The Italians know their olive oil. That's why Monini outsells all other brands in Italy. Monini authentic Italian Extra Virgin Olive Oil has a rich, smooth, delicate flavour.

In a taste test carried out by Olive Oil experts, Monini was the only olive oil to receive the highest overall rating of "Excellent".

For texture, colour, bouquet, and that truely authentic Italian taste, do as the Romans do... choose Monini Extra Virgin Olive Oil.

MONINI
FIRST COLD PRESSING

The No. 1 BRAND IN ITALY
Judged the Best by Italian Experts & Consumers

Questions & Assignments

1. Do you think this illustration will be effective in helping to sell the product? Give a reason.
2. Explain the caption *'Do as the Romans do.'*
3. What facts about the product are to be found in this advertisement?
4. Does the advertisement make any claim that could be difficult to prove? Explain.
5. What words are used to describe the flavour of the product? Do these words actually mean anything in the way they are used? Explain.
6. '... *that truly authentic Italian taste* ...' Does this phrase succeed in making the product attractive? Give a reason.

Brush up with Macleans Whitening!

Why not set heads turning on the beach this summer with the hottest accessory of all - a dazzling white smile!
Macleans Whitening toothpaste from SmithKline Beecham is the perfect choice for beautiful, white teeth. Try it as part of your daily beauty routine and watch as its gentle and effective cleaning action reveals a sparkling, white smile. A superb formula based on a unique patented ingredient called Triclene means it's free from nasty abrasives and bleaches too.
Because you want to look stunning this summer, there's a super promotion currently running in stores nationwide. To *'Brush up with Macleans Whitening'* and be in with a chance of winning a voucher for the renowned *Peter Marks* range of hair and beauty salons, simply pick up an entry form next time you're shopping.

It's a winning combination, guaranteed to have you looking good and feeling great all summer long!

Questions & Assignments

1 What benefits does this product offer?
2 What words and phrases are used to make the product attractive?

Advertising

STIRA Attack Your Attic

Don't ignore the single largest storage area of your house. Make use of it with a Stira Folding Attic Stairs.

WITH A STIRA YOU GET:
- Safe easy access to your attic.
- Pine folding stairs. The comfort and strength of timber.
- Comes pre-varnished.
- An unbeatable guarantee.

WE FIT THE STIRA FOR YOU ANYWHERE IN IRELAND
- We install the Stira, no middle-men (not available in any stores).
- We will enlarge the existing opening if necessary.
- We manufacture a variety of sizes, we'll have one to suit you.
- Because we make it, we guarantee it.

YOU KNOW IN ADVANCE HOW MUCH IT COSTS
- We have set prices which start at £289 fully fitted for an 8 ft high ceiling.
- 8'6" high ceiling, £10 extra, 9 ft, £20 extra (standard 24" trapdoor). Wider openings cost up to £10 extra.

WHAT'S INVOLVED IN FITTING?
- Our fitter will enlarge your existing trapdoor, no mess.
- Supply and fit the stairs.
- Fit new trapdoor, new architrave.
- Fitting takes less than two hours.

WHAT GUARANTEE!
- Guaranteed Irish.
- ISO 9002.
- 12 months parts and labour.
- Plus 9 years parts only.

NOW THAT'S UNBEATABLE

Spring Special – £20 OFF

Irish Times Spring Special Offer

Spring Special Offer: £20 off with every Stira ordered today by phone, please quote 'Irish Times Spring Special Offer' or use the coupon and post to:

Michael Burke, Stira Folding Attic Stairs Ltd., Dunmore, Co. Galway

£20 off with this coupon, Irish Times Readers Only

Irish Times Special Offer

Name..

Phone Nos. (H) ....(W) ....

Address ....

Please note: The £20 offer is only available with purchase of Stira Attic Stairs as a result of this Advertisement.

Folding Attic Stairs Ltd.
DUNMORE, CO. GALWAY

Phone Monday to Saturday between 9 am–5 pm

1850 639 639

Phone Number: 093 38055

9 am to 9 pm - Mon to Sat

Questions & Assignments

1. Outline clearly the product being advertised here.
2. What kind of people is the product likely to interest?
3. Explain how (i) the text and (ii) the illustrations make the product attractive.

hot Scotch

From purple-headed mountains to crystal clear lochs, Scotland offers great walks on the wild side as well as grand, cultured cities

The delights of Dundee

'We arrived by train, catching our first view of Dundee across the spectacularly wide River Tay,' says Louise Johnson who, with husband Barry and children John, six, and Lizzie, four, made the city their base for a week's holiday.

'As Dundee is a former ship-building town, many of its sights are connected with the sea. Our favourite family outing was to the Discovery Point museum on the waterfront, where Captain Scott's polar research ship, *Discovery*, is berthed. The interior of the ship has been kept as it was during Scott's voyages to the Antarctic at the beginning of the century, complete with all the crew's cabins and galleys.

'Of course, we couldn't resist a trip to Shaw's Dundee Sweet Factory. Here, the Shaw family are still turning out ten tonnes of boiled sweets, humbugs and fudge a week, all made to traditional recipes. A visit to the factory shop on the way out was a must!

'We hired a car for a few days because the beautiful Angus Glens and the Perthshire lochs are only a 1½ hour drive away. If you're keen on golf, you'll be in paradise here: Dundee is surrounded by more than 40 golf courses – including the famous St Andrew's and Gleneagles – all within an hour's drive away.

'Also near is Glamis Castle, near Forfar, famous as both the Queen Mother's childhood home and the setting for Shakespeare's *Macbeth*. You can see the enormous dining rooms and surprisingly cosy living rooms, as well as the elegant gardens with an ornate sundial more than 21 feet high. Our stay passed all too quickly, but we returned refreshed from our breath of fresh Scottish air.'

Louise and family stayed at the four-star Angus Thistle Hotel (tel: 01382 226874). Prices start at £32.50 per person per night for b&b. Family rooms are also available.

Questions & Assignments

1. (i) How did the Johnson family travel to Dundee?
   (ii) How long did they spend there?
2. What do we learn from the report about the Discovery Point Museum?
3. Explain how the Shaws make money from the visitors to their factory.
4. What places did the family visit outside Dundee?
5. What does the report say about golf facilities in the area?
6. What features of Glamis Castle did the Johnson family find interesting?
7. Is there evidence in the report that they enjoyed the holiday? Explain.
8. Describe each of the photographs accompanying the report and explain how they are connected with the report.
9. Study the caption in the top photograph and say what four attractions are mentioned.
10. Select a town or village in Ireland with which you are familiar and write a similar style report on a week's holiday you have spent there.

Questions & Assignments

1. What is the main selling point in this advertisement?
2. Comment on the phrase *'Simply light years ahead'*.
3. Do you think that the illustration is effective? Give reasons.

Spectrum 1

DOG LOVERS

SAY goodbye to winter morning getting-out-of-bed to let the dog out misery — thanks to

DOGGO-DOOR

Operated by infra-red remote control hand set Doggo-Door opens your door automatically at the press of a button. Fido's out 'n' about — you're nice 'n' snug. (Operates up to 6 ft. range.)

● £799.99

BATHROOM NOVELTY from SWITZERLAND

The SONY SHOWERMAN

The new experience for shower-users! Water-proof belt with soap holder — shampoo holder — spectacle receptacle plus waterproof stereo walkman and headphones.
As used by astronauts

£350.99

SAVE POUNDS WITH THIS MIRACLE OF KITCHEN TECHNOLOGY — FROM NOW ON NO NEED TO THROW AWAY THAT LOAF-END YOU CAN'T SLICE

Just insert the end of the loaf in your

Loaf.O.Cut

and hey presto! there's two or three extra slices you never thought you'd get! Plays "Ravel's Bolero Theme" from Torvill and Dean.

£8.63p *(postage extra)*.

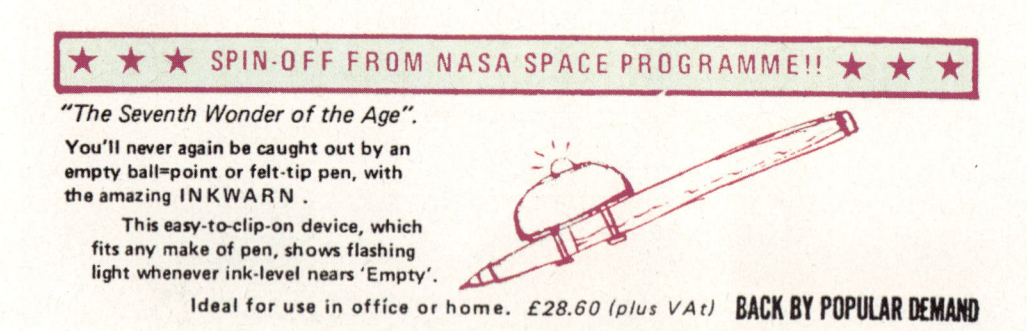

★ ★ ★ **SPIN-OFF FROM NASA SPACE PROGRAMME!!** ★ ★ ★

"The Seventh Wonder of the Age".

You'll never again be caught out by an empty ball-point or felt-tip pen, with the amazing **INKWARN**.

This easy-to-clip-on device, which fits any make of pen, shows flashing light whenever ink-level nears 'Empty'.

Ideal for use in office or home. £28.60 (plus VAt) **BACK BY POPULAR DEMAND**

£££'s SAVING

New from NORWAY

The luxurious, Scandinavian-style "WOOD BATH" in polished stripped-pine (ex works).

"The Greatest bathroom revolution of the century"

Just fill with water and get clean NATURE'S WAY. Easy to assemble kit. £200.16 (plus VAT)

AN IDEAL GIFT FOR ALL THE FAMILY

Questions & Assignments

1 At what target group is each of these products aimed?
2 What words and phrases are used to make the products attractive?
3 Rate the products in order of (i) usefulness and (ii) value for money.

Questions & Assignments

1 Tell the story of Dicky's first trick in your own words.
2 Find suitable words to describe
   (i) Mum's expression in frame three
   (ii) Dicky's expression in frame four.
3 What features of the cartoonist's drawings helped you choose your answers to Question 2?
4 What do you think will happen after frame five when Dicky warns his dad about the frog?

BOPPO
THE HOPELESS HOOLIGAN
HAW! HAW! A SITTING DUCK! GEROFF THAT WALL.
SHOVE!
WAA!
TOMMY JOE, BOPPO'S ONLY PAL
BAH! I KNEW BOPPO COULDN'T RESIST THAT!
HAWR! TAKE A CLOSE LOOK DOWN THERE!
YOWPS!
BARROOM!
DRAIN REPAIRS
ENJOY YOUR TRIP, WIMP! HEESH!
TSK!
TRIP!
WURF!
SPLATT!
CACKLE! ANOTHER SHRIMPOID TO ANNOY.
WHO? ME?

Questions & Assignments

1 Write an accurate description of Boppo's appearance.
2 Describe what Boppo does in the first three frames and say what kind of person Boppo is.
3 In frame four Boppo is laughing. Is it a pleasant laugh? Explain.
4 What happens in the next five frames?
5 Describe the expression on Boppo's face in the final frame. Why is he looking like this? What is likely to happen next?

Spectrum 1

Questions & Assignments

1. Explain clearly what Danny's tranny is.
2. *'I can't mend your stilts but I can . . .'*
   What else do you think Danny said to the man with the broken stilts?
3. (i) Describe the man talking to Danny in frame three.
   (ii) What did he want from Danny?
4. Write a detailed account of how Danny improved the circus.
5. In the last frame the clown says to Danny – '*. . . this is really pulling in the crowds*'. What do you think he meant by these words?
6. Imagine that you had a tranny like Danny's. Write an account of some of the things that you would do with it.

Advertising

Spectrum 1

Questions & Assignments

The first three frames and the final frame from a Roger the Dodger are included here but the remaining frames are omitted.

1. Explain clearly what is happening in the first frame.
2. Roger faces a new problem in the second and third frames. What is the problem?
3. How do you think he solves the problem.
4. What is happening in the final frame?
5. Explain clearly how the artist depicts (i) anger, (ii) disappointment, (iii) shame, (iv) shock and (v) happiness in this selection of frames.
6. Are there any examples of exaggeration in these scenes? Explain.

324

Advertising

Questions & Assignments

1. These six frames are from an episode of the Bash Street Kids. In what order did they appear? Give an explanation for your answer.
2. What kind of children are the Bash Street Kids?
3. Are the teachers as they are depicted in the cartoon true to life? Give reasons.
4. Are there any examples of exaggeration in these scenes? Explain.

325

Spectrum 1

Cork Heritage Trail

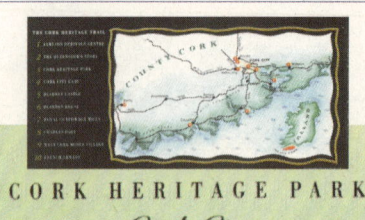

JAMESON HERITAGE CENTRE
Midleton

1

The award winning Jameson Heritage Centre is a lovingly restored 18th-century distillery. Visitors are shown an audio-visual presentation, available in 6 languages, and a guided tour through the old distillery. The tour culminates in the Jameson Bar, where all visitors are invited to sample the world-famous Jameson Whiskey (minerals for children). Afterwards, you can visit the gift or coffee shop.

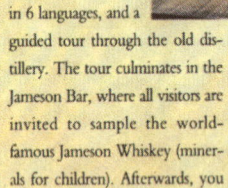

Opening times:
Mid March to October.
7 days a week 10am – 6pm.
Last tour commences at 4pm.
Admission charge.
Tel: 021-613594
Fax: 021-613642

CORK HERITAGE PARK
Cork City

3

Cork Heritage Park is situated beside a picturesque estuary of Cork harbour. Located in a restored courtyard, amidst the beautiful landscaped grounds of the old Pike estate at Bessboro, Blackrock. Visitors are given an exciting and varied introduction to the rich heritage of Cork. This historic journey covers the Pike contributions, Quaker influence, ecology of the area, the fire service and Cork's maritime traditions.

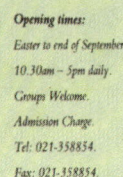

Opening times:
Easter to end of September
10.30am – 5pm daily.
Groups Welcome.
Admission Charge.
Tel: 021-358854.
Fax: 021-358854.

THE QUEENSTOWN STORY
Cobh

2

Cobh's unique origins, history and legacy is now shown in a multi-media permanent exhibition in the restored Victorian Railway Station and Customs Hall. This award-winning centre traces the story of Irish emigration via Cobh on sailing ships, early steamers and great ocean liners. Relive the dramas of the ill-fated Titanic and Lusitania. Afterwards you can visit the restaurant or browse through the gift shop.

Opening times:
February 18th to end of
December 10am – 6pm daily.
Last admission at 5pm.
Admission charge.
Tel: 021-813591
Fax: 021-813595

Opening times:
Summer daily
9.30am – 6pm.
Winter
Saturday and Sunday
10am – 4pm.
Admission charge
Groups by prior arrangement.
Tel: 021-305022
Fax: 021-307230

CORK CITY GAOL
Cork City

4

Despite its majestic appearance, this prison building housed 19th-century prisoners, often in wretched conditions. Furnished cells, amazingly lifelike characters, sound effects and fascinating exhibitions allow the visitor to experience day to day life for prisoners and gaoler. Incorporated in the Gaol visit is a spectacular sound and image presentation showing contrasting lifestyles in 19th-century Cork.

Questions & Assignments

1 Using the information in this brochure compose the text for a radio advertisement aimed at tourists intending to visit the Cork region. Your answer should be around 100 words in length.

✎ Functional Writing

Using this brochure as a model, devise a similar brochure for your own town or region.

Advertising

Questions & Assignments

Many children feel a little lost and confused on their first few days at second level school. Design and write out a short brochure with some useful tips and information to help them through these days. Consider what things you would include in a brochure on your school; what would new first year students need to know to help them through their first few days at your school?

GIVING DIRECTIONS

Below is an example of someone telling another person how to reach the nearest doctor's surgery from the school. Read it carefully and use it as a model for the assignment below.

EXAMPLE

> At the school gate, turn right along Church Street and go down it towards the traffic lights. About twenty yards before you reach them, cross over Church Street and go along Fish Street until you come to the Londis Supermarket and Carr's Newsagents at the far end. Straight after the newsagents turn left into Dromore Road. Follow it round until you come to a large house, number 22, with a red door and a long driveway. The gate has a sign on it saying 'Dr Carson and Dr Bradford'.

POINTS TO REMEMBER
- Aim to be clear and exact.
- Use landmarks (traffic lights, shops etc.) in your directions.
- Give every new part of the directions a new sentence.
- Try to start each sentence in a different way so you are not always beginning with 'Then' or 'Next'.

Questions & Assignments

Write directions for a stranger on how to get from your school to the following different places in your neighbourhood:
1. Post Office
2. Library
3. The nearest park/playing fields
4. The Garda Station
5. The dentist
6. Shopping Centre
7. A place of your own choice

Spectrum 1

Describing Pictures

General Description
- Begin with a general description of the subject of the photograph, e.g. This is a photograph of . . . a crowded street . . . a bridge . . . a family . . . an old house . . . a group of people watching a street musician . . . etc.
- Next describe, in more detail, the main subject of the picture. You must decide what details to include here. Give the most important ones. Bear in mind such things as size, number (of windows, people, trees etc), material from which it is made, weather conditions etc.

Background Details
- Describe briefly the background details. (Indoors, countryside, street.)
- If you are asked to describe a colour photograph then you will need to give details of the colours of the main elements in the picture.
- If possible state the location of the picture. Sometimes this will be obvious, sometimes impossible to tell. Make a guess by studying the picture carefully.

Describing People in Pictures
- Begin by stating the obvious details – sex, approximate age, race, noticeable or striking features, hairstyle, clothing.
- Describe the expression on the face – amused, angry, sad, worried, puzzled, surprised, contented, frightened etc.

(Perhaps there is evidence in the background of the picture which may tell you more about the person or why she or he appears to be in a certain mood.)

Purpose of the Picture
- Finally, state what you think is the purpose of the photograph, e.g. to show the beauty of nature (a lake/a river/a garden/a park) . . . to capture the joy of a family gathering (a wedding/an outing) . . . to show off the attractive features of a car/a motorbike/a building . . . to capture the excitement of a sporting event . . . to illustrate some feature of a news story (a traffic accident/a flood/a strike) . . . to illustrate some kind of hardship that people may be suffering (poverty/war/homelessness).
- These are broad guidelines only. Select only those which you think apply best to any photograph you are describing.

Questions & Assignments
1. Write a complete description of the pictures on pages 329, 330, 331.
2. Cut out some pictures from magazines and write a description of each one.

Advertising

329

Spectrum 1

Advertising

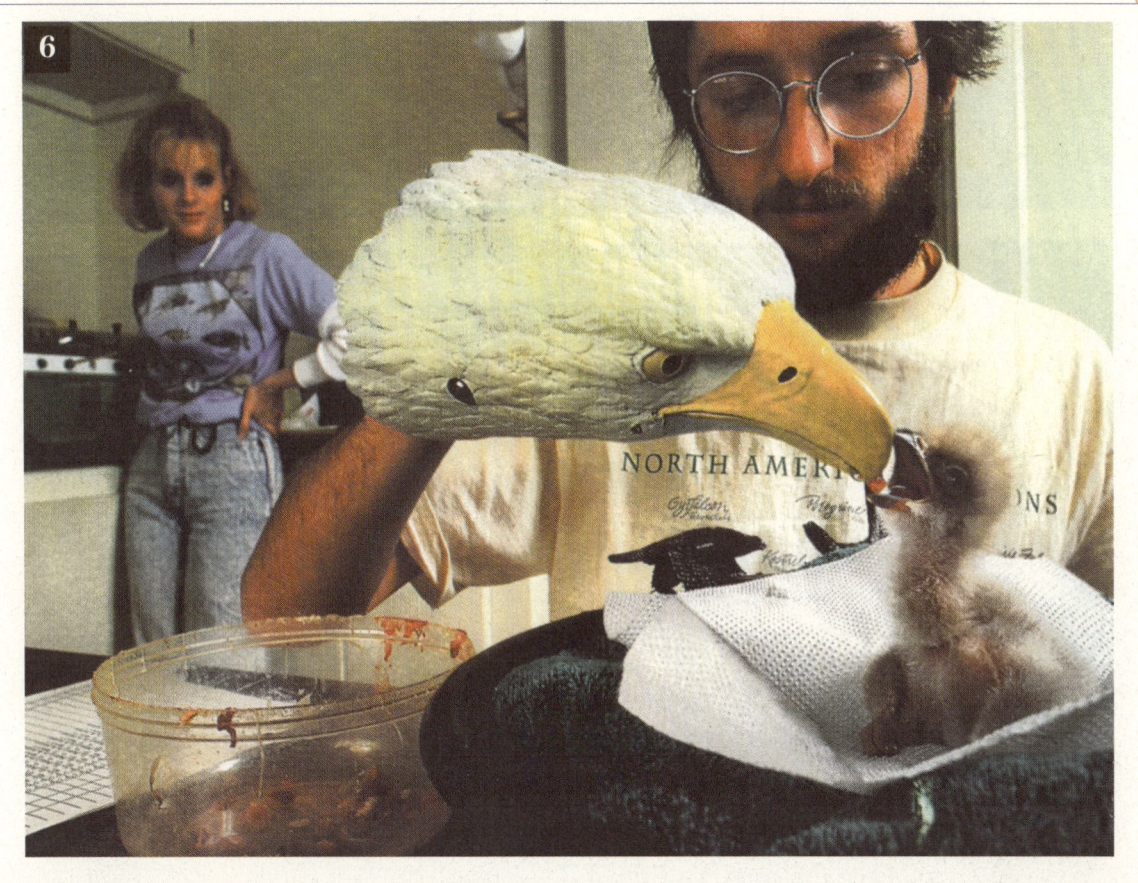

Spectrum 1

Report Writing

Performance Report

COMMUNITY REPORT

A report is usually written following an investigation into a particular event, incident or item. It should be descriptive and informative, and be presented in a well-planned format. A good report should present the facts clearly and is a perfect opportunity for conveying your own impressions and suggestions for improvements.

> **The following are some guidelines which should be adhered to when writing a report:**
> - Give the report a title and a date.
> - Begin with a clear objective description of the incident, event, item or place on which you are reporting. Use short sentences. Be clear and specific on aspects such as size, cost, appearance, sequence of events, damage etc.
> - Conclude with your own impressions, covering such aspects as are relevant to the topic of your report, e.g. cause, value for money, suggested improvements, other relevant recommendations.
> - Sign your report.

Questions & Assignments

Write a report on each of the following:
1. The condition of a local park or other amenity.
2. Shopping facilities in your neighbourhood.
3. Traffic in your town or neighbourhood.
4. Youth facilities in your area.

How to Write Instructions

It is important to learn to write clear and precise instructions. Simple, well-written instructions will aid the successful completion of any job and are essential for children and adults to avoid the many hazards involved in daily life.

> **Some basic points to remember when writing instructions:**
> - Begin by stating clearly the aim of the instructions.
> - List the items of equipment and the materials needed to carry out the instructions.
> - Specify quantities needed if necessary.
> - Aim for complete clarity in every sentence. Avoid puzzling or ambiguous language.
> - Explain clearly any technical terms used.
> - Aim for a logical step-by-step order.
> - Break the task into manageable steps.
> - Occasionally, a 'question and answer' approach might be effective.

Questions & Assignments

1. Imagine that you are a supermarket manageress or manager and you employ many temporary workers. Your service motto is 'The customer comes first.' Write a brief set of instructions for the temporary staff to deal with each of the following situations.
   (a) A customer who is trying to 'jump' the queue.
   (b) A spillage on the shop floor.
   (c) A customer asking for a refund or an exchange.
   (d) A customer who asks directions to a department or an item.
   (e) A customer with a defective trolley.
   (f) A customer in a wheelchair.
   (g) An angry customer.
2. You are going on holiday for a week. Write instructions for a friend who is to look after your pet.

Answer Guidelines

1. (g)
   - Listen carefully.
   - Do not interrupt.
   - Put the customer at ease.
   - Ask the customer to accompany you to the information desk.
   - Explain the customer's problem to your colleague at the information desk.
   - Leave the staff at the information desk to deal with the problem.
   - A wrong approach to this problem may make the complaint more difficult to settle.

Spectrum 1

The following is an advertisement warning children of the dangers involved in playing near electricity wires and pylons.

FOUR SIMPLE RULES
FOR CHILDREN PLAYING AND FOR EVERYONE ENJOYING OUTDOOR LEISURE

PLAY SAFE!

Beware of Overhead Wires!
Don't fly kites or model aircraft nearby – watch out when pitching tents, stepping dinghy masts, casting a fishing line etc.

DANGER HIGH VOLTAGE

Do Not Climb Pylons
It's extremely dangerous. Pylons carry hundreds of thousands of volts: even getting near the wire, you risk a fatal shock. And there's the risk of falling.

Stay Out of Substations
Climbing into transformer stations is very risky – and unnecessary. If your ball or frisbee is lost, don't try to retrieve it – wait for an ESB man to get it out.

Report Fallen Wires
Fallen wires are very rare. If you see one – don't touch it or go near it. Tell the ESB or the Gardaí as soon as possible.

Questions & Assignments

1. Using the above as a model, devise a set of simple guidelines for children playing near:
   (a) a railway line
   (b) a river
   (c) a busy road
   (d) a building site.
   You may include a line drawing to illustrate each point.

Newspapers

How a Newspaper is Produced
There are four main departments in each newspaper. These are the **advertisement**, **printing**, **circulation** and **editorial** departments.

Advertising in Newspapers
The advertisement department is responsible for persuading companies and private individuals to advertise their products and services in the newspaper. Most newspapers depend for their profits on the income they receive from advertisers. Around seventy per cent of a newspaper's income comes from publishing advertisements – with the remainder coming from sales of the paper.

Printing
The printing department is responsible for laying out news stories, features and advertisements and, from this, printing copies of the paper. Many people used to work in this department in the past. However, advances in computer technology over the past decade or so have made newspaper production less labour intensive.

Circulation Department
The circulation department is responsible for ensuring that the paper is delivered, as rapidly as possible, to all the areas of the country that it serves.

Editorial Department
The editorial department is responsible for producing everything that a newspaper prints, with the exception of advertisements. The **editor** controls this department. The editor is the person who decides what stories and features are printed in a newspaper. He or she will know the kinds of stories that the readership (the people who buy and read the paper) like best.

Spectrum 1

The editor is helped in this task by **assistant editors** or **deputy editors** who are each in charge of a section such as Sport, Business, Politics, Foreign News etc. **Reporters** and **special correspondents** are assigned to cover stories at home and abroad.

SUB-EDITORS

Sub-editors work on preparing each page of the paper for printing. The tasks of the sub-editor include:

- **PAGE LAYOUT:** This involves deciding on which part of the page different stories will be printed and deciding on the length of each story and the use of photographs or illustrations.

- **WRITING HEADLINES:** Good headlines catch the reader's attention as well as helping the reader to find a particular story that interests him or her.

- **REWRITING STORIES:** Stories filed by reporters sometimes have to be shortened or rewritten to fit available space, or to suit the style of the paper.

- **PROOF CORRECTION:** This involves checking the story or copy before it is printed to make sure that there are no mistakes in spellings and punctuation.

Questions & Assignments — NEWSPAPER HEADLINES

1. Rewrite each of the following headlines in sentence form.
2. Find words in the headlines that mean the following: child; criminals; occurence; road accident; dismissed; investigate; raid; close down; company.

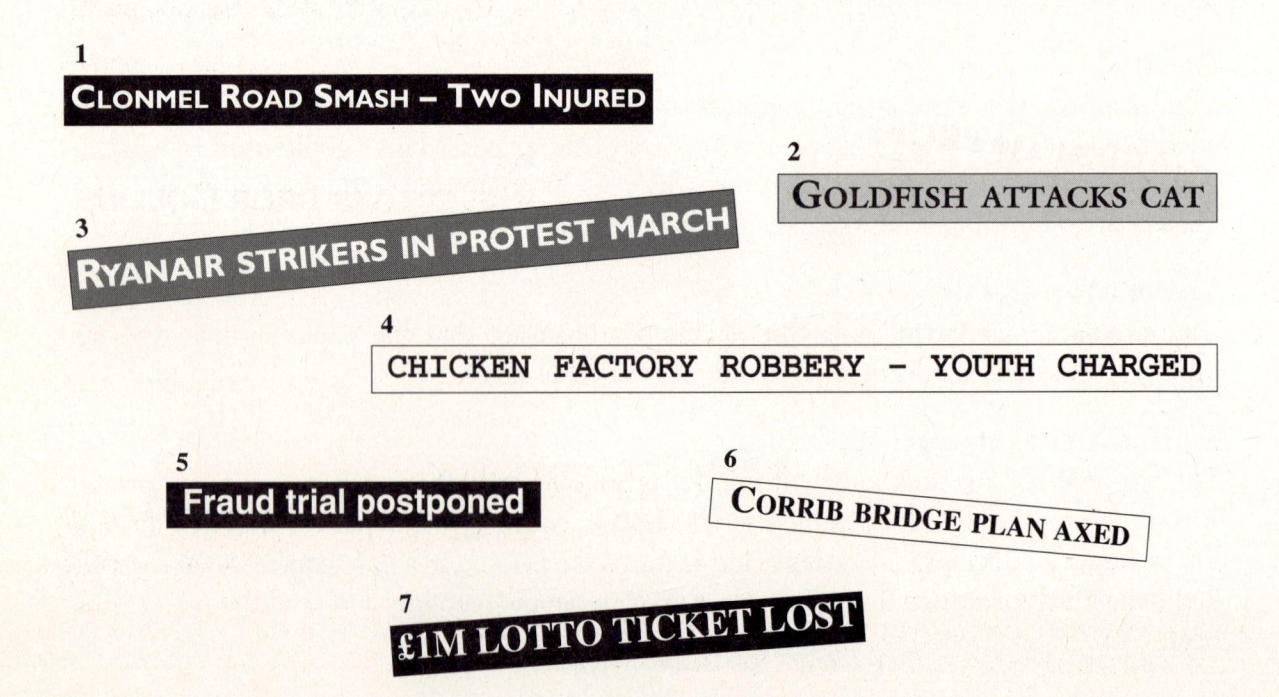

1. **CLONMEL ROAD SMASH – TWO INJURED**

2. **GOLDFISH ATTACKS CAT**

3. **RYANAIR STRIKERS IN PROTEST MARCH**

4. **CHICKEN FACTORY ROBBERY – YOUTH CHARGED**

5. **Fraud trial postponed**

6. **CORRIB BRIDGE PLAN AXED**

7. **£1M LOTTO TICKET LOST**

Newspapers

8 POP STAR HELD AFTER DRUGS SWOOP

9 **NEW HOSPITAL FOR CASTLETROY**

10 MAN ATTACKS ALLIGATOR IN THEME PARK INCIDENT

11 Action by neighbour saves toddler from fire

12 MONEY PROBLEMS BIGGEST WORRY – SURVEY FIND

13 Oakdale Community Hall vandalised: damage £9,000

14 Balbride toy firm to fold

15 TWO GUNMEN IN SHOOTING INCIDENT: EYEWITNESS REPORT

16 THUGS ROB PENSIONER IN KILLARNEY

17 GARDAI TO PROBE G.A.A. ROW

18 SELECTORS DROP COLLINS

19 YOUTH IN TRAGIC BIKE ACCIDENT

20 HORRIFIC SMASH CLAIMS ONE LIFE

21 UFO LANDED IN MY GARDEN — CLAIM BY LAOIS MAN

TREE-DWELLERS READY FOR A FELL SWOOP

The whine of chainsaws broke the tranquillity of the Glen of the Downs yesterday as workers began felling trees to make way for infill and tarmac worth £18 million pounds.

About 20 protesters, who have been camping in the glen since last September, reacted by occupying trees earmarked to be cleared for the road-widening scheme.

The workers, in bright yellow jackets and hard hats, did their best to ignore the defiant environmentalists by working around them. They did not attempt to fell the trees the protesters clung to.

One local farmer, Mr Michael Kerrigan, placed himself repeatedly in the path of the falling trees and ignored warnings by Wicklow County Council workers as branches crashed around his head.

The ash trees on the fringes of the forest which Mr Kerrigan stood beneath were small, and he was wise enough to position himself where he would receive only minor injuries.

"The next thing you know there'll be a ski slope on Sugar Loaf mountain," he said. "It's just reckless planning. They don't care about Wicklow anymore, it's just seen as part of greater Dublin."

As the work continued, the protesters, who call themselves vigil-keepers, darted among the tree trunks and undergrowth from the base camp on one side of the road to the tree-top dwellings on the other, passing on news.

Some took to their tree houses, suspended on platforms in the giant ancient oaks they are trying to save. Others videoed council workers and interrogated them about the environmental impact of their actions.

Apart from two noisy outbursts by protesters, the atmosphere during the day was calm and restrained.

Mr Jeff Colhoun, a protester's spokesman, who has lived in a tree-house on the side of the forest overlooking the road since last September, said they were committed to "non-violent direct action".

> The crews of council* workers, including tree surgeons, began arriving at the controversial section of the N11 at about 8.30 a.m.
>
> Gardai controlled traffic through the scenic valley while workers at either end of the disputed stretch of road set about felling the small straggly trees lining it.
>
> Curious drivers slowed and blew their horns in support of the campaigners. Some stopped to shout words of support to those clinging precariously to branches.
>
> At noon, the environmentalists heard through their solicitor that an injunction hearing was set for the High Court in the afternoon.
>
> After lunch, the environmentalists positioned themselves directly in front of the trees to be felled, preventing the workers from reaching them. The workers soon abandoned their chopping efforts and began clearing the felled branches off the road and loading logs on to a lorry.
>
> As the crews and gardai conceded defeat at around 2.30 p.m., Mr Colhoun said the protest would continue. "Hopefully the council will have to give us notice of evictions from our homes, if they want to move us," he said.
>
> *by Nuala Haughey*

*council – *employees and contracted*

Questions & Assignments

1. Explain clearly why the trees were being cut down.
2. Why did the protesters try to prevent this happening?
3. What do we learn about the protestors and their methods?
4. Who supported the protesters?
5. Which side 'won'? Give a reason for your answer.
6. Do you think that the term *'Tree-dwellers'* was a good choice for use in the headline? Give a reason.

Functional Writing

What are your views on the action of Wicklow County Council? Write a letter to the editor outlining these views.

BBC SAYS SORRY FOR ITS OIRISH EASTENDERS

The BBC has apologised for any offence caused by its portrayal of Ireland in Monday night's episode of its soap opera, *Eastenders*, which was set in and around Dublin.

All this week the London-based drama is set in Ireland, as Pauline Fowler, played by Wendy Richards, visits her long-lost half-sister.

After scenes depicting cows, sheep and donkeys wandering around a street, a menacing drunk, an unhelpful hotelier and resentful locals, many viewers were offended at the way Ireland and its people were portrayed.

The BBC received "a number of calls," according to a spokeswoman for the programme. One report put the figure at well over 100. RTE's public relations office received six calls, although it does not screen the programme. Some of the calls were from British people, a spokeswoman said.

Yesterday morning, the controversy was aired on *Morning Ireland*, where John Boland, the *Irish Independent* television reviewer, pointed out how bad the programme became when it left its London location.

There were also many calls to phone-in programmes, including *The Pat Kenny Show*, with listeners ringing in to protest.

The BBC issued a statement saying: "We are sorry if we have offended Irish people and we had no wish to misrepresent them."

Pauline did track down her half-sister, who lives in a house full of rowdy children and surly family members. She is married to a drunk, who turned up earlier pouring drink all over Pauline.

A BBC source suggested that the characters had now been introduced and would be give "context" over the rest of the week. Pauline comes from a "multifaceted family background," said the source, with some understatement.

The programmes were filmed in Ireland about two months ago.

Questions & Assignments

1. Explain clearly why people in Ireland were offended by the episode of *Eastenders*.
2. How did people express their annoyance at the programme?
3. Comment on the use of the word *'Oirish'* in the headline.
4. Rewrite this report in a much shorter form (120 words approx.). You should only include the most important pieces of information in your answer.

Gardai bust forgery scam at top school

Gardaí have busted a forgery scam at a top Dublin School.

Pupils were being offered forged cash by a fellow student.

Dectectives were alerted when the teenager – who is studying for his Leaving Certificate – told friends to bring extra money to school to buy his forgeries.

ARRESTED

Officers from Harcourt Terrace station went to the school where they arrested the boy.

He was in class when he was summoned by the investigation team. They found £120 in dud notes on him.

"The fakes were quite good. We don't know yet where he got them but he seems to have been running a lucrative trade in passing on these forgeries," a source said.

The teenager was taken to Harcourt Terrace station and questioned.

The college where the arrest took place is regarded as one of Dublin's top secondary schools.

Staff were totally unaware of the student's activities.

Gardai under Det. Supt. P.J. Brown first became suspicious when forged notes were being passed in local shops and they mounted a surveillance operation.

Their investigations led them to the school and enquiries then revealed the teenager at the centre of the forgeries was selling them for a fraction of their apparent face value to friends.

Questions & Assignments

1 Explain the words 'bust', 'scam' and 'top' in the headline.
2 How did the Gardai find out about the forgeries?
3 Where was the forger arrested?
4 Where, according to the report, was the boy getting the forged notes?
5 Write an alternative headline for this story.

Spectrum 1

First Train Ever to Fly The Atlantic

The world's first flying train – a 112 tonne, 3,200 horse-power Iarnród Éireann locomotive, mounted on its own rails in the cargohold of a Ukrainian Antonov 124 Russian aircraft – became the first train ever to fly the Atlantic when it landed at Dublin Airport at 0730 hrs this morning with the heaviest load ever flown in Irish aviation history.

When the cargo door at the nose of the aircraft opened it revealed a 60 ft. long locomotive in shining new Iarnród Éireann colours and the most dramatic air cargo ever landed at an Irish airport. The locomotive is the first of 10 ordered by Iarnród Éireann from General Motors of Canada.

Delivery of the first 201 Class locomotive is being made by air in advance of the remaining nine – which will be transported by sea – to allow for trials, driver training and performance checks so that the other locomotives can go into service immediately after their arrival in Ireland.

The new locomotives with 100 mph capacity are the fastest and the most powerful ever to operate in Ireland and are being built at the General Motors Electro Motive division's manufacturing plant at London, Ontario, in Canada.

HISTORIC FLIGHT

The historic flight, which will attract the attention of rail and air enthusiasts everywhere, left London Ontario at 18:20 Irish time on June 8 and stopped for refuelling at Montreal (Canada), Gander (Newfoundland) and Reykjavik (Iceland), arriving at Dublin Airport at 0729hrs on Thursday, June 9.

To airlift the locomotive, the Antonov 124 aircraft had train tracks installed for loading and unloading through the giant cargo door in the nose of the plane.

This loading operation was co-ordinated by UK based Air Foyle, Antonov's Worldwide General Sales Agent, who also ensured that one of their flight managers, Kevin Creighton, accompanied the flight from Ontario.

It will be unloaded onto a multi-wheeled 12-axle truck, which will remain at the airport until late Thursday night and will then travel to Inchicore Works – a journey of over eight miles.

The truck will have a Garda escort and ESB and Telecom will clear any wires obstructing the route.

The 112 tonne locomotive is the second heaviest air cargo in the history of aviation. The world record for the heaviest single load ever transported by air was a 135.2 tonne generator from Siemens, Düsseldorf to New Delhi, India on September 22, 1993. This load was also carried by the Antonov 124.

The locomotive is to be used for high-speed InterCity and freight services planned for the Irish rail network. It will take eight hours to unload from the Antonov and will not be transported to Inchicore until after midnight, to avoid disrupting traffic on the Airport road.

Questions & Assignments

1. Why do you think the headline to this news story would make a reader curious to read the entire report?
2. State five separate facts about the locomotive that can be found in the article.
3. (i) How many locomotives were ordered?
   (ii) How will they all be delivered?
4. What will be done before the locomotive goes into service?
5. (i) How long did the total air journey take?
   (ii) How many stops were made for refuelling?
6. What person is named in the article? Explain why this person is named.
7. Why are the Gardaí, ESB and Telecom mentioned in the report?
8. Why is the journey to Inchicore taking place after midnight?
9. What fact in the report could be included in the Guinness Book of Records?
10. Look at the two photographs accompanying this story.
    (i) Write a sentence describing each one.
    (ii) If you were a newspaper editor, which photograph would you use to go with the report? Give a reason for your answer.

COLD SNAP SET TO 'MARCH' ON

Winter continues to hold the country in its icy grip with severe frost plunging temperatures to some of their lowest levels of the year.

The west and south of the country once again bore the brunt with heavy snowfalls causing chaos.

The Met. Office said there was more to come, with bitterly cold conditions and snowshowers forecast for tomorrow and Monday.

With the east coast expected to finally get a taste of snow this weekend, there were fears of more flooding in some parts of the country when the thaw starts.

Temperatures were expected to plummet overnight to as low as minus five degrees celsius in some areas.

Donegal, Sligo, Leitrim, Roscommon, Monaghan, Galway, Limerick, Tipperary and Cork were worst hit by the weather.

Barring blizzard conditions, today's Five Nations rugby clash between Ireland and France will go ahead at Dublin's Lansdowne Road.

A Met. Office spokesman said the cold snap was expected to last for the next few days and the indications were that it would be well into the week before temperatures rise.

Questions & Assignments

1. (i) In what month of the year do you think this report was published? Explain your answer.
   (ii) On what day of the week was this report published? Explain your answer.
2. Explain the phrases *'bore the brunt'*, *'causing chaos'*, *'plummet'*.
3. What, according to the report, is likely to cause more flooding?
4. What event may be affected by the bad weather?

Don't Look Down

Brad Pitt arrives by helicopter. He has been filming all day along sheer blue ice on a mountain ominously called Razorback. Blond hair flops forward, his face pinched against the cold and a look of fear in his eyes. Spending relentless hours pretending to fall over the edge of a cliff has proved a shattering experience. Yet, Brad Pitt feels a kind of safety amid the danger on snow-capped Canadian peaks of 10,000 feet. For once in his life, he's far from prying eyes in snowy white seclusion where there are more moose than people and the nearest town is an hour's precarious drive along icy roads. There is a part of him that doesn't want this experience to end.

In marked contrast, the film crew are going stir-crazy. They've been holed up near Bluff Lake, British Columbia in giant Portacabins, nicknamed Cell Blocks A, B and C, with an incongruous thread of Christmas fairy lights to lighten the gloom. There is one telephone between 120 people, a pool table and shared video room, surrounded by an ocean of mud and congealed ice and snow. Mountain ranges with such forbidding names as Chaos and Scimitar stretch from Vancouver and one hell of a road journey is required to get this far.

"Great, isn't it?" enthuses Pitt. "The film is over-running, but I could not care less. It gives me more time out here. If I don't think about the heights, then there's nothing to do but relax and enjoy the whole experience."

Pitt's luxurious trailer sits next to a wooden chipboard partition in what amounts to a private backyard, stretching to the trailer of his underemployed English minders, Paul and Dave. They have stopped worrying about fanatical girls and the paparazzi, which they faced in abundance for weeks while filming in Argentina, and are reduced instead to discussing yesterday's sighting of a cougar.

"There is nothing to do but to work and eat," continues the ecstatic Pitt. "If only it could always be like this."

. . . Brad Pitt's story has, like himself, a streak of morality and open-eyed wonder. He expected to suffer – and did. He expected fame and fortune like every other 22-year-old who has hitched from Hicksville to Hollywood. But unlike hundreds of thousands of thirtysomethings in Los Angeles who are still waiting tables, serving petrol and cleaning pools, he actually made the dream work. And he can't quite believe it. There is a sense that, aside from getting the big roles, part of him wonders whether he's got too much and if it's worth all the incessant clamour.

"I slept on a floor for the first year-and-a-half in Los Angeles," he says, as if to prove he's served his dues. "I had a friend in Missouri who said his father had a place in Burbank and I could stay there. It was run by a woman who didn't speak English and I didn't know what to expect. There were eight guys in one room, no furniture, each with our own pile of clothes stacked up and a separate sheet for all of us on the floor. I did not mind going through it at the time. It was part of the gig."

A few hours before our dinner, sitting under pine trees, listening to the click of pool balls in the recreation room, the growl of four-wheel drives crawling their way through snow and mud, and the tuneless, manic whistle from one of the crew, *Empire* had been regaled with stories from those who can't speak enough of Pitt's enormous kindness.

In Argentina, he had adopted 14 starving stray dogs and found them all homes. And to prove that he considers people even more than animals, he helped his housekeeper to buy a new $40,000 home in Argentina. He paid $5,000 toward a heart operation for crew member; bought flight upgrades for his voice coach; forked out for wives to visit lonely technicians; and had a new Ford Mustang convertible waiting in Los Angeles for his long-serving make-up lady. The list goes on. Fractious crew members, as a rule, can hardly wait to rubbish egomaniac, pain-in-the-arse, overpaid and overinflated stars, particularly when their salary is a cool $12 million. Brad Pitt, it turns out, is genuinely popular with those he works with. Even on the touchy subject of fame and being photographed in private moments, he is philosophical.

"I try not to think about it too much," he muses. "First of all, I thought, 'Man, what do I have here?' I went and hid for a time, but realised I can't always do that. It means a lot to me if people say that I have just given a great performance on screen or they've seen something that has moved them. I like that. I can't pretend that I don't. As for the paparazzi and intrusions, I just have to grit my teeth and do the best I can to avoid them."

One solution has been the purchase of one of the oldest houses, built in 1911, within view of the Hollywood sign and boasting "the first swimming pool built for private use in Los Angeles" and known for its seclusion and security.

"I may have to spend some time there one day," he laughs. "I searched for a year-and-a-half to find it and now it's empty. I'm not missing much, though, apart from my dog and family."

Brad Pitt has found an inner peace which works remarkably well for *Seven Years in Tibet*. But he knows, probably more than most in his position, that should he slip along the way, there is a long way to fall.

Questions & Assignments

1. From your reading of the passage, why do you think the actor has a *'look of fear in his eyes'*?
2. Why does Pitt feel safe in the dangerous snow-capped mountains?
3. How is the isolation of the film location emphasised in the passage?
4. Why do the actor's minders not have to worry about fanatical girls and paparazzi?
5. Describe Pitt's living arrangements when he first arrived in Hollywood.
6. What sounds does the writer hear when he is sitting under the pine trees?
7. What is Brad Pitt's attitude to fame?
8. What do you understand by the statement: *'should he slip along the way, there is a long way to fall.'*?
9. Do you think this is a flattering portrait of the actor? Explain.
10. What is your opinion of celebrity interviews? Is it possible for them to give a true and accurate picture of their subject? In what way do you think they are limited?

Making his Mark

Irmalin DiCaprio was enjoying her visit to the Uffizi Gallery in Florence. Though pregnant, she moved easily among the Raphaels and Giottos before taking her appointed place in her beloved Da Vinci section. It was while she was concentrating on one of the master's more celebrated efforts that she felt a hammer-blow of a kick in her womb, the first sign of life from her first child. Immediately seizing upon the artistic symbolism of the moment, the German legal secretary decided to name her unborn son Leonardo. One day, she felt sure, DiCaprio junior would make his mark on the world.

Twenty-three years after that assertion of his existence, Leonardo DiCaprio is arguably the most celebrated actor of his generation, his talents recognised by film critics and lustful teenagers the world over. He has shone in cult films and survived appearances in box office duds. Next week, however, sees the release of a film which should decide whether DiCaprio takes his place at the A-list top table.

James Cameron's *Titanic* is the sort of big budget extravaganza which can launch reputations or sink studios in its tow. In this case, there are two studios involved, Fox and Paramount, and with a budget exceeding 200 million dollars and an opening date which was originally set for July 4, the stakes are extremely high. DiCaprio toplines as Jack Dawson, a humble chap who wins his passage in a poker game and then falls for socialite Kate Winslet en route to the fateful iceberg. "The most incredible movie experience I've ever had," is how Leonardo described it. "It was the longest film I've ever done and it was a long journey. It made a man out of me."

Since the film premiered in Tokyo last month, critics and audiences alike have been in raptures. In order for *Titanic* to make a profit, however, it will need to take more than $500 million dollars at the global box office. That's a huge burden to place on the slim shoulders of DiCaprio because, no matter how superb the special effects may be (and you can be sure with James Cameron they will be state-of-the-art), it takes a true Hollywood superstar to put that many bums on that many seats. If the crowds do flock to see *Titanic*, DiCaprio will find himself in Cruise/Carrey territory.

For a young actor who has deliberately avoided the big-budget features (he turned down a huge paycheque to play Robin in the Batman franchise) to concentrate on smaller, more personal films, *Titanic* is the culmination of a career in the public eye which began when DiCaprio made an appearance on *Romper Room* at the age of five. Growing up in an impoverished part of LA ("I would walk to my playground and see, like, a guy open up his trench coat with a thousand syringes"), the young DiCaprio went on to nearby Hollywood where he filmed tons of commercials and made guest appearances on shows ranging from *Lassie* to *Roseanne*.

A co-starring role in the popular series *Growing Pains* brought him to the attention of some Hollywood producers and he was cast in such gems as *Critters 3* and *Poison Ivy* before beating over 400 hopefuls to his ground-breaking film, *This Boy's Life*. DiCaprio's superb performance in the adaptation of Tobias Wolff's novel matched those of his co-stars Robert De Niro and Ellen Barkin and led to his being cast opposite that other tortured young soul, Johnny Depp, in *What's Eating Gilbert Grape?*

At this stage, with only two major movies behind him, Leonardo was already a sought-after actor. Sharon Stone hand-picked him for *The Quick and the Dead*, and Baz Luhrmann considered no other actor for the difficult role of Romeo in his modern retelling of the Shakespeare classic. Though his films to date haven't always been commercial successes, Hollywood likes DiCaprio because he has both *critical and sex appeal*. When he travelled to Japan recently for *Titanic*, he was greeted by 3,000 screaming fans, some of whom had queued for three days and three nights to see their idol. Cries of "Leo!" and "Romeo!" filled the air as he attended the screening.

That other barometer of popular appeal, the Internet website, also speaks volumes about DiCaprio's fan-base. Tap the name of Leonardo DiCaprio into the net and you will be connected to the following sites: *Oh-so-so lush Leonardo; Totally Luvin' Leo; Lovin' Leo; Lusciously Leo; Leo, My Hero; Leo, The Most Gorgeous Man in the Universe; Admiring DiCaprio, Leo-lovers Worldwide...* and more.

For the actor, whose upcoming projects include *The Four Musketeers*, opposite Gabriel Byrne and John Malkovich, and the next Woody Allen film, opposite Winona Ryder, the time is ripe to justify Mrs DiCaprio's selection of such an artistic name.

And he can be eternally grateful that his mother's favourite artist wasn't Hieronymous Bosch.

Questions & Assignments

1. Why was Imalin DiCaprio enjoying her visit to the Uffizi Gallery in Florence?
2. Why did she decide to name her unborn son after Leonardo DaVinci?
3. In the second paragraph how does the writer show that Leonardo DiCaprio is *'arguably the most celebrated actor of his generation'*?
4. From your reading of the passage, briefly describe DiCaprio's role in the film *Titanic*.
5. What do you learn about the actor's early life from the passage?
6. Why do you think the passage refers to the internet as a *'barometer of popular appeal'*?

COPPERS SPOTLIGHT TREE RAIDERS

Garda helicopters have been drafted in to root out Christmas crooks in the nation's forests.

Airborne gardai are targeting gangs of Yule yobs who steal tens of thousands of pounds worth of Christmas trees every year.

For the first time, gardai are using infra-red equipment to detect night raiders in young tree plantations.

ATTACK

Truckloads of trees have already been stolen and one forest ranger has been attacked. Armed gangs of up to 20 people move into forests by night and get away with up to 240 trees in each truck.

One million Christmas trees are harvested each year in Ireland and sold for up to £20 each but a significant number are stolen.

Each truckload of stolen trees can be worth more than £4,000 on the open market.

"Thieves are a huge problem – they're as traditional as carol singers each Christmas," says Flannan Moloney, sales and marketing manager of Coilte, the state forestry company.

"We are very determined to stop them this Christmas. There have been liaison meetings with gardai in each region in the country."

"The thieves can be very inventive – in one instance, they tied a flashlight to a dog and sent him up through a forest at night. The security man followed the lamplight while a gang stole trees nearby," he said.

GUARD

Some owners of smaller plantations are sleeping with their trees.

They camp out nightly to guard their trees, said John Sheridan, secretary of the Irish Christmas Tree Growers Association.

"Theft is a double blow. Not only have the owners lost their trees, but they must then compete against the robbers who sell their trees in the marketplace," he said.

The association are seeking a documentation system for tree sellers.

Questions & Assignments

1. Who are the *'Yule yobs'* referred to in the passage?
2. How are Gardai planning to tackle the problem?
3. How do the thieves remove the trees?
4. Why are Christmas trees such an attractive target for thieves?
5. Give an example from the passage of how thieves can be very inventive in the way they operate.
6. In what sense is theft a *'double blow'* to plantation owners?
7. (i) Is the headline a suitable one? Give a reason for your answer.
   (ii) At what time of year do you think this report appeared in the newspaper? Give a reason for your answer.

STRESS

I feel nearest to having a heart attack when I am trying to wrench my way into the packaging surrounding four batteries or attempting to find an article on page 148 of a glossy magazine which has no page numbers between 38 and 206.

I'd like you to try this quiz. Count your score at the end and how long you have to live:

- Finding, just as you've finished stirring it, that your tea bag has disgorged its contents into the cup: **2 points.**
- Answering your front door bell, just as you're going out, and finding five total strangers standing there, whom you then recognise as your cousins, who you then suddenly remember inviting over for the afternoon: **8 points.**
- Vainly attempting to remove the sticky, dirty mark made by shop labels on glass or crockery: **10 points.**
- Finding a large ink stain on the inside of your jacket: **5 points.**
- Finding a large ink stain on the outside of your jacket: **35 points.**
- Being rung by someone in a call box, taking their number, putting the phone down, ringing them back and finding them engaged: **22 points.**
- Turning to introduce your friend to someone and forgetting his/her name: **50 points.**
- Settling down to watch the video you made of that great movie, and finding you actually recorded a programme on another channel: **15 points.**
- Queuing in a bank behind someone who is trying to persuade the cashier that although he has an account elsewhere, no cheque book on him and no proof of identity, the cashier should give him lots of money: **10 points**
- Queuing behind someone in a supermarket who has chosen to buy lots of things with no price labels on: **100 points**
- Queuing behind someone in a health food shop: **1,000 points.**
- Knocking over and trying to restack a pile of magazines all of which have a free lipstick taped to the front: **3 points.**
- Going to the loo in someone else's house, finding that it doesn't seem to flush properly: **15-45 points**, depending on the time.
- Seeing the stamp becoming detached from a letter just as you post it: **5 points.**
- Racing to a telephone and getting there just as it stops ringing: **10 points.**

Questions & Assignments

1 Rewrite the above quiz, using irritating events with which you and your friends can identify. Invent your own scoring system.

Index of Key Terms

A
abstract noun 250
advertising 306
adverb 273
alliteration 16
apostrophe 251, 292
assonance 16, 17
atmosphere 164
autobiography 241

B
biography 241
brainstorming 29

C
capital letters 276
characters 83, 146, 156
cinema 228
collective noun 250
comma 257
common noun 249
conflict 160
conjunction 286
consonant 16
costume 173

D
describing pictures 328
dialogue 149

E
editor 335
exclamation mark 149

F
fairy tale 114, 156
film drama 228
foreshadowing 162
formal letter 92

G
giving directions 327

H
haiku 52

headline 336
humour 63

I
idiom 288
image 23
informal letter 92
interjection 286
internal conflict 163

L
letter writing 92

M
main selling point 307
mass media 305
media studies 305
metaphor 20
metre 13
mood 26
musical quality 16

N
noun 247

O
omniscient point of view 147, 157
onomatopoeia 9

P
past participle 272
past tense 272
personal writing 265
plot 76, 142, 147
plural noun 247
poetry workshop 29
point of view 142, 147, 157
possessive pronoun 251
preposition 285
pronoun 251
proper noun 249
props 173
protagonist 156
proverb 280
punctuation 255

Q
question mark 149
quotation marks 149

R
radio 229
repetition 19
report writing 332
response 10
rhyme 12, 14
rhythm 13

S
satire 27
scenery 173
sentence 255
serial 229
set 173
setting 122, 145, 156
short story workshop 145
simile 20, 21
singular noun 247
situation comedy 230
special effects 173
suffix 262

T
target market 307
technical terms 9
tense of verb 272
theme 156
tone 26

V
verb 271
vowel 16

W
writing instructions 333

351

Alphabetical List of Poems and Short Stories

POEMS

A Boy Thirteen	36
A Crabbit Old Woman Wrote This	42
A Recipe for Happiness	29
Blackberry-Picking	22
Bodybuilders' Contest	28
But You Didn't	35
Carolling Around the Estate	39
Christmas Thank Yous	32
City Dweller	54
City Lights	20
Claims	11
Dad	45
Haiku	52
Happiness	56
If The Earth Should Fall Tonight	13
It Makes Me Furious!	26
Mid-Term Break	24
Miller's End	18
Mother To Son	46
Notice	34
Old Dog	43
Orders of the Day	31
Sheepkiller	44
Shelter	40
Smithereens	8
Snow Storm	9
Stopping by Woods on a Snowy Evening	38
Take One Home for the Kiddies	19
Teacher	47
The Choosing	48
The Great Blasket Island	55
The Hunter	27
The Listeners	15
Things People Do	32
Tich Miller	50
Winter Days	37

SHORT STORIES

SWALK	57
First Confession	64
Christmas Morning	71
The Secret Life of Walter Mitty	78
Uncle Ifor's Welsh Dresser	86
The Wolves of Cernogratz	97
The Choice is Yours	102
The Giant with the Three Golden Hairs	110
The Hitch-Hiker	116
The Scream	124
A Rat and Some Renovations	130
The Monkey's Paw	133
After Twenty Years	140